The Which? Book of Tax 1987/1988

THE
WHICH?
BOOK OF
TAX
1987/88

Which?
BOOKS

Published by Consumers' Association and Hodder & Stoughton

Which? Books are commissioned and researched by
The Association for Consumer Research and published by
Consumers' Association, 14 Buckingham Street, London
WC2N 6DS and Hodder & Stoughton, 47 Bedford Square,
London WC1B 3DP

First edition 1984
Second edition 1985
Copyright ©1987 Consumers' Association Ltd

British Library Cataloguing in Publication Data

The Which? book of tax
   1987/88
   1. Taxation–Great Britain–periodicals
   336.2'00941   HJ40

   ISBN 0–340–41357–3

Designed and typeset by DP Press, St Julians, Sevenoaks, Kent
Text illustrations by John Workman
Cover illustration by Greg Tansey
Printed and bound in Great Britain by Butler & Tanner Ltd,
Frome and London

Inland Revenue forms reproduced by permission of the
Controller of Her Majesty's Stationery Office

Acknowledgements

Editors:
Jonathan Shephard
Helena Wiesner

Revision Editor:
Jane Vass

With thanks to the following for their help:
Jane Alexander, Anthony Bailey, Tim Crawley-Boevey,
Thomas Crawley-Boevey, Jane Fann, Lynette Gilbert,
Michelle Goreham, Jill Greatorex, Stephen Hoyle, John
Kimmer, Pamela Le Gassick, Jonquil Lowe, Gareth G. Marr,
Veronica McGrath, Carole Slingsby, Nigel Smith, Philip
Sweetman CBE, Sue Thomas, Nick Turner, Virginia Wallis,
Sara Williams, John Willman.

CONTENTS

Section 4: Houses, Investments, Pensions

Section 5: Passing your money on

Section 6: The Revenue, Checking your tax, Tax facts, Index

1 HOW TO USE THIS BOOK

Many different sorts of people will be using this book. Some will be having a first go at understanding the tax system; others will already know it quite well. And quite a number of our readers will be people who give tax advice to others. The first thing is to decide what you want the book to do for you. So where do you fit in?

A beginner

The best starting-place is Chapter 3 – *How your tax bill is worked out*. This gives a step-by-step guide through the basics of the income tax system. Once you've mastered this chapter, the rest of the chapters on income tax should fall into place.

A general reader

If you're reading for interest, or if you want to sharpen up your knowledge of tax, the whole book is your oyster. The book is in six sections – so you can, if you like, go straight in to Section 2: *Tax and the family*, or skip this section and read about tax and your job in Section 3, or about investments in Section 4.

Checking a specific point

Start with the *Index*, which should give you a fast guide to the right place. Wherever there's space, we've given *Examples* to illustrate what we say in the text. And we give *references* to Finance Acts – so that you can, if you want, give chapter and verse to your tax office, or your tax adviser. See p11 for the abbreviations we use.

Planning ahead

One of the major worries for many people is how to pass their money on to their children. Section 5 gives practical advice.

Checking your tax bill

Chapter 34 – complete with a tax calculator – guides you through working out how much tax you should pay. And Chapter 35, *Tax facts*, is a handy reference section, with tax

rates for the past six years. You may need these if you're trying
to adjust your tax bills for past years.

Trouble with the Revenue

Chapter 33 gives advice if you're in dispute with the taxman,
and tells of tax penalties you might face.

The taxes covered in this book

Income tax

Income tax – inevitably – takes up most of the book. It's by
far the most important tax – not only for the Government, for
whom it brings in more money than anything else, but also for
ordinary people. Anyone with more than a very modest wage
has to pay income tax. So do many people with no earnings
but with money coming in from investments. The main aim of
the book is to help you realise:
- what income tax is
- how it affects you
- how you can check your tax bill
- how you can make the most of the tax rules and pay less tax.

Capital gains tax

You may have to pay capital gains tax if you sell some of your
possessions at a profit – or even if you give them away. Over
the years, the rules have become very complicated, and, when
you've worked your way through them, you're quite likely to
find that there's no tax to pay. But it's as well to skim through
our explanation in Chapter 32 to make sure that you're not at
risk. And if you *are* at risk, we suggest ways of cutting down
the amount of tax you have to pay.

Inheritance tax

This was first introduced in the 1986 Budget, replacing capital
transfer tax as a tax on the value of what you give away in your
lifetime or leave behind when you die. It differs from capital
transfer tax mainly in that there's no tax to pay on gifts you
make more than seven years before your death. But keep a firm
hold on common sense. Don't – in the rush to save tax – give
away money and possessions which you might need later.
Chapters 28 to 30 describe ways of cutting your tax bill, but
they take common sense into account in advising you.

Corporation tax

Corporation tax is the tax which companies pay. There's no attempt in this book to give more than the barest outline of corporation tax. It's mentioned only where it's relevant to individual taxpayers. The chief example is of someone who is self-employed and paying income tax (at high rates) on his or her profits. Someone like this should certainly consider becoming a company. More advice in Chapter 15.

Value added tax (VAT)

Again, we don't go into detail. But there's a basic guide in Chapter 18, and a guide to VAT for the self-employed in Chapter 15.

References to statutes

Here's an explanation of what the letters and figures mean:

FA	Finance Act	*s*	Section
ICTA	Income and Corporation Taxes Act 1970	*Sch*	Schedule
		IR	Inland Revenue Leaflet
TMA	Taxes Management Act 1970	*ESC*	Extra-statutory concession
CGTA	Capital Gains Tax Act 1979		
CAA	Capital Allowances Act 1968	*SI*	Statutory Instruments
IHTA	Inheritance Tax Act 1984	*SP*	Inland Revenue Statement of Practice

Schedules come at the end of Finance Acts. Lists of Inland Revenue leaflets and of Extra-statutory concessions are in Chapter 35 (p494). In addition, some *Tax cases* are mentioned – see overleaf.

Here are some examples:

FA 1976 s8	Finance Act 1976, Section 8
ICTA s437 (1)	Income and Corporation Taxes Act 1970, Section 437 subsection 1
CGTA Sch 1 para 4	Capital Gains Tax Act 1979 Schedule 1 paragraph 4
SI 1975/610	Statutory Instrument number 610 of 1975
IR 47	Inland Revenue leaflet 47
SP 5/80	Inland Revenue Statement of Practice number 5 of 1980

Sometimes you'll see several references together. Where this happens, and the references are to different topics, we put the topic (in brackets) after the reference:

ICTA 1970 s181 (income from jobs); s219 – 219A (pensions, social security benefits).

Where to find the sources

Inland Revenue leaflets are free from tax offices or PAYE enquiry offices (for exceptions, see p508). Tax cases and statutes should be in central reference libraries.

We give references to tax cases when the outcome of the case has an important effect on tax rules. Tax cases may be reported in more than one publication. References in this book are to *Tax cases* (TC) and to the *All England Law reports* (All ER). So, for example, *1976 1 All ER p272* means that the case is found on page 272 of volume 1 of the 1976 All England Law Reports.

How the book is arranged

The Which? Book of Tax is divided into six sections. Within the sections, there are separate chapters – see *Contents* on pages 6 and 7. On this page, we give a guide to what's in the different Sections.

Section 1: Introduction
pages 9 to 48

As its name suggests, this introductory section is designed to make you familiar with the book itself, and with the tax system. In addition, the main tax planning advice is summarised in Chapter 4. In Chapter 2, we provide a quick checklist of the main tax changes made in the 1987 Budget.

Section 2: The family
pages 49 to 135

Your tax bill doesn't simply depend on how much income you have. Your family circumstances – ie whether you're married, single, living together, separated, divorced – can drastically affect the amount of tax you pay. And if you (or your wife or husband) are 64 or more, you may get extra *personal allowances* to reduce your tax bill. Section 2 explains the way your age and circumstances affect your tax, and has practical advice on how to make the most of the rules. And Chapter 10 – *Social security and special tax allowances* – sets out the tax rules for social security benefits, and explains how some people who need help can claim extra tax allowances.

Section 3: Your job
pages 136 to 234

Section 3 explains the tax rules if you're employed, or self-employed, or employing others. There are special chapters for people who work abroad, for people with spare-time earnings, and for people who are in partnership. Value added tax (VAT) – also in Section 3 – is important for many people who are self-employed.

Section 4: Houses, Investments, Pensions
pages 235 to 350

Everything in Section 4 is really about investments. Buying your own home is likely to be the largest investment you make. Building up a pension is a way of investing for your retirement. And of course there are the more typical investments – in building societies, banks, National Savings, shares, unit trusts, and in life insurance policies. Section 4 tells you about the tax rules, and describes the new Personal Equity Plans.

Section 5: Passing your money on
pages 351 to 446

The five chapters in Section 5 take up a sizeable part of the book. The aim is twofold: to set out the tax rules for **capital gains tax** and **inheritance tax**, and to help you make sensible use of the rules in planning your gifts. The message is that the biggest tax saving may not be the best solution.

Section 6: The Revenue, Checking your tax, Tax facts, Index
pages 447 to 524

Chapter 33 helps you understand how the Inland Revenue works. More important, it guides you to the best approach if you find yourself in dispute with the taxman. If you don't check your tax, you'll never be sure that you're paying the right amount. Chapter 34 takes you step by step through checking your income tax bill. *Tax facts* – starting on p494 – is 23 pages of useful information: tax rates, allowances, Inland Revenue Concessions, and more.

2 TAX CHANGES

In this chapter we take a quick tour through the changes made by the 1987 Finance Act. It was a fairly low key Finance Act, rushed through in shortened form because of the June general election. Some of the Chancellor's 1987 Budget proposals were shelved – in particular, the introduction of tax relief on 'profit-related pay', and a new tax regime for personal pensions. The Government has said that it will re-introduce the proposals which were shelved – throughout this book we've marked them with this symbol: ▉

Tax rates

Income tax bands for the 1987–88 tax year were increased in line with inflation. The basic rate tax band rose to £17,900 from £17,200, and the basic rate of tax was reduced to 27% from 29%.

Tax rates for the 1987–88 tax year

Taxable income of:	Taxed at:
first £17,900	27%
next £2,500	40%
next £5,000	45%
next £7,900	50%
next £7,900	55%
anything more	60%

Allowances

The main personal allowances were increased by around 3.7%, in line with the rate of inflation, and a new higher age allowance for people aged 80-plus was introduced. A full list of the new allowances is on p22.

Separate taxation of wife's earnings

The changes in allowances and tax bands mean that the income level at which it becomes worthwhile to have the wife's earnings taxed separately in the 1987–88 tax year is £26,870 or more (£26,520 in the 1986–87 tax year). If you can claim extra allowances or outgoings, the figure rises by the total of the amounts you can claim (see p78).

Company cars

The taxable value of your company car will be increased in the 1987–88 tax year by around 10% (see p171 for this year's and next year's values). The taxable value of petrol provided by your employer for private use has not been increased.

VAT

If you supply goods or services which are liable for VAT (see p227), and you aren't registered, you'll need to tell Customs and Excise if you believe that the value of these supplies in the year ahead will be more than £21,300 (was £20,500), or £7,250 (was £7,000) in any one quarter.

If your annual turnover is less than £250,000, you now have the option of accounting for your VAT yearly rather than quarterly. You can also wait until you have received money owing to you before you have to pay VAT on it (although this change will have to be approved by the EEC).

Profit-related pay

In his Budget, the Chancellor proposed that an employee who takes a proportion of pay as 'profit-related pay' should get full tax relief on half of it, up to the point where profit-related pay equals 20% of total pay or £3,000 (whichever is lower). To qualify for tax relief, employers would have to register their schemes with the Inland Revenue before the start of their profit year, and schemes would have to meet certain statutory conditions. See p141.

Business expansion scheme

From 6 April 1987, if you invest in a business expansion scheme in the first half of the tax year (between 6 April and 5 October) you can claim up to half the tax relief on the investment against your income in the previous tax year. The maximum amount you can carry back in each tax year is £5,000 (see p293).

Capital gains tax

For the 1987–88 tax year, there's no tax to pay on the first £6,600 of net taxable gains (was £6,300 in 1986–87). And most trusts can make £3,300 of net taxable gains before there's tax to pay (was £3,150).

If you dispose of a business when you retire, you may now be able to claim relief from capital gains tax on up to £125,000 (was £100,000). This relief is available for people aged 60 or over and for people forced to retire before then due to ill-health (see p434).

Inheritance tax

The tax thresholds for each rate of inheritance tax due on gifts made within seven years of your death and on your estate have been increased from Budget day, 17 March 1987. You now pay tax only if the value of the estate or gifts amounts to £90,000 or more. The original seven rates of tax have been reduced to four, though the top rate remains 60%.

Share option schemes

If you hold share options in your employer's company under an *approved* scheme and your company is taken over, you will now be entitled to exchange your existing options for options of equal value in the company taking over (see p176).

Pensions

The Chancellor proposed new tax rules for personal pensions and for people in employer's pension schemes:

● for those joining an employer's scheme on or after 17 March 1987, there will be a maximum tax-free lump sum on retirement of £150,000, and there will be a stricter definition of 'final pay' for calculating pension entitlement (see p335)

● from October 1987, additional voluntary contributions (AVCs) can be made into any scheme, not just one linked to an employer's scheme, and you'll get full tax relief on them provided your total pension contributions don't exceed 15% of earnings. You no longer have to make AVCs at a constant level for at least 5 years, but can vary the amount and timing (as scheme rules permit)

● from 7 April 1987, if you start to make AVC's into a new scheme, or to an existing employer's AVC scheme, your AVC's will have to be used to improve your pension – you won't be able to use them to obtain a tax-free lump sum

● from 4 January 1988, anyone not in an employer's pension scheme can take out a personal pension. Anyone presently in an employer's scheme will be able to take out a personal pension from 6 April 1988. You'll be able to contribute up to 17.5% of your earnings (more if over 50) into your plan (or plans) and get full tax relief on these. On retirement, you can take up to a quarter of your fund as a tax-free lump sum.

3 HOW YOUR TAX BILL IS WORKED OUT

In this chapter, we aim to give you a quick run through the stages of working out your income tax bill. The details – and the difficulties – are left until later chapters. All we're doing here is setting out the bare bones of the income tax system.

Start with the Diagram

The Diagram, overleaf, shows that you don't pay tax on all the money you receive. It starts with *Money*, and takes you to *Taxable income*, and then to *Tax. Taxable income* is the amount of income on which you pay tax. On the way towards taxable income, different sums of money are knocked out of the way. Each time, they cut down the amount of money on which you have to pay tax. For a start, anything that isn't income is knocked out. Things that aren't income include gifts, or things you inherit, or capital gains (these will be taxed separately).

Tax-free income, tax relief, tax allowances

Next to disappear is any income which is tax-free. Then goes any payment you make on which you get tax relief, often called *outgoings* (see p24). This leaves what the taxman calls your 'total income' (see p29 for why this figure can sometimes be important). Lastly, you take away any income tax *allowances* (see p22). These allowances reduce the amount of income on which you have to pay tax. When all these subtractions have been made, the result is your *Taxable income*.

Example

Horace Walpole received £20,000 in the 1987–88 tax year (for what a tax year is, see p20). He works his way through the Diagram. First, he takes away things which aren't income: £300 he inherited, and £1,550 of capital gains from selling shares at a profit. Then he knocks off his tax-free income – £50 interest from a National Savings Bank Ordinary account. The next things to go are his outgoings: £1,000 in contributions to his employer's pension scheme. Lastly he takes away his allowances: his single person's allowance of £2,425, and another £100 for supporting a dependent relative. Here's the result:

Money	**£20,000**
subtract things which aren't income	
– inheritance	£300
– capital gains on shares	£1,550
Income	**£18,150**
subtract tax-free income	
– NSB Ordinary account interest	£50
Income for tax purposes	**£18,100**
subtract outgoings which qualify for tax relief	
– contributions to pension scheme	£1,000
'Total income'	**£17,100**
subtract allowances	
– single person's allowance	£2,425
– dependent relative allowance	£100
Taxable income	**£14,575**
Tax: 27% of £14,575	**£3,935.25**

Money		£20,000
Income	ie **money** *less* **things which aren't income**	£18,150
Income for tax purposes	ie **income** *less* **tax-free income**	£18,100
'Total income'	ie **income for tax purposes** *less* **outgoings**	£17,100
Taxable income	ie **'total income'** *less* **allowances**	£14,575
Tax ie 27% of £14,575	£3,935.25	

What is income?

In any tax year, you're likely to receive money from a number of different sources. The main ones are likely to be your job (or pension), and perhaps some money from investments. It's important to know how much of this money counts as income for tax purposes. If it's not income – or if it's tax-free income – there's no tax to pay on it. Opposite we tell you what counts as income – and what doesn't. You'll also find a list of tax-free income.

The main sources of income

- earnings from your job
- any spare-time earnings
- fees for work you do, and profits you make from running a business
- any other earnings from being self-employed
- pensions
- social security benefits
- rents from letting out property
- regular payments from someone else, like maintenance payments or covenant payments
- income from investments – for example interest from bank and building society accounts, dividends from shares, distributions from unit trusts. More details on p268.

Things which aren't income

- gifts and presents
- money you borrow
- money you inherit
- profits (gains) you make when you sell something for more than you bought it for – unless you did this as a business venture or as part of your business
- betting winnings – unless you bet (eg on horses) for a living
- lottery winnings
- premium bond prizes.

Tax-free income

Not surprisingly, there's no tax to pay on income which is tax-free. So you can forget about it when you're working out your tax bill.

> **Tax-free income from investments**
> - First £70 interest from a National Savings Bank Ordinary account
> - Proceeds from National Savings Certificates
> - Proceeds from Ulster Savings Certificates (if you live in N. Ireland)
> - Part of the income from many annuities – see p319
> - Proceeds from Save-As-You-Earn contracts
> - Dividends paid by a credit union to its members
> - Proceeds from a regular-premium investment-type life insurance policy (if held for 10 years or three-quarters of its term – whichever is shorter)
> - Proceeds from a Personal Equity Plan – see p289.

Tax-free income from the State, or from local authorities
- Tax-free social security benefits – see list on p117
- Tax-free pensions (including the £10 Christmas bonus)
- Rate rebates, rent rebates and allowances
- Grants for improving or insulating your home
- Most grants or scholarships for education
- Some allowances paid under job release schemes from 1977 onwards.

Tax-free income from jobs
- Some earnings from working abroad – see p178
- Some fringe benefits – see p162
- In many cases, up to a total of £25,000 in redundancy pay, pay in lieu of notice, etc when you leave a job – see p158
- Gifts which are genuine personal gifts – ie not given to you because you're an employee
- Certain profit-related pay (see p141).

Miscellaneous tax-free income
- Income from family income benefit life insurance policies
- The first year or so's income from a permanent health insurance policy
- Interest from a delayed settlement of damages for personal injury
- Strike and unemployment pay from a trade union
- Interest on a tax rebate.

Tax year

Income tax is an annual tax. In other words, there's a separate income tax bill for each year's income. Tax 'years' are not the same as ordinary years. Tax years run from 6 April in one year to 5 April in the next. So the tax year running from 6 April 1987 to 5 April 1988 is called the *1987–88 tax year*.

Income for a tax year

Normally, your tax bill for a tax year is based on the income you actually receive during that tax year. But if you're self-employed, it's likely that your tax bill will be based on money you received in an earlier year. More details on p187. This can also apply to interest you get which is not taxed before it's paid to you – see p276.

Tax rates for the 1987–88 tax year

Basic rate tax of 27% is charged on the first **£17,900** of your taxable income. Income above £17,900 is taxed at a series of **higher rates** up to a top rate of 60%.

slice of taxable income	tax rate	tax on this slice	so if taxable income is	tax due is
first £17,900	27%	£4,833	£17,900	£4,833
£17,901 – £20,400	40%	£1,000	£20,400	£5,833
£20,401 – £25,400	45%	£2,250	£25,400	£8,083
£25,401 – £33,300	50%	£3,950	£33,300	£12,033
£33,301 – £41,200	55%	£4,345	£41,200	£16,378
£41,201 and above	60%			

Investment income surcharge

Investment income surcharge was an extra tax people had to pay on unearned income above a certain amount. For example, in the 1983–84 tax year, people with more than £7,100 of 'total investment income' (see p278), had to pay an extra 15% tax on the amount over £7,100.

Investment income surcharge was abolished in the 1984 Budget – so the difference between earned and unearned income is no longer as important as it was. But it can still be very important for a married couple. This is because the wife's investment income is taxed as though it belongs to the husband. For how this can affect a couple's tax bill, see p67.

The general election held on 11 June 1987 meant that the Finance Act confirming the tax rules for the 1987–88 tax year was rushed through in shortened form. Some of the Chancellor's 1987 Budget proposals were shelved, but the Government has said that it will re-introduce them. We've marked these pre-election proposals with this symbol:

Personal allowances for the 1987–88 tax year

Subtracting your personal allowances from your income is the last step before tax on your income is worked out. The more allowances you have, the smaller the amount of income on which you have to pay tax – so the less tax you pay.

allowance	how much
Single person's allowance	£2,425
Married man's allowance	£3,795
Wife's earned income allowance	up to £2,425

Age allowance:
  single person (under 80)
  married man (under 80)
  single person (80 or over)
  married man (80 or over)
	
	up to £2,690
	up to £4,675
	up to £3,070
	up to £4,845

Additional personal allowance	£1,370
Widow's bereavement allowance	£1,370
Housekeeper allowance	£100

Dependent relative allowance:
  single woman claiming [2]
  other person claiming
	
	£145
	£100

Son's or daughter's services allowance	£55
Blind person's allowance	£540
Death and superannuation benefits	half of what you pay for certain benefits
Life insurance premiums	15% of gross premiums, within limits
Personal pension payments [3]	what you pay, within limits
Investments under the Business Expansion Scheme	what you pay, within limits

[1] a married couple with the wife's earned income taxed separately (see p74) each get the single person's allowance. They don't get married man's allowance, or wife's earned income allowance, or age allowance

who gets it	more details
anyone who isn't married (including children, widows, widowers, most divorced or separated people) [1]	p49
most married men [1]	p64
wives with earned income [1]	p64
elderly people with modest incomes. Age allowance *replaces* single person's or married man's allowance [1]. It's reduced if your 'total income' is above £9,800	p104
many people who have to bring up a child on their own (eg single parents, widows)	p50
widows in the tax year in which their husband died, and in the following tax year if they haven't remarried	p86
a widow (or widower) who has someone living in the house to help them	p124
people who support a needy relative	p125
some people who are permanently ill, disabled, or 65 or over during the tax year, with a son or daughter living with them and looking after them	p124
anyone registered as blind	p125
people making trade union subscriptions, part of which is for superannuation (ie pension), funeral or life insurance benefits	p315
people with policies that qualify taken out before 14 March 1984, given as a subsidy rather than a relief	p310
people making payments to personal pension plans or for Section 226A life insurance policies	p339
people investing in certain unquoted companies	p292

[2] or a wife with earnings taxed separately (see p74)
[3] including premiums for s226A life insurance policies (see p340). Note that though the taxman classes them as allowances, he treats them as outgoings.

Tax relief

If you get tax relief, it means that some of your income escapes tax. For example, suppose you're buying your house with a mortgage, and you pay £1,000 a year in interest. This interest qualifies for tax relief. The effect is that you pay tax on £1,000 less of your income. For a basic rate taxpayer, tax relief on £1,000 means £270 less tax to pay. (Most people nowadays get tax relief on their mortgages by making lower payments to the lender.)

Example

Arnold Brown has a mortgage, on which he pays £2,500 a year in interest. Tax relief means that Arnold can knock his mortgage interest off his income – so he pays tax on £2,500 less of his income. Tax on £2,500 is £675 (ie 27% of £2,500) – so Arnold pays £675 less in tax. He gets this tax relief by making lower payments to the lender – ie £2,500 *minus* £675 *equals* £1,825.

The main tax reliefs

In general, you get tax relief on what are called your **outgoings**. The most important outgoings are:
● mortgage interest on loans of up to £30,000 to buy or improve your only or main home
● pension contributions
● maintenance payments you make after a divorce or separation
● expenses in your job.
    The list starting on this page gives the basic rules which decide whether or not you qualify for tax relief.

The main things which qualify for tax relief

The code letters **A B C D** etc tell you how you get your tax relief – details on pages 27 and 28.

outgoing	more details	basic rules
mortgage interest **A or B**	p235	You get tax relief on the interest you pay on up to £30,000 of loans to buy or improve your only or main home. The limit for a married couple is the same – ie £30,000. For an unmarried couple it's £30,000 each.

outgoing	more details	basic rules
interest on a home which you let B	p256	You get tax relief on a loan to buy or improve property which you let. There's no limit on the amount of loans you can get tax relief on, but to qualify for tax relief the property must normally be let at a commercial rent for more than 26 weeks in the year.
expenses in your job C	p142	You get tax relief on expenses you pay which are *wholly, exclusively, and necessarily* incurred in carrying out the duties of your employment.
a loan to buy an annuity A or B	p323	You get tax relief on the interest you pay on up to £30,000 of loans to buy an annuity, provided you're 65 or over, *and* your only or main home is used as security for the loans.
loans for business B	IR11	You can get tax relief on an unlimited amount of loans for: • buying a share in a partnership – provided you're a partner (but not a limited partner) • contributing capital to a partnership – again you must be a partner (and not a limited partner) • buying a share in an employee-controlled company which employs you more or less full-time • buying a share in, or lending to, an industrial co-operative which employs you more or less full-time • buying machinery or plant (eg a car or a typewriter) for use in your job or in your partnership.
loans to pay inheritance tax when someone dies B	p407	You get tax relief for up to 12 months on the interest you pay on a loan to pay inheritance tax, provided you actually pay the tax before the grant of probate or letters of administration.
covenant payments D or E	p127	You get tax relief on payments you make under a deed of covenant. For covenants to people, you get tax relief at the basic rate only, and the covenant normally has to last for more than six years. For covenants to charities you get tax relief at your top rate of tax, and the covenant must normally last for more than three years.

outgoing	more details	basic rules
alimony, aliment, or maintenance payments **D**	p90	You get tax relief at your top rate of tax on the full amount you pay – provided there's some enforceable obligation to pay (ie no tax relief on mere gifts).
pension contributions **F**	p330	You get tax relief on contributions you make to an employer's pension scheme which is 'approved' or 'statutory' (most are).
personal pension payments, Section 226A policies **G**	p339	People who are self-employed, or not in their employer's pension scheme, can get tax relief (at their top rate of tax) on payments they make to provide them with an income in retirement, or to provide a lump sum for their dependants. From January 1988 people in certain employers' schemes will get similar relief on additional separate pension arrangements – see p340
Business Expansion Scheme [1] **H**	p292	You can get tax relief in each tax year on up to £40,000 of investment in certain types of company. The £40,000 limit is the same for a married couple.

[1] Investments under the scheme don't reduce your 'total income' for tax purposes: they're subtracted from 'total income' when working out your taxable income. In most cases this (highly technical) distinction is of no importance. But for some people the exact size of 'total income' can matter, see p105.

How you get tax relief

The mechanics of getting tax relief aren't always the same. For example, you might get tax relief by:
● claiming money back from the Inland Revenue
● if you work for an employer, getting the tax relief in stages through the Pay-As-You-Earn system. The effect is that less tax is deducted from your wages or salary
● giving yourself tax relief by subtracting tax (from a payment you're making) before you make the payment.

In our Chart on pages 24 to 26 we've put code letters from **A** to **H** against the different things which qualify for tax relief. Opposite we give details for each code letter.

A: mortgage interest paid under the MIRAS system

Most mortgages are now under the MIRAS system – which stands for Mortage Interest Relief At Source. Your lender will be able to tell you whether your mortgage is under MIRAS. Under MIRAS, you get *basic rate* tax relief by making a lower payment to the lender. If you're entitled to tax relief at higher rates, you get this extra tax relief either under the PAYE system or by paying less tax when your tax bill for the year is worked out.

B: interest on other loans which qualify for tax relief

You write to your tax office, and *either* get tax relief through the PAYE system *or* by making a claim when your tax bill for the year is worked out.

C: expenses in your job

You enter the amount of the expenses in your Tax Return. You'll get tax relief *either* by being asked to pay a lower amount in tax when you get a Notice of Assessment, *or* under the PAYE system in the following tax year.

D: alimony, aliment, or maintenance payments; covenant payments to charities

You give yourself *basic rate* tax relief by subtracting an amount equivalent to the basic rate tax on the payments before making them. So for a payment of £300, you'd subtract £81 – ie 27% of £219 – and pay £210. If you pay tax at higher rates, you can get higher rate tax relief – either under the PAYE system or by making a claim when your tax bill for the year is worked out. **Note:** if your alimony or maintenance payments are *small maintenance payments* (see p90 for what these are), you make the payments *in full*, and get your tax relief either under PAYE or by making a claim when your tax bill for the year is worked out.

E: other covenant payments

You give yourself basic rate tax relief by subtracting an amount equivalent to the basic rate tax on the payments before you make them. You can't claim higher rate tax relief, even if you pay tax at higher rates.

F: pension contributions

Tax relief is given automatically by your employer by reducing the pay on which you are taxed by the amount of your

contributions (including any additional voluntary
contributions you make.)

G: personal pension payments; Section 226A policies

Write to the tax office when you take out the policy (the
company should give you certificate SEPC). The taxman may
send you **form 43** to give details of the payments. Normally
you'll get tax relief by making a claim when your tax bill for
the year is being worked out.

If you take out a pension plan and are in an employer's
scheme you get any *basic rate* tax relief due by making lower
payments. Higher rate tax relief will be given when your tax
bill is worked out.

H: Business Expansion Scheme

You get a certificate from the company you invest in, and send
it to your tax office. Tax relief is given either through the PAYE
system or by paying less tax when your tax bill for the year is
worked out. From April 1987 half the amount of BES
payments made in the first half of the tax year can be set
against income from the previous year (subject to a £5,000
limit for relief).

Gross and net – what they mean

Throughout this book, you'll come across references to *gross
payments* and *net payments*, and to *gross income* and *net
income*. Here we tell you:
- the difference between gross and net
- how to get from gross to net (or from net to gross).

Example

Spencer Percival has a mortgage of £24,000 under the MIRAS
system (see p241). His mortgage is the type where he pays
interest-only – which amounts to £2,400 in the 1987–88 tax
year. Like most people, Spencer makes his mortgage payments
monthly, so each month's payment is £200. Because his
mortgage is under the MIRAS system, he gets basic rate rax relief
by making lower payments to the lender. So instead of paying
£200 a month, he gives himself basic rate tax relief of 27% of
£200 = £54. So he pays the lender £200 − £54 = £146.
- the £200 is the *gross payment*
- the £146 is the *net payment*
- the difference between the gross and net payments is the £54
basic rate tax relief – see Diagram.

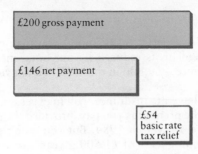

The same principle applies to **gross** and **net income**. If you receive income from which basic rate tax has been deducted, the amount you get is the *net income*, and adding back the basic rate tax brings you to the *gross income*.

How to find out the net amount

If you know the gross amount of a payment (or income), you find out the net amount by subtracting 27 per cent. If you've got a calculator, the quickest way is to *multiply* the gross amount by 0.73. So in the Example above, £200 (gross) × 0.73 = £146 (net).

How to find out the gross amount

If you know the net amount of the payment (or income), you find out the gross amount by adding the basic rate tax to the net amount. If you've got a calculator, the quickest way is to *divide* the net amount by 0.73. So in the Example above, £146 (net) divided by 0.73 = £200 (gross).

'Total income'

You may need to find out what the taxman calls your 'total income'. It's a very misleading name. Broadly, 'total income' equals income *minus* tax-free income, and *minus* outgoings.

income

less tax-free income

less outgoings
= 'total income'

Why it might be important

- if you're elderly (64 or more) you may get a special age allowance. This is reduced if your 'total income' is above a certain figure – £9,800 in the 1987–88 tax year. More details on p105

- if you have life insurance, you may get tax relief (at 15 per cent) on the premiums you pay, provided the policy was taken out before 14 March 1984. But you won't get tax relief on premiums in excess of £1,500 a year – or one-sixth of your 'total income' – whichever is less. See p310

- to qualify for dependent relative allowance (see p125), the 'total income' of the relative you support must not be more than the single person's basic retirement pension (which works out at £2,054 for the 1987–88 tax year).

Tax Schedules

Tax Schedules go back to the earliest days of income tax. But although they sound off-putting, it can be useful to have a rough idea of what they mean. It can – in some cases – save you money.

What they are

They're a way of dividing income up into different types. For example earnings from your job are taxed under Schedule E, whereas earnings from being self-employed are taxed under Schedule D. For a full list of what goes where, see below.

Why are Schedules important?

Dividing income into different bits may seem extremely unimportant. All income nowadays is taxed at the same rates, so why not lump it all together? But it's not quite that simple. Important differences still remain. The differences are in when you are taxed on the income, and in the **expenses** you can set against tax. Different Schedules have different rules – so it can be vitally important to be sure that income is taxed under a Schedule with generous (rather than stingy) rules about expenses. Because the more expenses you can set against tax, the less tax you have to pay.

Cases

To make life slightly more exciting, some of the Schedules are divided up into Cases. So you can have a Schedule divided into Case 1, Case 2, Case 3, and so on. Traditionally, Cases are given Roman numerals – so it's Case I, Case II, Case III, Case IV, Case V, and Case VI.

Rules about expenses can differ from Case to Case. For example Schedule D Case I income has fairly generous rules; whereas Schedule D Case III is the meanest of the lot.

Working through the Schedules

Schedule A

Schedule A income is investment income (unless it comes from carrying on a business).

What's taxed under Schedule A

Income from land – including income from unfurnished property. Income from furnished lettings is normally taxed under Schedule D Case VI or Schedule D Case I.

When the income is taxed

Schedule A income is taxed on a *current year basis* – ie your tax bill for the 1987–88 tax year is based on the income due to you in that tax year.

Expenses you can claim

● general expenses of managing the property, including maintenance, repairs, insurance (but not insurance of contents), fees of professional people, advertising costs, etc
● expenses connected with the land, including rent, rates (if you're liable to pay them), ground rent, easements, etc.

Costs of improving the property can't be set against tax, though you may get tax relief on interest on a loan to improve the property – see p256. Capital expenditure may qualify for capital allowances – see p198.

If the repairs you make are because the previous owner let the property become dilapidated, you won't get tax relief on the cost of repair (unless the property passes to you on death, and the previous owner was your wife or husband).

Schedule B

Schedule B income is investment income (unless it comes from carrying on a business).

What's taxed under Schedule B

Commercially managed woodlands in the UK. The rules are an oddity: instead of being taxed on your profits (if any), you're

taxed on one-third of the *gross annual value for letting purposes* of the property (ie what you might get in rent if you let the land on normal terms). For Schedule B purposes, it's assumed that the land is unimproved: broadly, this means uncultivated (ie woodland without trees). You can, if you wish, choose to be taxed under Schedule D Case I instead.

If you occupy woodlands wholly or mainly for the purpose of felling and removing trees for your business, you will be taxed under Schedule D Case I or Case VI for periods of occupation starting after 13 March 1984.

When the income is taxed

As we explain above, there's no real 'income'. The assumed income for a tax year is one-third of the gross annual value for letting purposes for that tax year.

Expenses you can claim

None – because the 'income' under Schedule B is calculated by an artificial method – see above.

Schedule C

Schedule C income is investment income.

What's taxed under Schedule C

Interest paid in the UK on some Government securities (UK Government and foreign Governments). Basic rate tax is deducted before the interest is paid to you.

When the income is taxed

Schedule C income is taxed on a *current year basis* – ie your tax bill for the 1987–88 tax year is based on the income due to you in that tax year.

Expenses you can claim

None.

Schedule D Case I, Schedule D Case II

Case I and Case II income is earned income.

What's taxed under Case I and Case II

These two collect tax on the profits of being self-employed.

If the profits are from a trade (eg window-cleaner, shopkeeper, manufacturer), you're taxed under Case I. If the profits are from a profession (eg barrister, architect, accountant), you're taxed under Case II. The tax rules in each case are virtually identical. Rent from lodgings in your own home may count as earnings from a trade.

When the income is taxed

You're normally taxed on a *preceding year basis* – ie your tax bill for the 1987–88 tax year is based on the income due to you in your accounting period ending in the previous tax year. If this sounds complicated, it's explained on p187.

Expenses you can claim

Any expense incurred *wholly and exclusively* for your trade or business. This definition is more generous than for people who are employed – see p142. More details on p193.

Schedule D Case III

Case III income is investment income.

What's taxed under Schedule D Case III

The main things are interest (eg interest from National Savings Bank accounts, interest from loans), income from annuities and income from Government securities (unless they're taxed under Schedule C). Other things taxed under this Case are annual payments – eg covenant or maintenance payments.

When the income is taxed

● **Interest** is normally taxed on a *preceding year basis* – ie your tax bill for the 1987–88 tax year is based on the income due to you in the 1986–87 tax year. More details on p276.
● **Covenant payments and maintenance payments** are normally taxed on a *current year basis* – ie your tax bill for the 1987–88 tax year is based on payments due to you in that tax year. Covenant payments are not liable to higher rate tax. And neither covenant nor maintenance payments were liable to investment income surcharge when it existed (see p21).
● **Bank interest** received (or credited to your account) up to 5 April 1984 was normally taxed on a *preceding year basis*. The rules have since changed – see p279.

Expenses you can claim

None. Case III income is often referred to as 'pure profit income' – ie it's assumed that you don't have any expenses.

Schedule D Case IV, Schedule D Case V

Case IV and Case V income is investment income (unless it comes from carrying on a business).

What's taxed under Case IV and Case V

These two are both concerned with income from abroad. Case IV covers income from foreign securities, except for securities covered by Schedule C. Case V covers most other types of income from abroad – eg rents, dividends, pensions, trading profits, maintenance payments. Broadly, if you're not domiciled in the UK, or (for UK or Irish citizens) you're not ordinarily resident in the UK, you're taxed only on money which comes to the UK. Otherwise, you're taxed on the lot – whether or not it reaches the UK. If the money comes from a pension a tenth of the income normally escapes UK tax.

When the income is taxed

This income is normally taxed on a *preceding year basis* – ie your tax bill for the 1987–88 tax year is based on the income due to you in the previous tax year (or in your accounting year ending in the previous tax year, if the money comes from a trade or profession).

Expenses you can claim

If the money comes from a trade or profession, tax is charged on your taxable profits – so you can subtract the usual expenses in working these out. Otherwise, normally none.

Schedule D Case VI

Case VI income is investment income (except for post cessation receipts).

What's taxed under Case VI

Case VI is a ragbag of odd bits of income which don't fit in anywhere else. Examples are income from furnished lettings (unless it counts as a trade – see p257); income from furnished holiday cottages; income from occasional freelance work; post-cessation receipts – ie after a business or partnership ends; income from investing in plays – unless you do this for a living.

When the income is taxed

This income is taxed on a *current year basis* – ie your tax bill for the 1987–88 tax year is based on the income due to you in that tax year.

Expenses you can claim

There's nothing in the tax acts about exactly what you can claim, but you have to pay tax on 'profits or gains'. So expenses necessarily incurred in making those profits are deducted when working out how much income is taxed. Losses can be set against other Case VI income for the same (or a following) tax year, but not against income from other Schedules or Cases.

Schedule E

Schedule E income is earned income.

What's taxed under Schedule E

- income from your employment – eg wages, expense allowances, tips, fringe benefits (if they're taxable)
- pensions from employers
- taxable social security benefits
- freelance earnings under a contract of employment. This can be a grey area, but if, for example, you're a teacher, and get some money from marking examination scripts the taxman will normally tax this extra income under Schedule E.

When the income is taxed

On a *current year basis* – ie your tax bill for the 1987–88 tax year is based on the income due to you in that tax year.

Expenses you can claim

The rules are harsher than for self-employed people: you can claim only expenses which are *wholly, exclusively and necessarily* incurred in the performance of the duties of your employment. For example, you could spend money on something which was entirely for use in your job, but unless it was *necessary*, you wouldn't be able to claim it against tax (see p142).

Schedule E is divided into three Cases, of which Case I is by far the most important. Broadly, Case I catches income from employments if the employee is resident and ordinarily resident in the UK; Case II applies to people who normally live and work abroad, but who have some earnings arising in the UK; Case III applies to income remitted to the UK (by people resident in the UK) earned in an employment abroad.

Schedule F

Schedule F income is investment income.

What's taxed under Schedule F

Dividends from companies resident in the UK, and distributions from unit trusts resident in the UK.

When the income is taxed

On a *current year basis* – ie your tax bill for the 1987–88 tax year is based on the income due to you in that tax year.

Expenses you can claim

None.

4 TAX ADVICE

There are three rules to follow if you want to keep your tax bill as low as possible:
- **keep in control.** If you let your tax affairs get out of hand, you'll store up trouble – and expense – for the future
- **make the right choices.** In planning your life, the choices you make can drastically affect your tax bill. There are 52 choices starting overleaf – any one of which might affect you
- **act in time.** Many of the choices you make have time limits attached to them. We give 20 time limits on p45.

Keep in control

George Selwyn gets occasional bits of income from spare-time work. He keeps hardly any record of what he's been paid, or of who's paid him, or of what expenses (if any) he had to pay out of his own pocket. George hasn't told the taxman about his spare-time income – not because he's dishonest, but because he hasn't got round to it.

George is storing up trouble for the future. One day, the taxman will catch on to the fact that George is making money on the side. And he won't know that George is honest. There's every chance that George will be summoned to a very unpleasant interview with a Tax Inspector, and asked to produce his non-existent accounts and receipts. Eventually, he's likely to be faced with a tax demand which he can't really afford to pay. It may be quite a lot higher than he thinks it ought to be – but he has no records to prove that it's too high.

George's brother Jack hasn't got around to claiming tax relief on a loan he took out two years ago to extend his house. There's no real danger here – provided Jack claims tax relief between six and seven years of taking out the loan. But meanwhile he's giving the Inland Revenue an interest-free loan.

These two examples are not unusual. They're ordinary, everyday, examples of carelessness which can cost money.

So here are a few tips on keeping your tax affairs in order.

1 Keep clear records of income you get, and of any expenses you can set against your income. And keep your records up to date.

2 Keep the taxman informed of what's going on. Tell him if there's any change in your circumstances – for example:
- you get married
- you separate or get divorced
- you move house
- you become unemployed, or retire
- you gain or lose a source of income
- you start or stop making a payment which qualifies for tax relief
- you start or stop supporting a dependent relative.

3 Check your tax. Whenever you get a tax bill, or a Notice of Coding, check to see that the figures are correct – and write to your tax office at once if they're not.

Make the right choices

Here are 52 tax choices – one for every week in the year. See how many of them apply to you – or might apply in the future. Making the right choice can reduce the amount of tax you have to pay.

Marriage – before, during, and after

1 Are you married? If your combined income is £26,870 or more, consider getting the wife's earned income taxed separately (p74)

2   Does one of you stay at home to look after the kids? If you could both earn the same amount, it pays handsomely if the *wife* goes to work, and the husband stays at home (p70)

3   Not married yet? Marriage can save – or cost you – hundreds of £££ in tax. Weigh up the pros and cons before going ahead (p67)

4   Wedding bells for the elderly? Once again, marriage may be a mixed blessing (p108)

5   Marriage on the rocks? There are more tax pitfalls when you're separating (or getting divorced) than at any other time. Make sure you make the best choices in deciding how to pay maintenance (p94) and get maximum tax relief on mortgage interest (p100)

6   Unmarried, and with children? Affiliation orders (p59) may save tax. So can covenant payments (on the same page)

7   Married this year? In this tax year only, the husband can choose not to take the married man's allowance – it could save tax (p73).

In a job?

8   Can you get any fringe benefits? Many perks are taxed at much less than their value to you (p161)

9   Can you set any expenses against tax? See the Table on p143 onwards

10   Approaching retirement? It may be worthwhile making additional voluntary contributions to your pension scheme (p336)

11   Not in a pension scheme? You can get tax relief (at your top rate) on premiums to a personal pension plan (p339)

12   A student? If you have vacation earnings, signing a form can save you the bother of paying tax now and claiming it back later (p55).

In business?

13   Self-employed? You may be able to save tax by employing your wife (p208)

14   Loans for your business? See if they qualify for tax relief (p25)

15   Entitled to capital allowances? It may pay you to claim less

than you're able to, and to roll on the balance to following years (p198)

16 Business losses? You have three choices of how to deal with them – and the choice you make can affect your tax bill and your cash-in-hand (p204)

17 Losses in a new business? You can get tax relief by setting them against other income (p207)

18 Should you register for VAT? See p209 for the answer

19 Should you form a company? Tax rates for money kept in the business could be much lower (p211).

On a low income?

20 Not a taxpayer? If you don't pay tax, and you've got money to invest, compare the *after-tax* return from a building society, bank, deposit-taker or local authority loan with the *before-tax* return from other investments (page 272)

21 Tax to claim back? Make your claim as soon as possible (p453). And if you'll be claiming tax back each year, arrange with the taxman to get it paid in instalments (p114)

22 Special tax allowances to claim? See the list on pages 124 to 126.

Elderly?

23 Not getting full age allowance? Consider switching to investments where the return is tax-free (p105). Beware of cashing in a life insurance policy where the return is taxable (p305). If you've got income to spare, a covenant to grandchildren, for example, can transfer more money to them than it costs you (p115)

24 Need more income? One solution might be to buy an annuity (p319). Or consider a home income plan (p323)

25 Can you make use of your husband's pension contributions? A married woman can get a state retirement pension based on her husband's contributions. It's worth doing so if this would be higher than the pension you would have got on your own contributions. And – when you get the pension – the amount you would have got on your own contributions counts as your earned income (p110)

26 Retiring from a business? You may be able to claim

retirement relief from capital gains tax on up to £125,000 of gains (p434)

27 Coming up to retirement – and with a personal pension plan? You may be able to get yourself a larger pension – and cut your recent tax bills (p347). If you haven't got a personal pension plan, it's not too late to take one out now.

Investments, life insurance

28 Buying British Government stocks? If you buy them through the National Savings Stock Register, income is paid to you without tax being deducted (p279) – and the costs of the transaction are lower

29 Do you pay tax at higher rates? Investing for capital gains, rather than income, may give you a better after-tax return (p273)

30 A large amount to invest, and worried about inheritance tax? Consider investing in 'favoured property' (p394)

31 Getting tax relief on a pre-March 1984 life insurance policy? Beware of extending the policy, or of altering it to increase the benefits. You may lose your tax relief (p315)

32 Self-employed, or in a job but not in an employer's pension scheme? You can get tax relief on a life insurance policy (p312)

33 Willing to take a risk? The Business Expansion Scheme gives you tax relief on your investments (p292)

34 Life insurance for your family? Cut your inheritance tax bill by making sure the proceeds aren't added to your estate (p316)

35 Married – and with capital gains tax to pay? You may be able to reduce your CGT bill by asking for the losses of each of you to be treated separately (p430).

You and your home

36 Thinking of buying? Tax relief on your mortgage could make buying your own home one of your best long-term investments (p235)

37 A home to let? If you're borrowing to buy or improve the home, see whether you can get tax relief on the interest you pay (p259). For the expenses you can claim, see pages 255 and 258

38 Selling your house and garden separately? Sell the garden first (p247)

39 Working at home? See p249 for expenses you can claim

40 More than one home? Be careful about which home you choose as your 'main home' for capital gains tax purposes (p243)

41 A home with your job – and another which you own? Make sure that the home you own is free from capital gains tax (p250)

42 Moving house? You can get tax relief on two loans at once (p240)

43 Moving house when you marry? You may be able to get tax relief on three loans (p74)

44 Buying a home for around £30,000? Juggling with the price could save you more than £300 in stamp duty (p266).

Passing your money on

45 Student children? Paying your parental contribution under a deed of covenant could save you tax – or give more money to them (p132)

46 A family business? Think now about ways of passing it on (p389)

47 Married, with valuable property – and one of you owns it all? Sharing some of it between you can cut down your inheritance tax bill (p360)

48 High income, and young children? Consider an accumulation and maintenance trust (p403)

49 Inheritance tax to pay when you die? Making regular gifts out of income can get rid of a lot of the value of your estate. And you can give away at least £3,000 a year tax-free (p360)

50 Capital gains tax to pay on a gift? You can delay a tax bill – perhaps for ever – if you claim hold-over relief (p427)

51 An executor? Think about whether you want values for probate to be high or low (p408)

52 A beneficiary under a will? You may be able to pay any inheritance tax by instalments (p408).

Act in time

Tax rules are hedged round with time limits. They can be as short as 30 days, and as long as six years or more. We start by explaining how far back you can go to claim personal allowances or tax relief that you've missed. After that, we give time limits for 20 tax choices.

The normal (6-year) rule

You may have forgotten to claim personal allowances in past years. Or, more likely, you may have forgotten to claim tax relief on, for example, a loan which qualifies for tax relief. Is it too late to make a claim? How far back can you go?

The answer is that you can go back six tax years into the past – ie you can claim tax relief, or allowances, for the six tax years before the current tax year.

Tax years run from 6 April in one year to 5 April in the next. So if you act *before* 6 April 1988, you can go back six tax years before the 1987–88 tax year – which takes you to the 1981–82 tax year. (See overleaf for later tax years.) This 6-year time limit applies in a number of other cases – see pages 45 to 47.

How much can you claim?

The *allowances* you can claim are the amounts which applied in the relevant tax year – the figures are on p496.

Together with any extra tax relief you can claim, these will (in normal cases) reduce your taxable income for the relevant tax year. Your tax bill for that tax year will be recalculated, using the tax rates that applied at the time – the rates are on p495.

Example

Charles Fox looks through his tax bills for previous years. In the 1981–82 tax year, his taxable income was £14,000, and his tax bill was £4,512.50.

Charles realises that he forgot to claim tax relief on the £950 interest he paid on a loan to buy machinery for his business. And he also forgot to claim the additional personal allowance, which he was entitled to for that year. In the 1981–82 tax year, this allowance was £770 (see p496). So Charles can subtract £770 *plus* the £950 interest from his taxable income – leaving him with a taxable income of £12,280. Tax (at 1981–82 rates) on that amount was £3,787. So Charles can claim back the difference between £3,787 and the £4,512.50 he paid – £725.50.

The six-year rule

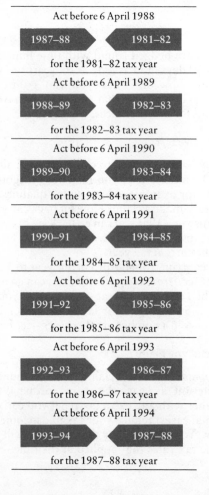

Act before 6 April 1988

1987–88 ⟩ ⟨ 1981–82

for the 1981–82 tax year

Act before 6 April 1989

1988–89 ⟩ ⟨ 1982–83

for the 1982–83 tax year

Act before 6 April 1990

1989–90 ⟩ ⟨ 1983–84

for the 1983–84 tax year

Act before 6 April 1991

1990–91 ⟩ ⟨ 1984–85

for the 1984–85 tax year

Act before 6 April 1992

1991–92 ⟩ ⟨ 1985–86

for the 1985–86 tax year

Act before 6 April 1993

1992–93 ⟩ ⟨ 1986–87

for the 1986–87 tax year

Act before 6 April 1994

1993–94 ⟩ ⟨ 1987–88

for the 1987–88 tax year

Time limits for 20 tax choices

1   Appealing against a *Notice of Assessment* (p468).
    Time limit 30 days from the date on the notice. You may
    also need to apply to postpone paying the tax asked for.
    Again, you have 30 days from the date on the notice.

2   Getting the wife's earned income taxed separately (p82).
    Time limit up to a year from the end of the tax year for
    which you want separate taxation – ie by 5 April 1989
    if you want separate taxation for the 1987–88 tax year.
    A longer time limit may be allowed in some cases. Once
    you've made the choice, you'll continue to be taxed
    separately unless you tell the taxman you've changed
    your mind – see below *(FA 1971 s23)*.

3   Changing your mind about getting the wife's earnings
    taxed separately.
    Time limit up to a year from the end of the tax year for
    which you want to be taxed together. A longer time limit
    may be allowed in some cases *(FA 1971 s23)*.

4   Getting husband's and wife's income separately assessed
    (p84).
    Time limit before 6 July in the tax year for which you
    want to be separately assessed – ie before 6 July 1988 if
    you want to be separately assessed for the 1988–89 tax
    year.

5   Changing your mind about separate assessment.
    Time limit before 6 July in the tax year for which you
    want to be assessed together.

6   In the tax year of marriage, choosing not to take the
    married man's allowance (p73).
    Time limit the normal 6-year rule applies *(TMA 1970 s43)*.

7   In the tax year of marriage, transferring unused
    allowances to your wife or husband (p73).
    Time limit the normal 6-year rule applies *(TMA 1970 s43)*.

8   In later tax years, transferring the married man's
    allowance, or part of it, (and any other unused
    allowances) to the wife (p70).
    Time limit the normal 6-year rule applies *(TMA 1970 s43)*.

9   Asking for business losses to be set against future profits
    from the same business (p204).
    Time limit within six years of the end of the tax year in
    which the losses (if they had been profits) would have
    been taxed *(TMA 1970 s171)*.

10 Asking for business losses to be set against other income of the year in which the losses were made (p204).
Time limit within two years of the end of the tax year in which the losses (if they had been profits) would have been taxed *(ICTA 1970 s168)*.

11 Asking for business losses to be set against other income of the following year (p205).
Time limit within two years of the end of the tax year in which the losses (if they had been profits) would have been taxed *(ICTA 1970 s168)*.

12 Asking for losses in the closing year of a business to be carried back against past profits of the same business (p207).
Time limit within six years of the end of the tax year for which you want to recalculate the profits *(ICTA 1970 s174)*.

13 Asking for losses in a new business to be set against other income from previous years (p207).
Time limit within two years of the end of the tax year in which the losses were made *(FA 1978 s30)*.

14 Claiming retirement relief (p434). This can reduce your capital gains tax bill when you dispose of your business.
Time limit the normal 6-year rule applies *(TMA 1970 s43)*.

15 If you own more than one home, choosing which one will be your 'main home' for capital gains tax purposes (p243).
Time limit within two years of the date on which you acquired the second home *(CGTA 1979 s101)*.

16 Claiming *hold-over relief* (page 427).
Time limit the normal 6-year rule applies, but hold-over relief can't be claimed for gifts made before 6 April 1980 *(TMA 1970 s43; FA 1980 s79)*.

17 Choosing to pay an inheritance tax bill by instalments (p408).
Time limit within six months of the end of the month in which the gift was made. This time limit applies strictly for gifts on death, and it's advisable to stick to it for gifts during life – though for lifetime gifts made between 6 April and 30 September you could wait until 30 April of the following year *(IHTA 1984 s226–229)*.

18 Claiming a first-year capital allowance (p199).
Time limit no formal limit, but you need to make a specific claim in your accounts *(CAA 1968 s70)*.

19 Adding extra contributions to a personal pension plan (p336).
Time limit see the detailed rules on p336.

20 Continuing a partnership when a partner joins or leaves (p219).
Time limit within two years of the change *(ICTA 1970 s154)*.

Tax advice – where to find it

No one person – and no one book – can answer every tax problem. On this page, we suggest sources of advice which, depending on your circumstances, you might find useful.

Start with this book

It's the obvious starting place. With over 500 pages of information and advice, it covers the great majority of tax situations.

Use Inland Revenue leaflets

These vary considerably in the amount of detail they give. Some are easy to read, but quite sketchy. Others are labyrinthine. In between, they provide relatively straightforward information, often with worked examples. Not all leaflets are up to date – though sometimes there are supplements, which should be given to you with the main leaflet. All leaflets are free from tax and PAYE offices. We list them on p507.

Go to PAYE enquiry offices

These are Inland Revenue advice centres for people who are taxed under PAYE. They should be able to sort out most PAYE problems.

Use the Which? Tax-Saving Guide

This is the best short guide to the tax system, and takes you step by step through filling in your Tax Return. It's published in March each year.

Try 'Pinson on Revenue law'

Only if you're feeling brave – it's written mostly for professionals and for law students. It's a difficult book to find your way around. But if you can get to grips with it, it's a very useful book. The latest edition came out in December 1986. (A supplement taking the 1987 Finance Act changes into account is due to be published.)

Try 'Simon's Taxes'

This is a nine-volume looseleaf tax encyclopedia. Certainly not worth buying unless you're a tax professional. But it's the best place to consult statutes. One of the problems for the ordinary person is that Finance Acts very often make changes to sections in earlier Acts. So you need to find a version of the earlier Acts which contains all the changes. Simon's Taxes (Volumes G and H) do just that. Your local library might have a copy – or try a reference library or University Library.

Accountants or solicitors

Only if your tax affairs are complicated, or you're making a will. If you're setting up a trust, or engaging in detailed inheritance tax planning, you'll need a professional adviser. The level of competence and expertise varies enormously – and there's no easy way to find someone who's good. Try asking friends, or your employer.

5 TAX AND SINGLE PEOPLE

The size of your tax bill doesn't only depend on how much income you have – it can also be affected by whether or not you're married. This chapter describes the tax position of people who – in the eyes of the taxman – are single.

Who is single?

The taxman regards the following people as single:
- anyone who has never been married (this includes children)
- a married woman in the tax year that she marries (unless the wedding was on 6 April)
- a married woman who is separated from her husband (see p89 for the definition of *separation*)
- a married man who is separated from his wife, except during the tax year in which the separation takes place, or unless he is wholly maintaining his wife by voluntary payments (see *Separation and divorce*, p89)
- anyone who is divorced
- a widow
- a widower, except during the tax year in which his wife dies
- unmarried people who live together
- in some respects, a man and his wife who have chosen to have the wife's earnings taxed separately (see *Tax and marriage*, p74)

Single person's allowance

If you fall into any of the categories above, you're entitled to the *single person's allowance* (unless you qualify for the larger *age allowance* – see below). In the 1987–88 tax year, the single person's allowance is £2,425, which usually means that you won't have to pay any tax on the first £2,425 of your income – see Example 1 below. You don't have to claim this allowance – the taxman gives it to you automatically.

Example 1

Rupert Parkin is a 37 year old bachelor. The only allowance he gets is the single person's allowance. During the 1987–88 tax year, his earnings were £9,655, and his only other income was £105 interest from investments.

His tax bill was:

	£
Income – earned	9,655
– investment	105
	9,760
less *Allowances*	2,425
leaves taxable income of	7,335
tax on this at 27%	1,980.45

So Rupert doesn't pay tax on the whole of his income – the first £2,425 is tax-free.

Age allowance

If you are aged 64 or more before the start of the tax year, you can claim *age allowance*, instead of the single person's allowance. Age allowance is a larger allowance for elderly people who don't have particularly high incomes. For the 1987–88 tax year, the single person's age allowance is £2,960 if you are 64 or more before the start of the tax year, £3,070 if you are 79 or more. But if your 'total income' (broadly, income less payments you make which qualify for tax relief) is more than £9,800, your age allowance will be reduced on a sliding scale – although it won't ever be reduced to less than the ordinary single person's allowance. You can't claim age allowance if you're married, but have chosen to have the wife's earnings taxed separately. See *Tax and the elderly*, p104, for more details.

Additional personal allowance

If you have a child living with you, and you don't have a husband or wife to help you bring the child up, you may be able to claim the *additional personal allowance*, as well as the single person's allowance. Example 2, opposite, shows the difference this can make.

For the 1987–88 tax year, the additional personal allowance

is £1,370. It can be claimed by people who get the single person's allowance (excluding married people who have chosen to have the wife's earnings taxed separately), and by married men, if their wife is totally incapacitated throughout the tax year.

In order to claim it, you must have one or more 'qualifying' children living with you for all or part of the tax year. A qualifying child is one who is under 16 at the start of the tax year, *or* who is in full-time education, *or* who is undergoing full-time training (lasting at least two years) for a trade, profession or vocation.

The child must be either:
● your legitimate (or legitimated) child, stepchild, or legally adopted child; or
● any other child who is under 18 at the start of the tax year, and whom you maintain at your own expense (a younger sister, say).

If two people can claim the additional personal allowance for the same child (ie if the child lives with each of them for part of the year), the allowance is divided between them in agreed proportions. If they can't agree, the allowance is divided in proportion to the time the child spends with each of them during the year.

Note that you can't claim the additional personal allowance if you get *housekeeper allowance* (see p124). And note also that the amount you can claim doesn't depend on the number of children you're bringing up – the most each person can get is £1,370, whether they have one child or ten.

Single people may also be able to claim other allowances – see *Social security and special tax allowances* (p124) for details.

Example 2

If Rupert Parkin (see Example 1 opposite) had a young child, and could claim the additional personal allowance, his tax bill would be worked out as follows:

	£	£
Income – earned	9,655	
– investment	105	
	9,760	
less *Allowances*		
– single person's		2,425
– additional personal allowance		1,370
	3,795	3,795
leaves taxable income of	5,965	
tax on this at 27%	1,610.55	

So Rupert's tax bill is £369.90 less than in Example 1 (£1,980.45 minus £1,610.55). This is because the additional personal allowance gives him an extra £1,370 before he has to start paying tax – and tax at 27% on £1,370 is £369.90.
ICTA 1970 s8, s12(1)(iv), s14, s14A, Sch 4; FA 1987 s26; IR 22.

Tax and children

This section describes how children's income is taxed – and how to make the most of your child's tax-free allowances.

Income

No matter how young your children are, they will be taxed on their earned income just as if they were adults. They will also be taxed on their investment income, unless the investment was given to them by their parents – in which case it will usually be taxed as the parent's income (see opposite).

Grants or scholarships to pay for children's education don't count as their income, and so don't affect their tax bill. But if the scholarship is paid by the parent's employer as a perk of the job, the parent may be taxed on it – see *Fringe benefits* (p166) for details.

Allowances

Children can also claim *allowances* in the same way as adults. All children are entitled to the single person's allowance (£2,425 in the 1987–88 tax year) – which means that they can have income of £2,425 before they have to pay any tax. And if they qualify for any other allowances, this figure will be even higher. For example, a 17 year old bringing up a younger brother or sister at his or her own expense, could claim the additional personal allowance – £1,370 in the 1987–88 tax year – on top of the single person's allowance.

If your child has little or no income, you aren't making the most of its tax-free allowances. In this case, a friend or relative might like to give the child money under a deed of covenant – see p131 for how this works. But note that *parents* can't take advantage of their special tax rules which apply to covenants, unless their child is 18 or over, or married.

If you are separated or divorced, and one parent is paying maintenance for the child, the payments could be made direct to the child, to set against its allowances – see *Separation and divorce*, p89 for more details.
ICTA 1970 s52–53, s434 (covenants); ICTA 1970 s65(1b) (maintenance).

Children's investment income

Remember that children can have income of at least £2,425 before they have to pay tax. But investment income is often paid after basic rate tax has been deducted – see below. So if your child gets investment income, and its income (including the gross amount of the investment income) is £2,425 or less, any tax deducted can be claimed back from the taxman. For how to claim tax back, see overleaf. However, if the income comes from a building society or bank (other than the National Savings Bank) account, normally no tax can be reclaimed – for details, see pages 279 and 280.

So a building society or bank may not be the best place to invest your child's money, and it could well get a higher return elsewhere – eg with a National Savings investment account. If the child isn't a taxpayer, you'll need to compare the interest it gets from a building society or bank account *after* tax, with the interest it gets from other investments *before* tax.

Investment income which is taxed before the child gets it, but on which tax can be reclaimed, includes:

- dividends from UK companies
- distributions from unit trusts
- income from trusts and settlements.

But note that if *parents* give a child something which produces investment income – eg if they open up a National Savings Investment account for their child – the income is usually taxed as the parents', unless the child is 18 or over, or married.

There are two exceptions to this rule:

- if the income which comes from investments given by the parents is less than £5; or
- if the parents set up an **accumulation trust** for the child and the interest is 'accumulated' (ie not spent) until the child reaches 18 or marries.

ICTA 1970 s119, s232, s242, s354 (investment income); ICTA 1970 s343 (building society interest); ICTA 1970 s375, FA 1976 s62A (scholarships); ICTA 1970 s 437–444, FA 1975 Sch 5(15) (settlements on children).

How to check your child's tax bill

Write down all the sources of your child's income, the *gross* (ie before deduction of tax) amounts, and how much tax (if any) has already been deducted. It might help if you fill in a Tax Return for your child – you can ask your tax office to send you one.

Then write down all your child's outgoings and allowances, to work out how much tax-free income it's entitled to. If the gross income is less than or equal to its tax-free income, then

your child shouldn't be paying tax – and you can claim back
any that has already been deducted. See Example 3.

If its gross income is *more* than its tax-free income, work out
how much tax is due on the difference. If this is less than the
amount already deducted, you can claim back the difference.

If you find that your child is owed money by the taxman, you
can reclaim it using the Special Tax Claim Form **R232** – get
it from your tax office. And the child can make its own claims
if the tax was deducted from income 'within its control' – eg
if it was deducted from the child's earnings from a holiday job.

Check your children's tax bills every year – and make sure
you reclaim any tax overpaid. Don't forget that you can also
reclaim any tax owing from the previous six years – see *You
and the Inland Revenue*, p447 for more information.

But note that if your child *owes* any tax, then you – as the
parent or guardian – are responsible for paying it out of your
own income, if the tax isn't paid out of the child's.

Example 3

In the 1987–88 tax year, Jemima Melville got £292 in
distributions from a unit trust company. The 'tax credits' on
the distribution (ie the tax that had already been deducted)
totalled £108. However, this investment was given to Jemima
by her mother, and so the income counts as her mother's. For
this reason, it isn't included in the sums to work out Jemima's
tax bill.

Jemima also got £1,825 in dividends, and £675 in tax
credits, from shares given to her by her grandparents; this *does*
count as Jemima's income.

She also has a National Savings Investment account opened
for her with money given by her aunt – again, the interest
counts as Jemima's. In the 1987–88 tax year, Jemima got £100
interest on her account. This sort of income *isn't* taxed before
you get it – so it has to be added to the rest of Jemima's income,
to find out if she owes any tax on it.

Jemima has no other income.

Jemima works through the figures

Source	Gross income [£]	Tax deducted or tax credits [£]
dividends, including tax credits	2,500	675
interest from National Savings Investment account	100	
	2,600	
less single person's allowance	2,425	
leaves taxable income of	175	
tax on this at 27%		47.25
less tax already deducted (£675) leaves		627.75

So Jemima can reclaim £627.75 from the taxman.
TMA 1970 s 72–73, s118 (children's returns and claims).

Tax and students

Here we describe your tax position if you are a student. You may have to pay tax, just like anyone else. But certain things don't normally count as income for tax purposes:
● student grants from a local education authority (LEA)
● parental contributions – unless paid under a deed of covenant (see p132)
● certain non-LEA discretionary grants – eg from the DHSS
● post-graduate grants from one of the research councils
● most other awards or scholarships – but always check with your tax office.

If you are being sponsored through college (eg by a company or by one of the armed forces), or if you are on a sandwich course, the money paid to you to cover the time spent *at college* is usually tax-free – but, again, check with your tax office. The money paid to cover the time you spend *at work*, however, does count as your income for tax purposes.

Any income which isn't tax-free is added together and, if it comes to more than your outgoings and allowances, you'll have to pay tax on the excess.
ICTA 1970 s375; SP4/86; IR59.

Vacation jobs
Earnings from vacation jobs count as income. But you and your employer can fill in a form to say that your total earnings, plus all your other income for the year, won't exceed the single person's allowance – and then tax won't be deducted under PAYE. You can get the form (called **P38S**) from tax offices.

Unemployment and supplementary benefit

If you are studying *full time*, you may be entitled to *unemployment benefit* during the summer vacation, though not in the Christmas and Easter breaks. You will be able to claim it if you:

● are out of work, and
● are available for, and capable of, work, and
● have paid enough of the right National Insurance contributions at the right time.

Broadly, if you claim in the 1987 calendar year, your entitlement depends on the contributions you paid in the 1985–86 tax year.

If you find that you haven't paid enough contributions to qualify for unemployment benefit, you may be able to claim *supplementary benefit (SB)*. This is paid to people whose weekly 'resources' (income) are less than their 'requirements' (needs). But LEA grants (and certain other awards) are supposed to cover the Christmas and Easter vacations, as well as term-time, so – unless you're disabled, for example, or a single parent – you probably won't qualify for SB during these periods. You can, however, register for work during the *summer* vacation, and claim SB then.

Part or all of the unemployment or supplementary benefit you get during the vacations may be taxed – see *Social security and special tax allowances*, p117, for details. The taxable part is added to the rest of your income, and if the total comes to more than your outgoings and allowances (not very likely for most students), you'll owe tax. But you may be able to pay it at a later time – for example, when you leave college and start earning.

FA 1981 s27–29; FA 1982 s32; SI 1982/66 (unemployment benefit).

Changes on the way

From April 1988 supplementary benefit will be replaced by a new benefit – **income support**. Full details of this benefit and whether it will be taxable in full or in part are not yet available.

Allowances

Unmarried students are entitled to the single person's allowance – £2,425 in the 1987–88 tax year. Married male students get the *married man's allowance* (£3,795 in the 1987–88 tax year), and married women students can get the *wife's earned income allowance* – which means they can earn up to £2,425 in the 1987–88 tax year before paying tax.

Students may also be entitled to other allowances – such as

the additional personal allowance if they have a dependent child.
ICTA 1970 s8, s14.

Tax-saving tips

- children can receive income under a **deed of covenant** to set against their allowances – see p131

- children can receive **maintenance** paid direct to them, to set against their allowances – see p91

- a **building society or bank** may not be the best place to invest your child's money – see p280

- **check your child's tax bill** each year – and reclaim any tax overpaid. See p53.

6 LIVING TOGETHER

This chapter sets out the tax advantages – and disadvantages – of living with your partner without being married.

The taxman treats an unmarried couple as two separate, single people. This means that you each get your own Tax Return, and are each legally responsible for paying the tax on your own income.

Allowances

You and your partner each get the single person's allowance, plus any other allowances that you're entitled to. In the 1987–88 tax year, the single person's allowance is £2,425 – so your combined allowances will be at least £4,850.

If you were married, however, you'd get the married man's allowance (£3,795), plus the wife's earned income allowance (of whatever she earns, up to £2,425), making a total of up to £6,220. So staying single can mean a loss of £1,370 in allowances – and an extra tax bill for basic rate taxpayers of 27% of £1,370, ie £369.90.

If you have one or more children, however, your tax position is different. This is because a single parent with a 'qualifying' child (see *Tax and single people*, p51 for what this means), can claim the *additional personal allowance* on top of their single person's allowance. (Married people can't claim the additional personal allowance unless the wife is totally incapacitated.)

In the 1987–88 tax year, the additional personal allowance is £1,370. This means that:

- **if you have one child,** either you or your partner can claim the additional personal allowance, and your combined allowances will be £4,850 + £1,370 = £6,220: the same as a married couple
- **if you have two or more children,** you and your partner can *each* claim the additional personal allowance, bringing your combined allowances up to £7,590: ie *more* than a married couple.

Note that you can't claim the additional personal allowance if you're not the child's parent, unless you are maintaining it. So if your partner has two children, and you're the parent of neither, you should arrange your finances so that you maintain one child, and your partner the other – then you can *both* claim the allowance.

Make the most of your allowances

If one partner doesn't have enough income to make use of all his or her allowances, there are two possible solutions:
- transfer income to the partner with spare allowances, *or*
- transfer unused allowances to the partner with spare income.

However, the tax rules put limits on when you can use these methods to reduce your joint tax bill:
- **if you are married,** you can't save tax by transferring income, and the wife can't transfer her wife's earned income allowance. But the husband can transfer his married man's allowance – see p70.
- **if you are single,** you can't transfer any of your unused allowances – but you may be able to transfer income in one of two ways: we explain them below and overleaf.

Affiliation orders

If you and your partner live together and have a child, the woman can apply to the Court for an affiliation order saying that the man is the father of the child, and ask for a court order for maintenance. The man may be able to get tax relief on the maintenance payments he makes and the payments will normally count as the *woman's* income – against which she can set her allowances. Either of you can then claim the additional personal allowance – so make sure it's claimed by whoever can use it most – but see *Warning* on p61.

Covenants

If your partner doesn't have enough income to make use of all his or her outgoings and allowances, a covenant to your partner can reduce your joint tax bill. See Example 1, below.

A covenant is a legally binding agreement under which one person promises to make a series of payments to another – for more details, see p127. You can get basic rate tax relief on the covenant payments you make, *provided*:

- the covenant is capable of lasting for more than six years (although your partner can agree to end it before then), **and**
- *you* don't benefit from the payments. So it's no good covenanting, say, money to pay off the mortgage on the house you're both living in – because you would clearly benefit from that.

How to work out how much to covenant

Add up all your partner's outgoings and allowances. Then subtract all your partner's income (the *gross* amounts). Provided you're left with a positive number, this is the size of the gross covenant payment which will save you the most tax.

ICTA 1970 s8, s14 (allowances); Affiliation Proceedings Act 1957 s4; ICTA 1970 s65 (maintenance); ICTA 1970 s52, s53, s434 (covenants).

Example 1

Tony and Tina are an unmarried couple who live together. Tony earns £18,750, and has outgoings (loan interest) of £1,135. He gets the single person's allowance (£2,425) and the additional personal allowance (£1,370) – a total of £3,795. Tina stays at home looking after their two children. She's also entitled to the single person's and the additional personal allowances, but can't use them because she has no income.

Tony:	£
Income	18,750
less *outgoings* – loan interest	1,135
leaves 'total income' of	17,615
less *allowances*	3,795
leaves taxable income of	13,820
tax on this at 27%	3,731.40

Tina has no income, and so no tax to pay.

Tony and Tina realise that Tina is making no use of her personal allowances. So Tony decides to covenant enough

money to Tina to cover her unused allowances – ie £2,425 +
£1,370 = £3,795. Their tax bills are now as follows:

Tony:	£	£
Income	18,750	
less *outgoings* – loan interest		1,135
– gross covenant payments		3,795
	4,930	4,930
leaves 'total income' of	13,820	
less *allowances*	3,795	
leaves taxable income of	10,025	
tax on this at 27%	2,706.75	

Tina:		
Income – gross covenant payments	3,795	
less *allowances* – single person's		2,425
– additional personal allowance		1,370
	3,795	3,795
leaves taxable income of	nil	

So Tina has no tax to pay.

Their joint bill has gone down by **£1,024.65** (£3,731.40 minus
£2,706.75). This is because they've gained an extra £3,795 of
tax-free income, by using Tina's allowances – and tax at 27%
on £3,795 is £1,024.65.

Tina could have applied instead for an affiliation order
against Tony, and asked for a court order for maintenance of
£3,795. This would have given them the same tax saving.

> *Warning:* you may not be allowed tax relief on payments you
> make under an affiliation order if you benefit from them too – eg
> the money is used for general housekeeping.

Income

Your income is treated as separate from that of your partner,
which means that you each have the first £17,900 of taxable
income taxed at the basic rate only. The incomes of a married
couple, however, are normally added together, with the first
£17,900 of *joint* taxable income taxed at the basic rate:
anything more is taxed at higher rates. So a couple with a high
joint taxable income may find that less of it will be liable to
higher rate tax if they stay single.

But remember, unless one of you can claim the additional
personal allowance, your joint allowances may be £1,370 less
than a married couple (see p64). As a rough guideline:

● **if neither of you** can claim the additional personal allowance, *and* your joint income is less than £26,870, staying single normally means that you lose more in allowances than you gain in higher rate tax savings. At £26,870 or more, however, you could be better off staying single – or, if you marry, having the wife's earnings taxed separately (see p74). But you'll need to do your sums to check (see pages 80 to 81)

● **if one or both of you** can claim the additional personal allowance, you'll normally be as well off, or better off, staying single – whatever your income.

Separate taxation
Note that a married couple can choose to have the wife's earned income taxed separately – see p74. This gives them both the full basic rate band of £17,900 – but at the cost of £1,370 in allowances. And they can't choose to have the wife's *investment* income taxed separately.

The investment income trap

An unmarried woman gets the single person's allowance (£2,425). A married woman gets the wife's earned income allowance up to the same amount. But the wife's earned income allowance – unlike the single person's allowance – can be set only against the wife's earnings. It can't be used to reduce the tax on her investment income.

So if a woman has earned income of less than £1,055 *and* her investment income is more than £1,370, she'll be able to make better use of her allowances if she's single. (The first £1,370 of her investment income would be covered by the extra £1,370 of the married man's allowance.) See p67 for more details.

Other points

● two single people can each get tax relief on the interest they pay on up to £30,000 of **mortgage loans** – ie on up to £60,000 in total. But a married couple can get tax relief on only £30,000 between them – see *Homes and land*, p235 for more details.

● two single people can each make net taxable gains of £6,600 in the 1987–88 tax year before having to pay **capital gains tax** – see p415. But a married couple can make gains of only £6,600 between them.

● gifts between a husband and wife (but not between unmarried partners) are exempt from **inheritance tax** – see p356.

FA 1974 Sch 1 para 5; FA 1982 s25 (mortgage interest); IR22; IR29; IR30; IR31.

7 TAX AND MARRIAGE

Getting married can dramatically affect your tax bill. Some couples pay less tax after marriage; others find that the taxman asks them for more than before. But there are ways of keeping down your tax bill after marriage – this chapter explains them. First, though, we tell you how married people are treated by the taxman, and how their tax bills are worked out.

Changes on the way

In 1986 the Government published a Green Paper on the reform of the personal tax system. One of the main proposals was that there should be equal and independent taxation for married couples. This would mean that the married man's allowance would be abolished and each partner would have the same personal allowance. If one partner did not have enough income to make full use of his or her allowance, the unused part could be transferred to the other person. In addition a wife's investment income would no longer be treated as her husband's for tax purposes but as her own income. This would be a fundamental change in the tax system and no decision has yet been taken on whether – or when – to implement it.

What happens to your tax bill when you marry?

The taxman normally treats a married couple as one person: the income of both of them is added together, outgoings and allowances are subtracted, and tax is charged on the joint taxable amount.

So if you are married, anything over £17,900 of your joint taxable income is normally taxed at higher rates. This can mean a larger tax bill, since:
● two single people, each with taxable income of £17,900 or less, would have paid basic rate tax only
● when they marry, their *combined* taxable income may be more than £17,900 – so they become liable to higher rate tax.

Any extra higher rate tax liability may be offset by a rise in your allowances – see overleaf. If not, think about having the wife's earned income taxed separately – see p74. Doing this gives each of you the full basic tax band of £17,900 – but in return, you have to give up some allowances.

Generally, only the husband is sent a Tax Return, on which he has to give details of his own and his wife's income. (This applies even if they've chosen to have the wife's earned income taxed separately.) He is also, in most cases, legally responsible for paying their joint tax bill – although tax on the wife's earnings will probably be collected under PAYE – see p147.

Allowances

Before you marry, you each get the *single person's allowance* (£2,425 in the 1987–88 tax year) – making a total of £4,850. You may also be able to claim other allowances – but for this comparison between single and married people, we consider only those allowances which everyone gets.

After marriage – unless you qualify for the larger *age allowance* (see p104) – you get:
● the *married man's allowance* (£3,795 in the 1987–88 tax year), plus
● the *wife's earned income allowance* of whatever earned income she has (*less* allowable expenses in her job, and *less* any personal pension payments she makes) – up to a maximum of £2,425 in the 1987–88 tax year.

This makes a total of up to £6,220. So marriage can mean that an extra £1,370 of your combined income is free of tax – giving a saving, to basic rate taxpayers, of £369.90. But don't forget that your *combined* income may be taxable at higher rates than either of you paid before you married.

Example 1

Nigel earns £12,000 a year, and his fiancée, Nicola, earns £8,000. Neither of them has any other income or *outgoings* (payments which qualify for tax relief). Their tax bills are:

	£
Nigel's income	12,000
less allowances – single person's	2,425
leaves taxable income of	9,575
tax on this at 27%	£2,585.25
Nicola's income	8,000
less allowances – single person's	2,425
leaves taxable income of	5,575
tax on this at 27%	£1,505.25
total tax bill	£4,090.50

After they get married, Nigel's and Nicola's incomes are added together, and they get the married man's and the wife's earned income allowances. Their tax bill is as follows:

	£	£
Nigel's income	12,000	
plus Nicola's income	8,000	
	20,000	
less allowances – married man's		3,795
– wife's earned income		2,425
		6,220
leaves taxable income of	13,780	
tax on this at 27%	£3,720.60	

So getting married has saved Nigel and Nicola £369.90 in tax (£4,090.50 – £3,720.60 = £369.90).

Exceptions to the normal rules

You and your spouse *aren't* treated as one person by the taxman:
● in the tax year in which you marry – unless the wedding was on 6 April – see p72
● if you've chosen to have the wife's earnings taxed separately – see p74
● if either you or your spouse is resident overseas, or absent abroad for the whole of the tax year – see p87
● if you and your spouse are permanently separated – see p89

How to make use of your allowances

Before you marry, you each get the single person's allowance to set against your own income (both earned and investment income).

After marriage the wife loses her single person's allowance, and it's only if she has *earned income* (see p67) that she gets the wife's earned income allowance in its place. This allowance can be set only against her earned income – it can't be used to reduce the tax on her investment income (which counts as her husband's for tax purposes), nor can it reduce the tax on her husband's earned income.

The man gets the married man's allowance to set against:
● his own earned income
● his own investment income
● his wife's investment income
● any of his wife's earnings not covered by her allowances.

Tax effects of marriage on your allowances – a bird's eye view [1]

Allowance	Husband	Wife
Single person's allowance (£2,425)	• replaced by *married man's allowance* of £3,795	• replaced by *wife's earned income allowance* of up to £2,425
Additional personal allowance	• can claim only if wife totally incapacitated throughout tax year	• can't claim
Age allowance	• can claim married man's age allowance (£4,675 if he, or his wife, is 64 or more before start of tax year; £4,845 if he, or his wife, is 79 or more before start of tax year) [2]	• can't claim
Housekeeper allowance	• can't claim	• can't claim
Dependent relative allowance	• can claim in respect of any of his (or his wife's) relatives	• can claim in respect of any of her relatives [3]
Allowance for son or daughter on whose services you depend	• can claim if he is (or his wife is) 64 or more before start of tax year, or permanently ill or disabled. But can't claim for himself if his wife is 64 or less and healthy	• can claim – unaffected by marriage
Blind person's allowance	• can claim – unaffected by marriage	• can claim – unaffected by marriage

[1] effects are different in the tax year of the marriage – see p72. For effect of having the wife's earnings taxed separately, see p74.
[2] replaces married man's allowance.
[3] the amount a wife can claim is £100. A single woman – or a wife in the tax year of marriage – can claim £145. A wife whose earnings are taxed separately can also claim £145.

Wife's earned income

The following counts as the wife's earned income:
- earnings from a job
- any pension from a previous job of hers
- a state pension paid as a result of her own contributions
- any taxable unemployment or supplementary benefit paid to her because of unemployment

income from a trade, profession or vocation carried on by her personally, or as an active partner in a partnership.

The following does **not** count as the wife's earned income:
- a pension she gets as a result of her husband's previous job
- a state pension paid as a result of her husband's contributions. (But if a wife who is entitled to a pension of her own, chooses to get a pension based on her husband's contributions because this is higher, she can count as earned income the amount of pension she was entitled to on her own contributions.)

So is marriage worth it?

Provided the wife has no investment income, marriage usually means that she's no better off, and no worse off. But her husband gets the extra £1,370 from the married man's allowance – which means less tax to pay, unless their combined income is taxable at higher rates than before.

If, on the other hand, the wife does have some investment income, things are more complicated. There are two ways that their tax bill can go up:
- if the wife's investment income, when added to her husband's, has tax charged on it at a higher rate than before
- if the wife has investment income of more than £1,370 *and* her earned income is less than £1,055. The catch here is that the wife's earned income allowance, unlike the single person's allowance, can't be used to reduce the tax on her investment income (because her investment income counts as her husband's). Suppose, before marriage, the wife had no earned income and investment income of £2,425. This would be covered by her single person's allowance and she would have no tax to pay. After marriage, the £2,425 investment income counts as her husband's income. He has extra allowances of £1,370 to set against it. But that leaves £1,055 of the previously untaxed investment income now liable for tax. If she'd had at least £1,055 of *earned* income before she married, then the £1,055 of investment income would have been liable to tax both before and after marriage. See Example 2, overleaf.

There's no escape from these situations except permanent separation (or divorce) – because you can't choose to have the wife's investment income taxed separately.

When marriage can lose you money

Example 2 (below) shows how two couples with identical incomes are taxed. First, we see the tax bill for Daniel and Dinah – who aren't married. Then, we look at Karen and Kevin, who are. By being married, Karen and Kevin gain £1,370 in allowances – see p64. But Karen can use up only £1,000 of her wife's earned income allowance of £2,425 – so the 'gain' of £1,370 is wiped out by the loss of £1,425 in unused allowances. In contrast, Dinah uses nearly all her £2,425 single person's allowance. The net result is that Karen and Kevin pay £13.50 more in tax.

Example 2

Daniel's income is £12,000. His fiancée, Dinah, earns only £1,000, and has £1,420 of investment income. The tax on their income is worked out like this:

	£
Daniel's income	12,000
less single person's allowance	2,425
leaves taxable income of	9,575
tax on this at 27%	£ 2,585.25
Dinah's income – earned	1,000
– investment	1,420
	2,420
less single person's allowance	2,425
leaves taxable income of	nil
tax on this at 27%	nil
total tax bill	£ 2,585.25

For Karen and Kevin, the calculation is different. Karen's investment income counts as Kevin's, and since her earned income is only £1,000, she can't make full use of her wife's earned income allowance of £2,425. The result is a higher tax bill – see opposite:

	£	
Kevin's income	12,000	
plus Karen's income – earned	1,000	
– investment	1,420	
	14,420	
less allowances – married man's		3,795
– wife's earned income		1,000
		4,795
leaves taxable income of	9,625	
tax on this at 27%	£2,598.75	

Other points to think about

● two single people can each get tax relief on the interest on up to £30,000 of **mortgage loans** – ie on up to £60,000 in total. But a married couple can get tax relief on only £30,000 between them – see *Homes and land*, p235

● if one (or both) of you can claim the **additional personal allowance** (see *Tax and single people*, p49), you could be as well off (or better off) staying single – because married people can't claim this allowance, unless the wife is totally incapacitated throughout the tax year

● two single people can each make net taxable gains of £6,600 in the 1987–88 tax year before having to pay any **capital gains tax**; a married couple can only make £6,600 of gains between them – see *Capital gains tax*, p430

● for the purposes of **inheritance tax**, a husband and wife are treated as two separate people, each with their own exemptions and tax bands. And gifts to each other are tax-free – see *Inheritance tax*, p351

● two single people may be able to use **covenants** to lower their tax bill – see *Living together*, p58. But a married couple can't save money in this way

● two single people can't transfer any unused outgoings or allowances to each other – but a married couple may be able to. See *Who's going to look after the kids?*, overleaf

● a husband and wife are each allowed £70 of interest tax-free from a National Savings Ordinary account. But if the man has, say, £110 interest, and his wife has £30 interest, he'll still have to pay tax on £40 – even though their *combined* interest isn't more than £140. If a husband and wife have a joint account, they can have £140 interest tax-free.

If, after reading all this, you've decided to take the plunge and get married, p72 describes how you're taxed in the first year of marriage.

ICTA 1970 s8, s37, s42; IR 31.

Who's going to look after the kids?

If you and your spouse could both earn the same amount, but only one of you can work (eg because the other has to stay at home to look after the children), you'll be better off if the *wife* goes out to work.

This is because:

- if the husband is the sole breadwinner, he gets the married man's allowance of £3,795, but can't get the wife's earned income allowance
- if the wife is the sole breadwinner, she gets the wife's earned income allowance (£2,425) *and* the married man's allowance to set against her earnings – a total of £6,220.

If the husband has some income (eg taxable unemployment benefit) but it's less than the married man's allowance, the

unused part of his allowance can be transferred to his wife –
Example 3 shows the difference this can make. If this applies
to you, contact your tax office to arrange the transfer.

Example 3

Jeremy Scarbrook is a married student; his wife, Katie, is at
work. Jeremy gets a full grant from his LEA, but this doesn't
count as income for tax purposes, and so isn't included in the
calculations.

For eight weeks during the summer vacation, Jeremy gets a
job, and earns £1,000 in total; for the remaining five weeks of
the vacation he gets unemployment benefit (UB) totalling
£157.25. (He gets this because he'd been working before he
went to college, and had paid enough contributions to qualify.)

Jeremy also has £50 of investment income not taxed before
he gets it, so his total income is £1,207.25 – leaving £2,587.75
of his married man's allowance unused.

This is transferred to Katie, to set against her earnings of
£10,400. The couple have no other income, and no outgoings
which qualify for the relief.

Their tax bill is worked out as follows:

		£	
Jeremy's income	– earned	1,000	
	– investment	50	
	– taxable UB	157.25	
Katie's income	– earned	10,400	
		11,607.25	
less allowances	– married man's		3,795 [1]
	– wife's earned income		2,425
			6,220
leaves taxable income of		5,387.25	
tax on this at 27%		£1,454.56	

[1] £1,207.25 to set against Jeremy's income, and £2,587.75 to
transfer to Katie

If Jeremy hadn't transferred his unused allowances to Katie,
their tax bill would have been £698.69 more. This is because
tax at 27% on the unused £2,587.75 is £698.69.

Tax in the year of marriage

In the tax year in which you get married, you and your spouse aren't treated as one person by the taxman – **unless** you marry on 6 April, in which case the normal rules for married couples apply immediately.

Otherwise your tax position is as follows:

● **the wife** continues to get the single person's allowance (£2,425 in the 1987–88 tax year), plus any other allowances to which she is entitled. She gets her own Tax Return, and is responsible for paying her tax on her own income (including her investment income)

● **the husband** gets all or part of the married man's allowance (£3,795 in the 1987–88 tax year), depending on the date of the wedding. If he gets married before 6 May, he gets the full allowance. If he marries on or after that date, he loses one-twelfth of the difference between the single person's and the married man's allowance (one-twelfth of £1,370) for each complete month after 6 April that he remains single – see the Chart below.

Married before . . .

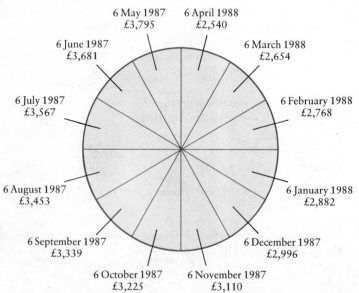

6 May 1987
£3,795

6 April 1988
£2,540

6 June 1987
£3,681

6 March 1988
£2,654

6 July 1987
£3,567

6 February 1988
£2,768

6 August 1987
£3,453

6 January 1988
£2,882

6 September 1987
£3,339

6 December 1987
£2,996

6 October 1987
£3,225

6 November 1987
£3,110

So if, for example, you marry on 10 September 1987, you lose five-twelfths of £1,370 = £570. Taking £570 from £3,795 leaves you with a married man's allowance of £3,225 for the 1987–88 tax year.

How to claim the married man's allowance

Tell your Tax Office as soon as possible after the wedding that you want to claim the married man's allowance. If you pay tax under PAYE, use **form 11PA**, available from tax offices.

Other allowances

If you get the married man's allowance in full or in part, you can't claim housekeeper allowance (see *Social Security and special tax allowances*, p124). Nor, unless your wife is totally incapacitated throughout the tax year, can you claim the additional personal allowance. But, in the first year of marriage only, the man can choose to keep either of these allowances (and the single person's allowance) instead of claiming the married man's allowance. This is worthwhile only if you marry between 6 March and 5 April 1988, for those who can claim housekeeper allowance. But if you can claim the additional personal allowance, it's worthwhile whenever you marry.

If the woman was claiming the additional personal allowance before the wedding, she can continue to claim it afterwards – but for the first year only.

Child allowance

This allowance was abolished completely from 6 April 1982.

Parents can now claim **child benefit**, which is a tax-free social security benefit and doesn't affect your tax position.

Unused allowances or outgoings

If your income in the year of marriage is less than your allowances and outgoings, you may be able to transfer the unused part to your wife or husband – thereby reducing your combined tax bill. Example 3 on p71 shows the difference this can make. The man can transfer *any* of his unused allowances, and any of the interest he pays which qualifies for tax relief.

The woman can transfer only:
- the dependent relative allowance
- the blind person's allowance
- the allowance for a son or daughter on whose services she depends
- any unused interest she pays *after* the marriage which qualifies for tax relief – except mortgage interest paid under the MIRAS system. Under MIRAS you get tax relief automatically whether or not you've got any income to set it against – by paying a reduced amount to the lender.

What happens to your mortgage(s) when you marry?

If you both had mortgage loans which qualified for tax relief before you married, and you intend to sell both old homes and buy a new one, you can:
● continue to get the tax relief on the old homes for up to twelve months, and
● jointly get tax relief on up to £30,000 of loans to buy the new home.

Alternatively, if you decide to live in one of the existing homes, and sell the other, you can:
● continue to get the tax relief for up to twelve months on the home you're selling, and
● continue to get tax relief as before on the home you live in.
ICTA 1970 s8, s12, s14, s15, s37; FA 1976 s36; FA 1983 s15(2) (allowances); SP 10/1980, ESC A38 (mortgages).

Separate taxation of the wife's earnings

The increase in allowances that you get when you marry usually means a lower tax bill right up to the point where your combined income is £26,870 (more than this, if you can claim other outgoings or allowances). But at £26,870 or more, the higher rate tax that you have to pay on your combined income might outweigh the extra £1,370 you get from the married man's allowance – and you could be better off having the wife's earnings taxed separately.

How does separate taxation work?

● **the wife** is taxed on her earnings (eg from a job or pension) as if she were a single woman with no other income. She gets the single person's allowance (£2,425 in the 1987–88 tax year) instead of the wife's earned income allowance
● **the husband** continues to be taxed on his earnings, his own investment income, and any investment income of his wife's. But he loses the married man's allowance (£3,795 in the 1987–88 tax year) and gets the single person's allowance instead – a loss of £1,370 in allowances.

This would normally mean an increase in your combined tax bill of at least £369.90. But with separate taxation, *each* of you can have £17,900 of your income taxed at the basic rate. For those in the higher income bracket, less income will be taxed at higher rates. This can more than compensate for the loss in allowances, see Diagram opposite, and Example 4 on p76.
ICTA 1970 s23, s37; FA 1971 s23.

Simplified example of separate taxation

If a husband (H) and wife (W) each earn £22,500 and they have investment income (I) of £10,000 between them, here's the difference that separate taxation of the wife's earned income makes in the way their income is taxed. For this simplified example, we assume they have no outgoings.

Without separate taxation

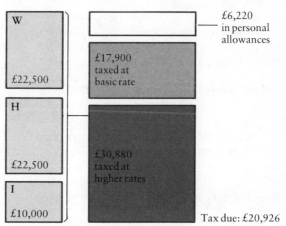

W £22,500

H £22,500

I £10,000

£6,220 in personal allowances

£17,900 taxed at basic rate

£30,880 taxed at higher rates

Tax due: £20,926

With separate taxation

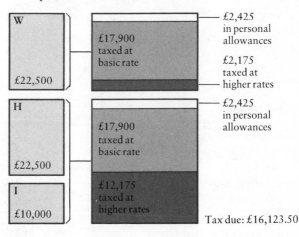

W £22,500

H £22,500

I £10,000

£2,425 in personal allowances

£17,900 taxed at basic rate

£2,175 taxed at higher rates

£2,425 in personal allowances

£17,900 taxed at basic rate

£12,175 taxed at higher rates

Tax due: £16,123.50

Example 4

Jonathan King earns £16,880 (including £480 in taxable fringe benefits), and has £2,020 of investment income. He makes *outgoings* (payments which qualify for tax relief) of £2,380.

Jonathan's wife, Caroline, earns £15,450 (including £200 in taxable expenses). She has investment income of £100 – but this always counts as the husband's, whether they're taxed together or separately. So Jonathan is treated as having £2,120 of investment income. Caroline makes outgoings of £330.

Taxed together, their tax bill is:

	£	
Jonathan's income – earned	16,880	
– investment	2,120	
plus Caroline's income – earned	15,450	
	34,450	
less outgoings – Jonathan's		2,380
– Caroline's		330
		2,710
leaves 'total income' of	31,740	
less allowances – married man's		3,795
– wife's earned income		2,425
		6,220
leaves taxable income of	25,520	
tax on first £17,900 at 27%	4,833	
tax on next £2,500 at 40%	1,000	
tax on next £5,000 at 45%	2,250	
tax on remaining £120 at 50%	60	
total tax bill	£8,143	

Taxed separately their tax bill is:

Jonathan:

	£
Income – earned	16,880
– investment	2,120
	19,000
less outgoings	2,380
leaves 'total income' of	16,620
less allowances – single person's	2,425
leaves taxable income of	14,195
tax on this at 27%	3,832.65

Caroline:

	£
Income – earned	15,450
less outgoings	330
leaves 'total income' of	15,120
less allowances – single person's	2,425
leaves taxable income of	12,695
tax on this at 27%	3,427.65
total tax bill	£7,260.30

So their joint tax bill, when taxed separately, is only £7,260.30 – a saving of £882.70 (£8,143 minus £7,260.30). This is because none of their income has been taxed at higher rates.

Example 5

Maurice earns £10,000, and has £3,000 of investment income. His wife, Doris, earns £9,000 and has £10,000 investment income – this counts as Maurice's, so he's treated as having investment income of £13,000.

The mortgage on their home is in Doris's name, and she's paying off the loan. (The loan is not paid under MIRAS.) She is also paying interest on a loan to buy a house in Wales for holiday letting. The gross interest payments (which qualify for tax relief) come to £4,000. If they choose to be taxed separately, these outgoings can only count against any earned income Doris has – not Maurice's income, or any investment income. See p77.

Taxed together, their tax bill is:

	£	
Maurice's income – earned	10,000	
– investment	13,000	
plus Doris's income – earned	9,000	
	32,000	
less outgoings (interest)	4,000	
leaves 'total income' of	28,000	
less allowances – married man's		3,795
– wife's earned income		2,425
		6,220
leaves taxable income of	21,780	
tax on first £17,900 at 27%		4,833
tax on next £2,500 at 40%		1,000
tax on remaining £1,380 at 45%		621
total tax bill		£6,454

If Doris and Maurice are taxed together (see previous page), Doris's outgoings of £4,000 reduce the higher rate tax on their joint income. The next column shows the effect of separate taxation.

Taxed separately their tax bill is:

		£	
Maurice:			
Income – earned		10,000	
– investment		13,000	
		23,000	
less allowances – single person's		2,425	
leaves taxable income of		20,575	
tax on first £17,900 at 27%			4,833
tax on next £2,500 at 40%			1,000
tax on remaining £175 at 45%			78.75
Doris:			
Income – earned		9,000	
less outgoings (interest)		4,000	
leaves 'total income' of		5,000	
less allowances – single person's		2,425	
leaves taxable income of		2,575	
tax on this at 27%			695.25
total tax bill			£6,607.00

With separate taxation, their joint tax bill has gone up by £6,607 *minus* £6,454 *equals* £153, because Doris's outgoings can no longer reduce the couple's higher rate tax bill – they can only reduce the basic rate tax on Doris's earned income.

Make sure that outgoings are paid by whoever will save the most tax – if *Maurice* had been paying off the mortgage, separate taxation would have saved them £203.50.

Is separate taxation right for you?

Unless you're in the higher income bracket, separate taxation isn't worthwhile – because you'll lose more in allowances than you'll save in higher rate tax. The level at which it becomes beneficial depends, first, on your combined income and secondly, on the income of the less well-off partner. (The wife's income is her earnings only; the husband's is his earnings, his own investment income and his wife's investment income.)

The Chart opposite helps you work out whether it's beneficial for *you* – but, broadly, your combined income should be at least **£26,870** (more, if you can claim other

Tax-saving in 1987–88 tax year if a married couple chooses to have the wife's earned income taxed separately

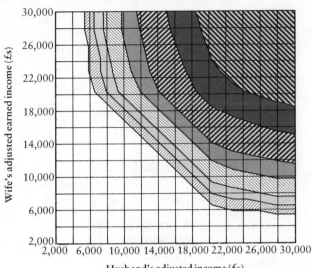

Key

Tax saving over £3,500

Tax saving between £2,500 and £3,500

Tax saving between £1,500 and £2,500

Tax saving between £1,000 and £1,500

Tax saving between £500 and £1,000

Tax saving between £250 and £500

Tax saving up to £250

No tax saving (normally extra tax payable)

outgoings or allowances), with the less well-off partner having at least £6,545. As your combined income increases, the minimum lower income reduces on a sliding scale – but you'll *never* be better off with separate taxation if either of you has income of less than £4,916. Two points to watch:

● with separate taxation, neither of you can get the additional personal allowance, housekeeper allowance, or age allowance (though with an income of £26,870, age allowance would anyway be reduced to nil). Nor can you transfer to your spouse any of your unused outgoings or allowances. But if the wife can claim *dependent relative allowance*, she'll get £145 instead of £100 – see *Social Security and special tax allowances*, p125

● if the wife has substantial outgoings, you may find that separate taxation *increases* your tax bill – even if your combined income is over £26,870. This is because, if you're taxed together, the wife's outgoings can be used to reduce the tax on *any* of your joint income. But with separate taxation, they can only reduce the tax on *her earned income* – they can't be set against the husband's earnings, or any investment income, and so the tax on these may rise. Example 5 on p77 shows what this can mean.

Interested in separate taxation?

You'll have to do some sums. On these pages, we set out the steps to follow – and to help you, we go back to Example 4 (see p76) and show you how Jonathan and Caroline work it out.

Work out what we call the **husband's adjusted income**	Jonathan's adjusted income £
STEP 1 Add together:	
● his before-tax earned income (minus any deductions to his employer's pension scheme)	16,400
● the taxable value of any fringe benefits he gets	480
● any taxable expenses he gets	nil
● his before-tax investment income (including grossed-up interest from building societies, banks and licensed deposit-takers)	2,020
● his wife's before-tax investment income (including grossed-up interest as above)	100
● **total A**	19,000
STEP 2 Add together:	
● any personal pension payments he makes	nil
● the gross amount of any interest payments he makes which qualify for tax relief	2,380
● the gross amount of any enforceable maintenance payments he makes	nil
● the dependent relative allowance *(but only if he gets it)*	nil
● the blind person's allowance *(but only if he gets it)*	nil
● **total B**	2,380
STEP 3 Deduct *B* from *A* to get the **husband's adjusted income**	19,000 (2,380)
● **total C**	16,620

Work out the **wife's adjusted earned income**	Caroline's **adjusted earned income**
	£

STEP 1 Add together:
- her before-tax earned income (minus any deductions to her employer's pension scheme) 15,250
- the taxable value of any fringe benefits she gets .... nil
- any taxable expenses she gets 200
- **total D** 15,450

STEP 2 Add together:
- any personal pension payments she makes ... 330
- the gross amount of any interest payments she makes which qualify for tax relief .... nil
- the gross amount of any enforceable maintenance payments she makes .... nil
- the dependent relative allowance *(but only if she gets it)* .... nil
- the blind person's allowance *(but only if she gets it)* .... nil
- **total E** 330

STEP 3 Deduct *E* from *D* to get the **wife's adjusted earned income** 15,450
(330)
- **total F** 15,120

Now look up each figure on the Chart on page 79. If they meet in a coloured band, separate taxation should save you tax.

Jonathan and Caroline look up their adjusted incomes on the Chart, and find that they should save between £500 and £1,000 if Caroline's earnings were taxed separately. They do their sums accurately, and find that the tax-saving is **£882.70**.

Don't confuse *separate taxation of the wife's earnings* (the proper name is the **wife's earned income election**) with *separate assessment*, which doesn't affect the couple's total tax bill at all – see p82 for more details.

How to 'elect' for separate taxation

If, after reading this section, you work out that you'd be better off having the wife's earnings taxed separately, ask your tax office for **form 14**. Both of you must sign it within twelve months of the end of the relevant tax year – so if you want to be separately taxed for the 1987–88 tax year, you've got until 5 April 1989 to return the form (send it to the *husband's* tax office).

The wife's earnings will then continue to be taxed separately until you withdraw your choice. To do this, you must both sign **form 14.1** – again, you've got twelve months after the end of the tax year to return it to the husband's tax office.

So if you've chosen to be taxed separately for the 1987–88 tax year, but later want to change your mind (because of changes in the tax rules, or in your circumstances), you can do so before 6 April 1989.

ICTA 1970 s23, s37; FA 1971 s23; IR13.

Separate assessment

Don't confuse this with *Separate taxation of the wife's earnings* (see p74). Separate assessment doesn't affect your total tax bill. But it *does* mean that the bill is split differently – with the aim of making each of you legally responsible for filling in your own Tax Return and paying the tax on your own income.

The wife may prefer separate assessment because it makes her feel more independent, or because she doesn't want her husband to know how much income she has. (But note that, in order to check your total tax bill, *one* of you will need to have details of the other's income.) The husband may prefer separate assessment because it makes the wife responsible for filling in her own Tax Return and paying the tax on her own income.

How it works

The couple's tax bill is first worked out as normal. Then the special rules for separate assessment are applied.

The couple still get the married man's allowance (£3,795 in 1987–88) and the wife's earned income allowance (of whatever she earns, up to £2,425 in 1987–88) – plus any other allowances that they're entitled to. But the allowances are split between the two partners on a different basis:

First, the gross income of each partner is worked out (and for this purpose, the wife's investment income counts as *hers*, not her husband's)

Second, any outgoings are deducted from the gross income of whoever makes the payments, to arrive at each partner's 'total income'

Third, the allowances are divided up in proportion to each partner's total income, to arrive at the taxable income of each.
There are three exceptions to this:
● the dependent relative allowance is given only to the partner who maintains the relative
● the allowance for a son or daughter on whose services you depend is given only to the partner who maintains the son or daughter
● when dividing up the allowances, the wife won't be given less than the amount of wife's earned income allowance she was entitled to *before* separate assessment.

Finally, the couple's original tax bill (worked out in the normal way) is divided up in proportion to each partner's taxable income. See Example 6, overleaf.

For couples who have also chosen to have the wife's earnings taxed separately (see p74), the same rules will apply *except* that their single person's allowances will be divided between them in proportion to their 'total incomes'.

Example 6

Nigel and Nicola (see Example 1 on p64) have a joint tax bill after marriage of £3,720.60. They decide to opt for separate assessment.

First, the gross income of each is worked out. Nigel has £12,000 and Nicola has £8,000.

Second, their total incomes are worked out. As neither Nigel nor Nicola has any outgoings, their 'total incomes' are also £12,000 and £8,000 respectively.

Third, their allowances are divided up in proportion to each partner's 'total income', ie 3:2.

They get the married man's allowance of £3,795, plus the wife's earned income allowance of £2,425, making a total of £6,220. This, divided on a 3:2 basis, gives:

Nigel an allowance of	£6,220 × 0.6 = £3,732
and Nicola an allowance of	£6,220 × 0.4 = £2,488

So Nigel's taxable income is

$$\begin{array}{r} £12,000 \\ -\ £3,732 \\ \hline £8,268 \end{array}$$

and Nicola's taxable income is

$$\begin{array}{r} £8,000 \\ -\ £2,488 \\ \hline £5,512 \end{array}$$

Finally, their original tax bill (£3,720.60) is divided up in proportion to each partner's taxable income, ie also 3:2.

So Nigel pays	£3,720.60 × 0.6 = £2,232.36
and Nicola pays	£3,720.60 × 0.4 = £1,488.24
making a total of	£2,232.36 + £1,488.24 = **£3,720.60**

Their total tax bill remains unchanged, but they have each paid the tax on their own income.

How to 'elect' for separate assessment

Either husband or wife can do this, by signing **form 11S** (available from tax offices), and sending it to the *husband's* tax office. The form must be returned within the six months before 6 July in the tax year for which you want to be separately assessed. So if you want separate assessment in 1988–89, you must return the form between 6 January and 5 July 1988.

You will then continue to be separately assessed until you withdraw your choice. Either husband or wife can do this – by signing **form 11S–1**, and sending it to the husband's tax office within the six months before 6 July in the tax year. So if you want to withdraw your choice in 1989–90, you can do so between 6 January and 5 July 1989.
ICTA 1970 s38, s39; FA 1976 s36 (3); IR32.

Nigel and Nicola opted for separate assessment because Nicola wanted to keep her income a secret from Nigel. The only figures Nigel knows are:
- his income (£12,000)
- the allowances he's given (£3,732).

But he can also find out the total of the married man's and wife's earned income allowances (£3,795 plus £2,425 equals £6,220). This gives him all the information he needs to work out Nicola's income.
- first Nigel divides his allowances by £6,220 to get 0.6
- next, he divides his income by 0.6 to get £20,000
- lastly, he subtracts his income from £20,000 to get **£8,000**.

So in three easy moves he's got to Nicola's income. The calculation would be different if either Nigel or Nicola could claim other allowances. And it couldn't be done if the amounts of Nicola's other outgoings or allowances were unknown to Nigel, or if her earnings were below £2,425.

Death of a spouse

In the tax year in which your husband or wife dies, these rules apply:
- **before the death,** the couple get the married man's and the wife's earned income allowances to set against their combined income (unless the wife's earnings are being taxed separately – see p74)
- **after the death of the wife,** the husband continues, for the rest of the tax year, to get the married man's allowance to set against his own income. He can't, for that year, get the housekeeper allowance or (unless his wife was totally incapacitated), the additional personal allowance. In the following years, until he remarries, he gets the single person's allowance, and any other allowances he's entitled to. For example, if he has a 'qualifying' child living with him (see *Tax and single people*, p51), he can claim the additional personal allowance. If the husband remarries within the same tax year, he *doesn't* get the reduced married man's allowance (see p72). Instead, he continues to get the full amount

● **after the death of the husband,** the wife gets the full single person's allowance to set against her own income from the date of his death until the end of the tax year. She also gets the **widow's bereavement allowance** (see below) and any other allowances she's entitled to in that and the following tax year. In subsequent years, until she remarries, she gets the single person's allowance and any other allowances she is entitled to.

Widow's bereavement allowance

This can be claimed by a widow in the tax year of her husband's death, and in the following tax year – unless she remarries before that year begins. The allowance is £1,370 in the 1987–88 tax year – no matter when in the year her husband dies. But in the first year, it can be set only against her income (both earned and investment) from the date of the death to the end of the tax year – see Example 7 below.

ICTA 1970 s15A; FA 1983 s15 (widow's bereavement allowance); ICTA 1970 s8, s14 (other allowances); IR 23, IR 31.

If your spouse leaves any money when he or she dies, see *Inheritance tax*, p351, for the tax rules.

Example 7

Robin Williams died on 12 August 1987. From 6 April until his death, Robin had earned £6,000, and received £500 of investment income. His wife, Emily, had earned £2,000, and received £300 of investment income (which counts as Robin's for tax purposes). They had no outgoings. Their tax bill for 6 April–12 August 1987 was worked out as follows:

	£	£
Robin's income – earned	6,000	
– investment	800	
plus Emily's income – earned	2,000	
	8,800	
less allowances		
– married man's		3,795
– wife's earned income (of what she earns – up to £2,425)		2,000
		5,795
leaves taxable income of	3,005	
tax on this at 27%	£811.35	

After Robin's death, Emily earned a further £4,000, and received £600 in investment income. Her tax bill for the remainder of the tax year was worked out as follows:

	£	£
Income – earned	4,000	
– investment	600	
	4,600	
less allowances – single person's		2,425
– widow's bereavement		1,370
		3,795
leaves taxable income of	805	
tax on this at 27%	£217.35	

So Emily has received the full single person's allowance and the widow's bereavement allowance to set against her income (earned and investment) from the date of her husband's death to the end of the tax year.

The foreign element

If your spouse is resident overseas, or resident in the UK but absent abroad for the whole of the tax year, you will both be taxed as if you were **permanently separated** – see *Separation and divorce*, p89, for what this means. But if your joint tax bill increases as a result of the treatment, you can claim the excess back from the taxman – see *You and the Inland Revenue*, p447.
ICTA 1970 s42(2).

Tax-saving tips

● the wife only gets the wife's earned income allowance if she has earned income (see p67). So if she doesn't have a job, and you run your own business, it pays to pay her. In the 1987–88 tax year, she can earn up to £2,425 tax-free – although it might be better to keep her salary below the starting point for National Insurance contributions (£2,028 from April 1987)

● if you and your spouse could both earn the same amount, but one of you has to stay at home, it pays for the wife to go out to work (see p70)

● in the tax year of marriage, check whether you'd be better off not claiming the married man's allowance – especially if you only get a reduced amount – and keeping your other allowances instead (see p70)

● check whether you can transfer any unused outgoings and allowances to your spouse (see pages 70 and 73)

● if you both had mortgage loans which qualified for tax relief before you married, make sure you continue to get relief on both loans for as long as possible afterwards (see p74)

● check whether you'd save money by having the wife's earnings taxed separately – on p74 we show you how. But you need to do your sums again every time there are changes in the tax rules (or in your circumstances)

● if you've chosen to have the wife's earnings taxed separately, make sure that outgoings are paid by whoever can save the most tax – see p79.

8 SEPARATION AND DIVORCE

After separation or divorce, the same income may have to support two households instead of one – so it's vital that you plan your finances carefully. This section shows you how to keep as much money as possible for yourself, your spouse (or ex-spouse), and your children – and how to keep the taxman's share to a minimum.

Typically, separation or divorce will involve one or both of these:
- the payment of maintenance
- two homes instead of one.

It's important that husband and wife decide *together* the most tax-efficient way of paying maintenance, and the best solution to the housing problem.

The end of a marriage

Your marriage can end by *divorce*, or (for tax purposes) by *separation* – almost the same tax rules apply in each case. The taxman treats you as separated if:
- there's a **deed of separation**, or
- there's a **decree of judicial separation**, or
- maintenance is payable under a **court order**, or
- the separation is likely to be **permanent**.

ICTA 1970 s8, s14, s16–19, s42.

If you separate, tell your tax office straight away. Even if you weren't paying tax before, still get in touch with the local tax office – you may have to have dealings with them later. You can find the address in the telephone directory, under *Inland Revenue*.

Maintenance – basic rules

Maintenance payments are regular payments made out of your income to maintain your divorced or separated spouse, or your children, or both. There are two types of maintenance payments:
- **enforceable payments** – if you're legally obliged to make them, eg under a deed of separation, or a court order
- **voluntary payments** – if you can't be made to pay up.

You don't get tax relief on any voluntary payments you make. If you *receive* voluntary payments, they don't count as income for tax purposes – so you won't have to pay any tax on them. But they *do* count as income when working out your entitlement to supplementary benefit.

If you make enforceable maintenance payments, they qualify for tax relief at your top rate of tax. If you *receive* enforceable payments, they are treated as income – and are taxable at your top rate of tax. But if you have little or no income apart from the payments, you may be able to *claim back* tax deducted by the person who makes the payments.

These rules mean that it may be possible for the wife to end up with **more** than the cost to the husband – which is what you should aim for. The flowchart on p93 will help you work out if this could apply to you.

Who pays maintenance?

In this section we have assumed that it is the husband who will pay maintenance to the wife – but you should follow the same basic strategy if it is the wife who will make the payments.

How the flowchart works

The flowchart tells you the most tax-efficient way of paying maintenance. It takes as its starting point the *amount received* (by the people who receive the maintenance), *after allowing for any tax they have to pay, or can claim back*. In other words, the chart shows you cases where, for the *same net benefit to the getter,* the *cost to the giver* can be lower. Opposite we mention individually the main cases where this can happen, and there are worked examples starting on p95. Other things to think about are:
- security – enforceable payments may be better (see p93)
- cash-flow problems – see pages 94 and 97.

Where do you fit in?

Opposite we set out the situations where the method of payment can either save you, or cost you, money.

Can you cling on to the married man's allowance?

After the tax year in which the marriage ends, most men lose the married man's allowance and get the single person's allowance instead – which, in the 1987–88 tax year, is £1,370 less. But a separated (*not* divorced) man who wholly maintains his wife with voluntary payments can continue to get the married man's allowance. This means that if:

● you plan to make payments of less than £1,370, *and*
● you *can't* claim the additional personal allowance (£1,370, which takes you up to the level of the married man's allowance) you'll be better not getting the tax relief on enforceable payments, but making them **voluntarily** – and keeping the married man's allowance.

Children with unused allowances

If the wife is paid enforceable payments for the children, they are treated as the *wife's* income. But all children are entitled to the single person's allowance (see p52) – which means that they can have £2,425 of income free of tax in the 1987–88 tax year. If they don't have any income – or have less than this amount – they aren't making the most of their allowances. So it can be a good idea to make **enforceable** payments of £2,425 (or the amount of their unused allowances, if this is less) to each of your children. They won't have to pay any tax on the payments, but you'll still get tax relief – so the cost to you will be less than the benefit to the children.

Payments to a child **must** be made under a court order (otherwise they'll be taxed as though they were the income of the payer) – and the court order must specify that the payments are *to* (not *for*) the child. (If the payments are *for* the child, they'll be taxed as income of the wife.) Provided the correct wording is used, it doesn't matter if the payments are actually made to the wife on the child's behalf. A recent court case established that it's also possible to get a court order against yourself to make payments to children in your custody, so transferring income from you to them and getting tax relief in the process.

If the wife is a higher rate tax payer, or if adding maintenance to her other income would make her pay tax at higher rates, it can pay to make payments direct to the children of *more* than the amount of their unused allowances.

Children, like adults, have the first £17,900 of taxable income taxed at the basic rate only. So income of up to this amount, if treated as the child's, will be taxed at the basic rate only.

Sherdley v Sherdley 1987 2 All ER 54 (child in own custody).

School fees

Some court orders say that part of the maintenance should be paid direct to the child's school, to cover the cost of the school fees. But if the contract for payment of fees is between the wife and the school, that part of the maintenance will be treated as the *wife's* income. If she is a higher rate taxpayer, it's better for the fees to count as the child's income. So cover the cost by paying a larger amount in maintenance direct to the child.

If the wife has unused allowances

From the date of separation or divorce, the wife gets the single person's allowance – plus any other allowances that she's entitled to. If she has no income (or less than the amount of her allowances), you should make *enforceable* payments to her. She won't have to pay any tax on payments up to the amount of her unused allowances, but the husband will still get tax relief on the whole lot – so the cost to him will be less than the benefit to his wife.

If the wife's top rate of tax is lower than the husband's

The husband should make *enforceable* payments to her – because he'll get more in tax relief than she'll have to pay in tax on the payments.

If the wife's top rate of tax is higher than the husband's

In this case, the wife will have to pay **more** tax on enforceable payments than the husband will get in tax relief – so he would be better off making *voluntary* payments.

Allowances
- from the date of separation or divorce, the woman gets the single person's allowance: £2,425 in 1987–88
- she may also be entitled to other allowances – for example, if there is a child, she might get the additional personal allowance: £1,370 in the 1987–88 tax year
- in the tax year of separation or divorce, the man continues to get the married man's allowance: £3,795 in the 1987–88 tax year
- in later tax years, until he remarries, he normally gets the single person's allowance (£2,425 in 1987–88), plus any other allowances that he's entitled to. But see p91 for the exception to this rule
- for more details on allowances, see p99.

None of these applies?

If the wife would pay the same amount of tax on enforceable payments as the husband could claim back, it doesn't make any difference whether maintenance is paid voluntarily or enforceably – in both cases, the cost to the husband will be the same as the benefit to the wife. However, she may feel happier with enforceable payments – and the knowledge that she can take court action if the husband fails to pay.

The most tax-efficient way to pay maintenance

First, decide how much extra income the wife (and any children) will need. Then use this flowchart to work out the best way of paying it.

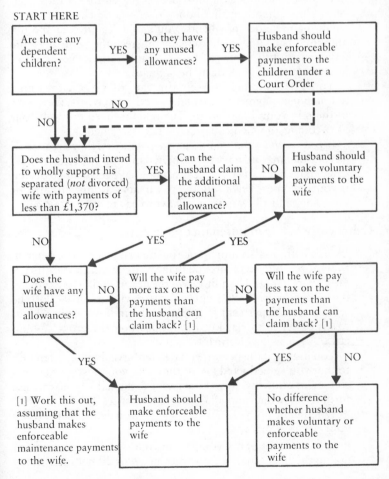

START HERE

Are there any dependent children? — YES → Do they have any unused allowances? — YES → Husband should make enforceable payments to the children under a Court Order

NO

NO

Does the husband intend to wholly support his separated (*not* divorced) wife with payments of less than £1,370? — YES → Can the husband claim the additional personal allowance? — NO → Husband should make voluntary payments to the wife

YES

YES

NO

Does the wife have any unused allowances? — NO → Will the wife pay more tax on the payments than the husband can claim back? [1] — NO → Will the wife pay less tax on the payments than the husband can claim back? [1]

YES

YES

NO

[1] Work this out, assuming that the husband makes enforceable maintenance payments to the wife.

Husband should make enforceable payments to the wife

No difference whether husband makes voluntary or enforceable payments to the wife

How to make the payments

Small maintenance payments

These are enforceable maintenance payments made under a UK court order which specifies that the payments are to be made weekly or monthly. They must not exceed certain limits.

If the payments are for your spouse (or ex-spouse), the limits in the 1987–88 tax year are £48 a week or £208 a month.

If the payments are made direct to your child (aged under 21), the 1987–88 limits are £48 a week or £208 a month.

If the payments are **for** your child (aged under 21), but made to someone other than the child, the 1987–88 limits are £25 a week or £108 a month.

If you make enforceable maintenance payments of more than these amounts, you must deduct basic rate tax (at 27 per cent) before handing the money over – see below. But with small maintenance payments, you simply hand over the full amount. This has cashflow advantages: the wife gets the payments in full, and – if she isn't liable to pay tax – doesn't have to claim tax back from the taxman.

You get tax relief at your top rate of tax on the small maintenance payments you make – and you have to give details of them in your Tax Return. The relief is given through your PAYE coding, or when you get your tax assessment.

If you *receive* small maintenance payments, they are treated as your income and have to be entered in your Tax Return. You can't claim back any tax, because none has been deducted. And if your income – *including* the payments – is more than your outgoings and allowances, you have to pay tax to the taxman.

Other enforceable maintenance payments

Except with small maintenance payments, you get tax relief on the enforceable payments you make by deducting basic rate tax (at 27 per cent) and handing over the net amount. For example, if Stephen Smith makes enforceable payments of £4,000, he will deduct 27 per cent (£1,080), and hand over only £2,920 to his ex-wife, Sheila. But he should enter the gross amount (£4,000) in his Tax Return.

You must tell the person you pay (enforceable) maintenance to that you've deducted tax. If they ask, you must give them a statement showing how much you deducted – you can use **form R185**, which is available from tax offices.

Whether or not you can keep the tax you deduct depends on your circumstances:

• if the amount of tax you pay on your own income (without taking the maintenance into account), *plus* 27 per cent of any

grossed-up building society or bank (other than National Savings Bank) interest you receive, is *less* than the amount you deducted, you'll have to hand over the difference to the taxman
● if the amount of tax you pay on your own income (without taking the maintenance into account), *plus* 27 per cent of any grossed-up building society or bank interest you receive, is the *same or more* than the amount you deducted, you keep it all
● and if you're a higher-rate taxpayer, you'll get extra tax relief. This is because you're entitled to tax relief on maintenance payments at your top rate of tax – but you've given yourself only basic rate relief by deducting 27 per cent.

Heating bills, etc

If you pay specific bills – electricity, rates etc – *direct*, you won't normally get tax relief on the payments. If you pay tax at higher rates than your wife, you should pay her enough extra maintenance so that (after tax) she can pay the bills. This will save you the difference between your top rate of tax and hers on the amount of the extra payments.

If you *receive* enforceable maintenance payments, the *gross* amount (not the net amount that you actually get) counts as your income. You should enter the gross amount in your Tax Return, and you might have to pay tax on it. If the payments include an amount to maintain the children, this may also count as your income – see p91.

But, except with small maintenance payments, basic rate tax has already been deducted. So you won't have to pay any basic rate tax.
● **if you pay no tax** (or less than the amount deducted), you can claim tax back from the taxman – see Example 1 below, and overleaf. To reclaim the tax, use the special repayment claim **form R40** (available from tax offices). Ask your ex-spouse to give you **form R185** (also available from tax offices), showing how much tax he or she deducted, and send both forms to your tax office
● **if you should pay higher rate tax,** you'll have to hand over the extra tax to the taxman.

Example 1

Sheila earns £2,000 from her part-time job, but doesn't pay tax under PAYE. She also receives £2,920 in enforceable maintenance from her ex-husband – a gross amount of £4,000. She gets the single person's allowance of £2,425.

Sheila works out her tax bill as follows:

	£
Income – earned	2,000
– maintenance (gross)	4,000
	6,000
less *allowance* – single person's	2,425
leaves taxable income of	3,575
tax on this at 27%	965.25

So Sheila should pay only £965.25 in tax. But £1,080 has already been deducted (by her ex-husband) from the maintenance payments. Sheila can reclaim £114.75 from the taxman (£1,080 minus £965.25).

The foreign element

If maintenance is paid under a foreign court order, then different rules apply:
● if you make the payments to an ex-spouse who is resident abroad, you can't normally get tax relief on them
● if you receive payments from an ex-spouse who is resident abroad, they will count as your income and you may have to pay tax on them. Contact your tax office for more information.

Voluntary maintenance payments

You simply hand over the full amount. You don't have to mention the payments in your Tax Return, and (except for the rules about the married man's allowance – see p91), they don't affect your tax bill.

If you *receive* voluntary maintenance payments, they don't count as your income, and you don't have to pay tax on them. Nor do you have to mention them in your Tax Return.
ICTA 1970 s52–55; FA 1982 s33; SP15/80.

Examples

The following examples show how three divorced couples work out the best way of paying maintenance in their circumstances. First, they agree how much extra income the wife will need – then they decide how it should be paid.

Example 2

Joe is a higher rate taxpayer (at 40%); his ex-wife, Joanne, is a basic rate taxpayer. They decide that she needs an extra £1,825. The next stage is to work out the best way of paying it. The options are:
● **voluntary payments of £1,825**
The cost to Joe is £1,825; the benefit to Joanne is £1,825

- **enforceable payments of £2,500**

Joe deducts basic rate tax (£675) and hands over only £1,825. But he pays higher rate tax (at 40%) on at least £2,500 of his income – so he should get an extra 13% relief on the £2,500 maintenance payments. He gets the extra £325 in his tax assessment – so the cost to Joe is only £1,500. But the benefit to Joanne is still £1,825

- **conclusion**

Enforceable payments are better because Joe's top rate of tax is higher than Joanne's – so he gets more in tax relief than she has to pay in tax.

Example 3

Jack and Jill are divorced. Jack is a basic rate taxpayer; Jill has no income, so, although she's entitled to the single person's allowance, she can't make use of it. They decide together that she needs £2,400 – but how should it be paid? The options are:

- **voluntary payments of £2,400**

Jack doesn't get tax relief, so the cost to him is £2,400.

The payments received by Jill don't count as income for tax purposes – so she still isn't using her single person's allowance. But she has no tax to pay, and so the benefit to her is £2,400

- **enforceable payments of £2,400**

Jack deducts basic rate tax (£648), and hands over £1,752. The tax on his own income is more than the amount deducted, so he can keep it all. The cost to him is £1,752.

The *gross* amount of the payment (£2,400) counts as Jill's income – but this is less than her single person's allowance (£2,425), so she shouldn't be paying any tax. She can reclaim from the taxman all the tax deducted – so the benefit to her is £1,752 + £648 = £2,400.

- **conclusion**

Enforceable payments are better because they make use of Jill's unused single person's allowance – so the cost to Jack is £648 less than the benefit to Jill. (They could decide to share the advantage: if, for example, Jack paid £2,835 enforceably, the net cost to him would be roughly £2,070, and the net benefit to Jill would be roughly £2,724.)

However, Jill has a cashflow problem while she's waiting for the tax to be repaid to her. Jack agrees to lend her money until she receives the repayment.

Example 4

Marion and Melvin are divorced; they are both basic rate taxpayers. They decide that Marion needs an extra £3,500 for herself and for their daughter, Zoe.

If Melvin pays the maintenance to Marion, it makes no difference whether they are voluntary or enforceable payments:

● **voluntary payments of £3,500**

Melvin doesn't get tax relief, so the cost to him is £3,500.

The payments received by Marion don't count as income, so she has no tax to pay. The benefit to her is £3,500

● **enforceable payments of £4,795**

Melvin deducts basic rate tax (£1,295), and hands over £3,500. He can keep the amount deducted, so the cost to him is £3,500.

Marion can't reclaim any tax because she has no unused allowances. The benefit to her is £3,500.

But then they realise that Zoe has no income, so she isn't using her single person's allowance (£2,425). Melvin pays a gross amount of £2,425 direct to Zoe in **enforceable payments under a court order**. He hands over a net amount of £1,770.25; the balance of £654.75 can be reclaimed for Zoe, so the benefit to her is £2,425.

The remaining £1,075 which Marion and Zoe need can be paid to either of them – as a gross amount in voluntary payments, or as a net amount in enforceable payments. So the benefit to them is still £3,500 – but the cost to Melvin is only £1,770.25 + £1,075 = £2,845.25

- **conclusion**

Enforceable payments direct to Zoe under a court order are better – because they make use of the child's unused allowances.

Allowances in the tax year of separation

Up to the date of separation or divorce, you get the married man's and the wife's earned income allowances to set against your combined income (unless you've chosen to have the wife's earnings taxed separately – see *Tax and marriage* p74).

So, as far as the husband is concerned, his wife's income (both earned and investment) up to the date of separation or divorce is treated as *his*. The full wife's earned income allowance can be set against her earnings to that date, and any other allowances the couple get can be set against any of their combined income to that date.

After the separation or divorce until the end of the tax year, the husband can continue to set the married man's allowance against his own income. He isn't liable to tax on any of his wife's income after that date. But he can't, for that year, get the housekeeper allowance, or – unless his wife was totally incapacitated – the additional personal allowance.

In later years, until he remarries, he normally gets the single person's allowance, plus any other allowances that he's entitled to. But a separated (not divorced) man who wholly maintains his wife by **voluntary payments** (see p90) continues to get the married man's allowance to set against his own income.

The woman immediately gets the full single person's allowance to set against her own income (both earned and from investments) from the date of separation or divorce until the end of the tax year – and for future tax years until she remarries. This means that, in the 1987–88 tax year, she can have income of at least £2,425 before having to pay tax. She may also be entitled to other allowances – for example, if she has a 'qualifying' child living with her, she can claim the additional personal allowance (see p50).

The additional personal allowance

The husband can't normally claim this allowance in the tax year that the marriage ends (see above). But in later years, provided he doesn't get the married man's allowance, he may be able to. If both parents claim the additional personal allowance for the same child (ie because it lives with each of them for part of the year), the allowance is divided between them. But if there's more than one child, and each parent has a child living with him or her for at least part of the tax year, then both parents can claim the allowance in full – see p59 for more details.

Inheritance tax

Gifts between husband and wife don't count for inheritance tax purposes – and this applies even after separation *right up to the moment of divorce* (ie when the decree absolute is granted).

After divorce, the following gifts are normally tax-free:
● maintenance for your ex-spouse or children
● transfers made under the divorce settlement
● gifts which would anyway be tax-free – eg those made out of your income as part of your normal spending. See *Inheritance Tax*, p351, for more details.

What happens to your home?

After separation or divorce, you and your ex-spouse will probably need *two* homes instead of one – and this can mean two mortgages. Below, we explain the rules about tax relief on mortgage interest – and show you how to keep your tax bill to a minimum.

The general rules

You get tax relief on the interest you pay on up to £30,000 (in total) of loans to buy or improve a home for yourself, and a home for your former or separated spouse. But note that:
● if the *total* of your mortgage loans exceeds £30,000, you won't get any tax relief on the excess
● the loans must be used to buy you an *interest* in the home (or homes). This normally means that they should be in your name – or in your name jointly with someone else. But if you are living in the home, **and** *you* pay the mortgage interest, you should be able to get tax relief, even if the home's not in your name. For more details, see *Homes and land*, p235.

Note also that a married couple can only get relief on the interest on up to £30,000 of loans between them – whereas if you're separated or divorced, you can *each* have relief on up to £30,000.

Who should pay the interest?

If, for example, the husband pays the interest on both mortgages, he could find that the total of the loans exceeds

£30,000 – and he won't get tax relief on the excess. Also, he'll only get relief on the mortgage on his wife's (or ex-wife's) home if he's got an *interest* in it – which may not be what you want. So it's normally best to arrange things so that you each pay the mortgage on your own home. If you and your ex-spouse each pay part of the interest, the relief is divided between you. Contact your tax office for details.

If your ex-spouse can't afford it

You can make larger enforceable maintenance payments, so that she (or he) can pay the mortgage interest out of the extra amount. Although this means that her income will rise, her tax bill will stay the same – because she'll get tax relief on the mortgage interest payments. And you'll get relief on the larger sum you're now paying in maintenance – which will save you tax. See Example 5.

Example 5

Mary and Michael have separated, and their old home has been transferred to Mary.

Michael still pays the interest (£2,000) on the outstanding mortgage – plus gross maintenance payments of £3,000. But he can't get tax relief on the mortgage interest because the home is now in *Mary's* name (and so he no longer has an interest in it).

Michael earns £17,000 and Mary earns £3,000; they both get the single person's allowance. Their tax bills are worked out as follows:

	Michael £	Mary £
Income – earned	17,000	3,000
– maintenance (gross)		3,000
		6,000
less *outgoings* – maintenance (gross)	3,000	
leaves 'total income' of	14,000	6,000
less *allowances* – single person's	2,425	2,425
leaves taxable income of	11,575	3,575
tax on this at 27%	3,125.25	965.25

If, however, Michael increased the maintenance payments to £5,000, and Mary paid the mortgage interest out of this increased amount, their tax bills would be:

	Michael £	Mary £
Income – earned	17,000	3,000
– maintenance (gross)		5,000
		8,000
less *outgoings* – maintenance (gross)	5,000	
– mortgage interest		2,000
leaves 'total income' of	12,000	6,000
less *allowances* – single person's	2,425	2,425
leaves taxable income of	9,575	3,575
tax on this at 27%	2,585.25	965.25

So although Mary's income has gone up by £2,000 her tax bill stays the same – because she's used the extra money to pay off the mortgage interest and this qualifies for tax relief.

And Michael's tax bill has fallen by £540. This is because he gets tax relief on the extra £2,000 maintenance – and tax at 27% on £2,000 is £540.

Raising a lump sum

You might need to raise a lump sum for your ex-wife – to enable her to buy a new home while you stay on in the old one. But if you have to borrow to raise the lump sum, make sure you get tax relief on the interest you pay.

You could raise a lump sum by taking out a mortgage (or second mortgage) on the old home – and the interest on this loan would qualify for tax relief *provided* it's used to buy you an interest in the old home. So if, for example, the old home is owned jointly by you and your ex-spouse, you can specify that the lump sum is being used to buy out their share.

Even if the house is in your name only, your ex-spouse may still have an interest in it which you can buy out. For example, the interest could be the right to occupy the home. Make sure that the separation or divorce agreement says that you're buying out this interest – and then you'll still get tax relief.

Transferring the home

You don't normally have to pay **capital gains tax** if you sell or give away your only or main home – see p242. But if you transfer the home to your ex-spouse, things are more complicated.

If you move out and transfer the home to your ex-spouse, you won't have to pay CGT, provided the transfer takes place within two years of the separation. But after two years, part of the gain you make on the transfer *is* taxable, unless:

- your ex-spouse has lived in the home ever since you moved out, *and*
- you haven't yet chosen another home as your main residence for CGT purposes.

If you stay in the old home and your ex-spouse moves out, you can later transfer it to them without having to pay CGT, provided you haven't chosen another home as your main residence.

FA 1972 Sch 9; FA 1974 Sch 1 paras 4 and 5; CGTA 1979 s101–102; FA 1982 s26; ESC D6.

Capital gains tax implications

A husband and wife are allowed only £6,600 of net taxable gains *between* them before having to pay CGT. But if you're separated or divorced, you can *each* make gains of £6,600.

In the tax year of separation, the husband has to include in his £6,600 limit *his wife's gains up to the date of separation*. But the wife gets the full £6,600 exemption for her own gains from the date of separation to the end of the tax year.

Gifts between husband and wife don't count for CGT purposes – but this doesn't apply if you're divorced nor (except in the tax year of separation) if you're separated. And if your 'gifts' are really part of a bargain, such as a divorce settlement, you may not be able to claim *hold-over relief* – see p427 for what this means.

CGTA 1979 s44; FA 1980 s79(1); FA 1982 s82.

Tax-saving tips

- use our flowchart (see p93) to decide whether to make voluntary or enforceable maintenance payments

- make use of everyone's allowances when paying maintenance – including the children's allowances. See pages 91 and 92

- if you receive enforceable maintenance payments, check whether you can claim back any of the tax deducted – see p94

- if there are two children, try to make sure that each parent has one living with them for at least part of the tax year. Then *both* parents can claim the *additional personal allowance* in full – see p99

- where possible, arrange for you and your ex-spouse to each pay the mortgage interest on your own homes. You can cover the cost by paying a larger amount in maintenance – see p100

- if you raise a lump sum for your ex-spouse, try to ensure you get tax relief on the interest on the loan – see opposite

- if you transfer your home to your ex-spouse, make sure you avoid having to pay any capital gains tax – see above.

9 TAX AND THE ELDERLY

Elderly people are liable to tax on their income in the same way as anyone else. But many people over 64 will pay less tax than a younger person would on the same amount of income, because of a special *age allowance*. In this chapter we look at aspects of income tax which are likely to be of special concern to retired or elderly people.

Age allowance

If you were 64 or over before the start of the tax year, you qualify for age allowance. For a single person this means your personal allowance will be £2,960 instead of the normal £2,425. Paying basic rate tax on £535 less of your income means a tax saving of £144.45. If you were 79 or over before the start of the tax year you get a higher age allowance of £3,070 in 1987–88. If you pay basic rate tax this means a further saving of £29.70 (27% of £110).

A married couple can get married age allowance of £4,675 if either of them was 64 or over before the start of the tax year or a higher age allowance of £4,845 if either was 79 or over before that date. This means a basic rate tax saving of £237.60

over the normal married man's allowance of £3,795 (with a further £46.71 saving if either is 79 or more). A married woman still gets wife's earned income allowance of £2,425 to set against her earnings or pensions.

But the amount of age allowance you get is reduced on a sliding scale if your 'total income' is over a certain limit – £9,800 for the 1987–88 tax year (see Table overleaf). If your 'total income' as a single person is £10,603 or more (£10,768 or more if you are 79 or more) your age allowance will be reduced to the level of the ordinary single person's allowance. It won't ever be reduced to less than this – so you can't lose out by claiming age allowance. If you're married, the age allowance will be reduced to the ordinary married man's allowance if your 'total income' is £11,120 or more (£11,375 if one of you is 79 or more by the start of the tax year).

Your 'total income' is, basically, your gross income less your outgoings. It doesn't include any tax-free income, but *does* include the grossed-up amount of any building society or bank interest you've received – see pages 279 and 280. If you're married it includes the income of both husband and wife. The deductions you can make to arrive at your 'total income' include interest you pay which qualifies for tax relief, pension contributions you pay, and maintenance and covenant payments you make. If you've retained the basic rate tax when you made any of the payments (as you will have done with mortgage interest under MIRAS, covenant payments and some maintenance payments) it's the *gross* amount of the payments you deduct, not the amount you've actually paid.

ICTA 1970 s8 (age allowance); ICTA 1970 s528 ('total income'); FA 1987 s26.

'Total income' over £9,800 – beware

If your 'total income' for the tax year looks as though it will be above £9,800 but below the point at which you lose the benefit of age allowance altogether (see above), you should select your investments carefully. If you have investments which produce income which is included in your 'total income', you would almost certainly benefit by exchanging them for investments which are tax-free (like National Savings Certificates). This applies equally to interest from building societies and banks (which is 'tax-paid', *not* tax-free) and to gains on certain life insurance policies – see Example 2.

The sliding scale

If your 'total income' is more than £9,800, your age allowance is reduced by two thirds of the excess. For example, if you're single and under 80 your full age allowance would be £2,960. But if your 'total income' was £10,100, this is £300 more than £9,800, and your age allowance would be reduced by ⅔ of £300 = £200. So your allowance would be £2,960 − £200 = £2,760.

The Table below shows what your age allowance would be for different levels of 'total income'.

'total income'	single	single 80-plus [1]	married	married 80-plus [1]
9,800	2,960	3,070	4,675	4,845
9,850	2,927	3,037	4,642	4,812
9,900	2,894	3,004	4,609	4,779
9,950	2,860	2,970	4,575	4,745
10,000	2,827	2,937	4,542	4,712
10,050	2,794	2,904	4,509	4,679
10,100	2,760	2,870	4,475	4,645
10,150	2,727	2,837	4,442	4,612
10,200	2,694	2,804	4,409	4,579
10,250	2,660	2,770	4,375	4,545
10,300	2,627	2,737	4,342	4,512
10,350	2,594	2,704	4,309	4,479
10,400	2,560	2,670	4,275	4,445
10,450	2,527	2,637	4,242	4,412
10,500	2,494	2,604	4,209	4,379
10,550	2,460	2,570	4,175	4,345
10,600	2,427	2,537	4,142	4,312
10,650	2,425	2,504	4,109	4,279
10,700	2,425	2,470	4,075	4,245
10,750	2,425	2,437	4,042	4,212
10,800	2,425	2,425	4,009	4,179
10,850	2,425	2,425	3,975	4,145
10,900	2,425	2,425	3,942	4,112
10,950	2,425	2,425	3,909	4,079
11,000	2,425	2,425	3,875	4,045
11,050	2,425	2,425	3,842	4,012
11,100	2,425	2,425	3,809	3,979
11,150	2,425	2,425	3,795	3,945
11,200	2,425	2,425	3,795	3,912
11,250	2,425	2,425	3,795	3,879
11,300	2,425	2,425	3,795	3,845
11,350	2,425	2,425	3,795	3,812
11,400	2,425	2,425	3,795	3,795

[1] At any time during the tax year

Example 1

Anne Oakman is 67 and single. In the 1987–88 tax year she gets £2,137 in state pensions and £6,500 pension from her former employers. She has a National Savings Investment account, which is taxed on a preceding year basis, so in 1987–88 she'll be taxed on the £1,700 interest she received in the 1986–87 tax year. She pays £100 a year under deed of covenant to her young niece. Anne works out her 'total income':

state pensions	£2,137
employers' pensions	£6,500
National Savings interest	£1,700
	£10,337
less covenant payment (£100 grossed up)	£137
'total income'	£10,200

As Anne's 'total income' is £400 over the £9,800 limit, her £2,960 allowance is reduced by ⅔ of £400 = £266, so the allowance is £2,694. Her tax bill will be 27% of (£10,200 − £2,694) = £2,026.62.

If £400 of Anne's interest payments had come from a source which was tax-free, she would have got the full age allowance of £2,960. Her tax bill would then have been 27% of (£9,800 − £2,960) = £1,846.80. This is around £180 less. So Anne is paying £180 tax on the top £400 of her National Savings interest – effectively a tax rate of 45%.

If Anne closed her National Savings account before she received £1,300 income from it in the 1987–88 tax year, she would get her full age allowance. This is because the taxman would now tax her on the amount she received in the current tax year. But she would have to check that she wouldn't lose out in the 1986–87 tax year, as the taxman would tax the National Savings interest for that year on a current year basis if it came to more than the tax she had actually paid (see p278).

Example 2

Lawrence Duval is 63, and his wife Betty is 66 – so they qualify for the married age allowance. In the 1987–88 tax year Lawrence earns £11,200 in his job as a film director, and Betty gets £730 interest from a building society. They paid £1,095 interest on their mortgage under MIRAS. They work out their 'total income':

Lawrence's salary	£11,200
building society interest (grossed up)	£1,000
	£12,200
less mortgage interest under MIRAS (grossed up)	£1,500
'total income'	£10,700

As their 'total income' is £900 over the £9,800 limit, their age allowance is reduced by ⅔ of £900, ie by £600. So their age allowance is £4,675 − £600 = £4,075. Their tax bill is 27% of (£11,200 − £4,075) = £1,923.75.

If Betty's building society money had been in an investment which was tax-free, their 'total income' would have been only £9,700 and they would have got the full age allowance of £4,675. Their tax bill would then have been 27% of (£11,200 − £4,675) = £1,761.75. So they have had to pay an extra £162 tax (ie £1,923.75 − £1,761.75) because of their building society interest.

Getting married

Whereas most people can save tax by getting married, if either of you is over 64 the saving will be less. For example, two people over 64 who each have a 'total income' under £9,800 are going to gain little in allowances by getting married if their *combined* 'total income' is over £11,120. Instead of two full single age allowances of £2,960 (£5,920 in total) they'll get the ordinary married man's allowance and (if the wife's earned income is at least £2,425) the wife's earned income allowance, totalling £6,220. This is an extra £300 in allowances, saving £81 in tax. (A couple under 64 would gain £1,370 in allowances and save £369.90 in tax.)

If the woman's earned income is less than £2,425, she will not be able to claim the full wife's earned income relief in the tax year after the marriage. If her earned income – see box – is less than £2,125, and she has some investment income, the couple could be paying more tax. This is because a wife's investment income is treated as the husband's income – see p67.

ICTA 1970 s8(1) (allowances); ICTA s8(2) (wife's earned income).

A wife's earned income

This includes pensions from her former employers, pensions from personal pension plans and any state pension she is entitled to on her own National Insurance contributions. If she is entitled to a pension of her own but chooses to get a pension based on her husband's contributions because this is higher, she can count as earned income the amount of pension she is entitled to on her own contributions.

Tax in the year of marriage

If you get married on 6 April, you are treated as a married couple for the tax year and taxed on your joint income. This means that, in the 1987–88 tax year, your age allowance will be reduced if your *joint* 'total income' is over £9,800. If you marry *after* 6 April, you're each treated as a single person, and your incomes are taxed quite separately for that tax year. This means a woman over 64 gets a single person's age allowance, which will not be reduced unless her *own* 'total income' is over £9,800. If you're planning a spring wedding, make it *after* 6 April.

In the tax year in which a man gets married, he is taxed on his own income only. If he's over 64, he gets an allowance between the single person's age allowance he was entitled to and the married man's age allowance he becomes entitled to – see Example below.
ICTA 1970 s37, FA 1976 s36; ICTA 1970 s8(3).

Age allowance in the year of marriage

The Table below shows how much age allowance a man born before 6 April 1923 gets if he marries in the 1987–88 tax year and his 'total income' is no more than £9.800.

married before	age allowance if: born between 6 April 1908 and 5 April 1923	born before 6 April 1908
6 May 1987	£4,675	£4,845
6 June 1987	£4,533	£4,698
6 July 1987	£4,390	£4,550
6 August 1987	£4,247	£4,402
6 September 1987	£4,104	£4,254
6 October 1987	£3,961	£4,106
6 November 1987	£3,818	£3,958
6 December 1987	£3,675	£3,810
6 January 1988	£3,532	£3,662
6 February 1988	£3,389	£3,514
6 March 1988	£3,246	£3,366
6 April 1988	£3,103	£3,218

Example 3

Joe and Joyce Wallace (who are both 75) got married on 10 September 1987. Joyce's 'total income' for the tax year is £8,000, so she gets the full single person's age allowance of £2,960 to set against her income (investment plus earned).

Joe's 'total income' is £9,950. As this is £150 more than £9,800, his age allowance will be reduced by ⅔ of £150 = £100. The amount of single person's age allowance he's entitled to is therefore £2,960 − £100 = £2,860. If he were married for the whole tax year he would be entitled to married age allowance of £4,675 − £100 = £4,575. As Joe was married on 10 September, he was married for 6 whole months and part of a 7th month. His age allowance is therefore the single person's age allowance he'd be entitled to (£2,860) plus 7/12 of the difference between £4,575 and £2,860. This comes to £3,860.

If the Wallaces' incomes and the amounts of allowances and the £9,800 limit were the same in the 1988–89 tax year, they'd lose all their age allowance because their joint 'total income' would be well over £11,120. So their total allowances would be the ordinary married man's allowance and (as long as at least £2,425 of Joyce's income was earnings or pensions) full wife's earned income relief – a total of £6,220.

How pensions are taxed

Some pensions are tax-free. But the following pensions are taxable – and normally count as earned income:
- **state retirement pension** (including any graduated pension, additional pension or invalidity addition you get)
- **old person's pension** (or non-contributory retirement pension)
- **pension from former employer** – paid to you or your widow, widower or other dependants
- **personal (or self-employed) pension** – provided you got tax relief on all the payments you made into the plan (if you didn't, part of the pension counts as investment income)
- **partnership retirement annuity** – but some of this may count as investment income if certain conditions are not met.

ICTA 1970 s208–219.

Wife's state retirement pension

A married woman's state retirement pension counts as her earnings if the amount she gets is based on her own National Insurance contributions. If a wife gets a pension based on her husband's contributions, her pension normally counts as her husband's earnings, and wife's earned income allowance cannot be set against it. If a wife is entitled to a pension of her own but chooses to get a pension based on her husband's contributions because this is higher, she can count as her earnings the amount of pension she was entitled to on her own contributions.

ICTA 1970 s8(2), s219.

Tax on state retirement pensions

Although the state retirement pension is taxable, tax isn't deducted from it before it is paid. If you get age allowance, and the basic state pension is your only income, you won't have to pay any tax – because the pension comes to less than age allowance. But there may be some tax to pay if your state pension, added to any other taxable income you get (eg a pension from your former employer or investment income), comes to more than your total outgoings and allowances.

The amount of pension which will be included in your income is the total of the weekly amounts payable over the tax year. This applies even if your pension was paid monthly or quarterly.

Annuities

An annuity you've bought voluntarily is taxed differently from an annuity which comes from an employer's or personal pension scheme. If you've bought a life annuity voluntarily, part of it is treated as return of capital and is tax-free; the rest is treated as investment income (so the wife's earned income allowance can't be set against it). The insurance company will normally deduct basic rate tax from the interest part of each payment. But if that means too much tax will be deducted, ask the company if they have an arrangement with the Inland Revenue to pay the annuity in full.

If the annuity was provided by a pension scheme you've belonged to, the full amount of what you get is taxable but treated as earned income. Many insurance companies will deduct tax from each payment under PAYE, so the correct amount of tax should be deducted. Other companies will deduct tax at the basic rate, but if your income is too low to pay tax, ask the company for a form which you can send to your tax office to tell them your income. The company can then make each payment in full, without deducting tax.

ICTA 1970 s230 (annuities); FA1970 Sch 5 Part II para 1 (pensions).

Pensions from abroad

You are normally liable for tax on *nine-tenths* of any pension from abroad, whether or not it is brought into the UK. With certain pensions, only half the amount is taxable, and certain war widows' pensions are tax-free. Pensions from abroad are generally taxed on a *preceding year* basis – so your 1987–88 tax bill will be based on nine-tenths of any pension you got from abroad during 1986–87. Further details are given in leaflet IR25.

How tax is collected on pensions

If you get a pension from your former employer, the tax due on the whole of your income will, as far as possible, have been collected under PAYE from your employer's pension. You may find on your Notice of Coding that the amounts of state pension and any untaxed investment income the taxman expected you to receive over the tax year have been subtracted from your allowances – see Example below. This can make it look as though your employer's pension is being taxed at a higher rate than your earnings were before you retired – see diagram on p114.

If you don't get a pension from a former employer, and your state pension including any other income comes to more than your total outgoings and allowances, you will be sent a special Notice of Assessment – unless the tax on the excess comes to £40 or less.

Example 4

Peter and Marion Green get the basic state retirement pension for a married couple (Marion isn't entitled to a state pension herself). Peter gets £5,000 pension from his former employers, and Marion gets £2,000 from hers. They also got £500 a year interest from their National Savings Investment account in the 1986–87 tax year (taxed on a preceding year basis). They check the Notice of Coding the taxman has sent them.

The taxman has estimated their 'total income' at £3,289 state pension + £5,000 + £2,000 + £500 = £10,789. As this is £989 more than £9,800, Peter's £4,675 age allowance is reduced by ⅔ of £989 = £659, so it's £4,016. The only income which can count as Marion's earnings is her £2,000 employer's pension, so her wife's earned income allowance is £2,000. This gives them total allowances of £4,016 + £2,000 = £6,016.

The taxman decides to collect the tax due on their £3,289 state retirement pension and £500 Investment account interest under PAYE from Peter's employer's pension by reducing his PAYE code. He subtracts the total (£3,789) to find his *Net Allowances* (£2,227) and then knocks off the last figure to get his PAYE code (222). This will be followed by a letter T because he gets a reduced amount of married man's age allowance.

Marion's PAYE code will simply be BR to indicate that the whole of her pension is to be taxed at the basic rate. (Her wife's earned income allowance has gone into Peter's code.)

Peter's code of 222T means that no tax will be deducted from £2,229 of his pension, and 27% tax will be deducted from the remaining £2,771 – so he'll pay £748.17 tax. The tax deducted from Marion's pension will be 27% of £2,000 = £540, so the total they'll pay will be £1,288.17. Because their PAYE coding gave them an extra £2 allowances, this is very slightly less than the £1,288.71 tax due on their taxable income of £10,789 – £6,016 = £4,773.

A form P3 (PAYE coding guide) is enclosed or was sent to you with a previous notice of coding

How your PAYE code is calculated

Expenses	....
Death and Superannuation Benefits	....
Interest unless payable net of tax	....
Personal allowance	
Age allowance (estimated total income £ _10,789_) ...	_4,016_
Wife's earned income allowance	_2000_
Additional personal allowance	....
Dependent relative allowance	....
Widow's bereavement allowance...	....
Total allowances	_6,016_

Less allowances given against other income

Untaxed interest...	_500_	
Occupational pensions	....	
State pension/benefits	_3,289_	
		_3,789_
Net allowances		_2,227_

Less adjustments for

Tax unpaid for earlier years
198 -8   £............................
equivalent to a deduction of   ....
198 -8   (estimated £.....................)
equivalent to a deduction of

Allowances given against pay etc.	_2,227_

Your code is shown overleaf   Printed for HMSO by A. Pettitt Ltd 9/86 8976678

Notice of coding

Year to 5 April 198

Code
See form P3 | _222_ | _T_ |

Why you might think your employer's pension is being taxed too highly

Tax before you retire
if your income is £9,000
(all from earnings)

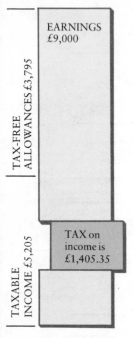

TAX-FREE ALLOWANCES £3,795

EARNINGS £9,000

TAXABLE INCOME £5,205

TAX on income is £1,405.35

Tax is collected under PAYE from your earnings – works out at 15½% of your income in our example

Tax after you retire
if your income stays at £9,000
(all from pensions)

TAX-FREE ALLOWANCES £4,675

TAXABLE STATE PENSION £3,289 (paid without tax being deducted)

EMPLOYER'S PENSION £5,711

TAXABLE INCOME £4,325

TAX on income is £1,167.75

Your tax-free allowances go up (assuming you get age allowance). So there's less tax to pay – works out at 13% of your income in our example. But the tax is all collected under PAYE from your employer's pension – works out at over 20% of this part of your income

If you've paid too much tax on your investments

With many types of investments, such as certain British Government stocks, income is paid after tax at the basic rate has been deducted. The same applies to income you get from a covenant (and from certain types of trusts), and to some alimony or maintenance payments. With dividends and most unit trust distributions, you will get tax credits. If you don't pay tax – or if your tax bill comes to less than the total of tax deducted plus tax credits received – you will have paid too much tax. So you should claim a rebate.

If you are in a situation like this you may well be sent a special **Tax Claim form R40** instead of the normal kind of Tax Return. You should fill it in and send it back to your tax office with your tax vouchers (which give details of tax deducted and tax credits). You don't need to wait until the end of the tax year to do this – claim as soon as you have received all your relevant investment income for the year (ie income paid with a tax credit or after tax has been deducted).

The taxman will work out how much tax you are owed (if any) and send you a rebate. Arrangements can be made for repayment of tax by instalments during the year – ask your tax office for details.

If you have to claim tax back regularly but aren't sent form R40, ask your tax office for it. If you claim only occasionally, write to your tax office, giving details of why you are claiming, and how much (if you know).

Using Covenants

Covenant payments to you

If your income is too low for you to pay tax, and a relative (or anyone else) is willing to give you money on a regular basis, it can save them tax if the payments are made under a *deed of covenant*. For example, if your income (excluding tax-free income and building society interest) is £500 less than your outgoings and allowances, you could receive £500 at a cost to the relative of only £365. See p127 for details of how to write a deed of covenant and how to reclaim the tax deducted by the payer.
ICTA s52

Making covenant payments

If you are a taxpayer, and want to give money on a regular basis to a friend or relative whose income is too low to pay tax (eg a grandchild), consider making the payments under a deed of covenant. For each £73 you pay over, the recipient will be able to claim £27 from the taxman, getting £100 in all.

If your income is in the band where each extra £ loses you age allowance – ie if your 'total income' is between £9,800 and £10,603 if you're single (£9,800 and £10,678 if, during the tax year, you are 80 or more), for each £73 you pay over, the taxman will not only pay the recipient £27 but he'll reduce your tax bill by £18. For married people this will happen if your 'total income' is between £9,800 and £11,120 (£9,800 and £11,135 if you or your spouse is 80 or more during the tax year). So the recipient gets £100 at a cost to you of £55. This is because your age allowance is increased by 2/3 of the gross amount of the covenant payments – see Example.

Example 5

Graham Jones's 'total income' is £10,250, and his age allowance is £2,660. His tax bill is 27% of (£10,250 − £2,660) = £2,049.30.

If Graham writes a deed of covenant to his granddaughter for a gross amount of £200 a year, he need hand over only £146 (ie 73% of £200) and his granddaughter gets the remaining £54 from the taxman. Graham's 'total income' is now £10,250 − £200 = £10,050 and his age allowance is £2,794. His tax bill is now 27% of (£10,250 − £2,794) = £2,013.12, a reduction of £36.18. So the cost of the covenant payment to Graham is the £146 he's paid over, *less* his £36.18 lower tax bill, a net cost of under £110, though the benefit to his granddaughter is £200.

Tax-saving tips

• If your income is in the region where each extra pound of taxable income loses you age allowance, investments where the return is tax-free may give you a higher after-tax return than ones like building society or bank accounts where the interest is included in your 'total income'. Be wary, too, of cashing in all or part of a life insurance policy on which you'll make a taxable gain

• Making covenant payments is particularly worthwhile if your income is in the band above

• Marriage often saves little (if any) tax for people over 64. But if you're planning a spring wedding, make it *after* 6 April

• If you aren't liable to tax but have income from which tax is deducted at source, ask to have repayments made at intervals during the year. You will also be able to benefit from covenant payments from anyone who is a taxpayer.

10 SOCIAL SECURITY AND SPECIAL TAX ALLOWANCES

If you're getting social security benefits, you may think you don't have to worry about tax at all. For many people this will be true, as the majority of benefits are not taxable. But pensioners, widows, sick and unemployed people could all find themselves in the tax net. This Chapter explains the rules. It also covers special tax allowances which you may be able to claim if you are widowed or elderly, disabled or permanently ill. These could mean less tax to pay – see p124.

Changes on the way

From April 1988 a new benefit **income support** will replace supplementary benefit. It will be taxable for unemployed people in a similar way to supplementary benefit. At the same time, **family credit** (not taxable) will replace family income supplement.

Tax and benefits

	tax-free	taxable
Unemployed or on strike	Additions for children paid with unemployment benefit. Part (or all) of supplementary benefit (income support from April 1988).	Unemployment benefit. Sometimes part (or all) of supplementary benefit (income support from April 1988).
Families with children	Maternity allowance. Maternity payments from social fund. Child benefit. One-parent benefit. Child's special allowance. Guardian's allowance. Family Income Supplement (family credit from April 1988).	Statutory maternity pay.
Elderly people	Supplementary pensions. Job release allowance under schemes open only to men aged 64, women aged 59.	Retirement pensions (except additions for children). Old person's or over-80s pension. Job release allowance under schemes for men aged under 64.

	tax-free	taxable
Widows	Additions paid for children. War widow's pension (including allowances for children and rent).	Widow's allowance. Widowed mother's allowance. Widow's pension.
Disabled or sick	Sickness benefit. Invalidity benefit (pension and allowance). Severe disablement allowance. Attendance allowance. Mobility allowance (or grant for maintaining a vehicle owned by a disabled person). Industrial death benefits paid for a child. Disablement benefits paid because of injury at work or an industrial disease. Disablement pensions paid as a result of service in the forces and to merchant seamen or civilians for war injuries. Extra pension paid to policemen and firemen injured on duty, beyond what they'd have got if retired through ill-health.	Statutory sick pay. Invalid care allowance (except additions paid for children). Industrial death benefits. Invalidity allowance paid with retirement pension.
Other benefits	Supplementary benefits (if not unemployed or on strike). £10 Christmas bonus. Housing benefits (ie rate and rent rebates). Funeral payments from social fund. Some annuities and pension additions for gallantry awards such as the George Cross. Benefits paid by foreign government similar to tax-free UK benefits. YTS training allowance. From 6 April 1986, special pensions paid by the governments of West Germany and Austria to UK victims of Nazi persecution.	Enterprise allowance. Community programme earnings.

ICTA 1970 s219; FA 1977 s23(1) (child benefit); F(No2)A 1979 Sch 1 para 4 (child's special and guardian's allowances); FA 1982 s30(1) (mobility allowance), s32(1) (unemployment benefit); FA 1987 s29.

How are benefits taxed?

Taxable benefits are paid gross – ie before any tax is deducted – and are taxed as the earned income of the person claiming benefit. If a married woman is getting any taxable benefits based on her own National Insurance contributions, or Invalid

Care Allowance, she will be able to set the wife's earned income allowance against them. But if a man is claiming extra benefit for his wife (or a woman living with him as his wife), it is taxed as his income. Tax-free benefits shouldn't be entered on your Tax Return, but you should enter the total amount of any taxable benefit you've received during the tax year.

At current rates of benefits and tax-free allowances, if your only taxable income is state benefits, you won't owe any tax. But if you have other income so that your taxable income is above your total outgoings and allowances, there'll be tax to pay. Special rules apply if you're off sick (see p123) or claiming unemployment benefit or supplementary benefit because you're unemployed – see overleaf. For other benefits, if you are working (or getting an employer's pension), any tax due will be collected through PAYE. It will look as if you are paying much more tax than others earning the same amount. But this is because *all* the tax due on your benefits is being collected at the same time as tax on your pay. See Example on p114.

Special codes

If your taxable state benefits are greater than your tax-free allowances and you're taxed under PAYE, your earnings (or employer's pension) will have to be taxed at a higher-than-normal rate – eg at 40% rather than 27% – to collect the tax on your state benefits. Your tax code will then include the letter F. With the level of benefits and tax-free allowances in the 1987–88 tax year, very few people are likely to have a tax code containing the letter F.

If you're not taxed under PAYE

You will be sent a Notice of Assessment telling you how much tax you owe on your benefits. But the Inland Revenue don't want to be bothered with collecting small amounts of tax, so won't normally send you an assessment if your total tax bill (*including* the tax on your benefits) would be less than £40. Above £40, you pay tax on the lot.

In the past, this **assessing tolerance** was quite important to some people (particularly widows and single women aged 60 to 64) receiving taxable state benefits, because the total amount of benefit they had in a year was a little bit higher than their personal allowance. They would technically have had to pay tax on their benefits – even if they were their only source of income. But because the tax due was less than the assessing tolerance, they didn't have to pay the tax.

Tax if you're unemployed

If you are unemployed and have to be available for work to be able to get benefits, some or all of the benefits you get will be taxable. The same applies if you're claiming benefits because you've been laid-off or are on short-time work. To find out how much of what you get is taxable, have a look at the Table opposite. If you're in any doubt, check with your local social security office.

Note that if you are on strike or involved in a strike you won't get benefits for yourself. But you can claim supplementary benefit (SB) for your partner (whether you're married or not) and for any dependent children. The taxable part is either the SB you get for your partner *or* the standard weekly scale rate of SB for a single non-householder whichever is smaller – see Table opposite.

A tip for unemployed couples
Until November 1983, a woman living with a man (whether married to him or not) couldn't claim supplementary benefits. But now either partner can claim so long as certain conditions are met (for details see DHSS leaflet NI248). If both partners are unemployed and want to claim supplementary benefit, part of this money could be taxable (see opposite). It will count as the income of the person who is claiming it. So if you have a choice of who claims benefit, you could pay less tax by making sure it is the partner who has the most tax-free allowances left.

How much of your benefit is taxable?

To work out what part of your benefit is taxable in the 1987–88 tax year, you'll need to know the standard weekly amounts of benefit. Benefits are uprated every year, nowadays at the start of the tax year (April).

Standard weekly rates of benefits 1987–88

Unemployment benefit
Couple	£50.85
Single person	£31.45

Supplementary benefit: standard weekly scale rates
single non-householder
aged 18 or over	£24.35
aged 16–17	£18.75

How much of your benefit is taxable?

If you get only unemployment benefit (UB)

	taxable	tax-free
	What you get for yourself and your husband or wife (or someone who looks after your child)	Any increase for children (but since November 1984, there is no extra benefit for children unless you are over pension age)

If you get supplementary benefit (SB), whether or not you also get UB:

	taxable	tax-free
For a couple	What you get in SB (or in SB plus UB) *or* the standard weekly rate of UB for a couple, whichever is smaller	The rest of your benefit
For a single person who is classed as a householder or boarder	What you get in SB (or in SB plus UB) *or* the standard weekly rate of UB for a single person, whichever is smaller	The rest of your benefit
For a single person who lives in someone else's household	What you get in SB (or in SB plus UB) *or* the standard weekly scale rate of SB for someone of your age, whichever is smaller.	The rest of your benefit

How much tax?

If you are unemployed and living on benefits for a full year with no other taxable income, your total taxable benefit is likely to be below your personal allowance – see p22. So there'll be no tax to pay.

Because of the way the PAYE system works, if you become unemployed part way through the tax year, you may have paid more tax on your earnings than you need to have done (see Example overleaf). But if you're claiming benefits, you won't get your tax rebate at once. Instead, you'll get it when you start work again or (unless you're on strike or involved in a strike) at the end of the tax year – whichever comes first. In most cases, the rebate will be paid to you by your unemployment benefit office and you'll also get a statement showing how much taxable benefit you have been paid. If you think the figure is wrong ask the benefit office to explain it. If you're still unhappy, you should write to the benefit office within 60 days of the date on which the statement was issued. Your tax office will then send you a Notice of Assessment after the end of the tax year, which you can appeal against in the normal way (see p455) – but *only* if you've made a written objection to your statement.

If you are unemployed and not claiming *any* benefit, you can claim a tax rebate after being unemployed for four weeks. You'll have to claim on **form P50** – get this from your tax office.

Example

Joe Doyle becomes unemployed on 4 October 1987, having earned £4,500 so far in the 1987–88 tax year. He's paid £702 in tax on these earnings under PAYE. He gets unemployment benefit and supplementary benefit – of which £50.85 a week is taxable. So his taxable benefit for the 1987–88 tax year is £1,322 (assuming he's unemployed until the end of the tax year). He has no allowances or outgoings other than the married man's allowance. His tax position for the year is shown below. He won't get his rebate until after the end of the tax year. (If he started work before the tax year ended, he'd get his rebate from the unemployment benefit office, when he went back to work.)

earnings	£4,500
taxable benefit	£1,322
	£5,822
less married man's allowance	£3,795
taxable income	£2,027
tax at 27%	£ 547.29
tax paid under PAYE	£ 702.00
rebate due	£ 154.71

If you owe tax while unemployed

If you start work again before the end of the tax year, your benefit office will give you a new form P45 showing how much taxable income you've had and how much tax you've already paid. Your new employer will then deduct the right amount of tax, including that due on your benefit, from your earnings for the rest of that tax year. You will also be sent a statement of how much taxable benefit you've had.

If you are still unemployed at the end of the tax year, your benefit office will send you a form **P60U** which includes details of how much taxable benefit you've had in that tax year.

Although you won't get a tax demand from the Inland Revenue straight away, once you're working your PAYE code will be adjusted so that the tax you owe on benefits will be collected from your earnings.
FA 1981 s27–29; FA 1982 s32; SI 1982/66.

Tax if you're off sick

Since April 1986, employers have been responsible for providing their employees with statutory sick pay for their first 28 weeks of a spell of illness. This statutory sick pay is treated just like your regular earnings – so tax is deducted from it under PAYE. If the amount of sick pay you get is lower than the amount you can earn each week (or month) before paying tax, your employer will give you a refund of some of the tax you've already paid in each pay packet.

After you've been off sick for 28 weeks, you'll start getting invalidity benefit instead (providing you've paid enough in National Insurance contributions). This benefit is not taxable. If you get any further sick pay from your employer, it will continue to be taxed in the same way as your normal earnings. But if you don't, you will have paid too much tax on your earnings since the start of the tax year – and you'll get a refund on your usual paydays.

Tax if you're having a baby

Since April 1987 employers have been responsible for paying statutory maternity pay for up to eighteen weeks to women who leave work or take time off work to have a baby providing they have worked for the firm for long enough. Statutory maternity pay is taxed in the same way as your regular earnings – so tax is deducted under PAYE. If the amount of maternity pay you get is lower than the amount you can earn each week (or month) before paying tax, in each pay packet you will get a refund of some of the tax you have already paid.

Extra benefit for children
Since the 1979–80 tax year, the child additions paid with all benefits have been tax-free and do not need to be entered on your Tax Return even where the basic benefit is taxable. To find out how much of your benefit is for children ask at your local social security office. Before that year, some additions for children were taxed.

Special tax allowances

Tax allowances reduce your tax bill. As well as the main personal allowances (see p22), there are a number of smaller allowances aimed at people with particular needs – for example, those who are blind, or who support a dependent relative. We give details of these allowances here. You'll find details of an allowance for people bringing up a child on their own on p50, and for widows in the tax year of their husband's death (and the following one) on p85.

How much?

For each £100 you get in allowances, you are let off paying tax on the most heavily taxed £100 of your income. So it's well worth checking whether or not you qualify.

Are you widowed?

If you're widowed and have someone living in your home acting as a housekeeper, you can claim a *housekeeper's allowance* for him or her. But you can't claim if he or she is a relative and someone else is claiming any allowance for them (including the married man's allowance), nor if the relative is a man claiming the married man's allowance.

If you have a child, you'd be better off claiming the much higher additional personal allowance (see p50) if you can, instead of this allowance – you can't have both. If the housekeeper is a relative, you might also qualify for the dependent relative allowance (see opposite).

See also p85 for details of *widow's bereavement allowance*.

How much?

The housekeeper's allowance is £100, so your basic rate tax saving will be up to £27.
ICTA 1970 s12; FA 1971 s15, s33; FA 1978 s19(2).

Does your son or daughter look after you?

If you (or your wife) are 64 or over or permanently ill or disabled, you might be able to claim an allowance for a *son or daughter on whose services you have to depend*. To qualify, he or she must live with you and look after you. But if you are a married man you won't qualify if your wife is under 64 and healthy. You can't claim this allowance if you claim housekeeper's or blind person's allowance.

If you are a widow or widower, you'd be better off if you class your son or daughter as your housekeeper (if you can) and claim the housekeeper's allowance which is higher (see above).

How much?

The allowance is £55, so your basic rate tax saving will be up to £14.85.
ICTA 1970 s17; FA 1971 s33(2); FA 1978 s19(5).

Are you blind or poorly sighted?

Anyone who is registered with a local authority as blind can get *blind person's allowance*. Many people who have some sight may be able to register – the rule is that you have to be so poorly sighted to make it impossible to perform any work for which eyesight is essential. Your local social services department should be able to help.

You can't have both this allowance and a son's or daughter's services allowance. Claim the blind person's – it's much larger. A widow or widower can have both the blind person's and the housekeeper's allowances.

How much?

The allowance is £540 so your basic rate tax saving will be up to £145.80. If you and your wife are both blind, the allowance is £1,080 (a basic rate tax saving of up to £291.60).
ICTA 1970 s18; FA 1978 s19(6); FA 1981 s23; FA 1987 s28.

Looking after a relative?

You can claim *dependent relative allowance* if you look after, or help to support:
• any of your or your wife's relatives who cannot look after themselves because of permanent illness, disablement or old age ('old age' means being 64 or over before the start of the tax year in which you're claiming)
• your mother or mother-in-law if she is widowed, separated or divorced, whether or not she is old, ill or disabled.

You can get an allowance for each dependent relative you support. If a relative is supported by two or more people, you can't each claim the full allowance: one allowance is divided between you in proportion to what you each contribute to your relative's upkeep.

If a couple have the wife's earnings taxed separately (see p74), the husband can claim only for his relatives, the wife for hers.

To get the allowance for a dependent relative:
• his or her income must be below a certain level. To get the *maximum* allowance, the relative's 'total income' (see p29) must not be more than the single person's basic retirement pension. For the 1987–88 tax year, this would work out at

£2,054. This limit applies to pensioners over 80 too, even though their small age addition may take their pension over the limit. If your relative's income is greater than the basic pension, your allowance will be reduced by £1 for each £1 of income over the limit

● the relative must live with you *or* you must contribute £75 or more towards his or her upkeep during the tax year. This can't be paid by deed of covenant. If you contribute less than £75 in a tax year, your allowance will be reduced to the same amount as your contribution.

How much?

If the person claiming is a single woman or a married woman who has her earnings taxed separately from her husband's, the maximum allowance is £145 – so the basic rate tax saving is up to £39.15.

For everyone else, the maximum allowance is £100 – so that the basic rate tax saving is up to £27.

In the 1987–88 tax year, a single woman would not be able to get an allowance for a relative whose 'total income' is £2,199 or more; a man wouldn't for a relative whose 'total income' is £2,154 or more.

ICTA 1970 s16; FA 1973 s12; ESC A15.

11 COVENANTS

Since the earliest days of income tax, tax relief has been available on **annual payments**, where some of your income for a number of years is effectively signed over to someone else (even if the actual payments are made more than once a year). Since you are forgoing such income, the theory is that you should not be expected to pay the tax on it – it should be the recipient who foots the bill. If the recipient does not pay tax because their income is too low, neither they nor you should have to pay tax on the money that you sign over to them.

One way of signing away income in this fashion is by using a **covenant** – a legally binding agreement under which one person promises to make a series of payments to another. You can get tax relief on covenant payments if the following conditions are met:
- neither you nor your husband or wife benefit from the payments
- if the payments are to your own child (or stepchild), he or she must be 18 or over, or married
- the covenant is drawn up so that the payments will last for more than six years (more than three years for covenants to charity) – though the covenant may be ended before then.

You can get tax relief at the basic rate only on covenant payments, unless the payments are to a registered charity.

How covenants work

Suppose you agree to pay a **gross** amount of £100 a year by covenant. If it qualifies for tax relief, you deduct tax from this gross amount at the 27% basic rate, and hand over the **net** amount of £73 (ie £100 − £27). You can keep the £27 tax you have deducted, provided you pay at least this much tax on your income. If you pay less tax than you've deducted, you'll have to hand over the difference to the taxman.

If the income of the person who gets the money – including the *gross* amount of the covenant payment – is low enough for there to be no tax due on it, he or she can claim a refund of £27 from the taxman. So at a cost to you of £73 a year, a total of £100 is received.

If the person getting the money is liable for some tax but less than the amount you have deducted, the refund payable is the difference between the two amounts. There is no tax advantage in making payments by covenant to someone who already pays tax, since there will be no tax refund – you part with £73, and £73 is received.

If the person getting the money is married, there will be no tax to claim back unless the tax bill on the *combined* income of husband and wife (including the gross amount of the covenant payments for the year) is less than the tax you've deducted. This is because covenant payments received are taxed as investment income – ie the tax liability always depends on the joint income of husband and wife (see p67).

ICTA 1970 s52 (deduction of basic rate tax); ICTA 1970 s434 (minimum periods); ICTA 1970 s437 (covenants to children); ICTA 1970 s447 (no tax relief if giver or spouse benefits); ICTA 1970 s457 (tax relief at basic rate only); FA 1980 s55, 56; FA 1986 s32 (charities)

Wife's earnings taxed separately?

Couples who have opted to have the wife's earnings taxed separately should beware of a complication which might crop up if the wife makes covenant payments. Her investment income may be worked out on the basis of the covenant payments she makes, rather than on her actual investment income.

Since her investment income is added to her husband's for tax purposes, there could be a higher rate tax bill to pay on his income, which would reduce or even eliminate the basic rate tax relief the wife gets.

Ang v Parrish 1980 2 All ER 790.

Example

Henry Philips pays a gross amount of £1,000 by covenant to his 19 year old student son, George, in the 1987-88 tax year. He can get tax relief on the £1,000 at the basic rate of 27 per cent only. This comes to £270 (27 per cent of £1,000), so he hands over £1,000 *less* £270 = £730.

Henry can keep the £270 tax relief since he will pay much more than that in tax on his earnings in the 1987–88 tax year.

George's income for the 1987–88 tax year is as follows:

gross amount of covenant	£1,000
holiday earnings	£540
interest on National Savings Investment account	£50
total	**£1,590**

£1,590 is less than the single person's allowance for the 1987–88 tax year of £2,425 (George isn't entitled to any other outgoings or allowances). So George can claim back the £270 tax relief deducted by Henry in full.

Note that if George landed a bumper vacation job, and earned £1,800 instead of £540, his income would be £2,850 – ie over the single person's allowance. He would have to pay tax on £2,850 less £2,425 = £425 at the basic rate of 27 per cent. The amount of tax due would be 27 per cent of £425 = £114.75, and George would be able to claim back only the difference between the tax due (£114.75) and the tax relief Henry deducted (£270) – ie £155.25.

Will you be able to get tax relief on covenant payments?

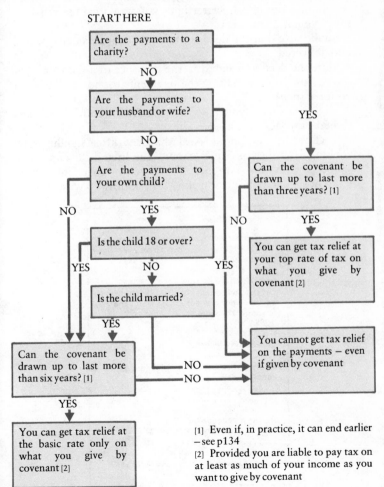

START HERE

Are the payments to a charity?
NO

Are the payments to your husband or wife?
NO

Are the payments to your own child?
NO → YES

Is the child 18 or over?
YES ← NO

Is the child married?
YES

YES

Can the covenant be drawn up to last more than three years? [1]
NO → YES

Can the covenant be drawn up to last more than six years? [1]
NO

YES

You can get tax relief at your top rate of tax on what you give by covenant [2]

You cannot get tax relief on the payments – even if given by covenant

You can get tax relief at the basic rate only on what you give by covenant [2]

[1] Even if, in practice, it can end earlier – see p134
[2] Provided you are liable to pay tax on at least as much of your income as you want to give by covenant

Drawing up a covenant

The agreement to make payments by covenant is known as a **deed of covenant**. It is a legal document, and there are pitfalls in devising one yourself. Many charities and insurance companies provide standard forms – as does the Inland Revenue for covenants to student children. However, you can draw up your own deed of covenant by following the drafts given in this chapter – the wording shown below is suitable for a covenant to anyone you are prepared to make payments to for at least seven years. Replace the words and figures in colour with your own details.

If using a DIY draft, it is essential to copy the wording exactly and follow any instructions to the letter – if the deed of covenant is not legally watertight, you won't get tax relief on the payments. You must:
- make sure that the deed contains the words 'signed, sealed and delivered'
- date the deed and sign it in the presence of a witness – not the person you are making the payments to, nor a relative of yours or theirs
- make the first payment on the covenant after the date it was signed – no backdating is possible.

Technically you should seal the deed after signing it by sticking on a disc of paper (though the Inland Revenue have said they won't insist on this). To deliver the covenant, simply hand or send it to the person you are making the payments to.

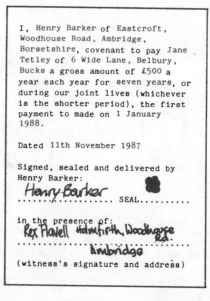

```
I, Henry Barker of Eastcroft,
Woodhouse Road, Ambridge,
Borsetshire, covenant to pay Jane
Tetley of 6 Wide Lane, Belbury,
Bucks a gross amount of £500 a
year each year for seven years, or
during our joint lives (whichever
is the shorter period), the first
payment to made on 1 January
1988.

Dated 11th November 1987

Signed, sealed and delivered by
Henry Barker:
    Henry Barker
..................... SEAL.........

in the presence of:
  Rex Flavell  Holmfirth, Woodhouse Rd.
...........................
            Ambridge
(witness's signature and address)
```

Note for readers drawing up a covenant in Scotland: you don't need to seal or deliver the deed, nor is a witness required (though there's no harm in one or two). And if the deed is not written in your own handwriting, you must write 'adopted as holograph' above your signature and on each preceding page, if any.

Covenants to charity

You can get tax relief at your top rate of tax on unlimited covenant payments to registered charities, provided the covenant is drawn up so that the payments are capable of lasting for more than three years.

If you prefer to make gifts to different charities each year, you can still get tax relief by making covenant payments to a charity which acts as an intermediary and passes money on to charities of your choice.

If you are eligible for higher rate tax relief on covenant payments to charity, you should still deduct tax at the basic rate only before handing over the money. Any extra relief you're due comes from the taxman when he works out your tax bill for the year.

The charity receiving your covenant payments reclaims tax from the taxman – but can do so at the basic rate only.

Covenants for children

Covenants to unmarried children under the age of 18 qualify for tax relief if made by someone other than the parents. Gifts to a grandchild, godchild or to other favoured children can therefore benefit from tax relief if made by a covenant drawn up so that the payments last more than six years. The draft on the left can be used to make the gifts – replace the words and figures in colour with your own details.

If the money from the covenant is to be invested for the child, take care in the choice of investment. The child is unlikely to have enough income to pay tax; investments should be avoided where income is paid out after deduction of tax which cannot be claimed back (for example, building societies or banks – other than the National Savings Bank).

Elderly?

The benefit of making gifts by covenant can be even higher if you are 64 or over and have a 'total income' of more than £9,800 but below the level at which you lose the benefit of age allowance (see p104): the tax relief on the payments can work out at almost £55 for each £100 of gross payments – see p115 for why.

Covenants for students

Covenants can be particularly useful for making regular payments to student children in further education: since they are usually 18 or over, payments by their parents qualify for tax relief if made by covenant (payments by a parent to younger children qualify for tax relief only if they are married). If the parent is expected to make a contribution towards the student's grant, using a covenant to make the payment could mean tax relief of 27 per cent on it. Alternatively, a generous parent could hand over more than the parental contribution, at no extra cost after the tax relief is taken into account – it only costs 73 pence to hand over £1 with 27 per cent tax relief on the payment.

To get the tax relief on covenant payments to a student child, the covenant must be drawn up so that the payments will last more than six years – rather longer than the normal higher education course. However, you can still get tax relief if the covenant is drawn up to last more than six years, *or until the child ceases full-time education.*

Covenant payments from parents don't affect the amount of grant if the student gets a **mandatory grant** (the type of grant paid for most first degree courses, teacher training and HND courses), unless the student counts as independent (broadly 25 or over, or self-supporting for at least three years). If the student counts as independent, or the payments are from anyone other than the parents, the covenant payments count as part of the student's income: if this exceeds a set limit, the student's grant is reduced by £1 for each £1 of income over the limit. With courses which do not qualify for a mandatory grant, check with whoever pays the grant.

The commonest form of covenant for students is the one on the left of the page opposite, to pay a fixed amount each year (£900, say) in three equal instalments. It is used so often that the Inland Revenue has produced a pre-printed form with similar wording (**Covenant form IR47**) which is available from local tax offices as part of the **Students Tax Information Pack (IR59)**. Alternatively you can copy out our draft, replacing the words and figures in colour with your details. If you later decide you wish to alter the amount of payment, you can simply end the old covenant (see p134) and draw up a new one, or draw up a new one just for the extra amount.

An alternative form of student covenant allows a parent to hand over the parental contribution deducted from mandatory grants in full, in three equal instalments – even though the amount of the parental contribution tends to vary each year. You can use the wording in the right-hand example of the two

I, Simon Grace of 18 Windermere Close, Borchester, Borsetshire, covenant to pay my son Sebastian of the same address a gross amount in respect of each academic term of £300 on each of the following dates in each year, namely 1 October, 1 January, 1 April, for the period of seven years, or for the period of our joint lives, or until he ceases to be receiving full-time education at any university, college, school or any other educational establishment (whichever is the shortest period), the first payment to be made on 1 October 1987.

Dated 15th September 1987

Signed, sealed and delivered by Simon Grace

Simon Grace .... SEAL..........

in the presence of:
Charles Ryman 16 WINDERMERE CLOSE BORCHESTER BORSETSHIRE
....
(witness's signature and address)

Fixed amount covenant

I, George Clark of Maltings, Wide Lane, Ambridge, Borsetshire, covenant to pay my son Anthony of the same address the gross amount in respect of each academic term as specified below on each of the following dates in each year, namely 1 October, 1 January, 1 April, for the period of seven years, or for the period of our joint lives, or until he ceases to be receiving full-time education at any university, college, school or any other educational establishment (whichever is the shortest period), the first payment to be made on 1 October 1987.

The gross amount of the payment in respect of each academic term shall be one-third of the parental contribution towards Anthony Clark's student maintenance grant for the year in which the payment is made, calculated according to any regulations for the time being in force relating to mandatory awards by local education authorities.

Dated 15th September 1987

Signed, sealed and delivered by George Clark

George Clark ..SEAL........

in the presence of:
Charles Brown Ivy Cottage Wide Lane Ambridge Borsetshire
....
(witness's signature and address)

Variable amount covenant

covenant forms shown above (replacing the words and figures in colour with your details) to draw up this type of variable covenant. Note, however, that using a variable amount covenant could (in very exceptional circumstances) lead to complications if your student child gets the minimum grant – it may be advisable to use a fixed amount covenant if this applies.

The dates on the covenant

Both the drafts given in this chapter for student covenants make payments on 1 October, 1 January and 1 April. These dates can be varied – or more than three instalments paid – by making appropriate changes to the wording. If the student intends to claim supplementary benefit during the holidays, all covenant payments should be made during term-time – otherwise they could count as the student's income, reducing the amount of benefit payable. Note that if the final payment in the academic year is made after 5 April, the student might not be eligible for a tax refund on it in the last year at college, since later in the same tax year he or she may be earning enough to pay tax.

Ending a covenant

A covenant is normally worded so that it comes to an end after a fixed period of time. The covenant will usually also say that payments stop if either the person making them or the person getting them dies before the end of the period. Some covenants have other clauses which can end the covenant early – for example, with covenants for students, when the child finishes full-time education.

A covenant can usually be ended at any stage by mutual consent, but it must not be agreed in advance that it will be. If the person who gets the payments does not agree to end the covenant, he or she can insist on you making the promised payments – and can take you to court if you don't.

Suitable words for a **deed of revocation** to end a covenant are given below – replace the parts in colour with your own details.

> We, George Gladstone of 23 Acacia Avenue, Slagthorpe and Henry Gladstone of the same address, agree that the covenant dated 25th September 1984 under which payments are to be made by George Gladstone to Henry Gladstone is hereby forthwith revoked.
>
> Dated 15th September 1987
>
> George Gladstone *George Gladstone*
>
> Henry Gladstone *Henry Gladstone*
>
> in the presence of:
> *Alfred Marley   25 Acacia Avenue Slagthorpe*
> ....
>
> (witness's signature and address)

Deed of revocation

Claiming the tax refund

When you have made all the payments due in a tax year under the deed of covenant, you should complete Inland Revenue **form R185AP** (see opposite) and give it to the person you are paying (with small payments to charity, this often needs to be

Certificate of deduction of Income Tax - Annual payment under Deed of Covenant

Person making the payment
Only complete this form if you have made the payment and deducted tax from it. If you are deducting the tax on behalf of your employer as a secretary, cashier, etc, you should say so after your signature. Send the completed form to the person who receives the payment.

For official use
District stamp

'Duty assessed 'stamp'

Your name and address
SIMON GRACE
18 WINDERMERE CLOSE
BORCHESTER
BORSETSHIRE   Postcode KVI 6PQ

Your employer's name and address or, if a company or business, the business address
BORCHESTER MEAT PACKAGERS LTD
39-43 FELPERSHAM ROAD
BORCHESTER
BORSETSHIRE   Postcode KVI 3DR

District (and reference) to which you make your tax returns
BORCHESTER

National Insurance number
NAO 77600C

I certify that • I have made the payment, details of which are given below, and deducted the income tax shown
• this tax has been or will be paid by me either directly or by deduction from other income when I receive it.

Name and address of person receiving the payment
SEBASTIAN GRACE
18 WINDERMERE CLOSE
BORCHESTER
BORSETSHIRE   Postcode KVI 6PQ

Gross payment £ 300
Income tax I have deducted £ 81
Net payment £ 219

Payment made under Deed of Covenant executed on	Consecutive number of the annual payment	Date payment made
15 09 1987	01	01 10 1987

Signature ... Simon Grace   Date 2nd October 1987

Person receiving the payment
Keep this form until you claim repayment. Then send it with your claim as evidence of the tax deducted.

R185(AP)New   Printed for Her Majesty's Stationery Office by Harvest Printers Ltd. 8/86 Dd. 8975754

done in the first year only). The person you're paying (or a parent if under 18) should send the completed form R185AP to their tax office to claim the tax refund. It may be possible in some circumstances to claim the tax refund after each payment – with a fixed amount covenant to a student, say, as above.

The taxman may require the person you're paying to complete a Tax Return or **Tax Claim form R40** (a child under 18 may get **Tax Claim form R232**). You and the recipient may also be asked to complete a **Certificate of non-reciprocity** (**form R111** for a covenant to a child under 18, **form R110** for covenants to anyone else) and perhaps answer some questions designed to establish that the payments have actually been made. This checks that the covenant is above board – that you're not getting something back in return for the payments, for example.

Tax-saving tips

Use covenants to get tax relief on payments to:
• your own student children
• grandchildren, godchildren or any other child who is not your own
• charities
• anyone else who does not pay tax.

12 WORKING FOR AN EMPLOYER

Most of us work for an employer, and tax on our wages or salaries is collected under the Pay-As-You-Earn system (PAYE). Your earnings are taxed in the way described in this chapter if you are employed under a *contract of service* and are paid a wage or salary on a regular basis. If you are employed under a *contract* (or contracts) *for services*, and are paid when you send in a bill or invoice, you are likely to count as self-employed. Details of how self-employed people are taxed are given in Chapter 15.

Earnings from employment are taxed under the rules of Schedule E; earnings from self-employment under Schedule D (see p33). See Chapter 13 for detailed rules about fringe benefits, and Chapter 14 if your job involves working abroad for some or all of the time.

One basic tax rule to start off with: if you work for an employer, your earnings from your job are taxed on what's known as a *current year basis* – ie in the 1987–88 tax year you pay tax on the pay you receive in that tax year.

And a useful piece of advice. The PAYE system collects tax not only on earnings but also on pensions from a job, sometimes on regular freelance earnings and – often – on pensions from the state. There's not much you can do about that. But PAYE is also used – quite often – to collect tax on investment income. If this happens to you, you may be paying tax on the investment income sooner than you need to. You can ask the taxman for a separate, and later, bill instead.

ICTA 1970 s181; s219, s219A; Inland Revenue leaflet IR56.

> **Sub-contractors in the building industry**
> Even though you may regard yourself as self-employed, basic rate tax will be deducted from all your earnings unless you hold a sub-contractor's tax certificate. See *Inland Revenue leaflet IR40* for more details.

What counts as earnings

The basic rule is that any money you get from your employer is taxable, unless it's a genuine personal gift; or it's spent on an *allowable expense* (see p142); or it genuinely is not in any way a payment for the job you do. So all the following count as pay:

● normal wages or salary; commission; tips; bonuses; holiday pay; overtime; cost-of-living allowance; London weighting; arrears and advances of pay

● fees and other expenses you get for being a company director

● any expense allowance from your employer (though you won't be taxed on anything spent on *allowable expenses* – see p142)

● money your employer pays to cover expenses in your job. If you've paid the expenses out of your pocket and your employer pays you back, you're taxed only on any profit you make from the difference. If the expenses are *allowable* – see p142 – you're not taxed on what your employer pays

● the taxable value of certain fringe benefits your employer gives you – see Chapter 13

● sick pay from your employer (including *statutory sick pay*); sickness benefits payable from an insurance scheme your employer arranges – see p157

● maternity pay (including *statutory maternity pay*)

● pay in lieu of notice and redundancy or leaving payments in excess of £25,000 (though see p158)

● most lump sum payments on taking up a job, including payments made by your new employer before you leave your old job

● taxable unemployment benefit if it is paid to you by your employer under arrangements with the Department of employment

● earnings (including all the things above) from any additional jobs.

Other things that count as earnings are pensions from former employers, state retirement pension, and other taxable social security benefits. See p141 for the Government's proposals for *profit-related pay*.
ICTA 1970 s183.

Understanding your payslip

EMPLOYEE NAME						EMPLOYEE NO	DEPT
GEORGE WATKINS		BAILEY DELCO LTD				676	51
BASIC	OVERTIME ETC	HOLIDAYS	BONUS/OTHER PAY	ADJUSTMENT	TAX-FREE ALLOWANCE	PERIOD	DATE
916.67						3	30/6/87
E/E NI	E/E NI TO DATE	DED 1	DED 2	TAX CODE	GROSS TO DATE	TAX TO DATE	TAX THIS PERIOD
82.50	247.50	24.16		379H	2,750.01	460.08	153.36
E/R NI	GROSS PAY	CUMULATIVE PENSION	PENSION DEDN	PRE-TAX B	PRE-TAX C	TOTAL DEDUCTIONS	NET PAY
95.79	916.67	96.24	32.08			292.10	624.57

a   *b*   *c*   *d*

e *f* *g* *h* *i* *j* *k* *l* *m* *n* *o* *p* *q* *r*

How the figures match up

On the payslip above, there's a large difference between £916.67 (the figure for **gross pay**) and £624.57 (the figure for **net pay**). Here's how you get from one to the other. (We've left blank spaces for you to fill in the figures from your own payslip.)

1. Gross pay   £916.67 £ _____

Deductions

2. Pension contributions [1] £32.08 £ _____

3. Tax   £153.36 £ _____

4. National Insurance [1] £82.50 £ _____

5. Other deductions (in this case, for season ticket loan) £24.16 £ _____

6. Total deductions £292.10 £ _____

£916.67 *minus* £292.10   = £624.57 £ _____

[1] What *you* pay (not your employer's contributions).

A quick check on tax

If you're a **basic rate taxpayer**, you can use this to check that the tax deduction on your payslip is broadly correct.

Gross pay   A

Pension contributions [1]   B

Free-of-tax pay   C
(Take your current PAYE code – see *Tax code* in example payslip – add the figure 9 to the end [2] and divide by 12 if paid monthly or 52 if paid weekly).

Add B to C and subtract the total from A   D

Multiply D by 0.27 [3]   E

E should be roughly equivalent to the tax deducted for the month or week.

[1] Leave this box blank if your employer's scheme is not an 'approved' or 'statutory' one.
[2] For example, if your PAYE code is 242 (ignoring any letters), make this 2429; if it's 379, make it 3799.
[3] For 1987–88 tax year.

When you look at your payslip, you'll see that there's a large gap between your earnings before any deductions – *gross pay* – and your take-home pay – *net pay*. To help you understand what the entries on your payslip are for, we've illustrated an example payslip here. Your payslip may well be laid out rather differently, but the same type of information should appear.

Of course, not all the deductions on your payslip are to do with income tax. For example, National Insurance (NI) contributions you pay should also be shown – more details on p156. Other deductions could be for pension contributions, season ticket loans or gifts to charity under a Payroll Giving Scheme and of course the biggest deduction will probably be for income tax.

If your employer's pension scheme is a 'statutory' or 'approved' scheme any contributions you make to the scheme aren't taxable, and they will be deducted before tax is worked out on the rest of your pay. 'Statutory' schemes are for employees of nationalised industries, local authorities, etc; most other schemes have been approved by the Inland Revenue.

Form P60

At the end of each tax year, your employer will give you **form P60** (or an equivalent form). This is a record of your total pay (including overtime etc) for the tax year – and of how much tax you've paid. Note that some P60 forms don't include the contributions to an 'approved' or 'statutory' pension scheme under the figure for pay (ie what's shown is pay *less* pension contributions).

Key to payslip entries

a **Basic**
   Pay before additions for things like overtime or bonus

b **Holidays**
   Depends on company policy. May list here your pay while on holiday, or may list only exceptional payments (eg pay in lieu of holiday)

c **Adjustment**
   On this payslip, statutory sick pay and pay from company's own sick pay scheme (less any amount attributable to contributions you've made to the scheme) or statutory maternity pay are entered here

d **Tax-free allowance**
   Depends on company policy. Non-taxable payments (eg evening meal or travelling allowance) paid with salary may be entered here

e **E/E NI**
Employee's National Insurance contributions for the month

f **E/R NI**
National Insurance contributions for the employee which the employer has to pay for the month

g **E/E NI to date**
Total of employee's National Insurance contributions since the beginning of the tax year

h **Gross pay**
This is the figure for salary for the month before any deductions. Would include overtime and bonus if these were paid

i **Ded.1/Ded.2**
Deductions – such as repayment of company loan, an advance on salary, your contributions to your employer's medical bills insurance scheme, a payment under Payroll Giving Scheme – would be entered in these boxes. In this example, Ded.1 is the monthly repayment of a season ticket loan

j **Cumulative pension**
Total contributions to company pension scheme paid by employee since the beginning of the tax year

k **Pension dedn**
Employee's contributions to the company pension scheme for the period covered by the payslip. As the scheme is an 'approved' one (see opposite) contributions are deducted before tax is worked out

l **Tax code**
PAYE code number. For how this is worked out see p146

m **Pre-tax B/Pre-tax C**
Depends on company policy. Boxes like these could be used to show things like additional voluntary contributions to the company pension scheme (which are non-taxable and deducted from your pay before calculating tax due) and certain expenses or benefits (eg lunch allowance paid in cash) which have to be included in pay for the period and taxed under PAYE. On this payslip, amounts in these boxes will be included in pay to be taxed if marked by a plus sign

n **Gross to date**
Total pay (before deductions) since the beginning of the tax year

o **Tax to date**
Total tax deducted since the beginning of the tax year

p **Total deductions**
Total of all deductions from gross pay for the period covered by the payslip

q **Tax this period**
Tax deducted for the period covered by the payslip (a month in this case)

r **Net pay**
Take-home pay – ie what's left of gross pay after the figure for total deductions has been subtracted.

Profit-related pay

In his 1987 Budget, the Chancellor proposed that employers should be able to set up profit-related pay (PRP) schemes, under which employees would be able to get tax relief on up to half the proportion of their pay which is profit-related. This proposal was shelved when the Finance Act was rushed through Parliament before the June election.

Assuming the proposal is revived, under such a scheme the percentage of pay which is linked to the profits of the employer will rise if the profits rise and fall if profits fall. Tax relief on half your PRP will be available only if the scheme has Inland Revenue approval. And the relief will be given only up to the point where PRP forms no more than 20 per cent of your total pay which is taxed under PAYE (see p146) or £3,000 a year, whichever is less. Your employer will give you the relief through the PAYE system. National Insurance contributions will still have to be paid on PRP.

Approved PRP schemes will have to meet certain conditions:
● only private sector employers can run approved schemes
● a scheme must run for at least a year and be open to at least 80 per cent of the workforce. Part-timers can be excluded, and, for up to three years, so can new employees. 'Controlling directors' with a 25 per cent or more stake in the company or firm must be excluded
● a scheme must be set up for an 'employment unit'. This can be either the whole company, or firm, or a unit within it (eg a subsidiary company in a group of companies), and the scheme must establish a clear link between the PRP of each unit and the profits generated by it
● at outset, the total PRP must form at least 5 per cent of the total pay of participating employees.

Expenses in your job

Two questions people ask are:
● if they pay expenses out of their own pocket, can they get tax relief on what they pay?
● if their employer pays expenses for them, will they escape being taxed on what their employer pays?

The answer to both questions depends on whether the expenses are *allowable expenses* for tax purposes. The Table on the following four pages shows the main things that are – and aren't – allowable. If an expense is allowable, the answer to both questions is yes. If it's not:
● you get no tax relief on what you pay yourself
● you're taxed on what your employer pays, *less* anything you pay towards the cost.

For an expense to be allowable, the money must be spent *'wholly, exclusively and necessarily in the performance of the duties of your employment'* . So if you get a fixed expense allowance and don't spend all of it on allowable expenses, you are taxed on the difference. Note that *'necessarily'* means necessary within the context of your job, and not simply necessary to you. So if working late means that you'll have to stay in a hotel overnight because your home is a long distance away, the hotel bill won't be allowable if your job could be done by someone else living closer to your workplace. However, small differences in individual circumstances (or in a Tax Inspector's assessment of them) may mean that an expense disallowed for one person is allowable for someone else. Allowable expenses can be set off only against earnings from your job, not, for example, against investment income.

Expenses paid out of your own pocket

In trades where it's customary to provide your own tools or clothing (eg plumbing) many trades unions have agreed a **fixed deduction** for upkeep and replacement of these things. For example, there may be a fixed amount of £70. You can claim the whole fixed deduction as an allowable expense even if you don't spend it all. And if you spend more, you can claim more.

Equipment you buy (such as a car, typewriter or your initial outlay on tools) to use in your job counts as *machinery or plant* and what you spend can't be claimed as an allowable expense. If the equipment is necessary for your job, you can get tax relief by claiming a **capital allowance**. See Chapter 15 (capital allowance rules are the same as for self-employed people).

Note that if you borrow the money to buy the equipment, this counts as a qualifying loan (see p25), and you can claim tax relief on the interest you pay in the tax year you get the loan and the following three tax years.

Expenses your employer pays for

If an expense *isn't* allowable, it counts as part of your pay and you're taxed on it – either under PAYE or by getting a separate tax bill. If an expense *is* allowable, how it's dealt with varies:

● has your employer got a **dispensation** for the expense? Broadly, a dispensation means that your employer doesn't have to give details to the taxman of expenses he pays – and you don't have to declare them in your tax return. The taxman won't give a dispensation unless he's satisfied that it's for allowable expenses (and nothing else), and that your employer keeps proper control over expenses

● if there isn't a dispensation, and you count as higher-paid (ie earning at a rate of £8,500 a year or more – see p163), your employer has to tell the taxman, at the end of the tax year, about all expenses he's paid you (or for you) for which there isn't a dispensation. He does this on **form P11D**. You'll have to enter all these expenses in your tax return, and be taxed on any which aren't allowable. Allowable expenses have to be entered twice – as income and as outgoings. Entering them as outgoings means that you don't pay tax on them.

● if you don't count as higher-paid, expenses for which there's a dispensation are ignored; so are other allowable expenses – including 'scale payments' (eg a mileage allowance) which have been agreed between your employer and the taxman. Other expenses, if they're not allowable, haven't been taxed as part of your pay and total more than £25 a year, are declared by your employer on **form P9D** – and any tax due is normally collected under PAYE in a later tax year.
ICTA 1970 s189, s192, s411.

Expenses in your job

	Expenses normally allowed	Not allowed
To get a job	Cost of retraining provided by employer to acquire new work skills, if you have left or are about to leave your job.	Agency fees. Expenses of interview. Travelling and extra living costs (except for re-training – see left).

	Expenses normally allowed	Not allowed
To get a new or extra qualification	Cost of fees and essential books you buy for a full-time training course lasting 4 weeks or more. Your employer must either require you or at least encourage you to attend the course, and must go on paying your wages while you are on it. Possibly, extra cost of living away from home and extra travelling expenses, if away for under a year.	Fees and book purchases for other courses or evening classes – even if required to take course by employer. Examination fees. Re-sit courses or examinations.
Fees and subscriptions to professional bodies	Subscriptions to professional bodies provided membership is relevant to your job. Fee for keeping your name on a professional register approved by the Inland Revenue – but only if this is a condition of your employment.	
Clothes	Cost of replacing, cleaning and repairing protective clothing (eg overalls, boots) and functional clothing (eg uniform) necessary for your job and which you are required to provide. Cost of cleaning protective clothing or functional clothing provided by your employer, if cleaning facilities are not provided.	Ordinary clothes you wear for work (eg a pin-stripe suit) which you could wear outside work – even if you'd never choose to.
Tools, instruments	Cost of maintaining and repairing factory or workshop tools and musical instruments you are required to provide. Cost of replacing instruments and tools, less any amount from sale of old, provided new ones not inherently better than old. Often, fixed amounts agreed with trade unions – see p142.	Initial cost of tools and instruments but may be able to claim capital allowances (see p198).
Books and stationery	Cost of reference books which are necessary for your job and which you are required to provide (eg actuarial tables, government regulations). If the book's useful life is more than 2 years you may have to claim capital allowances instead (see p198). Cost of stationery used strictly for your job (eg business notepaper if you are a salesman). Possibly, cost of books essential for a full-time training course.	Cost of other books. Subscriptions to journals to keep up with developments. General stationery – eg pens, notepaper, etc.

	Expenses normally allowed	Not allowed
Use of home for work	Proportion of heating and lighting costs, and, possibly, proportion of telephone, cleaning, and insurance costs. If part of home is used *exclusively* for business, you may be able to claim a proportion of rent and rates. But these expenses allowed only if it is necessary that you carry out some of your duties at or from home (ie if it is an express or implied condition of your employment). Exclusive business use of part of your home may mean some capital gains tax to pay if you sell your home – see p249.	
Interest	Interest on loans to buy equipment (eg car, typewriter) necessary for your job.	Interest on overdraft or credit card
Travelling	Expenses incurred strictly in the course of carrying out job. *Running costs of own car*: whole of cost if used wholly and necessarily in carrying out your job, proportion of cost if used privately as well. Work out what proportion your business mileage bears to your total mileage, and claim corresponding proportion of cost. If your employer requires you to use your own car for business purposes, and he pays less for doing so than it costs you, work out full cost to you – and claim the extra here. *Company car*: if you pay for running costs (eg petrol, repairs, maintenance), claim proportion of cost of business mileage – see *Running costs of own car*, above.	Travel to and from work (but if you travel to or from a job abroad, see p181). Cost of buying a car and depreciation – may be able to claim a capital allowance (see p198) but only if the car is necessary for you to carry on your job and it is necessary for you to provide one.
Wives travelling with husbands (and vice versa)	Allowed only if cost paid by (or for) employer, and if wife or husband has and uses, practical qualifications directly associated with trip, or if their presence is necessary for essential business entertaining of overseas trade customers, or if your health is so poor that it is unreasonable to travel alone. Often only a proportion of cost is allowed.	

	Expenses normally allowed	Not allowed
Entertaining	Reasonable expenses of entertaining overseas trade customers (including cost of entertaining your own colleagues if it's necessary for them to be there). Expenses of entertaining UK customers (but only if you can claim these expenses back from your employer, or pay them out of an expense allowance given specifically for entertaining). (Note for employees of non-trading organisations like schools, local authorities and trade unions: you can claim all entertaining expenses, but only if spent *wholly, exclusively and necessarily in the performance of your job* – see p142 for what this means.)	Any other entertaining expenses.
Hotel and meal expenses	If you keep a permanent home, reasonable hotel and meal expenses when travelling in the course of your job. But if, say, you're a single person living in a hostel, and give up your room when travelling, you can claim only extra cost of reasonable hotel and meal expenses over your normal board and lodging.	Meals unless you wouldn't normally have had one at that time.

Pay as you earn (PAYE)

Principles

PAYE is a way of collecting tax bit by bit over the tax year. The taxman allocates a PAYE **code** to you which indicates the amount of free-of-tax pay he estimates you're entitled to over the tax year. Any excess over this free-of-tax amount will be taxed. For how the free-of-tax amount is worked out, see the illustrated Notice of Coding on p150. Each payday, you'll be allowed 1/52nd or 1/12th (depending on whether you're paid weekly or monthly) of the free-of-tax amount.

Mechanics

The taxman tells you on the *Notice of Coding* he sends you how your PAYE code is calculated, and also tells your employer what your code is. Your employer then uses your code, and the Tax Tables supplied by the taxman, to deduct the right amount of tax from your pay.

The *Free Pay Tables* allow your employer to work out how

much of each month's or week's pay is free of tax. For example, if your code is 307H, this gives you up to £3,079 free-of-tax pay for the tax year. Because of roundings in the Tables, code 307H actually works out at £3,079.08 over the year if you're paid monthly (£3,079.44 if paid weekly). On monthly pay, you'll get one-twelfth of £3,079.08 (= £256.59) of your pay free-of-tax each month. If you're paid weekly, you'll get one-fifty-second of £3,079.44 (= £59.22) of your pay free-of-tax each week. Any excess, after deducting pension contributions to 'statutory' or 'approved' schemes, payments to charity under a Payroll Giving Scheme and – if the proposal dropped because of the June election is revived – the tax-free part of profit-related pay under an approved scheme (see p141), is taxable. The *Taxable Pay Tables* tell your employer how much tax to deduct.

As the Tax Tables work on a cumulative basis, this makes dealing with a change to your PAYE code part-way through a tax year comparatively simple – see the examples of code changes overleaf. If you get a new code with a higher number, the first time it's used, the Tables will reveal that you've been allowed too little free-of-tax pay so far, and so paid too much tax. Your employer will automatically give you a rebate.

But if you get a new code with a lower number, the Tables will show that you have paid too little tax. Deducting what you owe the first time the new code is used could mean a dramatic drop in take-home pay. So normally, the taxman takes account of the underpayment when he sets your PAYE code for the *following* year – which means you repay the tax gradually. For the remainder of the current tax year, he tells your employer to apply your new code on a *Week 1* (or *Month 1*) basis. This will mean that each pay day you get the correct proportion (1/52 or 1/12) of your new, lower, free-of-tax pay.

A drawback to being on a Week 1 (or Month 1) basis is that changes (eg in the Budget) which are to your advantage can't be backdated to the beginning of the tax year. Any rebate due to you won't be paid until you get off Week 1 basis (usually when the next tax year starts) unless you especially ask the taxman to take you off it.

Working wives

A working wife earning more than £46.50 a week or £202 a month (for the 1987–88 tax year) gets her own code – but it usually takes account only of the wife's earned income allowance and allowable expenses in her job. All other outgoings and allowances are normally included in the husband's code – unless the couple have chosen to be

separately assessed, or to have the wife's earnings taxed separately (see p74).
ICTA 1970 s204 Regulations.

More than one job?

You get a separate PAYE code for each job in which your earnings are taxed under PAYE – and, normally, a separate Notice of Coding giving your code for each job. If possible, all your outgoings and allowances are included in the code for your main job.

For more details see Chapter 17.

PAYE code changes during the tax year

Boris Frank's code goes up

Boris's code for the 1987–88 tax year was 242L. This meant that he could earn £202.42 a month free of tax.

On 4 June, Boris got married and became entitled to the married man's allowance – a reduced amount of £3,681 for the year of marriage (see p72), but higher than the single person's allowance it replaces.

In August, Boris told the taxman he'd got married. The taxman sent him a revised Notice of Coding showing his new code, 368H. This meant that he was entitled to £307.42 free-of-tax pay for every month of the tax year (including April and May before his marriage) – ie £105 a month more than before.

As Boris is a basic rate taxpayer, his tax bill falls by £28.35 a month (27% of £105).

In addition to this regular monthly saving of £28.35, Boris got an extra £141.75 in his pay when his employer first used the new code in September. This was a rebate of tax for the first five months of the tax year when he paid (£28.35 × 5 = £141.75) too much tax. So Boris's total extra pay in his September pay packet was £28.35 plus a rebate of £141.75 = £170.10.

Avril Jackson's code goes down

Avril got a loan to modernise her kitchen two years ago. The interest she pays qualifies for tax relief and the taxman, when working out Avril's code for the 1987–88 tax year, estimated she'd pay a total of £215 interest. Avril's code was set at 290L which means she got £55.95 free-of-tax pay each week.

In July 1987, when Avril had paid £71 interest, (in the 1987–88 tax year) she paid off the loan, but forgot to tell the taxman until October. She got a new code – 276L – in

December. This entitles her to £53.25 free-of-tax pay for each
week of the tax year – £2.70 a week less than under her old
code. Avril is a basic rate taxpayer, so this puts her weekly tax
bill up by 73p (ie 27% of £2.70), and she also owes the taxman
for the 36 weeks when she was being taxed under the wrong
code – a total of 73p × 36 = £26.28. The taxman instructed
Avril's employer, by putting her new code on a *Week 1 basis*,
not to deduct this straight away. Instead, the tax owed will be
collected by an adjustment to Avril's 1988–89 code.

Notice of coding

Not everyone gets a Notice of Coding each tax year. But you're
likely to get one if, for example, certain of your outgoings this
year look like being more (or less) than last year. The majority
of Notices of Coding are sent out in January or February each
year, and apply for the tax year starting on the following 6
April. To work out your PAYE code for the 1988–89 tax year,
say, the taxman initially uses the allowances for the 1987–88
tax year and estimates what he reckons your outgoings will be.
When allowances change in the Budget, your PAYE code – in
most cases – changes automatically, and you don't normally
get a new Notice of Coding. For other changes, you may get
a new Notice of Coding part way through the tax year.

Whenever you get a Notice of Coding, you should check that
it's correct. If you think there's a mistake tell the taxman at
once. The same applies if your circumstances change during
the tax year – eg if you become entitled to a new allowance or
incur a new outgoing. If your PAYE code is not correct at the
end of the tax year you'll have paid the wrong amount of tax
under PAYE – and either have to claim a rebate, or be faced with
more tax to pay in a later year. To get your code changed, write
and tell the taxman why your code is wrong – send your most
recent Notice of Coding if you've still got it (keep a copy). If
not, quote the tax reference number which is on all forms and
letters the taxman sends you.
ICTA 1970 s204 Regulations 6(2), 7(b) (d), 8.

Not sent back your tax return?

If you've received a Tax Return but haven't returned it, you may
get a Notice of Coding showing a special deduction which reduces
your PAYE code – possibly to zero – (and as a result, the amount
of free-of-tax pay you can have). This is because the taxman thinks
you have income you haven't declared and has decided to estimate
the amount of tax you might owe. To get this sorted out – and,
if necessary, your code changed, you'll have to send back your
completed Tax Return.

Notice of coding

A form P3 (PAYE coding guide) is enclosed or was sent to you with a previous notice of coding

How your PAYE code is calculated

Expenses	
Death and Superannuation Benefits	
Interest unless payable net of tax	*380*
Personal allowance	*3,795*
Age allowance (estimated total income £..........)	
Wife's earned income allowance	
Additional personal allowance	
Dependent relative allowance	
Widow's bereavement allowance...	
INTEREST –	
HIGHER RATE	*840*
Total allowances	*5,015*

Less allowances given against other income

Untaxed interest...	*78*	
Occupational pensions		
State pension/benefits		
BENEFITS (CAR)	*1,100*	*1,178*
Net allowances		*3,837*

Less adjustments for

Tax unpaid for earlier years		
198 *6-8* 7 £ *75*	*277*	
equivalent to a deduction of		
198 -8 (estimated £.................)		
equivalent to a deduction of		*277*
Allowances given against pay etc.		*3,560*

Your code is shown overleaf   Printed for HMSO by A. Pettitt Ltd 9/86 8976678

Notice of coding

Year to 5 April 198 *8*   **Code** *See form P3* | *356* | *H* |

Here we show you what a Notice of Coding might look like, and then explain what might be entered under each heading on the form. More and more Notices of Coding are now computer-printed. They look different from the hand-written version shown above, because the computer only prints out the headings which are relevant to you, but they contain exactly the same information.

Outgoings (Expenses, Death and Superannuation Benefits, Interest)

The taxman will enter his estimate of your outgoings here. For example, if you're 'higher-paid' (see p163), he'll enter any allowable expenses in your job which aren't covered by a *dispensation* your employer has (see p143).

Mortgage interest won't feature in your Notice of Coding if it comes under the MIRAS system and the taxman expects that you'll pay tax at the basic rate only – see p241 for more details. But if you've got a mortgage or home improvement loan which doesn't come under MIRAS, the taxman enters his estimate of the interest you'll pay in the 1987–88 tax year.

If you make outgoings net of basic rate tax (eg covenant payments to charities, MIRAS interest) and you're entitled to tax relief at higher rates too, the taxman will add on an amount to your allowances to give you this – see *Adjustments* below.

Allowances

Details of the allowances you've claimed will be included here.

Note that if you've claimed age allowance, you may get a reduced amount if your 'total income' is above the limit (£9,800 for the 1987–88 tax year) for the full amount. The reduced amount won't be below the amount of the ordinary personal allowance (see p104 for more details).

Allowances other than those mentioned specifically on the Notice of Coding (eg blind person's allowance, housekeeper allowance) will be entered in the gap below *Widow's bereavement allowance*.

Allowances given against other income

If taxable income is paid to you without tax being deducted, the taxman may decide to collect the tax on it by deducting his estimate of the amount from your *Total Allowances* shown above. Income which may be treated in this way includes state retirement pension, unemployment benefit, taxable interest from a National Savings account, regular freelance earnings, and taxable fringe benefits.

Adjustments

If, for example, you pay tax at higher rates and have investment income which has been taxed at the basic rate only, the taxman might decide to collect the extra tax on this income by making a *taxed investment income* deduction. But you can ask him for a separate bill if you don't want to pay tax through PAYE.

If a husband and wife pay tax at higher rates on their joint earnings, the taxman might make an *excessive basic rate* deduction here. This deduction is made because the Tax Tables would charge tax at the basic rate (for the 1987–88 tax year) on the first £17,900 of both husband's and wife's taxable income – whereas they should, in fact, pay higher rate tax on anything over £17,900 of their *joint* taxable income (unless they've chosen to have the wife's earnings taxed separately – see p74). This excessive basic rate deduction is normally subtracted from the code of whichever partner has the higher earnings. But you can tell the taxman which code you want him to adjust.

If you deduct tax at the basic rate from covenant or maintenance payments there might also be a deduction here if your tax bill for the year is likely to be less than the tax you've deducted. On the other hand, with maintenance payments, and with covenant payments to charities, there might be an addition if you are a higher rate taxpayer, and entitled to extra tax relief.

Allowances given against pay etc

When the taxman has worked out the total amount of pay you can have free of tax in the tax year, he enters it in this box.

The number in your code

This is arrived at by knocking the last figure off your *Allowances given against pay etc.* So if these allowances come to £3,560, as in our example, the code number is 356 and this entitles you to tax-free pay of £3,569 (not £3,560). Note that if your allowances come to between £1 and £19, your code number is 1, and you get £19 of tax-free pay. (But if instead of collecting the tax you owe under PAYE, the taxman sent you a bill, he'd ask for the exact amount you owe, so you wouldn't benefit from this rounding up.)

Tax unpaid for earlier years

The taxman enters here any tax you owe from previous years which he has decided to collect from your pay. Notices of Coding for the 1987–88 tax year will have been sent to you normally before the end of the 1986–87 tax year. So the taxman had to estimate any underpaid tax for the 1986–87 tax year. If you pay tax at the basic rate, a deduction of a bit less than four times the tax you owe will bring in the tax required; if you pay tax at higher rates a smaller deduction will do the trick.

Example:
Say you're a basic rate taxpayer owing £75. A deduction here of £277 will mean an extra £277 is taxed at 27%. £277 × 27% comes to £74.79 – almost exactly the tax owed (the taxman will forget about the 21p you still owe).

But if you were a 45% taxpayer owing the same amount, a deduction of £166 would bring in very nearly the same amount. An extra £166 would be taxed at 45%. £166 × 45% comes to £74.70.

The letter in your code – which one for you?

L if you are getting the (lower) single person's allowance of £2,425, or the wife's earned income allowance

H if you are getting the (higher) married man's allowance of £3,795 or the additional personal allowance

P if you are getting the full age allowance of a single person aged up to 79, ie £2,960

V is you are getting the full age allowance for a married man aged up to 79, ie £4,675

T under certain circumstances – eg if you get a reduced amount of age allowance, or the higher age allowance for people aged 80-plus, or you don't want your employer to know what personal allowances you're getting. If you want letter T, tell the taxman.

(The amounts above apply for the 1987–88 tax year).

The letters L, H, P and V allow budget changes in the main personal allowances to be automatically reflected in a new PAYE code. Your employer will be told what the new code is and when to make the change. If your code doesn't end with one of these letters, or if any of the other allowances you may be getting are increased, a new code may take longer to come through.

If you are 80 or over (or will be during the 1987–88 tax year), you are entitled to the new higher age allowance for the over-80s. This is up to £3,070 (if single) or up to £4,845 (if married). Tax offices have been reviewing their records to identify as far as possible who does qualify. But if you think you do qualify and have not heard from the taxman, you should write to your tax office, giving your date of birth.

You should also write to your tax office if you are entitled to the increased blind person's allowance of £540 for 1987–88 if you haven't heard from the taxman about this.

Code BR and D codes

You may get one of the following codes if you've got a second job. With these codes, all your earnings from the second job will be taxed at the rate shown. (Any free-of-tax pay will be included in the PAYE code for your main job.)

code	BR	DO	DI	D2	D3	D4
rate of tax	27%	40%	45%	50%	55%	60%

For more details about second jobs, see Chapter 17.

Code F

You get this if the taxable state benefits you get come to more than your tax-free allowances and the taxman has to deduct the tax due on them by taxing your pay at a higher-than-normal rate.

Code NT

This means that no tax is to be deducted.

Code OT

This means that all your pay is to be taxed (ie no free-of-tax amount).

PAYE Enquiry Offices

If you pay tax under PAYE, it's possible that your tax office is a long distance away. This may make resolving any tax problems you have more difficult. In this situation, check to see if there's a local PAYE enquiry office – look in the telephone directory under *Inland Revenue*, or see *IR52*. Staff at an enquiry office can get details of your tax affairs sent to them by your tax office so that they can discuss your problems with you, give you advice, and chase up matters (eg a long overdue tax rebate) for you.

Starting work

Your first job

If you've started work for the first time after full-time education (and haven't claimed unemployment benefit) you won't be taxed on your earnings unless these are at least £46.50 a week (£202 a month) for the 1987–88 tax year. Once your earnings are more than this amount, your employer will ask you to complete **form P46**. This allows him to operate PAYE on your pay under an emergency code – 242L for the 1987–88 tax year – which assumes that the only allowance you've been entitled to since the beginning of the tax year is the single person's allowance. Code 242L entitles you to £202.42 of tax-free pay each month (£46.72 each week) – ie roughly 1/12 (or 1/52) of £2,429.

Tax won't be deducted until the free-of-tax pay since the beginning of the tax year has been used up. So, for example, if your first monthly payday is in the fourth month of the tax year, you are entitled to four months' worth of free-of-tax pay on code 242L – ie £202.42 × 4 = £809.68. So on your first payday tax will be deducted only on any excess over £809.68. If your total pay for the month is less than this amount, the balance of the free-of-tax pay owing to you will be given to you on subsequent paydays until it runs out. Note that if you don't complete form P46, the emergency code will be operated on a *Week 1* (or *Month 1*) basis. See *Returning to work* for what this means.

As well as form P46, your employer also gives you a **Coding Claim (form P15)** to complete in case you're entitled to other outgoings or allowances. When you return it to the taxman, he will work out what your proper code should be, send you a Notice of Coding and notify your employer. This new code may allow you a higher amount of free-of-tax pay than the emergency one. If so, any tax over-deducted will be refunded to you.

Working in the vacation

A student who gets a vacation job won't be taxed on weekly (or monthly) earnings even if these are more than £46.50 a week (£202 a month), if his or her earnings and other taxable income for the whole year won't exceed the single person's allowance of £2,425. Both the student and the employer have to complete **form P38(S)** to get this exemption.

Returning to work

If you haven't worked for some years (for example because you've stayed at home to look after the children), the procedure is broadly the same as that described in *Your first job* above.

However, if your earnings, for the 1987–88 tax year, are more than £46.50 a week (£202 a month) your employer will operate the emergency code (242L for the 1987–88 tax year) on a *Week 1 (or Month 1) basis*. This means that no account will be taken of any free-of-tax pay due from the beginning of the tax year to the time you started working, and tax will be deducted straight away. When the taxman has received your Coding Claim (form P15), and allocated your proper code to you, any tax you've overpaid will be refunded to you.

Changing jobs

When you change jobs, your employer should give you a **P45 form**. This shows your PAYE code and details of the tax deducted from your total pay for the year to date. Give this to your new employer on your first day so that he can take up where your old employer left off and deduct the correct amount of tax from your pay.

If you don't do this, your employer will follow the procedure described above in *Returning to work* – and you may pay too much tax for a while.

ICTA 1970 s204 Regulations 18 (changing jobs); 20(3)(a) (starting a job).

National Insurance contributions

If, in the 1987–88 tax year, you earn £39 or more a week (£169 or more a month), you'll have to pay Class 1 National Insurance contributions. These will be deducted from the whole of your pay on up to a maximum limit of £295 weekly earnings (or £1,279 monthly).

Social Security Act 1975 s1–4.

Temporary work through an agency

If you work through an agency – eg as a temp – you will be treated as an employee (normally of the agency) and taxed under PAYE. But there are exceptions to this rule: you can generally work through an agency and be treated as *self-employed* if you're an actor, entertainer, model, sub-contractor in the building industry, or if all your work is done at or from your own home.

F A (No 2) 1975 s38.

Other temporary or casual jobs

Tax won't be deducted unless your earnings are more than £46.50 a week (£202 a month). If you are paid more than this amount, the basis on which you are taxed depends on whether or not you can give your employer a **P45 form**. With a P45, the procedure is as described under *Changing jobs* above. Without a P45, the emergency code (242L for the 1987–88 tax year) will be used on a Week 1 (or Month 1) basis. Special rules apply to the building industry – see p137.

Interrupting work

Off sick

Statutory sick pay paid by your employer on behalf of the state, and sick pay you get from your employer's own sick pay scheme, is taxable under PAYE. But if the amount you get is lower than the amount of free-of-tax pay you are entitled to, your employer will refund some of the tax you've already paid, in each pay packet.

You can get statutory sick pay only for a limited period. After that you may get state invalidity benefit. This isn't taxable, though tax will still be deducted from sick pay you get from your employer's scheme.

Some employers have *sick pay insurance schemes* which they've arranged with an insurance company or trust fund. Tax will normally be deducted from payments you receive from these schemes. But if you contribute towards the insurance premiums, you'll only be taxed on the part of the payment attributable to your employer's contributions.

If you've taken out your own sick pay insurance policy, income from it won't be taxed at all until it has been paid throughout a complete tax year. Then it's taxed as investment income.

FA 1981 s30.

Maternity

Statutory Maternity Pay (SMP) was introduced on 6 April 1987 for babies due on or after 21 June 1987 and replaces maternity pay previously paid by employers. Like maternity pay, it is taxable under PAYE. But a woman whose baby was due before 21 June 1987 should receive the maternity pay under the old rules. If either SMP or maternity pay is paid when (or before) you stop working, the tax deducted will depend on your PAYE code. If it's paid *after* you've stopped working, tax is deducted at the 27 per cent basic rate. This could mean too much tax is deducted. If so, claim a rebate from the taxman.

State maternity benefits are not taxable.

ICTA 1970 s219A.

Laid-off, on short-time, on strike

In any of these situations, too much tax may have been deducted from your pay since the beginning of the tax year. If you've been laid-off or put on short-time, any tax refunds due will be given on your normal paydays by your employer. But

strikers (or those involved in strikes) will have to wait until they return to work for their tax refunds.
ICTA 1970 s204 Regulations 24, 53, 60, 63.

Unemployed?
For details of how unemployment benefit and supplementary benefit are taxed, see Chapter 10.

Stopping work
Redundancy

If you're made redundant, earnings your employer owes you – eg normal wages, pay in lieu of holiday, pay for working your notice period, commission – paid when you leave your job, are taxed in the normal way under PAYE. But the following payments are tax-free:
● any lump sum for any injury or disability which meant you couldn't carry on your job
● usually, compensation for loss of a job done entirely or substantially outside the UK
● gratuities from the armed forces (but if for early retirement, balance over £25,000 may be taxable)
● certain lump sum benefits from employers' pension schemes
● money your employer pays into a retirement benefit scheme or uses to buy you an annuity (provided certain conditions are met)
● Job Release allowances under schemes which are open only to women aged 59 and men aged 64. (Most other allowances are taxable.)
   Other payments are also tax-free if, added together, they total less than £25,000. These are:
● redundancy payments made under the Government's redundancy payments scheme
● payments under a redundancy scheme 'approved' by the Inland Revenue
● pay in lieu of notice – provided your conditions of service don't say you are entitled to it
● other payments made to you, so long as they are not payments for work done, not part of your conditions of service, and – technically at least – unexpected. This would normally cover redundancy payments over and above the government minimum.
   Anything more than £25,000 is added to the rest of your income; only half the normal amount of tax is charged on the first £25,000 of this excess, and only three-quarters the normal

amount is charged on the next £25,000. Anything more is liable to tax in the normal way as earned income.

Your employer has to deduct tax under PAYE on the excess over £25,000 before paying it to you. Unless a special, reduced tax payment is negotiated with your tax office, too much tax will be deducted because the Tax Tables don't allow for these special rules and you'll have to claim a rebate. If, on leaving a job, you received a lump sum of more than £50,000 between 6 April 1982 and 3 June 1986, you may have paid too much tax. This is because of a change in the interpretation in the law. So you should claim a rebate within six years of the end of the tax year in which you received the lump sum.

ICTA 1970 s188; FA 1977 s30; FA 1970, s19, s26, Sch 5 para 2 (tax-free payments); ICTA 1970 s188, Sch 8; FA 1982, s43 (tax-free payments under £25,000).

Employer going bust

Pay in lieu of notice is normally tax-free. But if you lose your job because your employer goes bust, and get pay in lieu of notice from the liquidator (or trustee in bankruptcy), 27% will be deducted from the whole amount. You can't claim a full rebate, but if this notional tax is more than the tax that would have been deducted if you'd received it as normal pay, you can get a refund of the difference. You get the refund from your local Redundancy Payments Office – not through the taxman.

Dismissal

Earnings your employer owes you will be taxed under PAYE. Pay in lieu of notice together with any other payments (provided they are not payments for work done, not part of your conditions of service and, technically, unexpected) totalling less than £25,000 are tax-free. See above for how any excess over £25,000 is taxed.

If you are awarded compensation for unfair dismissal by an Industrial Tribunal, the amount you get for loss of wages will be paid after deduction of 27% tax. As with pay in lieu of notice paid by a liquidator (see above), the only tax rebate you can get is the difference between the amount actually deducted and any (smaller) amount that would have been deducted if you'd received the money as normal pay.

Refunded pension contributions

If you leave a job before retirement age and get a refund of pension contributions from your employer's scheme, the trustees of the pension fund deduct any tax due before paying the refunds back to you.

> **Retirement**
> For details of how a pension paid to you by a former employer (and other pensions) are taxed, see Chapter 9.

Tax-saving tips

- **count as 'higher-paid'?** Check that what you enter in your tax return for expenses and fringe benefits tallies with what your employer tells the taxman on form P11D
- **checking your Notice of Coding?** Whenever you get a Notice of Coding, check that it's correct. If you think there's a mistake tell the taxman at once. Until he alters your code, you'll be paying the wrong amount of tax. See p149 for how to get your code changed
- **need a new PAYE code?** If your circumstances change during the tax year – eg if you become entitled to a new allowance or incur a new outgoing – tell the taxman straight away and ask him to change your code – but see Chapter 20 if the outgoing is a mortgage
- **expenses in your job?** Make sure you get tax relief on everything that counts as an allowable expense
- **left a job?** If you received a lump sum of more than £50,000 between 6 April 1982 and 3 June 1986, on leaving a job, you may have paid too much tax (see p159). Check with your taxman.

13 FRINGE BENEFITS

If your employer lets you use a company car, provides you with a cheap meal in a canteen or pays for private medical bills insurance, fringe benefits are a part of your life. Giving you fringe benefits like these is one of the ways your employer can reward you for the work you do, as well as paying you a wage or salary – and can tie you more closely to the firm you work for. Many fringe benefits are things you might choose to buy for yourself if they weren't provided by your employer.

Are fringe benefits worthwhile?

Yes – because the tax system treats most fringe benefits favourably compared with a rise in salary. Getting a fringe benefit can often be worth more to you than a salary rise costing your employer the same to provide. Some fringe benefits are much more worthwhile for you than others. A company car, say, can be worth £3,000 or more a year to you, but you would either pay no tax on it or very little.

But there are disadvantages to getting fringe benefits:
● no choice – you may find that your fringe benefits aren't the things you'd choose to spend your money on
● lower pension, life insurance and redundancy money – all these are often linked to your pay in £££, *excluding* the value of the fringe benefits you get.

What fringe benefits are worth

to basic rate taxpayer who counts as higher-paid

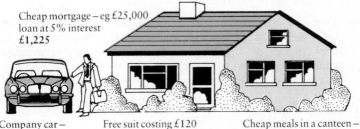

Cheap mortgage – eg £25,000
loan at 5% interest
£1,225

Company car –
eg 1.6 litre car
£3,250

Free suit costing £120
£120

Medical bills insurance
£400

Cheap meals in a canteen –
eg you pay 75p a meal
£400

A fringe benefit – or an expense?

There are some payments which you might get from your employer which are on the borderline between a fringe benefit and an allowable expense. These include mileage allowance, removal expenses and overnight allowances. These are normally regarded as expenses because your employer is reimbursing you for money you have to spend in the course of your job. They are all tax-free as long as they count as *allowable expenses* – see p142.

Your employer may have what's called a *dispensation* from the taxman for certain expenses and fringe benefits he pays you – such as a mileage or subsistence allowance. You don't have to pay tax on these expenses and benefits. If you get expenses and benefits for which your employer hasn't got a dispensation, he will give details to your Tax Inspector on **form P11D** if you count as higher-paid (see opposite).
ICTA 1970 s189, s192; ESC A5; FA 1976 s70(1).

How are fringe benefits taxed?

Fringe benefits are taxed in one of three ways:
● some are tax-free
● some are taxed only if you count as higher-paid (according to the tax rules)
● the rest are taxed whatever you earn.
See p164 for how individual benefits are taxed.

Swopping pay – a warning

No matter how much (or little) you earn, if you can swop some of your pay for a fringe benefit (or vice versa) the taxman may tax you on the amount of pay you give up if this is more than the taxable value of the fringe benefit under the normal tax rules.
Heaton v Bell 46 TC 211; Tennant v Smith 3 TC 158.

Tax-free fringe benefits

There's a large number of fringe benefits which you can get without having to pay any tax, provided certain conditions are kept. Some of the more common ones include pension contributions from your employer, free life insurance and sick pay insurance, cheap or free drinks and meals.

Taxable fringe benefits

With these benefits, you pay tax on what the taxman calls the *taxable value* of the benefit. This is also the amount you have to enter in your Tax Return. The way the taxable value is worked out will normally depend on whether or not you count as *higher-paid*.

If you count as higher-paid, you're normally taxed on the amount your fringe benefits cost your employer to provide, *less* anything you pay towards the cost. See p168 for exceptions.

If you don't count as higher-paid, you're normally taxed on the *second-hand value* of your fringe benefits – usually less than they cost your employer. And the taxable value of fringe benefits which don't have a second-hand value (eg free hairdressing at work) is nil.

Who counts as higher-paid?

For the 1987–88 tax year, you will count as higher-paid if you're paid at a rate of £8,500 or more a year. *At a rate of* means you'd be caught if, say, you were paid £4,250 for six months' work.

If you are paid at a lower rate than £8,500 a year, you will still count as higher-paid if the total of the following comes to more than £8,500:

● your earnings from your job

● your fringe benefits *valued as though you were higher-paid*

● any expenses reimbursed to you by your employer for which he hasn't got a dispensation (see opposite) even if these count as allowable expenses. *(FA 1976 s69.)*

Directors

A director normally counts as higher-paid whatever he earns. But a director earning at a rate of less than £8,500 a year doesn't count as higher-paid if:

● he (together with his close family and certain other associates) owns or controls 5 per cent or less of the shares in the company, *and*

● he is a full-time working director of the company, *or* works for a charity or non-profit-making company, *and*

● he is not a director of an associated company.

If he has more than one job with the same (or an associated) company and his *total* earnings and expenses from these put him into the higher-paid category, *all* these jobs are higher-paid.

FA 1976 s69(3), (5), s72(10).

Example

Joseph Jones is paid a salary of £8,300. His employer lets him use a new 1.3 litre car. To find out if he counts as higher-paid, Joseph needs to add the taxable value of the car assuming he is higher-paid to his salary. This is £525 for the 1987–88 tax year, which takes him over the limit of £8,500. So Joseph does count as higher-paid.

How each fringe benefit is taxed

benefit	
board and lodging – ie job-related accommodation (see also *living accommodation*) *FA 1976 s63A; FA 1977 s33(4), (7).*	
company car – including use of the car for private purposes; employer pays costs – eg repairs, insurance *FA 1976 s60, s63–65, Sch7; FA 1982 s46.*	
clothes specially needed for work – eg overalls *Ward v Dunn 52 TC 517.*	
crèche or day-nursery provided by employer at work *IR Press Release 24 April 1985*	
use of credit cards, charge cards *FA 1982 s44, s45; FA(2) 1975 s36, s36A.*	
discounts on goods and services, if employers sell their own products cheap to employees	
employees' outings; Christmas party	
fees and subscriptions to professional societies or associations *ICTA 1970 s192.*	
food and drink – includes free or cheap meals, tea, coffee, etc *FA 1976 s62(7).*	
gifts – if they are genuinely personal, such as wedding or retirement gifts (but not a gift of money on retirement) *Herbert v McQuade 4TC 489.*	
gifts of something previously lent – eg furniture, TV *FA 1976 s63(3A).*	
hairdressing at work *FA 1976 s63(1), (2).*	
life insurance – cost of providing this under a scheme approved by the Inland Revenue *FA 1976 s62(6).*	
living accommodation – eg rent-free or low-rent home *FA 1976 s63A; FA 1977 s33, s33A; FA 1983 s21.*	

how it is taxed if you count as higher-paid [1]	how it is taxed if you don't count as higher-paid
accommodation provided for you, tax-free; for other benefits, pay tax on what employer pays out *less* anything you pay towards his cost up to a limit (see p172)	accommodation provided for you, tax-free; other benefits tax-free, unless you are paid cash, in which case you are taxed on the amount paid (but see p174)
pay tax on the taxable value of car – see p169	tax-free
tax-free	tax-free
pay tax on what employer pays out *less* anything you pay towards the cost [2]	tax-free
taxed on what employer pays out *less* anything you pay towards his cost and *less* allowable expenses	taxed on what employer pays out *less* anything you pay towards his cost and *less* allowable expenses
tax-free, as long as employer doesn't end up out of pocket	tax-free, as long as employer doesn't end up out of pocket
normally tax-free	normally tax-free
tax-free if society or association recognised by Inland Revenue; if not, taxed on cost to employer	tax-free
tax-free, if provided for all employees – even if separate facilities are provided on the employer's premises for different groups of employees	tax-free, if provided for all employees – even if separate facilities are provided on the employer's premises for different groups of employees
tax-free	tax-free
pay tax on taxable value – see p174	pay tax on second-hand value
pay tax on cost to your employer	tax-free
tax-free	tax-free
sometimes tax-free – see p173	sometimes tax-free – see p173

[1] Or count as a director – see p163.
[2] applies from 6 April 1985. Any tax collected relating to periods before this date will be refunded.

benefit	
loans of money *FA 1976 s66 Sch8; FA(2) 1983 s4; SI 1982/1273.*	
loans of things – eg furniture *FA 1976 s63.*	
long-service awards – eg gifts of things or shares (but not a gift of money) *ESC A22; Weston v Hearn 25 TC 425.*	
luncheon vouchers *(ESC A2)*	
medical bills insurance *FA 1976 s62(8); FA 1981 s72.*	
mortgage – low-interest or interest-free *FA 1976 s66 Sch8.*	
pension contributions your employer pays into an 'approved' or 'statutory' pension scheme for you *FA 1971 s21(3), s22.*	
petrol – if you get any for private use in company car *FA 1976 s64A(6); FA 1982 s46.*	
removal expenses (if reasonable) – including solicitor's, surveyor's, estate agent's fees, stamp duty, removal costs, an allowance for carpets and curtains, temporary subsistence allowance, rent while you're looking for a new home *(ESC A5).*	
scholarship and apprenticeship schemes awarded to you by your employer *SP 4/86*	
scholarships awarded by your employer to your children *FA 1976 s61; FA 1983 s20; FA 1984 s31.*	

[1] Or count as a director – see p163.
[2] Amount is tax-free if scholarship awarded before 15 March 1983 as long as first payment was made before 6 April 1984 *and* your child is still

how it is taxed if you count as higher-paid [1]	how it is taxed if you don't count as higher-paid
tax-free, if loan qualifies for tax relief; pay tax on taxable value of other loans – see p171	tax-free
pay tax on taxable value – see p174	tax-free
tax-free, if given for service of 20 years or more with the same employer. From 13 March 1984, the cost must not be more than £20 for each year of service and you must not have had such an award within the past 10 years	tax-free, if given for service of 20 years or more with the same employer. From 13 March 1984, the cost must not be more than £20 for each year of service and you must not have had such an award within the past 10 years
15p each working day is tax-free	15p each working day is tax-free
pay tax on cost to your employer	tax-free
tax-free, if interest qualifies, or would qualify, for tax relief	tax-free, if interest qualifies, or would qualify, for tax relief
tax-free	tax-free
pay tax on taxable value – see p169	pay tax on cost of petrol unless directly provided by employer – see p169
normally tax-free, if have to move to take a new job or are transferred by your employer	normally tax-free, if have to move to take a new job or are transferred by your employer
tax-free if you are enrolled for at least one academic year and attend full-time for an average of at least 20 weeks a year. Rate of payment (including lodging, subsistence and travelling allowances but excluding tuition fees) must not be above £5,000 or the amount of a grant from a public body such as a research council, if higher – otherwise taxable in full. Payments for time at work taxable in normal way.	tax-free if you are enrolled for at least one academic year and attend full-time for an average of at least 20 weeks a year. Rate of payment (including lodging, subsistence and travelling allowances but excluding tuition fees) must not be above £5,000 or the amount of a grant from a public body such as a research council, if higher – otherwise taxable in full. Payments for time at work taxable in normal way.
normally pay tax on amount of scholarship [2]	tax-free

at the same full-time school or college. Special rules apply if scholarship comes from a trust fund.

benefit
season ticket loans   *FA 1976 s66 Sch8.*
shares bought cheap (or free) in your employer's company through an approved employee share scheme *FA 1978 s53–61; FA 1980 s47, Sch10. FA 1982 s42; FA 1984 s38–39, Sch 10.*
sick pay insurance – cost of insurance paid for you by employer *FA 1981 s30(3).*
social and sports facilities
staff suggestion schemes – awards from schemes
training – eg attending a course or studying on normal pay; tuition fees *Humbles v Brooks 40 TC 500; ESC announced 8 August 1986; FA 1987 s35.*
vouchers – such as travel voucher (eg British Rail season ticket) or any other voucher which can be exchanged for goods or services (eg a letter to a tailor telling him to give you a new suit) or for cash (eg a cheque) *FA(No 2) 1975 s36, s36A, s37; FA 1982 s44.*

[1] Or count as a director – see p163.

Some fringe benefits in more detail

Some fringe benefits have special tax rules – we give details for:
- use of cars and petrol
- cheap loans
- living accommodation
- loans of things and their subsequent gifts
- employee share schemes.

how it is taxed if you count as higher-paid [1]	how it is taxed if you don't count as higher-paid
most are tax-free as the taxable value of the loan is usually nil – see p171	tax-free
tax-free – but see p175 and p176 for capital gains tax rules	tax-free – but see p175 and p176 for capital gains tax rules
cost of insurance met by employer is tax-free if the scheme meets the taxman's conditions. Income from scheme normally taxed as part of your earnings. If you pay some of the premiums, only the income provided by your employer's contributions is tax-free.	cost of insurance met by employer is tax-free if the scheme meets the taxman's conditions. Income from scheme normally taxed as part of your earnings. If you pay some of the premiums, only the income provided by your employer's contributions is tax-free.
normally tax-free	tax-free
tax free up to an overall maximum of £5,000	tax-free up to an overall maximum of £5,000
pay is taxed in the normal way. Books and tuition fees paid for by your employer for some external training courses in the UK are tax-free. Provided you're not away for more than 12 months, extra travel expenses and living costs met by your employer while on the course may not be taxable either. Similar expenses if you are leaving or have left your job for retraining in new work skills are also tax-free	pay is taxed in the normal way. Books and tuition fees paid for by your employer for some external training courses in the UK are tax-free. Provided you're not away for more than 12 months, extra travel expenses and living costs met by your employer while on the course may not be taxable either. Similar expenses if you are leaving or have left your job for retraining in new work skills are also tax-free
pay tax on amount your employer pays out *less* anything you pay towards the cost	pay tax on amount your employer pays out *less* anything you pay towards the cost [2]

[2] If you work for a transport organisation, any transport voucher under a scheme in operation on 25 March 1982 is tax-free.

Cars and petrol

The taxable values of company cars are set each year. The Table on p171 gives these values if you count as higher-paid in the tax years 1987–88 (the figures in black) and 1988–89 (in red). If you don't count as higher-paid, the taxable value is nil. The right-hand column shows the taxable value of petrol for private use: the figures apply if you get *any* petrol for private use from your employer which you don't pay for in full – no matter how much or how little. If you're not higher-paid, you pay tax on the cost of the petrol unless it is provided directly by your employer. Travelling to and from work will normally count as *private use* of a car.

If you have a company car for only part of the tax year, the taxable values (both for the car and, if this applies, for petrol) are reduced proportionately. If you have to pay your employer a sum of money for private use of the car, you can subtract this sum from the value in the Table. For electric cars and cars with rotary engines, ask your Tax Inspector for details of the taxable values.

If you cover at least 18,000 miles on business in the tax year, the benefit (both for the car and for petrol) is half the figure in the Table. If you have the car for only part of the tax year, the 18,000 figure is reduced proportionately. If you drive no more than 2,500 miles on business during the tax year, the value is 1.5 times that in the Table. If you have a second company car, the taxable value for the car you use least for business travel is 1.5 times the figure in the Table. The charge for the other car, and for both cars' petrol, is the normal charge for cars of their engine size. If the second car is provided for another member of your family, these rules still apply.

Motoring costs for a company car paid by your employer

If your employer pays certain motoring costs – such as repairs, business petrol, insurance – direct (eg he settles a company account), they don't affect your tax position. But if *you* pay them, claim what you pay as *allowable expenses* in your Tax Return. If part of your use of the car is business use, part private, claim the proportion attributable to your business mileage. And if your employer reimburses you in full or in part (eg by a mileage allowance), also enter what he pays you under *expense allowances*.

FA 1976 s64, s64A, s65, Sch7.

Pool cars

A pool car doesn't count as a fringe benefit and there is no tax to pay by the people who use it. To qualify as a pool car, the car must be made available to (and used by) more than one employee, and it mustn't normally be kept overnight near an employee's home. Any private use of the car must be merely incidental to business use – eg occasional travel between home and office as part of genuine business trips.

FA 1976 s65.

Cars whose value when new was up to £19,250 [1]

size of engine	age of car at the end of the tax year				charge for petrol	
	under 4 years		4 years or more			
1400 cc or less	£525	£580	£350	£380	£480	£480
1401 to 2000 cc	£700	£770	£470	£520	£600	£600
more than 2000 cc	£1,100	£1,210	£725	£800	£900	£900

Cars whose value when new was £19,251 to £29,000 [1]

all sizes of engine	£1,450	£1,595	£970	£1,070	[2]	[2]

Cars whose value when new was more than £29,000 [1]

all sizes of engine	£2,300	£2,530	£1,530	£1,685	[2]	[2]

[1] 1987–88 figures in black, 1988–89 figures in red.

[2] Charge for petrol is the normal charge for a car of that engine size – see above.

Cheap loans

If your employer lets you have a loan on which you pay little or no interest, how it is taxed depends on whether you count as higher-paid or not and whether the loan qualifies for tax relief. The rules are:

● if you don't count as higher-paid, the low-interest or interest-free loan is tax-free

● if you do count as higher-paid, but the loan or part of it qualifies for tax relief, then the part which *does* qualify is a tax-free fringe benefit. So, for example, if you get a loan to buy or improve your only or main home, the first £30,000 of it is a tax-free fringe benefit because the interest qualifies for tax relief. The amount of the loan over £30,000 is a taxable benefit because it doesn't qualify for tax relief. If the loan is interest-free, this applies even if a second loan (eg from a bank or building society) is taken out at the same time as, or later than, the employer's loan. The second loan will take up the first slice of the £30,000 limit and any of the employer's loan over the limit counts as a taxable benefit. The £30,000 limit applies to the total of loans for you *and* your spouse. The excess over £30,000 is taxed in the same way as a loan not qualifying for tax relief – see below

• if you count as higher-paid, a cheap loan which doesn't qualify for tax relief counts as a taxable benefit and you will have to pay tax on the value your Tax Inspector puts on it. This value is the difference between the amount of interest you actually pay your employer and the amount you would pay if you were charged the *official rate of interest* – 10.5 per cent a year, at the time we went to press.

You don't have to pay tax if the value the taxman puts on all your cheap loans adds up to £200 or less. This means you could have an interest-free loan of £1,904 for the 1987–88 tax year (assuming the official rate stays at 10.5 per cent) completely free of tax. But if the value put on your loans comes to £201 or more, you are taxed on the whole value, not just the amount over £200.

Note that if your employer lets you off paying back a loan, the amount you're let off paying counts as part of your income, and is taxed in the normal way.

FA 1976 s66; F(No2)A 1983 s4.

Example

George Hamlyn borrowed £3,000 from his employer to buy some furniture. He will repay the loan in a lump sum after three years and will pay interest at a rate of 3.5% – ie interest of £105 a year. George counts as higher-paid and the interest on the loan doesn't qualify for tax relief. So he will pay tax for the 1987–88 tax year on the difference between the interest he pays his employer (ie £105) and the interest he would pay at the official rate – ie 10.5% of £3,000 = £315. So he'll pay tax on £315 − £105 = £210. Note that George will pay tax on this whole amount, even though he's only just over the £200 tax-free limit.

Living accommodation

A rent-free or low-rent home can be a tax-free fringe benefit if one of the following applies:

• it is necessary to live in the home to do your job properly (eg you are a caretaker)

• living in the home enables you to do your job better, *and* it is customary for people doing your sort of job to live in such a home (eg you are a policeman and live in a flat over the police station)

• there is a special threat to your security, and you live in the home as part of special security arrangements.

Where living accommodation is provided for a company director who comes into either of the first two categories, the home will not qualify as a tax-free benefit if the director owns more than five per cent of the company's ordinary share capital. If he owns five per cent or less, the home still won't qualify unless he is a full-time working director OR the company is non-profit making or a charitable body.

Even if the home does count as a tax-free benefit, if you count as higher-paid you will have to pay some tax on what your employer pays for heating, lighting, cleaning, decorating or furnishing (but the value put on these by your Tax Inspector cannot be more than 10% of your earnings without including these benefits).

If a rent-free or low-rent home doesn't count as a tax-free fringe benefit, the taxman values the benefit at the *gross value* of the home (the figure the rateable value is based on, but with an adjustment in Scotland) *less* any rent (and, in most cases, rates) you pay, *plus* anything your employer pays towards running the home (eg heating, lighting). This applies whether or not you count as higher-paid.

If the home costs your employer more than £75,000 to buy, there will be an extra tax bill. The extra tax bill is worked out by finding how much the accommodation cost to buy and set up and deducting £75,000. You then multiply this figure by the *official rate of interest* on cheap loans – currently 10.5 per cent. But you can deduct any rent paid in excess of the *gross value*.

Note that if you are a director who counts as higher-paid, a rent-free or low-rent home is never tax-free, unless you have to live there for security reasons. There are special rules for free or cheap accommodation abroad – see p182.

Agricultural workers whose employers give them free board and lodging may be able to take higher wages and arrange their own accommodation instead. That would normally make the value of their board and lodging taxable. But by a concession, agricultural workers who are not higher-paid will generally avoid the tax.

FA 1976 s63A s72; FA 1977 s33, s33A; FA 1983 s21; ESC announced 8 August 1986.

Loans of things and their subsequent gift

If you count as higher-paid and your employer lends you something like furniture or a TV, your Tax Inspector will value it at 20 per cent of the market value at the time your employer first loaned the thing out, *less* anything you pay for the use of it. For things first loaned out before 6 April 1980, the 20 per cent figure becomes 10 per cent. If your employer pays for servicing (or any other costs) the amount he pays is added to the taxable value.

If your employer gives you whatever it was he was lending you, your Tax Inspector will value it at the market value at the time your employer first loaned it out, *less* anything you've paid towards it, and *less* any amount you've already paid tax on (eg under the 20 per cent rule). But if this value is lower than the market value when the thing is given to you, you'll be taxed on the higher (market) value, *less* anything you've paid towards it. And if the thing was first loaned out before 6 April 1980, its value is taken as the market value when the thing was given to you (*less* anything you've paid towards it).

If you count as higher-paid and your employer lets you use a thing which he rents (eg a flat, a TV) your Tax Inspector can value the benefit at the amount your employer pays in rent, running costs, etc *less* anything you pay, if this comes to more than the value using the normal method.

If you don't count as higher-paid, there's no tax on a loan; and you're taxed on the *second-hand value* of a gift.

FA 1976 s63(3A), (4), (5), (6).

Employee share schemes

An employee share scheme is organised by an employer and is a way in which an employee can get a stake in the company he works for. The following sorts of schemes have considerable tax advantages if they are *'approved'* by the Inland Revenue:
- profit-sharing schemes
- share option schemes
- SAYE share option schemes.

Profit-sharing schemes

Under an *approved* scheme you can get shares in your employer's firm free of tax. The yearly limit is £1,250 worth of shares, or 10% of your earnings, whichever is higher, with an overall limit of £5,000-worth of shares a year. To get approval, the scheme must meet various conditions. For example, the shares must be held in trust for you. They can't normally be handed over to you for at least two years (unless you reach retirement age, are made redundant, or stop work through injury or disablement). And if you withdraw your shares from the trust within five years of getting them, there will normally be some income tax to pay (unless the shares are withdrawn because you die).

If you sell the shares for more than their value at the time you were given them, the gain you make counts as a taxable capital gain – and there may be capital gains tax to pay (see p415). And any dividends you get count as part of your income for the tax year in which you get them.

FA 1978 s53–61; FA 1982 s42; FA 1985 s45.

Share option schemes

A share option scheme gives you the right (or *option*) to buy shares in your employer's company at some future date, but at today's market price. From 6 April 1984, there has been no

income tax to pay on any gain you make when you exercise your option, if the scheme is an *approved* one. Instead, any gain you make when you sell (or give away) the shares will count as a taxable capital gain. Any tax will be based on the difference between the price you paid to buy the shares, and the price when you sell (or give away) the share – see p415. To get approval, the scheme must meet certain conditions. For example, you can't get an option of more than the greater of £100,000-worth of shares (valued at the time the option is granted) or four times your earnings (see p137) excluding the taxable value of your fringe benefits and after deduction of any contributions you make to your employer's pension scheme in the current tax year. The preceding year's earnings are used if they are greater.

When you exercise your option, you must be able to do so at the market price at the time the option was made. The option must be taken up at some time between three and ten years, but this can only be done at three-yearly intervals – ie three times during the seven years. Employees who work at least 20 hours a week (directors, 25 hours a week), will be allowed to get an option.

From 18 March 1986 you are liable for income tax on anything you receive for agreeing *not* to exercise the option or for granting someone else an option over the shares.

If you are in a share option scheme which is not *approved*, you will pay income tax on the difference between the market value when you exercise your option and the cost to you of the shares, including any amount paid for the option. You might have to pay capital gains tax when you sell (or give away) your shares, based on the difference between their market value when you exercise your option and their value when you dispose of them.

FA 1984 s38–39, Sch 102; FA1986 s26.

Savings-related share option schemes

Your company can run a savings scheme giving you the option to buy its shares some years in the future at a price fixed now. Provided the scheme is an *approved* one and you buy the shares with the proceeds of a SAYE scheme – which normally runs for five or seven years – there will usually be no income tax to pay when the option is given to you, nor on the difference between the value of the shares when you buy them and the price you pay for them. But if you sell (or give away) the shares, there could be capital gains tax to pay based on the difference between the price you buy at and the market value when you sell or give them away. The maximum saving is £100 a month

and the minimum can't be more than £10.
FA 1980 s47, Sch10; FA 1984 s39(5).

Company takeovers and share option schemes

It is now possible for employees in a company which is taken over to exchange their existing share options under an approved share option scheme (including savings-related schemes) for options to buy shares in the company which takes over. The replacement options can only be granted if certain conditions are met to ensure that the employees concerned will be no better or worse off than if the takeover had not happened.
FA 1987 s33, Sch 4.

Tax-saving tips

● consider asking for fringe benefits as part of your pay package. Some fringe benefits are tax-free – and with others the tax you pay is less than it would cost you to buy them yourself

● try not to go just over the limit for cheap loans. If the taxman values your cheap loans at £200, there's no tax to pay. If he values them at £201, you'll pay tax on the whole lot

● if you don't count as higher-paid, consider asking your employer to lend you things such as a car, TV or hi-fi. There'd normally be no tax to pay. Or you could ask for gifts with low second-hand values, such as made-to-measure clothes – there'd normally be little or no tax

● employee share schemes are a tax-efficient investment – though be wary if there's a risk of the company going bust.

14 WORKING ABROAD

If you want to keep the UK taxman's hands off your hard-earned guilders, dinars or even pounds, you'll have to earn them abroad. But just earning them abroad isn't enough. You'll have to be absent from the UK for at least a year to get your earnings free of UK tax.

Where you live – according to the taxman

In general, the UK tax system aims to tax all earnings made in the UK, and all earnings paid to people who are **resident** and **ordinarily resident** in the UK, even if the money is earned outside the country. But if you're paid money abroad and aren't allowed to take it out of the country (because of a ban on doing so, or a war, say) you can ask the taxman to let you off paying tax on it until it is possible for the money to be sent to the UK. You'll then have to pay tax on the income whether or not it is sent to the UK.

The terms resident and ordinarily resident have not been defined by Act of Parliament – so their interpretation is up to the courts. Whether you are resident and/or ordinarily resident is decided separately for each tax year. But you will always be treated as resident if you're in the UK for at least six months (183 days) of the tax year. The 183 days may be made up of one visit or a succession of visits. Under current Inland Revenue practice, the day of your arrival and the day of your departure do not normally count towards the 183 days. You're also likely to be treated as resident if:

● over a period of years (four years, say), you come to the UK for an average of three months or more each year, OR
● you visit the UK at all during the tax year, and have a home for your use here (even if you don't own it). This doesn't apply if you work wholly abroad full-time. But if you're married, and your husband (or wife) doesn't work abroad full time and comes back to the UK with you, he (or she) could count as resident, even though you don't.

The term ordinarily resident is less clear-cut and is to do with your intentions and way of life. If you are treated as being resident in the UK year after year, you are likely to count as ordinarily resident too.

A person can be resident (or ordinarily resident) in two or more countries at the same time – or even none at all.
ICTA 1970 s49–51, s181; IR 20.

How you're taxed

If you're resident and ordinarily resident in the UK, you'll be taxed on all you earn abroad unless you qualify for a *100% deduction*. If you do qualify, all your earnings from abroad will be treated as free of UK tax.

The 100% deduction

If you're abroad for a continuous period of 365 *qualifying days* (see next page) or more (not necessarily coinciding with a tax year), all your earnings will be tax-free. Where possible (eg you work for a UK company which has sent you abroad) the deduction is given in your PAYE code, and if the taxman is satisfied you'll get the 100 per cent deduction, you'll get a 'No Tax' code (see p154) for those earnings.

Even if you come back to the UK during your 365 days, you may still qualify for the 100 per cent deduction. The taxman adds together:
● the continuous days abroad immediately *before* your UK visit
● the number of days in your UK visit
● the number of days abroad immediately *after* your UK visit.

If the number of days in your UK visit come to more than one-sixth of this total *or* to more than 62 days, the continuity of your 365 days is broken at the end of your first period abroad. And a new period of 365 days starts at the beginning of your second period abroad. But if your UK visit is one-sixth of the total above (or less) and not more than 62 days, the whole time, including the days in the UK, counts towards your 365 days. If you come back to the UK for another visit, the whole period which counted towards your 365 days is included when working out the continuous days immediately before your second UK visit, and the total number of days that you've spent in the UK in previous visits is added to the number of days in your latest visit – see Example 1 overleaf. The 62-day limit doesn't apply to the cumulative total for UK visits. The process is repeated for each UK visit.

Note that the 100% deduction only applies to work done entirely abroad, unless your work in the UK is regarded as 'incidental' to the overseas employment. Things like getting further instructions, or reporting to head office would be treated as incidental; beyond this the taxman deals with each case on its merits.
FA 1977 s31, Sch 7.

Qualifying days

A qualifying day of absence is a day abroad spent mainly working, and which you are absent at the end of. The day you leave the UK to travel to your job also counts, but the day of your return doesn't. Aircrews and seamen count as working abroad during trips that take them to or from (or between) places abroad.

FA 1977 Sch 7.

Example 1

Angela Tavistock and Brian Duckworth work for the same company. They both have to go abroad three times in the next 16 months or so, for a total of 400 days away. They know when they have to be away and when they will come back for UK visits, so they work out if they are entitled to the 100 per cent deduction.

Neither of Angela's UK trips exceeds the limits, so her earnings will be free of UK tax.

Brian's first visit to the UK breaks the one-sixth rule, and his second and third trips abroad (including the 20 days of his visit to the UK) don't add up to 365 days. So he can't claim the 100 per cent deduction. If Brian could arrange another working trip abroad which linked to his third trip abroad without breaking the one-sixth rule, and he then met the 365-day requirement, he could claim the 100 per cent deduction for his second and third trips abroad and the final one that took him over the 365-day requirement.

Note that if Angela's or Brian's work (other than work incidental to their overseas employment) was done partly in the UK during their visits home, they would not get the 100 per cent deduction from all their earnings. The deduction would be given against the amount of earnings which is shown to be 'reasonable' given the nature of the duties, the time devoted to them in the UK and abroad, and all other relevant circumstances.

Angela	days	⅙th limit exceeded?	Brian	days	⅙th limit exceeded?
1st trip abroad	100		1st trip abroad	100	
1st UK visit	20		1st UK visit	60	
2nd trip abroad	150	no(20/270)	2nd trip abroad	150	yes (60/310)
2nd UK visit	60		2nd UK visit	20	
3rd trip abroad	150	no(80/480)	3rd trip abroad	150	no (20/320) *

* but Brian hasn't met the 365-day requirement since the beginning of his second trip abroad

Servants of the crown

Servants of the crown (eg UK diplomats and members of the Armed Forces) working abroad are, for most income tax purposes, always taxed as if they worked in the UK. But if an extra allowance is paid for working abroad, this isn't taxable. *ICTA 1970 s184, s369.*

Personal allowances while you're away

If you're resident in the UK, you'll get your full personal allowance for the tax year. So if, say, you get the 100 per cent deduction you'll be able to use all your personal allowances against other income you get in the UK – eg National Savings Bank interest, dividends, UK earnings.

If a couple has elected for *separate taxation of the wife's earnings*, and now one of them is working abroad and qualifies for a deduction, it may be worth revoking this decision if the couple's income after the deduction falls below £26,870. More details on p78.

Travelling expenses

You don't have to pay tax on what your employer pays towards the cost of travel to a job abroad (and back again when you've finished), or between countries where you're working. If your employer doesn't pay, you can claim such costs you incur as *allowable expenses* – see p142.

You can now make any number of visits to the UK, paid for or reimbursed by your employer, without being taxed on the travel expenses – so long as your job can *only* be performed outside the UK and you go abroad purely for work purposes. This provision was introduced in 1986 and is backdated to 6 April 1984. And, so long as you've worked abroad continuously for at least 60 days and there are no more than two return trips for each person per tax year, what your employer pays towards some other journeys is tax-free too:

- visits by your wife (or husband) or children under 18.
- return trips that you make to visit them.

But if *you* pay for these trips, the costs cannot count as *allowable expenses*. There's no tax to pay on costs, met by your employer, of travel in the UK at the beginning or end of your journey – eg from a UK home to the airport. This is also backdated to 6 April 1984.

FA 1977 s32; FA 1986 s34–38.

Working abroad for a short time

You can no longer get tax relief against your earnings from abroad if you are absent from the UK for less than 365 days. In the 1983–84 tax year, you could have got part of your income free of UK tax, if you:
- worked abroad for at least 30 qualifying days during the tax year, *or*
- worked wholly abroad for a non-resident employer (in which case there was no minimum number of days).

If you met either of these requirements, you could claim a 25% deduction from what you earned while you were abroad before the tax due on this income was worked out. The Finance Act 1984 reduced the percentage deduction to 12½ per cent in 1984–85 and the relief vanished altogether from the 1985–86 tax year onwards. *FA 1977 Sch 7; FA 1984 s30.*

Board and lodging abroad

If your job is done wholly abroad, and your employer pays (or reimburses) the cost of board and lodging which enables you to carry out your duties, there'll be no tax to pay on this fringe benefit. But you *will* be taxed on the cost to your employer of board and lodging for your wife and children, and of any board and lodging for a holiday abroad. If your employer doesn't pay, you can't claim any board and lodging as an *allowable expense*.

If your job is done partly in the UK and partly abroad, there'll normally be no tax to pay on what your employer pays towards *your* board and lodging – and if he doesn't pay, you may be able to claim the cost as an allowable expense. See p142 for details.

ICTA 1970 s189; FA 1977 s32.

Golden handshakes

If you're a UK resident, redundancy payments you get after working abroad may be wholly tax-free, even if they're over £25,000 (see p158). Payments you get are tax-free if any of the following apply:

● you worked abroad for at least three-quarters of the time you did the job
● you worked abroad for all of the last 10 years
● you did the job for over 20 years, and at least 10 of the last 20 years *and* at least half the total time was spent working abroad.

Where the payment isn't wholly tax-free, part may be. An amount will be deducted from the golden handshake equal to:

$$\frac{\text{number of years you worked abroad} \times \text{the amount which would otherwise have been taxable}}{\text{total number of years' service}}$$

You count as working abroad if either you weren't ordinarily resident or you got the 100 per cent deduction (see p179).

ICTA 1970 s188, Sch 8.

Double taxation relief

If you pay local income tax on what you earn abroad, you may be eligible for *double taxation relief*. The UK has a number of double taxation agreements with other countries, which prevent you paying tax both abroad and in the UK on the same income. This is done either by making certain types of income (eg earnings, dividends, business profits) taxable in one country and other types taxable in the other or by reducing the UK tax bill by the smaller of the overseas tax liability and the UK tax liability.

If there is no double taxation agreement, you can claim *unilateral relief* if you're a UK resident earning income which has been taxed abroad. You'll be allowed to offset the tax you paid abroad against the UK tax you have to pay. See IR6 for more details.

ICTA 1970 s497-498; IR6.

Domiciled abroad, but working in the UK

Broadly speaking, your **domicile** is the place you have your permanent home. It's likely to be the same as your father's – unless you've changed it, which can prove a complex process.

Before the 1984–85 tax year, if you were domiciled abroad (but resident in the UK) and worked for a non-resident company you could qualify for a 50 per cent deduction from your UK earnings (or 25 per cent if you had been resident in the UK for 9 out of the last 10 years). You could also have got these deductions if you worked abroad for a non-resident employer. But the Finance Act 1984 removed these deductions unless you got the 50 per cent deduction in 1983–84 tax year. If you did, you'll continue to get the deduction until you have been resident in the UK for 9 of the last 10 years, or (if this doesn't happen) until 5 April 1987 – after which it will be reduced to 25 per cent and removed altogether in 1989–90.

ICTA 1970 s181; FA 1974 s21, Sch2; FA 1984 s30.

Tax if you're non-resident

As a non-resident, you pay UK income tax on only your UK earnings – both at the basic rate and higher rates if your UK income is high enough. You'll also have to pay tax on your UK investment income. But there may be relief given under a double taxation agreement – see p183. (Note that there are some British Government stocks which have a tax-free return for people who are not ordinarily resident. And, by concession you won't normally have to pay UK tax on bank and building society interest.)

Becoming non-resident

If you leave to go and work abroad full-time (so that any work you do in the UK is 'incidental' to your work abroad – see p179, you'll count as non-resident and not ordinarily resident providing your visits back to the UK don't exceed the limits on p179 *and* providing your trip abroad spans a complete tax year or more. You'll count as non-resident from the day after you leave to the day before you come back.

If you're not employed full-time abroad, in addition to meeting the requirements above, you'll have to produce some evidence to support your claim to non-residence – for example, selling your home in the UK and setting up a permanent home abroad. If you can do this, your claim may be accepted provisionally. It will normally be confirmed when you've been away for a complete tax year during which visits back to the UK have not amounted to more than an average of three months a year. If you're unable to provide sufficient evidence, the decision is delayed for three years, and your tax liability will be worked out provisionally as though you were still resident (except for any tax year in which you don't set foot in the UK at all). After the three years are up, you'll be able to claim back any tax that you've overpaid if it's confirmed that you're non-resident.

IR 20; ESC B13 *(untaxed interest)*.

Personal allowances

In the tax year that you leave the UK and the one in which you return you can claim your full personal allowance and any other allowances and outgoings you're entitled to. If you're non-resident for a complete tax year, you may be able to claim a proportion of your personal allowances (see IR20 for more details).

If you are non-resident but your husband or wife is resident, you'll be treated as though you were permanently separated – see *Separation and divorce* on p89 – but only if it is to your advantage. This means that you'll be treated as single people with the one who is resident getting the single person's allowance; the one who is non-resident may be able to claim a proportion of the allowance as above.

ICTA 1970 s27, s42; IR20.

Tax saving tips

● for the 100 per cent deduction make sure you don't exceed the one-sixth or 62-day limits

● if you or your wife get the 100 per cent deduction and have elected for separate taxation of the wife's earnings, it may no longer be worthwhile

● try to arrange for your employer to either pay for or reimburse the cost of your board and lodging abroad. If he doesn't, you can't treat your expenses as allowable.

15 TAX IF YOU'RE SELF-EMPLOYED

Being self-employed includes all sorts of occupations – owning a shop, being a manufacturer or wholesaler, or working as a doctor, barrister, singer or writer, and so on. Most of this chapter is for people in business on their own – ie we give the tax rules for people taxed under Schedule D Case I or Case II (see p33) – but we also tell you something about companies on p210. Partnerships and casual earnings are dealt with in Chapters 16 and 17.

Do you count as self-employed?

Self-employed people can generally claim more in expenses to reduce their tax bills. Unlike employees, tax is not deducted from their earnings before they are paid. And they do not have to pay the tax they owe until some time – up to 20 months – after they have received the money.

So being your own boss has its attractions from the tax point of view. If you own a shop or offer a mobile car mechanic service, say, provide all your own equipment and find all your own customers, there is little doubt that you are self-employed. But there can be circumstances when though you may regard yourself as self-employed, the taxman says you are not.

In general, you are on dangerous ground if all (or nearly all) your work comes from just one source – from one company you have a contract with, say – and you are paid on a regular basis without having to send in an invoice. The taxman may decide you are an employee with a *contract of service* rather than a self-employed person with a *contract for services*. If the taxman says you have a contract of service, he may tax you under Schedule E as an employee and insist that the company deducts tax from your pay under the Pay-As-You-Earn system. This is particularly likely to happen if all the work you do is carried out on the company's premises.

Note that if you are a director of a limited company, no matter how small, you are an employed person, not self-employed.

Each Inland Revenue and DHSS local office now has someone responsible for saying whether or not you will be treated as self-employed, and who will confirm their decisions in writing if you wish. Also see Inland Revenue leaflet IR56.

What is trading?
You may be taxed as if you're a business, even if you don't think you are, if your Tax Inspector says you are *trading*. You might be said to be trading if, among other points:
- you frequently buy and sell similar items
- you sell items which you haven't owned for very long
- you alter the items so that you can sell them for more
- your motive in buying and selling is to make a profit.
ICTA 1970 s108, s109, s526.

When profits are taxed

A big advantage of being taxed as self-employed is that there can be a considerable delay before you pay tax on the profits you earn. There are two things you can do to get the longest delay you can:
- choose your *accounting year-end* carefully, and
- use the rules about which profits are taxed when your business starts – see Table 1, overleaf.

When your business has been going for two complete tax years, tax will normally be charged on a *preceding year basis* (see Table 1) – ie your tax bill for the 1987–88 tax year will be based on the profit you made in your accounting year ending in the 1986–87 tax year. This tax will have to be paid in two equal instalments on 1 January 1988 and 1 July 1988.

Occasional or spare-time earnings
If your 'business' is simply occasional freelance or spare-time work, it will normally be taxed on a *current year basis* – ie your tax bill for the 1987–88 tax year is based on the profit you make during that tax year. For more details, see p222.
ICTA 1970 s125; TMA 1970 s29, s55, s86.

Starting a business

Choice of accounting year

Your accounting year need not run from 1 January to 31 December, nor need it coincide with the tax year. If you choose your accounting year carefully – eg end it a little after the start of the tax year – there could be as much as 20 months before you start to pay tax on the profits you've earned. As long as your profits are rising, this could be an advantage, because you will be paying tax on lower profits than you are currently making.

Example 1

Accounting year end		dates tax due	time lag
31 December 1986		1 January 1988	12 months
	and	1 July 1988	18 months
31 March 1987		1 January 1988	9 months
	and	1 July 1988	15 months
30 April 1987		1 January 1989	20 months
	and	1 July 1989	26 months

Your first accounting 'year' doesn't have to cover exactly 12 months, but once you have chosen a date to make your first accounts up to, you should normally stick to that date in the following years as the rules about changing are very complicated – see Inland Revenue leaflet IR26. But if you think you may benefit by changing the date, get advice from an accountant. If you're certain that the profits for your first accounting period will be low, it can pay you to make your first accounting period longer than a year – see Example 2, opposite.

Table 1: What your tax bill is based on in the opening years of a business

	Tax is initially based on	But for some years, there is a choice
First tax year you are in business	*Actual profit* [1] in that tax year	no choice this year

	Tax is initially based on	But for some years, there is a choice
Second tax year	Profit in your first 12 months of operation	**your choice:** you can choose to have your tax bill for the second and third tax years (but not just one of them) based on the *actual profit* [1] for each of these tax years. **Do so if this would make the total tax for the two years less**
Third tax year	Profit in your accounting year ending in the preceding tax year (or, if your first accounting year hasn't come to an end, normally your first 12 months' profit)	
Fourth and subsequent tax years	Profit in your accounting year ending in the preceding tax year (ie *preceding year basis*)	no choice for these years

[1] Your *actual profit* for any tax year is the proportion of your profits (worked out on a time basis) which will be attributed to that tax year. Suppose your accounting period doesn't coincide with the tax year. If you need to attribute your profits, do it on this basis:

profits in accounting year × number of months of accounting period in tax year ÷ number of months in accounting period

If your first accounting period is more than 12 months, the *actual profit* for your third and fourth tax years will be apportioned – see Example below. Your tax inspector may insist that you apportion profits on a daily basis.

Note that if you want to choose to have your tax bills for the second and third year based on actual profits, you have to choose within six years after the end of the third year of assessment.

Example 2
Henry Haswell started in business on 6 November 1985. He decided to make his first accounting period last 18 months and end on 30 April 1987. He expected his taxable profits to be low for that period – £10,000, say. Assuming that he does in fact make taxable profits of £10,000 in his first accounting period, his assessments of taxable profits for the first five tax years are likely to be as follows:

tax year
1985–86   5/18 × £10,000 = £2,778
1986–87   12/18 × £10,000 = £6,667
1987–88   12/18 × £10,000 = £6,667
1988–89   12/18 × £10,000 = £6,667
1989–90   profits in accounting year ending on 30 April 1988.

If Henry had decided to end his accounting period on 31 March his assessment for the 1988–89 tax year would be based on his accounting year ending on 31 March 1988.

You and your tax inspector

When you've been in business for nearly a year, your Tax
Inspector will ask you for your accounts for your first
accounting period. If you can't provide them – because, for
example, your first accounting period isn't finished – he will
shortly send you an assessment of tax. You will receive two
assessments, one for each of the first two tax years. When you
get the assessments, if you don't agree with them you can
appeal, and apply to postpone payment. You normally need to
do this within 30 days – see p468. If it turns out in the end that
more tax is due than is shown on the assessment, interest can
be charged on the extra tax due, as well as on any tax you've
postponed paying.

Once your first accounting period is over, you should send
your accounts showing your taxable profit to your Tax
Inspector. You don't always need to send a balance sheet and
you don't need to have your accounts audited. But you will
need to be able to back up your accounts with your records,
if your Tax Inspector should challenge them. You need written
receipts for as many items as possible. Keep a record of your
cash payments in and out of your bank account and your petty
cash box.

There are some simple rules you can follow to cut down the
chances of being investigated by the taxman (see p460):
● find out the profit margin for people in similar businesses
and if your profit margin is lower, send a note saying why
● if the income you take out of the business is very low – eg
because you are living on savings – tell your Tax Inspector why
this is so
● try to send your accounts in on time
● don't miss out simple things, such as National Savings Bank
interest, from your Tax Return
● if possible, send a balance sheet and list of fixed assets as
well as a profit and loss account
● if you've made a loss, explain it.
ICTA 1970 s115–118; TMA 1970 s31, s55, s86.

Checklist: starting a business

● decide whether to register for VAT – see p209
● inform the Department of Health and Social Security
● inform your local tax inspector
● make a list of fixed assets – eg office equipment, car
● get cash books to show cash paid into (and taken out
of) the bank, and a book for petty cash

● set up an accounting system (eg in a book – or books) to show details of sales and purchases. Sort the purchases into different types – eg stationery, travel, heating and lighting
● if you need stocks of raw materials and other goods, keep records of what you've bought, what you've sold, and what has gone from stock
● get written receipts and file them in date order
● get a notebook to record items for which there's no receipt
● plan how you are going to pay your tax bill – eg by putting money aside each month
● if a car is used partly for your business, keep a record of business mileage, petrol, and all running costs
● if you are going to use in your business things you already own – eg a car, typewriter, computer – include them in your accounts. You will be able to claim capital allowances on them
● choose your accounting year-end to take advantage of delay in tax payments – see p188
● if profits are likely to be low in first year, take advantage of the rules about starting in business – see p188
● consider employing your wife or making her your partner – see pages 207 and 217
● ask for any expenditure before you start business to count as pre-trading expenditure – see p194
● if you make a loss in the first year, remember you can set it off against other income – see p206
● make sure you have adequate life insurance and pension cover. Think about *permanent health insurance* in case you're too ill to work.

Closing a business

In the last tax year in which you're in business you are taxed on the *actual profit* – see [1], on p189 – you make in that tax year. Profits are normally attributed to tax years on a time basis. In your last-but-two and last-but-one tax years your Tax Inspector can choose how to work out your tax bills. He can either base the bills on your profit in your accounting year ending in the preceding year. Or when you tell him that you've closed down your business, he can choose to base your tax bills for both years (but not just one of them) on the *actual profit* – see [1] on p189 – for each of these tax years. He will do this if it will make the total profits for the two years greater.

Income after you close a business

If you get any income after you have closed your business, it will be taxed under Schedule D Case VI (see p33) as earned income of the tax year in which you get it. However, if you get it within six years of closing the business, you can choose within two years to have it treated as income you got on the last day of your business. Your final assessment will be adjusted.
ICTA 1970 s149.

Working out taxable profits

The taxable profit of your business is the amount you are going to pay tax on. If you were working out your taxable profit from scratch, it would be your takings during your accounting year, ie cash received during the year for the sales you make, plus:
● money owed *to you* at the end of the accounting year
● money owed *by you* at the beginning of the year
● the increase in value of your stocks during the year
less the following deductions:
● allowable business expenses (see opposite)
● stock relief if you are working out taxable profits for an accounting year which included, or ended before, 13 March 1984
● money owed *to you* at the beginning of the year
● money owed *by you* at the end of the year
● capital allowances
● losses
● from the 1985–86 tax year onwards, half the amount of any Class 4 National Insurance contributions payable for the year of assessment.

In practice, you may start off working out your profit under normal accounting rules. You then turn this into your taxable profits by adding back things which aren't allowable business expenses and deducting things on which you can get tax relief.

In a very few cases, eg a barrister, your sales figure may be taken as the cash you receive during your accounting year for work done – regardless of when you actually did the work. So you can ignore money owed at the start or end of the accounting year.

If you take items out of stock for your own use you normally have to include these in sales at the normal selling price.
CIR v Gardner Mountain & D'Ambrumenil 29 TC 69; Sharkey v Wernher 36 TC 275.

Other income
If you have any other income which is not part of your trading income, it is not part of the taxable profits of your business. How any non-trading income is taxed depends on where it comes from. For example, bank interest is taxed as investment income.

Allowable business expenses

An expense is allowable only if incurred *'wholly and exclusively'* for the business. Table 2 overleaf lists expenses you probably will be allowed and those you will not. But business needs vary widely and an expense allowable for one business may not be for another. If in doubt, claim.

Note that the *'wholly and exclusively'* rule does not mean that you can claim nothing if, for example, you sometimes use your car for business, sometimes for private purposes. If the car is used wholly for business purposes on some occasions, then you can normally claim the proportion of car expenses which is attributable to business use – you'll have to agree the proportion with your Tax Inspector. You can usually claim the same proportion of your car expenses as your business mileage bears to your total mileage. However, if you use the car for a trip which is part pleasure, part business, you may not be able to claim any of the costs of the trip as an allowable expense. This is known as the *dual purpose rule*. For example, you can't normally claim the expenses of a business trip which is combined with a holiday. However, if you attend a conference during the trip, the conference fee will be allowable.

You can normally claim part of your home expenses – eg heating, lighting, rates – if you use part of your home for business. Home expenses are usually shared out on the basis of the number and size of rooms. If you claim costs of using your home for business, beware of a possible capital gains tax bill if you sell your home – see p252.

Capital expenditure – eg what you spend on buying cars, machinery, improving property – is not an allowable expense, nor is depreciation – eg of cars. But you may get capital allowances – see p198.
ICTA 1970 s130.

Pre-trading expenses

If you spend money – eg rent and rates – before your business actually starts, it will probably count as pre-trading expenditure. It will be treated as a loss in your first year of trading, and you can get loss relief – see p206.

FA 1980 s39; FA 1982 s50.

Table 2: Business expenses

	Normally allowed	Not allowed
Basic costs and general running expenses	Cost of goods bought for resale and raw materials used in business (see p197 for how much to claim). Discounts allowed on sales. Advertising. Delivery charges. Heating. Lighting. Cleaning. Rates. Telephone. Rent of business premises. Replacement of small tools and special clothing. Postage. Stationery. Relevant books and magazines. Accountants' fees. Bank charges on business accounts. Subscriptions to professional and trade organisations.	Initial cost of buildings, machinery, vehicles, equipment, permanent advertising signs – but see *Capital allowances*, on p198.
Use of home for work	Proportion of telephone, lighting, heating, cleaning, insurance. Proportion of rent and rates, if use part of home *exclusively* for business – but watch out for capital gains tax (see p252).	
Wages and salaries	Wages, salaries, redundancy and leaving payments paid to employees. Pensions for ex-employees and dependants.	Your own wages or salary, or that of any partner.
Tax and National Insurance	Employer's National Insurance contributions for employees. VAT on allowable business expenses if you're not a registered trader for VAT (and, sometimes, even if you are – see p209).	Income tax. Capital gains tax. Inheritance tax. Your own National Insurance contributions – but see p208.

	Normally allowed	Not allowed
Entertaining	Reasonable entertainment of overseas trade customers and their overseas agents (and normally your own costs on such an occasion). Entertainment of own staff – eg Christmas party.	Any other business entertaining – eg entertainment of UK customers.
Gifts	Gifts costing up to £10 a year to each person so long as the gift advertises your business (or things it sells). Gifts (whatever their value) to employees.	Food, drink, tobacco, or vouchers for goods given to anyone other than employees.
Travelling	Cost of travel and accommodation on business trips. Travel between different places of work. *Running costs of own car:* whole of cost, excluding depreciation, if used wholly for business, proportion if used privately too. See also *Business abroad* on p207.	Travel between home and business. Meals, unless any personal benefit is purely incidental to the business purpose. Cost of buying a car or van – but see *Capital allowances*, on p198.
Interest payments	Interest on, and costs of arranging, overdrafts and loans for business purposes – see p25.	Interest on capital paid or credited to partners. Interest on overdue tax.
Hire purchase and leasing	Hire charge part of payments (ie the amount you pay *less* the cash price). Rent paid for leasing car or machinery, for example.	Cash price of what you're buying on hire purchase (you may get *capital allowances* on cash price – but see p199).
Hiring	Reasonable charge for hire of capital goods, including cars.	
Insurance	Business insurance – eg employer's liability, fire and theft, motor, insuring employees' lives.	Your own life insurance, accident insurance, sickness insurance.
Trade marks, designs and patents	Fees paid to register trade mark or design; or to obtain a patent.	Cost of buying patent from someone else – but see *Capital allowances*, p203.

	Normally allowed	Not allowed
Legal costs	Costs of recovering debts; defending business rights; preparing service agreements; appealing against rates on business premises; drawing up a partnership agreement; forming a company; renewing a lease, with the landlord's consent, for a period not exceeding 50 years (but not if a premium is paid).	Expenses (including stamp duty) for acquiring land, buildings or leases. Fines and other penalties for breaking the law. Costs of fighting a tax case.
Repairs	Normal repairs and maintenance to premises or equipment.	Cost of additions, alterations, improvements.
Debts	Specific bad debts and, in part, doubtful debts.	General reserve for bad or doubtful debts.
Subscriptions and contributions	Payments which secure benefits for your business or staff. Genuine contribution to approved local enterprise agency. Payments to societies which have arrangements with the Inland Revenue (in some cases only a proportion).	Payments to political parties, churches, charities (but small gifts to *local* churches and charities may be allowable).
Training	Subject to certain conditions, cost of training employees to acquire and improve skills needed for their current jobs; cost of training employees who are leaving or who have left in new work skills.	
Secondments	Cost of seconding employers on a temporary basis to certain educational bodies including local education authorities and institutions maintained by them and to charitable institutions.	

ICTA 1970 s130; Coltness Iron Co v Black 1 TC 287 (machinery); ICTA 1970 s411 (entertaining); ICTA 1970 s411; FA 1985 s43 (gifts); Newsom v Robertson 33 TC 452, Caillebotte v Quinn 1975, 50 TC 222 (travelling); TMA 1970 s90 (interest on overdue tax); CIR v Pattison 38 TC 617 (hire purchase); ICTA 1970 s132, s378 (trade marks, patents, etc); Smith's Potato Estates Ltd v Bolland 30 T 267 (legal costs); FA 1980 s54; FA 1982 s48; Morgan v Tate & Lyle 35 TC 367; (subscriptions and contributions); FA 1987, s34, s35 (training and secondments)

Stock

You can claim as an allowable expense the cost of raw materials you use in your business, and the cost of things you buy for resale. But you can claim only the cost of business materials which you actually sell during your accounting year – ie the value of your stocks of these things at the start of the year *plus* anything you spend on buying more during the year, *minus* the value of your stocks at the end of the year. So an *increase* in the value of stocks will normally increase your taxable profits for the year. A *decrease* in the value of stocks reduces your taxable profits.

If you have stocks which can only be sold for less than you paid for them, you will normally be allowed to value them at what they would fetch if sold now. This means for tax purposes that you can value stock *at the lower of cost or market value*. No other method of valuing stock is allowed by your Tax Inspector – regardless of what is allowed under accounting rules.

For accounting years ending before 13 March 1984 or including 13 March 1984, you may be able to claim **stock relief** for all or part of the year – see below.

When you value your stocks at the start and end of the accounting year, you need to add in the value of *work-in-progress*. This is the value of work which has begun, but which isn't completed – eg products half way through the manufacturing process, or part-completed work if you're a builder, solicitor, engineer, etc. Work-in-progress can be valued in one of the following ways:

- cost of raw materials used
- cost plus overheads
- cost plus overheads plus profit contribution.

Once you've chosen a way of valuing work-in-progress, this is how it must be valued each accounting year.

If you are closing a business, your stock will be valued either at the price it's sold at, if sold to someone else in business, or at the price it would fetch if sold in the open market.

Stock relief

You can get stock relief for accounting periods which ended before 13 March 1984. If the accounting period included 13 March 1984, you can get relief based on the increase in stock prices up to March 1984.

To work out the amount of the relief, you:

- take the value of the stock at the start of the accounting year
- deduct £2,000
- multiply the result by the percentage increase in the **all stocks index** between the start and the end of the accounting year (or March 1984, if this is earlier). Figures are on p504.

FA 1981 Sch 9; FA 1984 s48.

Capital allowances

When you work out your taxable profits, you can't deduct anything you spend on capital assets or equipment – eg machinery or cars. Money spent in this way is not an allowable business expense. But you can still get tax relief on these sorts of things by claiming capital allowances on:

- motor cars

- plant and machinery (vans, machines, typewriters, for example)
- buildings (eg industrial, agricultural, hotels, in enterprise zones)
- patents, know-how and scientific research.

To get a capital allowance, expenditure must be *wholly and exclusively* for the business. But again, on anything used partly for business, partly privately, you will get a proportion of the capital allowance, depending on the proportion of business use.

If you buy equipment for private use, and then use it in your business, you can claim a capital allowance on its market value at the time you start using it. Detailed rules are overleaf.

How you pay for the equipment doesn't make any difference to the capital allowance. If you pay by a loan or by bank overdraft, the interest is an allowable business expense, not part of the cost of the asset. In the same way, hire purchase charges are a business expense.

CAA 1968 s1, s2, s18, s19, s28; FA 1971 Sch 8 para 5; FA 1984 s58, Sch 12.

VAT

For how to deal with VAT on items on which you claim a capital allowance, see p210.

Types of allowances

- **first-year or initial allowances.** You set this allowance (either all or part of it, if you choose) against the profits of the accounting period in which you buy the asset.

For example, if you're taxed on a preceding year basis, and you spend money on a machine in the accounting period ending 31 December 1986, you will get the allowance in the 1987–88 tax year. First-year and initial allowances have been phased out, and you won't normally be able to claim one for assets you buy after 31 March 1986 (except for buildings in enterprise zones and capital expenditure for the purposes of scientific research). For how much you can claim, see p202

- **writing-down allowances.** In most cases, you can claim a writing-down allowance each year until you have written-down the value of the equipment or building to nil.

In some cases, the writing-down allowance is worked out on the value (at the end of each accounting year) of your pool of written-down expenditure – see overleaf. In other cases, it's worked out on what the asset originally cost you – see p202.

With plant and machinery, you can get the writing-down allowance once you've started to pay for the equipment. Note that for periods ending before 1 April 1985, you couldn't claim the allowance until you had actually started using it. If you are claiming less than your full writing-down allowance, see Example 3 opposite.

> **Leasing**
>
> If, instead of buying a car or a machine, you choose to lease it, you can claim the rent paid as an allowable expense, as long as you are using it in your business. The person or company from whom you lease can in most cases claim the normal capital allowances.

New (and closing) businesses

You can get a capital allowance on all expenditure which qualifies, but you can't have more than one allowance on the same expenditure.

It becomes confusing working out capital allowances when you start (or close) a business, because some profits may be taxed twice and others not at all. But you get the allowances in the first tax year available (and not in the following tax year if the assessment is based on the same taxable profits).

If you've bought something in an accounting period and the profits for that period are *not* assessed for tax purposes, you get the allowance as if you had bought the equipment in the following accounting period. But if the following accounting year is the last year of the business (because you're closing it down), you get the allowance in the preceding year.

CAA 1968 s70–74.

Plant and machinery

You get a writing-down allowance of 25 per cent of the cost of the equipment for the accounting year in which you buy the capital equipment. The remainder of the cost (the **written-down value**) is added to your **pool of expenditure** at the start of the next accounting year. If you don't claim any of your writing-down allowance, all the cost will be added to the pool for the next accounting year. (If you claim only part of your writing-down allowance, see Example 3 for what happens.) Your **pool of expenditure** is the total written-down value of all the machinery and plant you've claimed capital allowances on in the past. Anything (including a car – see opposite) used partly for business, partly privately, has its own separate pool of expenditure. And from 1 April 1986, some plant and machinery can have its own pool – see *De-pooling* on p202.

You get the writing-down allowance on the value of each pool of expenditure at the end of each accounting year. You can normally claim up to 25 per cent of the value of each pool.

The pool is reduced by what you claim. If you sell something you have claimed capital allowances on, the proceeds (up to the original cost of the equipment) must be deducted from your pool of expenditure *before* working out your writing-down allowance for the accounting year in which you sell it. If the proceeds of sales come to more than the value of your pool, the difference (the **balancing charge**) is added to your profit.
CAA 1968 s18–19; FA 1971 s41, s42, s44; FA 1984 s58 Sch 12.

Example 3

Mary Worsley bought some machinery costing £1,000 in the 1987–88 tax year. She sees that she could claim a writing-down allowance of 25% – but she decides to claim only 20%. As she is claiming only 4/5 of the maximum allowance (i.e. 4/5 × £1,000 × 25% = £200), she adds the remaining expenditure of £1,000 – £200 = £800 to her pool of expenditure for the following year.

Computer software

The yearly writing-down allowance of 25 per cent for plant and machinery is normally available if the software is bought at the same time as computer hardware. But if software is bought separately from the hardware, you can either claim a capital allowance or treat it as a business expense.

Example 4

Herbert Hughes works out what he can claim in capital allowances for his accounting year ending on 30 April 1987. On 1 May 1986, his pool of expenditure was £16,784. In April 1987, he bought a computer costing £1,480. But he sold his old one (which he'd claimed capital allowances on) for £215. This left him with a pool of expenditure on 30 April 1987 of £16,784 – £215 = £16,569.

At the end of the year, Herbert claims a writing-down allowance of 25 per cent of £1,480 – ie £370. And he claims a writing-down allowance of 25 per cent of his pool of expenditure – ie 25 per cent of £16,569 = £4,142. The value of the pool of expenditure at the start of the next accounting year is £16,569 + £1,480 – £4,142 – £370 = £13,537.

Cars

As with plant and machinery, you can claim a writing-down allowance of up to 25 per cent for each year in which you own the car.

Cars bought after 31 May 1980 go into a separate pool of expenditure. In the main, cars bought before this go into your normal pool. And if the car was bought after 12 June 1979, and it costs more than £8,000, it will be dealt with separately – with a maximum writing-down allowance of £2,000 in any

one year. Lorries, vans and so on are treated like other machinery and plant.
FA 1971 s43, Sch 8 (10), (11); FA 1980 s69.

De-pooling

You can choose to have a separate pool of expenditure for any piece of plant and machinery (but not cars) which you buy on or after 1 April 1986, and which you expect to scrap or sell within five years. You must make this choice within two years of buying it.

If, when you sell the equipment, you sell it for less than its written-down value, you will be able to write off the difference in that year. If you sell it for more than the written-down value, the difference (the balancing charge) will be added to your profit. If you don't sell it in five years, its written-down value will be added to your main pool as if it had never been treated separately.
FA 1985 s57.

Table 3: Rates of capital allowance

asset on which capital allowances can be claimed	allowances		
	date	first-year/ initial	writing-down
plant and machinery – no definition by law – eg includes lifts and central heating, but not normal electrical wiring	from 1 April 1986	nil [1]	25% of written-down value of pool of expenditure at end of accounting year
cars		nil	25% of written-down value of pool of expenditure at end of accounting year
industrial buildings – eg factories, warehouses	from 1 April 1986	nil [2]	4% of original cost excluding land
agricultural buildings, such as farmhouses, farm and forestry buildings, cottages, fences, roads	from 1 April 1986	nil	4% of original cost excluding land
hotels or hotel extensions of 10 bedrooms or more which meet certain conditions	from 1 April 1986	nil	4% of original cost excluding land (unless in an enterprise zone)

asset on which capital allowances can be claimed	allowances		
	date	first-year/ initial	writing-down
buildings in enterprise zones, including factories, warehouses, shops and offices, and fixed plant or machinery in the buildings		100%	nil (but if you don't claim full first-year allowance you can get a writing-down allowance of up to 25% of original cost, starting the following year)
cost of buying a patent to use in business (not creating and registering your own patent)	from 1 April 1986	nil [3]	25% of written-down value of pool of expenditure at end of accounting year
know-how – ie any industrial information or techniques likely to assist in manufacturing, mining, agriculture, forestry or fishing	from 1 April 1986	nil [3]	25% of written-down value of pool of expenditure at end of accounting year
capital expenditure for the purposes of scientific research	from 1 April 1985	100% (but not land or houses)	nil

[1] From 1.4.85 to 31.3.86 you could claim a first year allowance of up to 50 per cent; from 15.3.84 to 31.3.85, allowance was up to 75 per cent and before 15.3.84, allowance was up to 100 per cent.

[2] From 1.4.85 to 31.3.86 first year allowance was up to 25 per cent; from 15.3.84 to 31.3.85, allowance was up to 50 per cent and before 15.3.84, allowance was up to 75 per cent.

[3] Before 1.4.86 you could claim a writing-down allowance of 1/17 of original cost with patents and 1/6 of original cost with know-how.

CAA 1968 s70–74; FA 1971 s41, s42, s44; FA 1985 s55–57, s59 (plant and machinery); FA 1971 s43, Sch 8 (10), (11); FA 1980 s69 (cars); CAA 1968 s1, s2, s7; FA 1980 s74, s75, Sch 13; FA 1982 s73; FA 1983 s30 (industrial buildings); CAA 1968 s68–69; FA 1978 s39; FA 1985 s59 (agricultural buildings); FA 1978 s38; FA 1985 s66 (hotels); FA 1980 s74–75, Sch 13; FA 1982 s73; FA 1983 s31 (other buildings); ICTA 1970 s378–386; CAA 1968 s90–92; FA 1985 s63–65 (patents, know-how, scientific research).

Losses

If you make a loss in your business there are several things you can do with it. Your choice depends on whether it is a new business, a business closing down, or one which has been going for a few years and which you don't intend to close.

Losses in an established business

Strictly speaking, with a loss in an accounting year which doesn't coincide with the tax year, you should apportion it to the correct tax years. In practice, your Tax Inspector will normally let you treat it as a loss for the tax year in which your accounting year ends.

You have three options about how you treat your loss:

Option A: set the loss against future profits from the same business. You start by setting the loss against profits in the same business in your following accounting year. Any losses left over can be carried to the year after, and so on.

The advantage of doing it this way is that it is relatively straightforward. The disadvantages are:
- the loss can only be set off against profits from the same trade
- there may be quite a time before the loss can be translated into a cash saving – see Example 6, opposite
- the whole loss has to be set off against the profits available which means you may not be able to take advantage of any outgoings or allowances you may be entitled to.

If you decide to set off losses in this way, you need to do so within six years after the end of the year in which you want the relief.
ICTA 1970 s171.

Option B: claim immediate relief. You can ask for the loss to be set off against any *other income* you have for the tax year in which your accounting year ends. This could include profits made in your *preceding* accounting year – because these profits will be counting as income for tax purposes in the current year. It could also include income received and taxable in the current year, such as earnings from a job, or dividends from shares.

If you ask for losses to be set off in this way, the whole of your losses have to be set off before you can set off any other outgoings or allowances you may have. So some of your outgoings and allowances may be unused because the losses could reduce your tax bill to zero. If you don't have enough income to cover your losses, you can carry forward the excess to the next tax year and get relief then against other income for that year – see Option C.

If you decide to set off losses in this way, you need to do so within two years after the end of the year in which you want the relief.
ICTA 1970 s168.

Option C: set the loss off against *other income* for the following tax year – eg earnings from a job, or dividends from shares. You can choose to do this rather than set losses off against other income in the same tax year, if you'd prefer it. You can't use Option C unless your business is still being carried on in the following tax year. If there are still any losses left over they can be carried forward, but not set against other income, only against income from the same business.

If you decide to set off losses in this way, you need to do so within two years after the end of the year in which you want the relief.

ICTA 1970 s168.

Example 5

Suppose you have other income of £10,000, and outgoings and allowances of £4,000. In this case your taxable income will be £6,000. If you have losses of £8,000, and ask for them to be set against other income, the whole of the £8,000 will be set off first against your other income, even though you only need £6,000 in losses to reduce your tax bill to zero. You will not be able to carry forward the remaining losses to the future, so you will have lost the benefit of £2,000 of outgoings and allowances.

Wife and husband

If both husband and wife have income, whoever makes the loss can choose whether or not to set it off against the other's income. This may mean that you don't waste allowances if you choose not to set the loss off against both incomes.

Example 6

Jessica Jones has a job as a part-time bookkeeper – she earns £10,000 a year. She has outgoings and allowances of £4,000 a year.

Jessica also runs a business on the side as a theatrical costumier. In the accounting year ending on 31 December 1986 her taxable profits were £10,000. But, in the following year, she makes a substantial loss of £20,000. Then, in the following years, she makes profits of £10,000 a year.

Her Tax Inspector allows Jessica to treat all the loss for the accounting year ending on 31 December 1987 as a loss for the 1987–88 tax year (strictly speaking he could insist that she splits the loss between tax years). As Jessica is taxed on a preceding year basis, she has no income from her business to be taxed in the 1988–89 tax year.

Jessica has to decide the best way of getting relief for her loss. She can set her loss off against future profits from her business (Option A); she can claim immediate relief against other income she has – ie from her job and income from her business for the preceding year (Option B); or she can set the loss off against other income of the next year (Option C). Here's how the options affect her tax bill:

	1987–88 tax year	1988–89 tax year	1989–90 tax year	1990–91 tax year
Income:				
business	£10,000	nil (loss of £20,000)	£10,000	£10,000
job	£10,000	£10,000	£10,000	£10,000
Option A	Setting off loss against future profits			
income [1]	£20,000	£10,000	£10,000 (from job)	£10,000 (from job)
allowances	£4,000	£4,000	£4,000	£4,000
tax to pay [2]	£4,320	£1,620	£1,620	£1,620
Option B	Claiming immediate relief against other income			
income [1]	nil	£10,000	£20,000	£20,000
allowances	*nil* [3]	£4,000	£4,000	£4,000
tax to pay [2]	**nil**	£1,620	£4,320	£4,320
Option C	Setting off loss against following tax year's other income			
income [1]	£20,000	nil	£10,000 (from job)	£20,000
allowances	£4,000	*nil* [3]	£4,000	£4,000
tax to pay [2]	£4,320	**nil**	£1,620	£4,320

[1] after setting off losses – for how losses can be set off, see previous page
[2] at 1987–88 rates
[3] with no income, Jessica's allowances can't be used

Although Option A would mean Jessica would pay less tax in total over the years, she decides that her best choice is Option B, claiming immediate relief. It cuts her tax bill at the time she makes the loss. Option A or Option C would mean waiting a long time to get relief, and – in this example – would mean £4,320 to pay in tax in the year in which she makes the loss.

Losses in a new business

If you make a loss in any of the first four tax years of your business, you can set it against other income (including earnings from a job) in the three years before the year in which the loss was made – and so get a rebate. You start by setting the loss off against the earliest year first. Note that you don't get this relief unless you can show that your business could reasonably have been expected to make profits in that period or within a reasonable time.

With losses in a new business you will have to apportion between tax years if your accounting year doesn't coincide with the tax year.

If you want to set off your losses in this way, you need to do so within two years after the year when the loss occurred. *FA 1978 s30.*

Losses in a closing business

If you're closing down a business which has made a loss in its final 12 months, you have two options. You can set the loss against profits from the same business in the three preceding tax years, starting with the latest year first. Or, you can set the loss against *other income* of the same tax year. If the loss is large enough, you can do both. Ask your Tax Inspector for more details.
ICTA 1970 s174.

Business abroad

It is no longer possible to escape tax on your business profits if you are abroad on business for part of the year. In 1984–85 and previous tax years, if you were resident in the UK and spent at least 30 days abroad, some of your profits were normally free of tax.

The cost of travel to and from the UK to carry on a business performed wholly outside the UK is an allowable business expense – provided any trips are exclusively for business purposes. And, provided you are working in the UK continuously for 60 days or more, the travel costs for up to two return visits a year from your spouse and each of your children may be allowed. These provisions are backdated to 6 April 1984. So you may be able to claim a rebate.
FA 1974 s23; FA 1978 s27, Sch4; FA 1984 s30; FA 1986 s34–36.

You as an employer

When you employ staff on a permanent basis you have several duties as an employer. These include:
- acting as a collector of taxes and deducting income tax and Class 1 National Insurance contributions from your employee's pay (assuming your employee earns more than a certain amount – £39 or more a week in the 1987–88 tax year)
- paying National Insurance as an employer – see Box overleaf for rates.

Your wife

If you employ your wife and she has no other earnings or pension, you can pay her up to £2,425 in the 1987–88 tax year before she has to pay any tax. But if she earns over a certain amount (£2,028 in the 1987–88 tax year) both of you will have to pay National Insurance contributions – see Box overleaf. Note that if your wife pays the reduced rate for married women she will pay 3.85% on her pay in 1987–88.

It can, though, be worthwhile to pay your wife considerably more than this if it pays to have her earnings taxed separately *and*, even then, you still pay tax at higher rates on the husband's earnings.

Your Tax Inspector will want evidence that your wife actually does the work she's paid for – and that she gets the money. He'll also need to be satisfied that her earnings are not above the market rate.

Your own National Insurance contributions

You will have to pay Class 2 National Insurance contributions (unless your earnings from self-employment will be less than £2,125 for 1987–88) and you may also have to pay Class 4 contributions depending on your earnings.

Class 2 contributions are payable each week. Class 2 is a flat rate payment of £3.85 a week for the 1987–88 tax year. You can pay it either by buying a special stamp each week from the Post Office and sticking it on to a contribution card or you can pay by direct debit. Paying Class 2 contributions entitles you to most contributory benefits, but not unemployment benefit, invalidity pension, widow's benefit or the earnings-related portion of the retirement pension.

Class 4 contributions are earnings-related and collected along with your tax payments. For the 1987–88 tax year the Class 4 contribution is 6.3 per cent of the amount by which your 'profit' exceeds £4,590 – up to a maximum contribution of £677.25. Your 'profit' for Class 4 purposes will normally be your taxable profit before deducting half your NI contributions – see below. But in certain situations you can make further deductions – see leaflet IR24. Paying Class 4 contributions doesn't entitle you to any benefits over and above those you get by paying Class 2.

You get tax relief on half the Class 4 contributions you pay.

There are special rules to prevent you paying more than a certain amount in all classes of NI contributions – see DHSS leaflet NP18.

National Insurance rates for employers

There's no National Insurance to pay on earnings below £39 a week. Above £39 rates are on a graduated scale. For earnings:
- from £39 up to £64.99 a week, 5% on all earnings
- from £65 up to £99.99 a week, 7% on all earnings
- from £100 up to £149.99 a week, 9% on all earnings
- from £150 a week, 10.45% on all earnings with no upper limit.

Note that rates are different where an employer runs a *contracted-out* pension scheme.

For employee rates, see p330.

Value added tax

The current rate of value added tax (VAT) is 15 per cent. There are some goods on which the rate is zero – most food, books, childrens' clothing, and transport, for example. And some goods are *exempt* – for example land, insurance, postage, education and so on (more details on p229). But if you buy any goods or services for your business, it's likely that on some of those things you will be paying VAT. If you are registered for VAT, you will be able to claim that tax back once every three months. By doing this, you are lowering your costs. However, you must add VAT on to all the bills you send out or sales you make if, of course, they are items on which VAT is payable at 15 per cent. By doing this you are increasing your selling prices, but not your income – because you have to hand over the VAT to HM Customs & Excise.

Handing over VAT on income you haven't yet received can cause cashflow problems. But, providing the EEC approves the scheme, it is proposed that from 1 October 1987 businesses with a yearly turnover below £250,000 will have the option of handing over VAT only on income actually received. As well as improving cashflow, it will be unnecessary to reclaim VAT on bad debts by including it in your claim for business expenses – see overleaf – because you will get this relief automatically.

Registering for VAT

At present, you have to register for VAT if your sales are likely to be more than £21,300 a year, (or £7,250 in a calendar quarter – but not if the yearly total from the start of the quarter comes to less than £21,300). Below these levels, you can choose whether or not to register. Your choice depends upon:
● how much you can cut your costs by claiming VAT back on things you buy for use in your business (which you can do if you register)
● whether your customers will be able to claim back VAT which you must add to your selling prices, and
● how tedious you find the record-keeping necessary to be registered for VAT.

Keeping records

If you are registered, you have to:
● give your customer a bill (and keep a copy yourself) which shows, among other things, your VAT registration number,

your name and address, the amount payable before VAT, the amount of VAT due. (If you're a shopkeeper and the bill, including VAT, is £50 or less, you needn't show all these)

● keep a VAT account in your books which shows the amount of VAT you are reclaiming and the amount of VAT you are handing over

● fill in a form (VAT return) every three months (normally) and send it to the VATman, showing what you are claiming and what you are handing over. A new scheme for yearly VAT returns instead of quarterly will be introduced in the summer of 1988. Only businesses which have been registered for VAT for at least a year, pay VAT regularly and have a yearly turnover of below £250,000 will be able to opt for a yearly return.

If you have charged more VAT on your sales than you can claim on your purchases, then you have to send the difference to the VAT Collector. If you can claim more on what you've bought than you can charge on what you have sold, the VAT Collector will pay you the difference.

Business expenses and capital allowances

If you *are not* a registered trader for VAT, include any VAT when claiming the cost of allowable business expenses. Also include VAT in the cost of any 'machinery or plant' on which you can claim a capital allowance.

If you *are* a registered trader for VAT, *don't* include VAT when claiming business expenses or capital allowances. However, you should include in your claim for expenses or capital allowances any VAT which you can't claim back through the normal VAT system – eg because it relates to part of your sales exempt from VAT.

But with cars (unless you're a car trader) and – usually – *bad debts*, include VAT in the cost you base your claim on for business expenses and capital allowances. The reason is that VAT on cars you buy can't be reclaimed (even if the expense is related to part of your business liable to VAT).

How companies are taxed

In this section we look at how a company's income will be taxed. Below and overleaf we look at the disadvantages and advantages of being self-employed or forming a company.

Tax on company profits

You pay **corporation tax** on a company's profits. If the company is UK-resident, corporation tax is payable on profits no matter where they are earned. Profits are worked out in much the same way as if you were self-employed, but all company income and gains from whatever source have to be included. If the company gets investment income, the gross amount is included (if tax has already been deducted, it can be set off against corporation tax). However, dividends or other distributions from UK-resident companies (called *franked investment income*) don't have to be included in your company's profits for tax purposes, because corporation tax has already been paid by the company distributing the dividend.

Any capital gains the company makes are included in its income for tax purposes.

If the company has to make any payments, such as royalty payments, where it has to deduct income tax before handing over the money, the amount of these payments is deducted from the company's income before arriving at the figure for profits liable to corporation tax.

ICTA 1970, s53, s54, s238, s243, s250, s265; FA 1972 s93, s104, Sch 20.

Advantages and disadvantages of being self-employed or forming a company

	self-employed	company
debts you owe	for money you owe there is full liability including personal assets – in the extreme you could be made bankrupt	your liability is limited to the amount unpaid on issued shares which you own. But as a director you may need to give personal guarantees to banks, suppliers, landlords and so on
starting-up	you can do it without formalities	it costs money to form a company, and you need at least two people (a director and a company secretary)
accounts	the form of accounts is not set out in detail by law – but they do need to show a *true and fair* picture	the form of accounts is laid down in detail by law
auditing	you don't need to get your accounts audited	you need to get your accounts audited and file them with the Registrar of Companies

	self-employed	company
national insurance (for you)	lower payments with some tax relief, but not eligible for some benefits	higher payments, especially for higher-paid employees earning over £150 a week – see p208
rates of tax	on taxable profits (ie the income you take out and the money you leave in the business), the rates of tax are up to 60 per cent	on salary, income tax rates of tax up to 60 per cent. On money left in business, corporation tax rates – see opposite
timing of tax payments	you can be paying tax on profits earned 20 months before	you pay tax nine months after profits are earned if money left in business; monthly tax – ie PAYE – for salary
losses	you can set off losses against future profits of the same trade or other income you may have in the year the loss happens or the year after – see p204	you can set off losses in one period against any profits of the same period (including capital gains); against profits of the previous period of the same length; or you can set the loss off against future profits
pensions	up to 17.5 per cent of before-tax earnings can be put in a pension scheme (higher limits apply for people aged over 50)	no limit on pension contributions free of tax if you are in a company scheme approved by the Inland Revenue
capital gains	you can get up to £6,600 free of tax each year	there is no exemption from tax on gains each year
finance	you can't raise finance through the Business Expansion Scheme – see p292	you can raise finance through the Business Expansion Scheme if your company is unquoted – see p292
selling part of business	it's difficult to do unless you take a partner or part of your business is easily separated	you can sell some of your shares. If company becomes quoted, you can sell in the stock market – but you will be liable for capital gains tax

Rates of corporation tax

The rate of corporation tax payable on a company's taxable income depends on the size of the profits. Below a certain amount you pay the *small companies rate*; above a certain amount you pay the full corporation tax rate. For *the financial year 1987* (running from 1 April 1987 to 31 March 1988), if profits are £100,000 or less you pay the small companies rate; if they're £500,000, or over, you pay the full corporation tax rate. If the profits of your company are between £100,000 and £500,000 you pay a rate of tax somewhere between the two.

Before the June 1987 election, the Government proposed that a company's capital gains should be taxed at corporation tax rates, rather than at the current rate of 30 per cent. This would mean that if you counted as a small company, capital gains would be charged at the small companies' rate.

To work out if you count as a small company for 1987–88, add:

● income on which corporation tax is payable; plus
● two thirds of capital gains; plus
● dividends and tax credits from UK-resident companies (ie franked investment income).

If the sum worked out above comes to more than £100,000 you won't be able to pay tax at the small companies rate. But if the figure is less than £500,000 you can still get some relief from the full rate. This is known as the *small companies relief fraction*. You deduct the amount of the company's profits (as worked out above for small companies rate) from £500,000 and multiply the answer by a stated amount – see Example 7 overleaf. This has the effect of reducing the amount of profits on which the full corporation tax rate is payable.
ICTA 1970 s243.

Table 4: Rates of tax from 1983 to 1987

financial year [1]:	1983	1984	1985	1986	1987
corporation tax rate	50%	45%	40%	35%	35%
small companies rate	30%	30%	30%	29%	27%
small companies relief fraction	1/20	3/80	1/40	3/200	1/50

[1] Financial years run from 1 April in one calendar year to 31 March in the following calendar year. So the 1987 financial year runs from 1 April 1987 to 31 March 1988.

Example 7

Lambert Lights has profits of £150,000, on which corporation tax is payable, in the 1987 financial year which runs from 1 April 1987 to 31 March 1988. If the company paid tax at the full corporation tax rate of 35 per cent, the tax bill would be £52,500. But Lambert will get some relief from the full rate, because the profits are less than £500,000 (but more than £100,000).

The relief is worked out by deducting the level of profits from £500,000, ie £500,000 − £150,000 = £350,000. Multiply this figure by the small companies relief fraction of 1/50, ie £350,000 × 1/50 = £7,000. This is deducted from £52,500 (ie the tax bill at the full corporation tax rate) and means there is tax to pay of £52,500 − £7,000 = £45,500.

If Lambert had capital gains or franked investment income, the tax bill would be slightly different. Suppose the company had franked investment income of £10,000 (ie dividends plus tax credits) in the 1987 financial year. The profit figure for small companies purposes would be £150,000 + £10,000 = £160,000. The small companies relief is:

$$(£500,000 - £160,000) \times \frac{£150,000}{£160,000} \times \frac{1}{50} = £6,375$$

Deducting this from £52,500 (ie the tax bill at the full corporation tax rate) means that there is tax to pay of £46,175.

When tax is due

Tax is worked out on a *current year basis* and is payable nine months after the end of the accounting period (which is not longer than 12 months), or 30 days after the date on the notice of assessment, whichever is later. If, however, your company was formed before April 1965, tax is payable on 1 January of the tax year after your accounting year-end – up to 21 months later. If you pay your tax late, you will have to pay interest – currently at 8.25 per cent.

The payment interval for all companies is to be standardised at nine months after the end of the accounting period for which it is due. This will be phased in over three years, beginning with a company's first accounting period starting on or after 17 March 1987.

Before the June 1987 election, the Government proposed the introduction of a new system called Pay and File. Companies would be required to pay corporation tax nine months after the end of an accounting period whether or not an assessment had been issued. At present, payment can be delayed by late submission of accounts so the assessment cannot be agreed on time.

ICTA 1970 s243, 244, 247; FA 1987 s36, Sch 6.

Paying dividends

When the company pays a dividend (either cash or in kind), it has to pay some corporation tax at the same time. So it is paying part of the corporation tax before it is normally due. This is called *advance corporation tax (ACT)*.

The current amount of ACT is as follows: **dividend** × 27/73 – ie £27 on a dividend of £73. As a result of paying this ACT, when a shareholder gets his dividend it is paid with a tax credit and no more basic rate tax is payable.

Note that if the company pays the dividend out of money it has received in dividends from another company (*franked investment income*), there is no ACT payable, but the shareholders still get the tax credit. If the dividend is paid partly out of other dividends received the ACT is reduced in proportion.

When it comes to working out the full corporation tax bill, after the accounting period, you can set off the amount of ACT you've paid, subject to certain rules. If you can't set it all off, then any *surplus* ACT can be carried back and set off against the tax bills for the six previous accounting periods (for accounting periods ending before 1 April 1984, you could only go back two accounting periods). You start with the latest period first.

FA 1972 s84–89, Sch 14; FA 1984 s52.

Making losses

If the company makes a loss in an accounting period, it can be set off against any profits of the same period (including capital gains); or carried back and set against the profits of the previous accounting period of the same length, but no further. You need to do either within two years from the end of the accounting period in which the loss was made. You can also carry the loss forward and set it against future profits.

Note that if, up to 31 March 1986, the loss includes first year capital allowances you have claimed on plant or machinery, you can carry back that part of the loss for three years.

ICTA 1970 s177–179; FA 1986 Sch 57.

Close companies

If there are five (or fewer) people controlling a company or it is controlled by its directors, it is likely to be a **close company**. The definition of who controls a company broadly means its shareholders and their family, their partners and the like.

Close companies have to meet certain requirements as well as the normal corporation tax rules. For example, a close company has to distribute a specified amount of its non-trading income, ie up to 50 per cent of net rents and income from woodlands, plus all other investment income after tax.

Details are complicated and you should ask your professional adviser.

ICTA 1970 s282–287A, s303; FA 1972 s94, Sch 16.

Tax-saving tips

- keep full and clear records. Get as many receipts as you can for your business expenses

- if you end your accounting year a little after the start of the tax year, there's a long gap between earning the profits and paying tax on them. This also increases the amount of profits which escape assessment when the business ends

- you don't have to claim all the capital allowances you're entitled to. It can pay you to claim less – ie if claiming them wouldn't reduce your tax bill for that year. You can carry the rest forward to next year

- beware of asking for losses to be set off against *other income* if they come to more than your taxable income for that tax year. You might waste some personal allowances and outgoings and it could mean more tax to pay in the future

- if your wife hasn't got a job consider employing her. She will get wife's earned income allowance to set against her earnings

- if you are a limited company, consider paying some dividends instead of a bigger salary – and save National Insurance contributions

- when you start a business, some profits may be assessed more than once. Try to plan your expenses to take advantage of this

- if you spend money before you start your business, ask for it to be treated as pre-trading expenditure and get loss relief

- if you are starting in business and using something you owned before – eg a car – take it into your accounts at its market value at the time you start using it in your business, and claim capital allowances on it.

16 PARTNERSHIPS

If you're already in a partnership, you may know it all already. But if you're not yet a partner, this chapter tells you the basic rules – including some of the extraordinary ways in which the tax on partnership income is worked out.

Basics

Partnership profits are worked out in the same way as profits for a trade or business. But when it comes to working out how much tax to pay on those profits, the rules can – in some cases – be strange:

- **Rule one:** all partners are *jointly and severally liable* for all tax on the profits from the partnership. Put into English, this means that if one partner doesn't pay up, the others can be made to pay up instead
- **Rule two:** rule one doesn't apply to the capital gains of a partnership, and it doesn't apply to non-trading income (eg interest from a bank deposit account). In these cases, each partner pays the tax on his share, and if he doesn't pay, the others don't have to
- **Rule three:** the amount of tax charged on the partnership profits depends on the rates of tax paid by the individual partners. For example, a partnership might have very modest profits – £2,000, say. But if one of the partners is paying tax at a top rate of 60 per cent, part of the profits (in normal cases) will be taxed at 60 per cent
- **Rule four:** When the taxman works out the bill on the partnership profits, he divides the profits between the partners in the same proportion as the partners themselves are sharing the profits in that tax year. So if the profits are £2,000, and there are two partners, sharing the profits equally, the £2,000 will be divided equally between them. If one partner pays tax at 27%, and the other at 60%, the tax bill on the profits will be 27% of £1,000 *plus* 60% of £1,000 = £270 *plus* £600 = £870
- **Rule five:** Partnership income is normally taxed on a preceding year basis – ie in any tax year, the partnership pays tax on the profits from its accounting period ending in the previous tax year

- **Rule six:** The way in which the tax on the partnership is worked out has nothing at all to do with how much tax the various partners actually pay. The partners can agree to pay the tax in any proportions they like.

The effect of rules four and five

Rule four is based on the division of profits in the current tax year. But the income taxed in that year will – because of rule five – be from an earlier year, and may have been divided quite differently.
ICTA 1970 s26.

Example 1

Alice, Barbara, and Caroline are in partnership. In the 1986–87 tax year, they decide to split the income of the partnership equally between them. But the income for the partnership is the profit for their accounting period ending in the *previous* tax year (ie the 1985–86 tax year). Those profits *weren't* shared on an equal basis. Alice took half the profits, and Barbara and Caroline took 25% each. The profits amounted to £30,000.

In the 1986–87 tax year, Alice pays tax at a top rate of 29% (the basic rate of tax for 1986–87). The other two both pay tax at a top rate of 60%. Here's how tax is calculated on the £30,000:

Total partnership profits for the 1986–87 year of assessment [1]   £30,000

partner	received	share [2]	equals	tax rate	tax
Alice	£15,000	one-third	£10,000	29%	£2,900
Barbara	£7,500	one-third	£10,000	60%	£6,000
Caroline	£7,500	one-third	£10,000	60%	£6,000
	£30,000		£30,000		£14,900

So the partnership has to pay £14,900 in tax.

[1] ie the profits from the accounting period ending in 1985–86
[2] Divided on the 1986–87 basis of sharing

It looks as though Alice has done very well – £2,900 in tax on her share of £15,000. But this may be totally false. Alice may in fact have paid very much more than £2,900 in tax. This is because of rule six.

A new partner

Each time a partner joins (or leaves) the partnership, the partnership can come to an end. In fact it *will* come to an end, unless everyone who was a partner before the change *and* everyone who is a partner after the change agrees that it should continue (technically, by making a *continuation election* to the taxman), *and* at least one of the partners before the change is still a partner after the change. If a partnership continues, the calculation of tax on partnership profits can be even more bizarre.

Example 2

Alice, Barbara and Caroline make a profit of only £9,000 in their 1986–87 accounting year. This is split equally between them (see Example 1), so they each get £3,000. They decide they need an injection of capital, and so a new partner, Daphne, joins them after the end of the 1986–87 accounting year. The arrangements are that Daphne will take two-thirds of the profits in 1987–88, and the other three will take one-ninth each. They all agree that the partnership should continue. The tax bill for the 1987–88 tax year is worked out on the profits for the accounting year ending in the 1986–87 tax year (rule five) and on the way the profits are shared in 1987–88 (rule four). So let's look at what happens to the tax bill on the £9,000. Alice, Barbara, and Caroline have a top rate of tax of 27% (the basic rate of tax for 1987–88). Daphne's top rate tax is 60%.

partner	received	share	equals	tax rate	tax
Alice	£3,000	one-ninth	£1,000	27%	£270
Barbara	£3,000	one-ninth	£1,000	27%	£270
Caroline	£3,000	one-ninth	£1,000	27%	£270
Daphne	nil	two-thirds	£6,000	60%	£3,600
	£9,000		£9,000		£4,410

So although Daphne actually received none of the £9,000, the tax on the partnership is worked out as though she received £6,000.
ICTA 1970 s154 (2).

If a partnership ceases

The same rules for opening and closing years apply to partnerships and to sole traders – see pages 188 and 191. But if the membership of the partnership changes (ie someone leaves or joins) and this results in the partnership being treated as coming to an end, special rules apply from 20 March 1985 onwards.

If all the partners before and after the change *do not* make a continuation election, the tax on the new partnership's profits will be assessed on a current year basis for the year of the change and the following three tax years. So the tax bills will be based on the actual profits earned each year. This will result in higher tax bills if profits are rising.
FA 1985 s47.

Losses

Partnerships have much the same options as individuals for dealing with losses – see p204. If a partnership makes a loss, the individual partners 'own' the losses in the same proportion as they would have actually received the profits. Carrying back of losses isn't allowed, except for a new partner. And carrying back isn't allowed if the new partner is married to an existing partner and the partnership continues.

Individual partners can treat losses in different ways – ie they don't all have to treat them in the same way. So, for example, one partner could set his or her losses against other income for the same tax year; another could carry them forward against future profits from the partnership.

Example 3

Suppose Example 2 is unchanged, except that the £9,000 profit becomes a £9,000 loss. Alice, Barbara and Caroline 'own' the losses in the same proportions as any profits would actually have been received: ie they each 'own' £3,000 of losses. They can each treat these losses in one of three ways:

● set them off against other income of the tax year in which the loss was made (ie the 1986–87 tax year in this Example)
● set them against future profits from the partnership
● set them against other income for the tax year in which the profits of the partnership (if there had been any) would have been taxed (ie the 1987–88 tax year in this Example).

There is no need for them to treat their losses all in the same way: each of them could use the losses in a different way from the other two.

Limited partners

For periods beginning after 19 March 1985, the amount of losses a limited partner can set against other income will be limited broadly to the amount of capital he has contributed to the business.

FA 1985 s48, Sch 12.

Pensions for partners

There are special rules where a pension is paid to a partner who has retired on the grounds of age or ill-health, or to the widow or dependant of a partner who has died. Briefly:

● take the partner's *actual profits* – ie what he or she actually declared in the Tax Return – for the last seven years in which he or she spent substantially the whole of his or her time in acting as a partner in that partnership (or in a collection of partnerships)
● separately for each year, multiply the profits by the Retail Price Index (RPI) for December in the final tax year and divide them by the RPI for December in the year in which the profits were charged to tax
● take the average of the three highest figures and divide by two.

The result is the maximum pension which counts as earned income. Payments above that limit are investment income. The payments reduce the partnership's income for tax purposes, but payments *within* the limit can't reduce the partnership's (or anyone else's) investment income.

FA 1974 s16 (3) (4).

17 SPARE-TIME INCOME

Many people who have jobs in their spare time don't realise that they almost certainly need to tell the taxman about the income they get. Nearly all income is taxable – and any taxable income must be declared to the taxman. This is true whether or not the income comes from your main business activity or employment.

This chapter tells you how income from spare-time work should be reported to the taxman, and how the taxman can find out about this income, even if you keep quiet about it.

Types of income

Read this list to see if you fit in anywhere. It contains the most common examples of how people get spare-time income:
● you have a second job in the evenings, or at weekends, completely different from your main job – eg working behind the bar at your local pub
● you're someone with a skill (eg electrician, plumber, carpenter, motor mechanic), and you normally work full-time for an employer. But you get spare-time income from doing work for other people – often for cash
● you're a professional person (eg school teacher, architect). Again, you use your professional skills and knowledge to get spare-time income – eg if you're a teacher, you may give private tuition, or mark examination papers for one of the examining boards
● you are married and your husband or wife has some spare-time income – eg commissions from running mail order catalogues or income from foreign students (both possibilities which the taxman has been looking at recently)
● you own a second home or a caravan which you let out; or you let rooms in your house.

The first three activities in the list are examples of what's often called *moonlighting*. The Inland Revenue are very concerned at how much of this goes on unknown to them. (They don't mind at all if they're told about it.) They're now making a concerted effort to track down the people involved and to tax them on the income they get from moonlighting.

Telling the taxman

If you get a Tax Return

If you get a Tax Return, you must list all your income on the Return. Where exactly on the form you need to show your spare-time income depends on what sort of income it is (eg from a second employer, or from renting out your house). If you're not sure where to show the income, don't worry too much: the important thing is for it to appear somewhere. The taxman can – if need be – transfer it to the right heading. Broadly speaking the income will probably fall under one of these headings:

- **income from employments**

If you get a wage or salary from your spare-time work (eg £20 a week for working in a chip shop in the evenings), enter the name and address of your employer and the amount of your earnings, including any tips, in the section of the Return dealing with employments. Enter any *allowable expenses* (see p143) separately

- **income from trades, professions or other business activities**

If your spare-time income comes from a trade or business (eg you put small ads in newsagents' windows saying that you decorate houses), use the section of the form dealing with trades, professions or vocations. Say what your trade or business is (eg painter and decorator), give the address from which you work (eg your home), and declare the amount of your profit for the tax year

- **income from lettings**

If you let property or rooms, you should show (in the section dealing with property) the gross rental income due for the tax year and all the expenses you're claiming

- **income from other activities**

If your income doesn't fit under any of the headings above, there's a special section of the Return which asks for details of any other income or profits. Enter full details of your income and expenses.

See Chapters 12 (p136) and 15 (p186) for details of the types of expenses which you can claim against your income.

If you don't get a Tax Return

If you don't get a Tax Return, you must still tell the taxman about your income within one year from the end of the tax year in which the income arose, eg income earned in August 1987 must be reported to the taxman by 5 April 1989 at the latest. If you fail to do this, the taxman can charge you a penalty of up to £100 – in addition to the tax due – when you eventually tell him about the income, or he finds out about it from other sources (see below). He will also charge you interest from the date on which the tax ought to have been paid to the date on which it is actually paid.

It is better to tell the taxman straight away about any income you have from spare-time activities. You will then be able to pay the tax as you go along and not be faced with a large bill for tax covering a number of years, plus interest and penalties. *TMA 1970 s7, s88; (see also p447)*

How the taxman can find out about your activities

- If you are employed, your employer should tell his tax office that you have started work, and should ask for a PAYE code number for you so that he can work out how much tax to deduct from your pay
- If your activities consist of a trade or business, or the letting of property, and you advertise in local or national papers, the Inland Revenue have a department which monitors these ads and checks to see that the income has been declared
- The Inland Revenue have wide powers to compel employers to send details of payments they make to freelance staff, consultants, caterers, etc – in short any people who do work for them
- The Revenue also get a number of letters from informants – some of them anonymous, and a few of them paid by the Revenue. What they say may or may not be taken seriously – but it may tie in with suspicions the Revenue already have, or it may alert them to taking an interest in your affairs.

Since the tax office can get to know of your income without your telling them, it makes it more important for you to report your income yourself. If the tax office starts an inquiry into your affairs as a result of information received (see *You and the Inland Revenue, p447*) the taxman is more likely to charge penalties in addition to the tax due than if you disclose your income voluntarily.
TMA 1970 Part III, Part X.

How will your income be taxed?

Income from spare-time activities can be taxed in a number of ways:
- under Schedule E if your income is from an employment
- under Schedule D Case I or II if it amounts to a trade or business
- under Schedule A if your income is from the letting of property. (It will normally be taxed under Schedule D Case VI if the property is let furnished, and under Schedule D Case I if your letting of furnished accommodation counts as a trade)
- under Schedule D Case VI if the income doesn't fit in anywhere else, or arises from activities which do not amount to a trade or business, and are not an employment – eg a casual commission. Income charged under this Case will almost always be taxed as investment income. If Case VI income is a married woman's (and is investment income), the income will count as her husband's for tax purposes, and the wife's earned income allowance can't be set against it.

For a more detailed explanation of the Schedules, see Chapter 3.

Why bother about the Schedules?

The most important reason is the type and level of expenses which you can claim. These differ from Schedule to Schedule. The rules for allowable expenses under Schedule E are more stringent than the rules under Schedule D Cases I and II. For example, the cost of travelling between your home and your place of work are not allowable under Schedule E. But if you're in business and work from your home, the cost of travelling to see your clients or customers is allowable under Schedule D Cases I and II. More details in *Working for an employer (p136)*, and in *Tax if you're self-employed (p186)*.

Note: the Inland Revenue are likely to say that teachers marking examination papers for a fee should be taxed under Schedule E.

18 VALUE ADDED TAX (VAT)

Most of the time we pay VAT without realising. It's only when we get a 'phone bill, or a garage bill, or some other bill where VAT is listed separately, that we notice the 15 per cent extra charge at the end. But VAT is the hidden element which bumps up the prices of a vast number of the things we buy – toothpaste, tampons, razor blades, clothes (except children's clothes), electrical goods, and so on.

This chapter gives a brief run-down of what VAT is, and how it's collected. If you're self-employed, it may be worth your while to apply to register for VAT, so that you can claim back VAT which you've paid to your suppliers, although, of course, you'll then have to charge VAT on your sales and invoices. (If your turnover is above certain limits, you *must* register for VAT – see p209). Sadly, the ordinary consumer can't claim back VAT.

How VAT works

As its name implies, VAT taxes the value added at each stage of production. Here's a simple example:

Stage one Alan is a sheep farmer and sells some wool to Boris, a coat manufacturer. He charges Boris £100 for the wool, and adds on 15 per cent VAT (ie £15). So Boris pays Alan £115.

Stage two Alan sends the £15 VAT to HM Customs & Excise. Boris *claims back* from Customs & Excise the £15 VAT he's paid to Alan.

Stage three Boris makes the wool into 20 coats and sells them to Clive, a retailer. He charges Clive £400 for the coats, and adds on 15 per cent VAT (ie £60). So Clive pays Boris £460.

Stage four Boris sends the £60 VAT to HM Customs & Excise. So Boris has (a) claimed back all the VAT he paid to Alan, and (b) paid to Customs & Excise all the VAT he's received from Clive. Clive *claims back* from Customs & Excise the £60 VAT he's paid Boris.

Stage five Clive sells the 20 coats to consumers. The price is £46 for each coat. This price *includes* VAT. Clive receives £46 × 20 = £920. The £920 is made up of £800 plus VAT at 15 per cent (ie £120).

Stage six Clive sends the £120 VAT to HM Customs & Excise. The consumers can't claim back the VAT they've paid.

What happens to Boris

Boris pays Alan £115, including £15 VAT.

Boris claims the VAT back from Customs & Excise

Clive pays Boris £460, including £60 VAT.

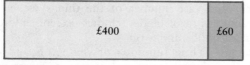

Boris pays the £60 VAT to Customs & Excise

So Boris has paid £15, claimed £15, received £60, and paid £60.

So at the end of it all, here's what's happened:

	VAT paid to supplier (input tax)	VAT claimed from Customs & Excise	VAT received from sale (output tax)	VAT paid to Customs & Excise	gain/ loss
Alan	nil	nil	£15	£15	nil
Boris	£15	£15	£60	£60	nil
Clive	£60	£60	£120	£120	nil
Consumer (one coat)	£6	nil	nil	nil	£6 loss

Input and output

In the Example, above, the second column is labelled *input tax*, and the fourth column is labelled *output tax*. Input tax is the tax you pay to a supplier; output tax is the tax you charge to your customer. If you're registered for VAT, you can reclaim input tax (as our Example shows). You have to hand over your output tax to Customs & Excise.

In practice there aren't so many transactions as in the Example above. Businesses keep accounts of their VAT – both input and output tax – and settle up with Customs & Excise every quarter (or, from the summer of 1988, yearly for some business – see p210). If output tax exceeds input tax, the business hands over the difference to the VATman; if input tax exceeds output, the VATman hands over the difference to the business.

Standard rate, zero-rate, and exempt

Most goods and services have VAT added to their cost at the *standard rate* of 15 per cent. But some goods and services are *zero-rated* – ie VAT is added to their cost at a rate of nil per cent (so there's no VAT to pay). Other goods and services are *exempt* from VAT.

The difference, for suppliers, between zero-rate and exempt, is that suppliers of zero-rated goods or services can claim back any VAT they've paid on the materials or services used to produce their end product. For example, books are zero-rated. So a publisher can claim back VAT on paper, authors' fees, typesetting costs, and so on. But if you supply only exempt goods or services, you can't claim VAT back.

You can register for VAT if you supply *standard-rated* or *zero-rated* goods and services. You can't register if all you supply are *exempt* goods or services.

Zero-rated

The main goods and services which are currently zero-rated include:

- **most food** – but VAT is payable on some items such as ice cream, confectionery, crisps, soft and alcoholic drinks, and pet food as well as meals in restaurants and hot take-away food and drink
- **books and newspapers** – but not advertisements in them
- **transport** – but not taxis
- **dispensing prescriptions**
- **young children's clothing and footwear**
- **some equipment for use by handicapped people and charities**
- **sales of new buildings and construction of most new buildings**
- **exports of goods**
- **water and sewerage supplies**
- **fuel and power** – but not petrol.

Exempt

The main goods and services which are currently exempt include:

- **insurance**
- **betting** (but not, for example, takings from gaming machines)
- **provision of credit**
- **certain education and training**

- services of doctors, dentists, opticians (but not, for example, osteopaths)
- certain supplies by undertakers
- membership benefits provided by trade unions and professional bodies
- land.

Home improvements

This was, until June 1984, a very grey area for VAT, as certain work – such as the installation of double-glazing – was zero-rated. VAT must now be paid on all work done to existing buildings except certain work done to help the disabled or handicapped – eg providing ramps, or installing a ground floor bathroom. Approved alterations done to most listed buildings are also zero-rated. Construction and demolition (of complete buildings) remains zero-rated. If you build a detached garage in your garden – although you might consider this construction of a complete building – you will have to pay VAT on the materials and labour unless it is constructed at the same time as your house.

For more information about VAT contact your local VAT office. (Look in your telephone directory under 'Customs & Excise'.)

19 TAX AND DOMESTIC STAFF

If you employ someone, it's your responsibility to collect income tax and National Insurance contributions from them under the PAYE system – assuming that the amount of pay the employee gets will mean that tax and National Insurance are payable. This chapter tells you how to collect the money if you are employing someone in the home – eg housekeeper, nanny and so on. If you employ someone foreign who has been living abroad, your employee will probably be taxed in the same way.

Another duty you have as an employer is to give your employee a pay slip. This should show the amount of pay and the amount of the deductions.

When you first employ someone

If you pay £46.50 or more a week (£202 or more per month) in the 1987–88 tax year, write to the local Tax Inspector (look up *Inland Revenue* in the 'phone book) and tell him:
- your employee's full name, type of work, National Insurance number and address
- the date your employee will start work, the amount of pay and if it's to be paid weekly or monthly
- the name and address of the previous employer (if any).

You should also let your local DHSS office know.

The forms you get

You will be sent:
- **P12 – Simplified Deduction Card** (see overleaf). This is where you will record all the details of pay and deductions
- **P16 – Simplified Tax Tables** These can be used for an employee who is paid a fixed amount each week or month. The tables show how much tax you need to deduct for different levels of taxable pay
- **P37 – Employer's Annual Declaration and Certificate** You will be sent this at the end of each tax year (ie 5 April). You need to fill this in and send it to the Collector of Taxes, plus the Simplified Deduction Card, by 19 April
- **CF391 – Contribution Tables** These show the amounts of employee's and employer's National Insurance contributions.

The first three are sent by the local tax office; the last by the local DHSS office.

1987-88 Simplified Deduction Card

Employee's National Insurance No.	YM 34 67 26 C
Employee's date of birth in figures — Day	13
Month	8
Year	1965
Enter here 'M' if male 'F' if female	F
Nature of employment	NANNY
Employee's Surname in CAPITAL LETTERS	ANTHONY
First two forenames	JANE EMMA
Employee's private address	32 GARDEN ROAD, HAYWARDS HEATH, SUSSEX
Tax District and reference	BRIGHTON 4
Employer's name and address	ELIZABETH JONES, 32 GARDEN ROAD, HAYWARDS HEATH, SUSSEX
Code	242 L
Free Pay	£202.42 per week/month *Delete as necessary

National Insurance Contributions

Earnings on which employee's contributions payable (1a)	Total of employee's and employer's contributions payable (1b)	Employee's contributions payable (1c)	Statutory Sick Pay in the week or month included in Column 2 (1d)	Statutory Maternity Pay in the week or month included in Column 2 (1e)	Pay Day	Total pay in the week or month including Statutory Sick Pay/Statutory Maternity Pay (2)	Free pay in the week or month (3)	Taxable pay in the week or month (4)	Tax deducted in the week or month (5)
£	£	£	£	£		£	£	£	£
25.00	12.50	—	—	—	30 APRIL	250.00	202.42	47.58	12.69

NI Letter
†When you make the first entry on the card or when there is a change of table letter enter letter showing contribution table you have used.

NI Totals
Enter in columns 1a, 1b and 1c separate totals for each table used.

†N.I. Cont'n Table Letter ►

TOTALS for quarter ending 5 JULY 1987 ▲

How to fill in the simplified deduction card

Code

The Tax Inspector will write in your employee's code – this will show the amount of allowances your employee is entitled to.

Free pay

The Tax Inspector will write in the amount of free pay which your employee is entitled to each week or month – depending on how often your employee is paid. Use this figure in Column 3.

NI Contributions – 1a, 1b, 1c

For the 1987–88 tax year, if the pay figure entered in Column 2 is £39 or more in any week (£169 or more in any month), look up the amount of your employee's contributions and your contributions as an employer in the tables you get from the DHSS.

Statutory Sick Pay or Statutory Maternity Pay – 1d, 1e

If you've paid your employee any Statutory Sick or Maternity Pay since the last pay day, enter the gross amount here. Also include that amount in pay and enter it in Column 2.

Pay day

Enter the date on which the payment is actually made.

Total pay – 2

Enter the full amount of pay before any deductions (eg National Insurance contributions), but including any sick pay or maternity pay under the statutory schemes.

Free pay – 3

Enter the amount of free pay shown on the left hand side of the card.

Taxable pay – 4

Deduct the amount in Column 3 (free pay) from the amount in Column 2 (total pay) and put the difference in Column 4 – this is your employee's taxable pay.

Tax deducted – 5

Turn to the Simplified Tax Table and look in the column headed 'Taxable Pay' for the figure you have just entered in Column 4. If the exact figure is not shown in the Table, take the next smaller figure. Then look in the column to the right, headed 'Tax Deduction' and find the tax to be deducted. Put this figure in Column 5. Deduct this amount (plus the amount of the employee's National Insurance contributions – Column 1b) from your employee's pay.

> **Board and lodging**
> There's no tax for the employee to pay if living accommodation is provided, as long as the job is one in which accommodation is normally available – eg nanny, nurse, housekeeper. And there's no tax to pay on free or cheap meals if they're provided to all employees you may have.

Paying tax

You have to pay the Collector of Taxes at the end of each quarter (ie 5 July, 5 October and so on) the amount deducted in tax from your employee's pay, and the amount of National Insurance contributions due from you and your employee.

If, during the quarter, you have paid any Statutory Sick Pay or Statutory Maternity Pay, you can deduct this amount from the National Insurance contributions.

When an employee leaves

You should fill up the Simplified Deduction Card up to the date of leaving and send what's due in tax and NI contributions to the Collector of Taxes, together with the completed Deduction Card. If you know the name and address of the new employer, you should fill that in the space provided for it on the Card. Note that you don't need to give your employee a form P45 (which shows earnings and tax to date – see p155).

> **Leaflets**
> P7 – Employer's Guide to PAYE
> NI227 – Employer's Guide to Statutory Sick Pay
> NI257 – Employer's Guide to Statutory Maternity Pay
> NP15 – Employer's Guide to National Insurance Contributions

20 HOMES AND LAND

Tax relief for buying your home

Buying a home is by far the largest transaction most people enter into, and few can afford to pay for their home outright. Even if they can afford to, the availability of tax relief on loan interest can make borrowing a sensible choice. Tax relief means that an interest rate of, say, 11 per cent costs a basic rate taxpayer only 8 per cent, a higher rate taxpayer even less. See Example 1.

In general, you can get tax relief on the interest you pay on up to £30,000 of loans used to buy your home or spent on improving it. The remainder of this section gives the detailed rules about tax relief.

> **Example 1**
> Diana Scott is buying her flat with a £30,000 endowment mortgage from her building society. Without tax relief, the interest charged this year would be £3,300. With tax relief, the cost to her is only £2,409, a saving of £891.

More than one home

If you have more than one home, you get tax relief only on loans used to buy your *main* home. In most cases, this is the one you in fact live in most of the time.

You can be away from this home for up to a year at a time and still get tax relief, and you can be away for longer if your employer requires you to live elsewhere, or if you live in a home which counts as a tax-free fringe benefit, or if you're self-employed and have to live in accommodation provided under the terms of your business – see *Your home and your work* on p253.

You can get tax relief on interest you pay on a loan used to buy or improve a home which is *not* your main home only if it is used as the only or main home of your former or separated wife or husband or a dependent relative. 'Dependent relative' means any of your (or your wife's) relatives who cannot look after themselves because of permanent illness, disablement, or old age. ('Old age' means being 64 or over by the start of the tax year.) It also includes your mother or mother-in-law if she is widowed, separated or divorced, whatever her age or state of health. The relative mustn't pay you any rent for living in the home but can contribute to certain outgoings, such as rates. *FA 1972 Sch 9 para 1; FA 1974 Sch 1 para 4; ESC A27 (absences).*

Example 2
John Hedges is buying his own home with a mortgage from his bank, and in 1987 (when his loan stood at £20,000) he got a building society loan to buy a home for his widowed mother. Both loans qualify for tax relief – but see Example 4 for how much tax relief he gets.

If you're separating
See p100 for what tax relief you qualify for if you're separating from your husband or wife, and how mortgage payments can be made most effectively after separation.

How much tax relief?

You get tax relief on the interest you pay on the first £30,000 of loans you take out. You can get tax relief on more than one home – eg the one you live in and the one your ex-wife lives in. But the £30,000 limit applies to the total amount you pay interest on. Before 6 April 1983, this limit was £25,000.

If you have a loan of over £30,000, you get tax relief on the interest you pay on £30,000 only – see Example 3.

If you have more than one loan which qualifies for tax relief (whether on one home or more than one) and the amount owing on them is more than £30,000, you get tax relief on what you owe on the earliest loans first – see Example 4.

Example 3

Richard Powell got a mortgage of £42,000 to buy his home in 1983, and he now owes £40,000. In the 1987–88 tax year he is charged £4,400 interest, and he gets tax relief on $\frac{30,000}{40,000} = \frac{3}{4}$ of this – ie on £3,300. If he pays tax at the basic rate only, his tax relief will be 27% of £3,300 = £891, so the cost of the interest to him will be £4,400 − £891 = £3,509.

Example 4

In 1987, John Hedges buys a home for his widowed mother with a £15,000 mortgage. He gets tax relief on the whole of the interest he pays on the £20,000 loan outstanding on his own home. This leaves £30,000 − £20,000 = £10,000 of available relief, so he gets tax relief on $\frac{£10,000}{£15,000} = \frac{2}{3}$ of the interest he pays on the loan on his mother's home. Strictly, he should be allowed tax relief on only 2/3 of the interest he pays in future years, but may be allowed relief on a larger fraction as the amount he owes falls.

Example 5

Miles Long and Tina Short jointly own the home they live in, which they bought with a £60,000 mortgage. They pay half the interest each – ie they each pay interest on £30,000. As both are single, they each get tax relief on all the interest they pay.

   Note that if Miles paid two-thirds of the interest (ie on £40,000), and Tina one-third (ie on £20,000), things would be different. Tina would get tax relief on all her interest, but Miles would get tax relief on only £30,000 of the loan – ie on 3/4 of his interest.

If you take out more than one loan on the same day, they are treated as a single loan. If you're taking out two loans which total more than £30,000 (eg a building society mortgage and a more expensive top-up loan) try to arrange things so that you take out the more expensive loan at least a day before the cheaper loan. You'll then get tax relief on more of the total interest you pay.

For a married couple, the £30,000 limit applies to the total borrowed between them. But anyone who is single, widowed, separated or divorced has their own £30,000 limit. This applies even if two (or more) single people each pay interest on a loan on a jointly-owned home which each uses as their only or main home – see Example 5.

If you get married and you each have a home with a mortgage, see p74 for the special concessions.

You can normally get tax relief on the interest you pay on a loan you use to buy or improve a home which you let. The

£30,000 limit does *not* apply to these loans. See p256 for details of letting property.

If at some time in the past you didn't pay all the interest which was due and it has been added to what you owe the lender, it doesn't count towards the £30,000 limit if the amount is £1,000 or less. If it's more than £1,000 the full amount counts.

FA 1974 Sch 1 para 5; FA 1982 s25(2).

Example 6

Bill and Linda Adams sold their London flat for £60,000 and paid off the £15,000 owing on their mortgage. Their new home in Norfolk is costing them £50,000, and their moving expenses total nearly £5,000. They have £60,000 − £15,000 − £5,000 = £40,000 to pay towards their new home, so only need a loan of £10,000. But they decide to get a £30,000 mortgage and keep the extra £20,000. They will get tax relief on the interest on the whole £30,000.

Which loans qualify for relief?

Interest on a loan qualifies for tax relief only if you spend the money you borrow on:
- buying the home; or
- buying an *interest* in the home (eg buying a half share, or buying out someone else's stake); or
- improving a home in which you have (or are buying) an interest (for what count as improvements, see opposite).

Part of the loan can be spent on the costs of acquiring the property – eg solicitor's fees, surveyor's fees, stamp duty, removal costs. The loan doesn't have to be secured on the home you're buying. Nor does it matter if you have other savings or made a profit on your previous home which made it unnecessary for you to borrow – see Example 6. But you can't get tax relief by arranging an artificial transfer of the property (eg between a husband and wife who aren't separated) or selling to an accomplice at an inflated price in the hope of getting tax relief.

The interval between getting the loan and acquiring the interest in the property must not normally be more than six months (it doesn't matter which comes first). If you get the money before acquiring the interest in the home, you mustn't spend it on anything in the meantime, though you can place it on deposit and get interest. If interest becomes payable on the loan in this period, you can claim tax relief on it when the purchase is completed. You can also claim tax relief on interest you've paid to the vendor because you haven't paid the full price, or because you moved in, before completion.

If you pay off a qualifying loan (or part of it) and, within six months, replace it with another loan on the same property, you get tax relief on the interest you pay on the new loan. But if the new loan is bigger than the amount you paid off, you don't get any relief on the interest you pay on the excess (unless the new loan is taken out within six months of buying the home, or you spend the extra money on something else which qualifies – eg improving the home). It doesn't matter if the loan you pay off was interest-free. See Example 7.

You can't get tax relief on a loan which has to be repaid within 12 months of being taken out – unless the interest is paid in the UK to a bank, stockbroker or discount house. Nor is there any relief on a bank overdraft or a credit card debt (except as a business expense) though you can get relief if you convert to another type of loan within twelve months.
FA 1972 s75(1), (1A); FA 1972 Sch 9 paras 1, 2, 8, 14; IR 11 paras 10–18.

Example 7

In 1980, Michael Davies was given an interest-free loan by his employer to buy his home. When he left the job in May 1987, he had to repay the £20,000 still owing, and got a mortgage of £25,000 from his bank. At the same time he had the house re-wired at a cost of £2,000. So he gets tax relief on £20,000 + £2,000 = £22,000 of his new mortgage, but not on the remaining £3,000.

Over 65?

If you are 65 or over, in addition to the £30,000 loans on which you can get tax relief described here, you can get tax relief on a further £30,000 of loans you take out to buy an annuity. The loan *must* be secured on your only or main home. A *home income plan* is an off-the-peg scheme which combines loan and annuity. For more about annuities and home income plans, see Chapter 26, p323.

Which homes qualify?

The home must be in the UK or Republic of Ireland. It can be freehold or leasehold. A caravan or mobile home can qualify if it is more than 22 feet long (excluding any drawbar) *or* more than 7½ feet wide *or* if you have to pay rates on it as the occupier. A houseboat can also qualify if it has been designed or adapted for living in.
FA 1972 Sch 9, paras 1, 5, 5A, 9.

What counts as improving a home?

Improvements cover all permanent alterations and

improvements to a building or land. This includes putting up a new building, extending the home, converting the loft, installing central heating (but not portable radiators or night storage heaters), installing double glazing (even if it's detachable), roof or wall insulation, installing fitted furniture, converting a house into flats, connecting to main drainage, building a garage, shed or greenhouse, landscaping gardens and building a swimming pool. It also includes making up a road adjoining or serving the property (including money paid to a local authority for making up a private road being adopted). It doesn't matter if you already have central heating, fitted cupboards or whatever, as long as you are having new ones installed, not just repairing the old ones.

A loan which you use to pay for a number of smaller improvements can also qualify for tax relief – for example, installing a hot water system or ring main, converting to smokeless fuel.

In certain cases, a loan raised to cover other major expenditure may qualify for tax relief. Possible cases are re-tiling or rebuilding a roof, underpinning a house, rebuilding a façade, installing or renewing a damp proof course, and rewiring. Whether works like these can count as improvements (rather than repairs) depends on the exact amount of work to be undertaken in each case, the current condition of the building, and so on. Check with your Tax Inspector.

Ordinary repairs and decoration don't in themselves qualify for tax relief, except in the following two cases:
• if you bought the property in a dilapidated condition, you can get tax relief on a loan for repairs resulting from its condition
• if you're getting a loan to pay mainly for improvements, it doesn't matter if a small part is spent on redecoration or repairs.

A loan used to buy things which you could take with you when you move (eg fitted carpets), can't qualify for tax relief.
FA 1972 Sch 9, paras 3, 4, 9; IR 11 paras 21–23 and Appendices A, B.

Moving home

If you have to take out a loan (eg a mortgage or a bridging loan) on the house you are buying before you've sold your old home, the loan on the old home is ignored when working out how much tax relief you're entitled to on the new loan. And for 12 months (longer in deserving cases) you can get tax relief on both loans. It doesn't matter which of the two homes you live in for these 12 months.

If you moved home before 6 April 1984, and had a loan of over £30,000 on your old home (over £25,000 before 6 April 1983) you could get tax relief on the full amount of the loan from the time you moved out until the time you sold it, or until 5 April 1984 if earlier (subject to the 12-month rule). If you are in this position and your relief was restricted to £25,000 or £30,000, you can claim a rebate.

FA 1974 Sch 1 paras 4 and 6; FA 1984 s22; IR Press Release 29 March 1984.

Example 8

Ian and Sandra Walters buy their new home with a £40,000 mortgage, before they've sold their old one. Although they have a £30,000 mortgage on the old home, they'll carry on getting tax relief on the interest on it for up to a year, and will get relief on the interest they pay on £30,000 of their new loan as well.

How you get tax relief

Basic rate tax relief is given on most loans by the borrower paying a reduced amount to the lender under the system known as MIRAS (Mortgage Interest Relief At Source). You get this 'tax relief' even if you pay little or no tax. The government pays the difference between the net amount you've paid and the gross amount direct to the lender. You'll get any relief from higher rate tax you're entitled to through your PAYE coding or in your tax assessment. For example, if over the tax year you pay £730 interest under MIRAS, this is taken to be a gross amount of £1,000 on which you've had 27 per cent tax relief. If your top rate of tax is 50 per cent, say, on at least £1,000 of your income, you're entitled to another 23 per cent relief on this gross amount. So you should pay 23 per cent of £1,000 = £230 less tax, and the actual cost to you is only £730 − £230 = £500. See Diagram overleaf.

Most lenders have government approval to operate MIRAS, but a few don't. If your lender is not in the MIRAS scheme you'll have to pay the gross amount to the lender and claim the relief you're entitled to from the taxman. You'll then get the tax relief in your PAYE coding or by getting a lower tax bill.

With a loan which takes you over the £30,000 limit, some lenders used to ask you to pay the gross amount on the whole loan and claim tax relief through your PAYE coding or tax bill. Others calculated your payment so that you paid the correct net amount of interest on the first £30,000 of the loan and the gross amount on the rest. Since 6 April 1987, lenders have had to apply the second method to all new loans above the limit which qualify for tax relief.

FA 1972 s75(1); FA 1982 s26; SI 1982/1236; FA 1985 s37.

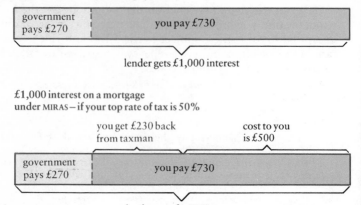

£1,000 interest on a mortgage under MIRAS — basic rate taxpayer

government pays £270	you pay £730

lender gets £1,000 interest

£1,000 interest on a mortgage under MIRAS — if your top rate of tax is 50%

you get £230 back from taxman · cost to you is £500

government pays £270	you pay £730

lender gets £1,000 interest

Claiming the relief

If your loan comes under MIRAS, the forms you fill in when you get the loan will entitle you to get your basic rate tax relief by making reduced payments. The lender will tell you the net amount to pay. If the loan doesn't come under MIRAS, or you need to claim higher rate tax relief, get a *Certificate of Interest Paid* from the lender at the end of each tax year and send it to your Tax Inspector.

Your home and capital gains tax

Any gain you make when you sell your home is normally exempt from capital gains tax. Exceptions are listed on p244. Any gains on other homes or land you own will normally be liable to capital gains tax (but see p244 for a home occupied by a dependent relative).

A married couple can get exemption on only one home. But a couple who are unmarried or separated can get exemption on one home each. See p102 for the position where a home is transferred between a couple who have separated.

A 'home' means a freehold or leasehold house, flat or maisonette. A caravan or a houseboat won't normally be liable to capital gains tax, whatever the circumstances (though the land on which a caravan stands won't be exempt unless you can show that the caravan was your only or main home for the whole time you owned the land).

For general details of capital gains tax (including how the indexation rules are applied), see Chapter 32, p415.
CGTA 1979 s101, s102(1).

More than one home

If you have two or more homes it's only your 'main' home which is exempt from capital gains tax. You can choose which home you want to be regarded as your main one – it doesn't have to be the one you spend most time at, though in most cases you must live in it at some stage. And it needn't be the one with a mortgage you get tax relief on. It's best to nominate the one on which you think you'll make the largest *taxable gain* (see p416 for what this means).

Make your choice by writing to the taxman within two years of acquiring the second home. You can alter the choice at any time, simply by telling the taxman. Your new choice can be backdated by up to two years. A married couple must both sign these letters, unless all the homes are owned by one of you.

If you don't tell the taxman within the two-year period which is your 'main' home, the taxman can decide for you. If his decision doesn't suit you, you can appeal within 30 days but you will have to prove that the home selected is *not* in fact your 'main' home.

If you live mainly in a rented home – or in one which goes with your job (eg as a caretaker or clergyman) – but also own

---

The two year limit

The two year period for telling the taxman which home is your 'main home' for CGT may be extended in certain circumstances. This may be the case, if you hadn't realised that you had to nominate a home, *and* all the homes – or all but one of them – are of negligible capital value to you (eg a weekly rented flat or accommodation provided by your employer). *(ESC D21.)*

a home where you spend some of your time or intend to live eventually, it is vital that you nominate the one you *own* as your main home. If this has applied for more than two years the taxman may accept a late request – see Box on previous page.
CGTA 1979 s101(5); SP D8.

Dependent relative

A home will normally be exempt from CGT for the period in which it has been occupied by a dependent relative. This means any of your relatives (or your wife's) who can't look after themselves because of permanent illness, disablement or old age ('old age' means being 64 or over by the start of the tax year). It also includes your mother or mother-in-law (whatever her age or state of health) if she is widowed, separated or divorced. The relative must not have given you the home, nor must they pay you any rent or perform any services for you as a condition of living there. But they can pay certain costs relating to the home, such as part or all of the rates, or the cost of repairs for normal wear and tear. Only one such home qualifies at any one time (even for a married couple), and if it's leasehold, *you* must pay any ground rent and maintenance charges.
CGTA 1979 s105; ESC D20.

When your only or main home isn't exempt

You may not get full exemption from capital gains tax on your only or 'main' home in any of the following cases:
- the home wasn't your main one for capital gains tax purposes for all the time you owned it
- you lived away from the home
- you let all or part of the home out
- you used part exclusively for work
- you converted it into self-contained flats and then sold them
- you built a second home in your garden and then sold it off
- you sold the house on its own, and the land around it afterwards
- the garden (including the house area) is bigger than one acre
- the home is one of a series of homes you bought, or spent money on, with the object of making a profit.

The detailed rules are given in the next three pages (except that aspects to do with your work are covered on p249 and property you let is covered on p260). In many cases, only *part* of the gain you make when you sell your only or 'main' home will be taxable – see p247.
CGTA 1979 s101–103.

If you have lived away from your only or 'main' home

The capital gain you are assumed to have made during periods when you were living away from your only or main home will normally be taxable. For example, if you have lived away from the home for 7 years out of the 15 you owned it, 7/15 of the gain you made would be taxable. But there are six situations in which absence from the property are ignored:

- **Before 6 April 1965** Any absence before 6 April 1965 will not affect exemption from capital gains tax.
- **The first year** If you can't move into your new home straight away because you're having a new home built on a plot you've bought, or because you're having the home altered or redecorated, or because you can't sell your old home, you will still get exemption from capital gains tax for up to a year (longer if there's a good reason). You must live in the home straight afterwards.
- **If you live in job-related accommodation** A home which you (or your husband or wife) own and which you intend to live in one day, can be exempt from capital gains tax while you are living in a home which goes with your job, or are self-employed and have to live in accommodation provided under the terms of your business – see *Your home and your work* on p249.
- **Because of your work** Certain periods when you have to be away from home because of your job are exempt – see p250.
- **The last two years** Any absences in the last two years before you dispose of a home which has been your only or main home at some time are always exempt. It doesn't matter why you're away, or if you have another home which you've nominated as your main home during this period. If you're away for more than two years before you sell, the gain for the excess over two years won't be exempt unless one of the other exemptions applies.
- **Any other absences** for any reason totalling up to three years will not affect exemption, as long as you use the home as your main one for a time both before the first such period and after the last one.

Except in the first year or last two years, you can't get the exemptions above if any other home of yours is exempt. None of the exemptions above is lost if you let the home while you're away.
CGTA 1979 s102; SP D4.

If you divide the property, or change its use

Exemption from capital gains tax for your only or main home is likely to be partly lost if you divide up the property or use part of it for something other than living in. For example, if you convert part of your home into self-contained flats, part of the gains you make when you sell the flats would not be exempt (see *Working out the taxable gain*, opposite). If you build a second home in your garden, the gain you make when you sell it would not be wholly exempt. If you use part of the property exclusively for a trade or business or some other non-residential use, you may also lose exemption on that part. The amount of the gain which is not exempt is whatever the Commissioners (see p457) consider to be just and reasonable, but will normally be based on the proportion of the property affected. For example, if you bought a home for £37,000 (after deducting buying costs) and spent £8,000 having part of it done up to sell, the cost of acquiring the whole home is taken to be £37,000 + £8,000 = £45,000. If you sell part for £40,000 when the whole home is worth £90,000, the cost of acquiring the part you sell is taken to be 4/9 of £45,000 = £20,000. So the gain (before allowing for selling costs or indexation) on the part you sell would be £45,000 – £20,000 = £25,000. Not all this gain is taxable. The taxable amount is the gain *less* what the Commissioners reckon your gain would have been (on that part) if you hadn't spent money improving the property. So if, without the additional expense, the gain would have been £15,000, the taxable part is £20,000 *less* £15,000 = £5,000.

If what you get for part of a property is no more than £20,000 (£10,000 before 6 April 1983) and its market value is not more than 20 per cent (5 per cent before 6 April 1986) of the value of the whole property, you can elect for the sale not to be treated as a disposal until you sell the rest of the property.

CGTA 1979 s35, s103(2), s107–108; FA 1986 s60.

Your garden

The garden of your main home is not normally liable to capital gains tax even if you sell off part of it while you still own the home. But if it's over one acre, the gain on the excess will not be exempt unless the taxman considers that a larger garden is appropriate for that house.

If you sell the home and retain some of the land, the gain you make on the land from the time when it stopped being part of your garden may be liable to capital gains tax.

CGTA 1979 s101(1)–(4); Varty v. Lynes, 1976 3 All ER p447.

The profit motive

If there is evidence that you bought your home wholly or partly with the object of selling it at a profit, you get no exemption from capital gains tax – even though it was your (or a dependent relative's) only or main home. Of course, it's not easy to prove what was in your mind when you bought it, but if you moved frequently from house to house – buying them in a derelict state and improving them, say – it would look as though your main aim was profit. The taxman might even class you as a property-dealer, and tax your gain as if it were income.

If you make major changes to your home (such as converting it into flats, buying the freehold if it's leasehold) *in order to increase the price you get for it*, the *extra* gain you make may not be exempt.

CGTA 1979 s103(3); ICTA 1970 s108.

> **Compulsory purchase**
> If part of your property is compulsorily purchased, special rules apply for working out any capital gains tax bill.
> *CGTA 1979 s110; IR booklet CGT8 para 117.*

Working out the taxable gain

In many cases, only *part* of the gain you make when you sell your home will be taxable. For example, capital gains tax came into effect on 6 April 1965, so any gain made before then is not liable to capital gains tax. Or if you have let your home while you lived away for a few years (unless you lived away for one of the reasons listed on p245), or nominated another home as your main one for part of the period you owned this one, you will be liable for tax on the part of the gain you are assumed to have made in that period. In general, the taxman assumes the value of your home has increased by even monthly steps from the price you paid for it to the price you sell it for.

First he works out the gain over the whole period as outlined in Chapter 32, p415. Broadly this is the amount you sold the home for *less* the amount you paid for it – but certain *allowable expenditure* (see below) may reduce your tax bill. So will the indexation rules (see p419) if you sell the home after 5 April 1982. The taxman then works out the taxable gain for the period when the home was *not* exempt from capital gains tax by the **time apportionment method**. This gain is:

$$\text{Gain over whole period} \div \frac{\text{Total number of months you owned it}}{} \times \frac{\text{Number of months it was liable for tax}}{}$$

See Diagram opposite and Example 9 for how this works in practice.

Allowable expenditure normally includes:
- any cost of acquiring *and* disposing of the asset (eg commission, conveyancing costs, stamp duty, valuation where necessary)
- capital expenditure which has resulted in an increase in the value of the asset (eg improvements, but not ordinary maintenance).

If you owned the home before 6 April **1945**, count only the period since that date as the *total number of months you owned it*.

If you owned the home before 6 April **1965**, do not include the period before then when counting up the *total number of months it was liable for tax*. See Example 10 for how the sums work out. Alternatively you can choose to have the gain worked out as though you bought the home on 6 April 1965 at whatever its market value was at that time (though this is unlikely to be beneficial). You must make this choice within two years of the end of the tax year in which you dispose of the home, and you can't change your mind.

There are special rules for limiting the taxable gain arising from letting your only or 'main' home – see p260.
CGTA 1979 s32, s102(2), s103, Sch 5 paras 11–12.

Example 9
Sarah Keighley bought her home in Wiltshire in April 1967 and sold it in April 1987 for £36,000, making a total gain of £30,000 (after deducting buying and selling costs).

Because Sarah lived in another home which she had nominated as her main home between 1972 and 1977, her Wiltshire home is not exempt for those 60 months. She owned the home for a total of 240 months. Her taxable gain is £30,000 ÷ 240 × 60 = £7,500.

Example 10

When Maurice Myner sold his only home in April 1987, he made a gain of £88,200. He'd bought the home in April 1940. As this is before 6 April 1945, he only counts the period since then as the time he's owned it – ie 42 years = 504 months.

From April 1960 to April 1970, Maurice used a quarter of his home for business. As part of this period is before 6 April 1965, Maurice counts the five years from 1965 to 1970 – ie 60 months – as the period for which his home was liable to tax.

His taxable gain is therefore:

$$£88,200 \div 504 \times 60 \times \frac{1}{4} = £2,625.$$

How time apportionment works

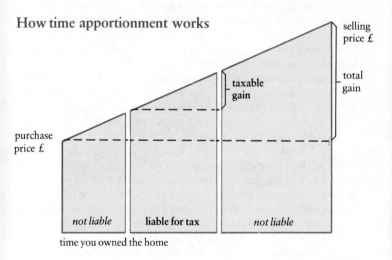

time you owned the home

Your home and your work

If you work for an employer

If you work at home

You may be able to claim as an allowable expense to set against your earnings a proportion of heating and lighting costs, and, possibly, of telephone, cleaning and insurance costs. If you use part of your home *exclusively* for your work, you may be able to claim a proportion of your rent and rates. But it's unlikely you'll be able to claim *any* of these expenses unless it's an express or implied condition of your employment that you carry out some of your duties at or from home.

Using part of your home exclusively for your employment should not mean you lose your home's exemption from capital gains tax, even if you are allowed tax relief for your expenses. But if you've been allowed a proportion of your rates or ground rent you might lose exemption on the proportion allowed.

ICTA 1970 s189.

Working away from home

If you're getting tax relief on the mortgage on your only or main home, you're allowed to be away from the home for up to a year at a time before you stop getting relief. And if your employer *requires* you to live away from home, you continue to get tax relief if you're likely to return to that home within four years. If you don't move back within four years (or if you sell the home without moving back) you don't lose any of the tax relief you've had. But there's no further tax relief for that home until you move back. If you move back for at least three months, you can have another four years' absence.

Being away from the home you've nominated as your 'main' home for capital gains tax purposes may not mean you lose exemption from the tax if the absences qualify because of your work. Any periods when you were employed (but not self-employed) and all your duties were carried on outside the United Kingdom are exempt, however long they are; taking leave in the UK or elsewhere doesn't affect this exemption. In addition, you can be away from your home for up to four years without losing exemption if you have to live away because of the location of your job or because your employer requires you to live somewhere else in order to do your job effectively. If you are away for more than four years in total, the excess won't be exempt (unless another exemption on p245 applies – eg it was the last two years you owned the home). To get any of the exemptions on account of your work, you must have lived in the home as your only or main home at some time before the first absence, and, unless you can't return home because your job requires you to work away from home again, you must also live in it after the last absence. A married couple still get these exemptions even if one owns the home and the other has the job causing the absence.

ESC A27 (interest relief); CGTA 1979 s102; ESC D3, D4 (capital gains).

If you live in job-related accommodation

You can get tax relief indefinitely on a loan used to buy a home which you (or your husband or wife) own and which you one day intend to live in. And, if you nominate the home you own as your 'main' one for capital gains tax purposes, any gain you

Example 11

In August 1987 Harold Garner sold his Edinburgh home which he bought in December 1970 (so he owned it for a total of 200 months). He has used the home as his main home for the whole time, apart from the following periods, during each of which he let the home:
- for 6 years between 1972 and 1978 while he was employed abroad
- for the following 5 years while he worked in London
- for 3 years from September 1984 to August 1987 (when he sold it) while he was again working in London.

In April 1986, Harold bought a new home in London which he moved into three months later after alterations had been carried out, and has occupied since.

Harold doesn't lose exemption for his Edinburgh home for his absence abroad, nor the following 5 years in London, as he lived in the home both before and after these absences. Although his period working in London was more than four years, the extra year is covered by the maximum of three years' absence for any reason.

The last two years of his ownership are also exempt, but the 12 months before that when he was working in London are not exempt because Harold didn't live in the home again. If he had used the house as his main home at some time during the last two years, those 12 months would have been covered under the three-year exemption.

As only 12 of the 200 months Harold owned the house are not exempt, his taxable gain is 12/200 of the actual gain he makes (after allowing for indexation).

Harold's new home in London will also be exempt from April 1986 for as long as he uses it as his only or 'main' home.

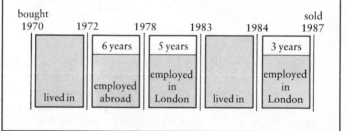

bought
1970   1972   1978   1983   1984   sold 1987

| lived in | 6 years employed abroad | 5 years employed in London | lived in | 3 years employed in London |

make when you sell the home is exempt from capital gains tax for any time after 30 July 1978 – providing that you are living in a home which goes with your job (before then the normal rules apply). It doesn't matter if you change your mind and sell the home without ever living in it, as long as you intended to live in it at some stage. To qualify on either count, at least one of the following must apply to your job-related accommodation:

- you need to live there to do your job properly (eg you're a social worker living in a childrens' home)
- living where you do enables you to do the job better *and* it is common for people doing your sort of job to live in such a home (eg you're a caretaker)
- you live there because there is a special threat to your security.

A director can qualify for the first two reasons above only if he owns or controls five per cent or less of the shares in the company, *and* is a full-time working director of the company *or* works for a charity or non-profit-making company.

FA 1974 Sch 1 para 4A (interest relief); CGTA 1979 s101(8) (capital gains).

Example 12

Gareth Jones is a school caretaker who lives in a house provided on site. In July 1973, Gareth and his wife bought a seaside cottage for their retirement, and in the meantime they let it. But in 1987, 14 years later, they changed their plans, and sold the cottage in July, without ever living in it.

As their absence was due to Gareth living in job-related accommodation, the whole of the period after 30 July 1978 is exempt from capital gains tax. The first five years are not, so their taxable gain is 5/14 of their actual gain (after allowing for indexation).

If the Joneses hadn't let the home, but had lived in it occasionally and nominated it as their main home, it would have been exempt for the whole time.

If you're self-employed

If you work at home

If you're self-employed (or do some freelance or spare-time work) and do part of your work at home, you can claim as an allowable expense the proportion of the cost of running your home that's attributable to business use (including rent and rates if part of the home is used *exclusively* for business – see p194).

But if you use part of your home *exclusively* for your business, the part you use will not be exempt from capital gains tax for the period you use it. The exact *proportion* of the gain you make when you sell the house which will be liable to tax will have to be negotiated with the Tax Inspector (in one of the same ways as if you had let part of your home – see p262). However, if your business is on a modest scale, and if you've got an understanding Tax Inspector, you may be able to get the best of both worlds by using a room *almost* exclusively for business – enough to be allowed rates and so on as an expense, but not so exclusively as to risk a capital gains tax bill.

Even if there is a taxable gain when you sell the home, you won't be liable for any tax at the time if you use the proceeds from selling the part of the home you used for your business to buy another property where you will carry on the same business or a similar one. The new building counts as replacement of a business asset, and the gain is *rolled over* (see p432). If you don't use all the proceeds in this way, only the part you use can qualify. If you eventually qualify for *retirement relief* (see p434), you may avoid a capital gains tax bill entirely.

ICTA 1970 s130 (expenses); CGTA 1979 s103, s115, s124 (capital gains).

Accommodation provided under the terms of your business

If you live in such accommodation (eg you're a licensee publican) and you're buying a home you intend to live in one day, from 6 April 1983 you get tax relief on your mortgage and exemption from capital gains tax as if you were an employee in job-related accommodation (see p250).
FA 1984 s25.

Pension mortgages

A tax-efficient way of buying your own home is available to self-employed people which isn't always open to others. Many insurance companies run personal pension plans with an immediate 'loanback' facility which you use to buy the home. You pay interest only on the loan (and make separate contributions to the plan); when you retire the loan is repaid from the tax-free lump sum you get. But you should watch out that this doesn't leave you with less pension than you need when you retire. For more details of personal pension plans, see p339.

Letting property

If you let land or property, there are two main things to consider:
● how rents you receive are taxed, and what expenses and interest you can set against the income
● capital gains tax when you sell the property. If a property is not your only or main home, the gain you make will be liable to capital gains tax. If you let part of your own home, the gain on the let part may be liable to tax, unless you were away from the home on a qualifying absence (see p245).

Income from land and property you let

In most cases, income from land or property you let is treated as investment income, and taxed under Schedule A. This includes rents you receive, ground rents, feu duties and premiums on leases. The main exceptions are:

● income from furnished property is generally taxed under Schedule D Case VI – see p34 – but receipts of a hotel or guesthouse are treated as earnings from a business and taxed under Schedule D Case I. Income from certain furnished holiday lettings is also treated as earnings from a business, although it remains assessable under Schedule D Case VI

● income from land and property abroad is taxed under Schedule D Case V, usually on a preceding year basis

● if you're entitled to rent from a property as a privilege of a job, the income is taxed under Schedule A but treated as earned income.

There are certain special rules for premiums on leases – see Inland Revenue leaflets *IR27 paras 6–9* and *CGT8 paras 174–188*.

The Case or Schedule under which your income is taxed may affect you if you have a loss on any property – see pages 30 and 257.

Other income from land and property

Most other income you get as a result of owning land, having an interest in it or rights over it is treated as investment income and taxed under Schedule A. The main exceptions are:

● mineral rents and mining royalties are taxed under Schedule D Case I

● income from commercially managed woodlands is taxed under Schedule B (though you can elect to be taxed under Schedule D Case I). There are more details of these in Inland Revenue booklet *IR27*.

Letting land and unfurnished property

In any tax year, you are taxed on the income you are entitled to receive in that year. This applies even if you haven't yet received the income, but not to debts you've tried unsuccessfully to recover, or ones you've waived to avoid hardship. Alternatively, you can ask to be taxed on your profits for your accounting year ending in the tax year, as long as they meet certain conditions (see *IR27 paras 4–5*). Once this is decided, you can't change back. You are allowed to deduct certain expenses and interest (see below) which you have actually paid during the tax year when you work out your profits. If the expenses and interest come to more than your income, you will have made a loss. For how losses are treated, see p257.

Tax on income from property is due on 1 January in the tax year (eg the tax on all the property income you are entitled to receive in the 1987–88 tax year is due on 1 January 1988). In many cases the taxman will only ask you to pay the basic rate tax then, and will ask for any higher rate tax later. As the taxman is collecting the basic rate tax before you've received all the income, he has to make an estimate of how much you should receive and what your expenses will be in the tax year. He normally uses last year's figures for this estimate, and adjusts your assessment when the actual amount is known. If you know that your income (before deductions) will be less than it was last year (because, say, you've sold off some property), you can ask the taxman before 1 January to reduce the initial assessment.

If you need more details than given here, see Inland Revenue leaflet *IR27*.

ICTA 1970 s69, s87.

Allowable expenses

You can deduct certain expenses from your income from letting when you work out your profits. If you let only part of your home, or let it for only part of each year, you and the taxman will have to agree on the proportion you can claim. You can't claim anything for your own time. The most common allowable expenses are:
- rates, water rates, ground rent, feu duty (in Scotland)
- normal repairs and decoration, but not repairs necessary when you bought the property, nor improvements, additions or alterations to the property
- management expenses as a landlord (eg stationery, phone bills, accountant's fees, cost of rent collection)
- cost of insurance and any necessary valuation for insurance

- legal fees for renewing a tenancy agreement (for leases of up to 50 years)
- estate agent's fees, accommodation agency fees, cost of advertising for tenants
- rent you pay for a property which you, in turn, sublet
- cost of lighting common parts of property
- cost of services you provide including wages of people who provide such services (eg cleaners, gardeners, porters)
- cost of maintenance and repairs made necessary by improvements you've made, as long as you haven't changed the use of the property
- cost of maintaining roads, drains, ditches etc on an estate you own, if for the benefit of tenants.

You can also deduct interest you pay on a loan used to buy or improve property – see below. If you buy any machinery or equipment (eg a lawnmower or ladder) for upkeep or repair of the property, you can either claim *capital allowances* as if you were self-employed (see p198), *or* claim on a *renewals basis* (see *Wear and tear* on p259). Once you have decided which basis to use you must stick to it.

If you incur expenses while the home isn't actually occupied by a tenant, they still qualify as long as you let it out at full rent straight afterwards and (unless you'd just bought the home) you had been letting it immediately beforehand. 'Full rent' means an amount which, over the years, is enough to cover all your expenses and the interest you pay (though you might still make a loss in any individual year).
ICTA 1970 s71–74.

Interest

You can get tax relief on interest on a loan (other than an overdraft or credit card debt) used to buy or improve a home you let out. In any 52-week period, you can get tax relief as long as it's let at a commercial rent for more than half the 52-week period, and provided that for the rest of the period it is available for letting (unless building or repair work is going on, or it's being used as the only or main home for you or your divorced or separated wife or husband or a dependent relative).

The interest you pay can be set off against any income from property but no other income. These loans don't count towards your £30,000 limit (see p236) except when the property is being used as an only or main home (when tax relief is given against your income in general, not just against income from letting).
FA 1972 Sch 9 Part 1; FA 1974 Sch 1 paras 4, 7.

Losses

Any part of a loss which consists of interest can be set off against any income from property. If you haven't enough other property income to set it all against, you can carry what's left forward and set it against any income from property in future years, as long as you're still letting the property you made the loss on.

The way a loss resulting from allowable expenses is treated is more complicated and depends on the type of lease:

● if the lease is at *full rent* (see previous page) and you are responsible for all or some of the repairs (*normal lease*), any loss can be set against income from other properties you let on a normal lease. If such income doesn't use up the whole loss, you can carry what's left forward and set it against income of the same type in future years

● if the lease is at full rent but the tenant pays for all or substantially all repairs (*tenant's repairing lease*), the loss can be set against income from any properties on a *normal* lease in the same or future years, *or* carried forward and set against future profits on the *same* property only

● if the lease is at a nominal rent (eg to a relative paying you little or no rent), a loss can only be carried forward and set against future income from letting the same home to the same person.

ICTA 1970 s72.

Letting furnished property

Income from letting furnished property is normally treated as investment income. But if you run a hotel or guest-house, the whole of your income will normally count as earnings from self-employment. For furnished holiday lettings, see p259.

If you let furnished accommodation to a tenant who pays you separately for services you provide (eg meals, cleaning, laundry), what he pays for these services may count as earnings from a business and be taxed under Schedule D Case I. What he pays for the rooms counts as investment income and is taxed under Schedule D Case VI.

If you pay someone else to provide such services in furnished accommodation, the wages you pay count as an allowable expense deductible from the rent you get. For the person you pay, they count as earnings. So if your wife, say, provides the services, what you pay her will be her earnings (as long as the amount you pay her is appropriate for the work she does). This can be useful if your wife's other earned income is less than the full amount of the wife's earned income allowance (£2,425 in the 1987–88 tax year).

Income taxed under Schedule D Case VI is taxed in the same way as income from land and unfurnished property (see p255) except that you're taxed on the amount you actually receive in the tax year instead of the amount you're entitled to.

You can ask (within two years of the end of the tax year) for the part of the rent which comes from the *premises* (as opposed to the furnishings or any services you provide) to be taxed under Schedule A instead of under Case VI of Schedule D. This could be useful if you have made a loss on furnished lettings which you want to set off against income from unfurnished property being taxed in the same tax year (or vice versa) in order to reduce your tax bill immediately. As well as apportioning the rent you get between the premises and for the furnishings, you'll have to apportion your allowable expenses. See Example 14, below.
ICTA 1970 s67.

Example 13

Brian Wallis lets out three furnished flats and gets £8,000 a year in rent. His wife Glenda provides the tenants with an evening meal, cleans the flats twice a week and collects the rents. Brian pays Glenda £2,700 a year for this (but has to deduct some tax and National Insurance from what he pays). As Glenda has no other earned income, £2,425 of this will be tax-free. Brian deducts the £2,700 wages from his letting income of £8,000, and will be taxed on £5,300, less the NI contributions he pays, and less any other allowable expenses.

Example 14

Brian Wallis also lets out an unfurnished house. In the 1987–88 tax year the mortgage interest and allowable expenses on the house come to £400 more than the rent he gets. As Brian wants to reduce his tax bill immediately, he asks for the income he gets from letting the *premises* of his furnished flats (see Example 13) which he reckons on being £3,700 after expenses on the property, to be taxed under Schedule A. He can now set the £400 loss on the unfurnished home against it, and only be taxed on £3,700 − £400 = £3,300.

Allowable expenses

When working out your profits, you can deduct all the expenses allowable for unfurnished property (see p255) *plus*:
- heating, lighting and tenants' telephone bills you pay
- wear and tear of fixtures and fittings (see opposite), cost of specific repairs to furniture
- cost of preparing an inventory.

If you get paid separately for services you provide and this income counts as earnings from a business, you can deduct other allowable expenses from it – see list on p194. Except in these circumstances, you can't claim capital allowances on furnished property.

Wear and tear

You can claim an allowance for wear and tear on fixtures, furniture and furnishings, eg chairs, cookers, lampshades, beds, sheets. You can claim *either* the actual cost of fixtures, furniture etc you replace during the year (called *renewals basis*), *or* a proportion (normally 10%) of the rent *less*, if you pay them, rates and service charges. Once you've chosen a basis, you must stick to it.

Interest

Interest you pay on a loan to buy or improve the property can also be deducted from the income you get. If it counts as investment income, the same rules apply as with unfurnished property (see p256).

If part of the income you get counts as earnings from a business, interest you set against it counts as a business expense (see p193). The rules on p238 don't then apply – so you could get tax relief on an overdraft or credit card debt, for example.

Losses

If the income is taxed under Schedule D Case VI, any part of a loss which consists of interest can be set off against any other income from property. But any part which results from allowable expenses can be set off only against other income taxed under Schedule D Case VI – eg other income from furnished lettings, or freelance earnings you've received. If you haven't any (or enough) other income of the right type in the same tax year, you can carry the loss forward and set it against any income of that type in future tax years.

If the income on which you've made a loss counts as earnings from a business and is taxed under Schedule D Case I, you have the options outlined on p204 for offsetting this loss.
ICTA 1970 s176.

Furnished holiday lettings

From 6 April 1982, income from letting property (including caravans) which is let as furnished holiday accommodation for part of the year has been treated as earnings from a business, even though it is assessed under Schedule D Case VI.

To qualify, both the following must apply:

• the property is available for letting to the general public at a commercial rent for at least 140 days (which need not be consecutive) during each 12 month qualifying period (not necessarily a tax year)

• it is actually let out as living accommodation for at least 70 of those days, and during at least seven months of the 12 month period it isn't normally occupied by the same tenant for more than 31 days at a stretch.

If you let more than one unit of accommodation, you can average the days they're actually let to pass the 70-day rule.

If a furnished letting counts as holiday accommodation, all the income you get from it in the tax year counts as earned income. But if only part of the let accommodation counts as furnished holiday lettings only a proportion of the income counts as earned income.

FA 1984 s50; IR Press Release 17 May 1984.

Example 15

Winston Fry started letting out a furnished bungalow in Skegness for holidays on 1 June 1987. It will count as a furnished holiday letting for the 1987–88 year of assessment, as long as it's available to the public at a commercial rent for 140 days during the 12 months from 1 June 1987 to 31 May 1988, and as long as he lets it out for 70 of those days, mainly for periods of 31 days or less. If Winston continues to let the bungalow in the 1988–89 tax year, it will count as a furnished holiday letting as long as it meets the qualifying rules during the 12 months from 6 April 1988 to 5 April 1989.

Capital gains on let property

Letting a property may mean a capital gains tax bill when you come to sell it. But this isn't always the case.

If a home has been your only home or nominated as your main one for the whole time you've owned it, the whole of your gain will be exempt from capital gains tax even if you've let it out while you were away, as long as all your absences count as qualifying absences (see p245). But the gain attributable to any other period you let it while you were away (worked out by the time apportionment method shown on p248) won't be exempt.

If you let part of your only or main home, you don't lose any exemption for having lodgers who are treated as members of your family, sharing your living rooms and eating with you, even though the lodgers have their own bedrooms. In other cases it depends on whether you have occupied the part of the

Example 16

Elizabeth Kerr bought a house in October 1975 for £38,000 which she sold in October 1987 for £190,000 (after deducting selling costs). Throughout this time, the house was her main home for capital gains tax purposes. But from June 1976 to June 1982 (ie exactly 6 out of the 12 years she owned the home) she let out half of the house as living accommodation. She works out her taxable gain as follows. First she applies the indexation rules (see p419). She chooses to base the indexation allowance on the value of the property on 31 March 1982: it comes to £29,000. She adds this to the price she paid for the house in 1975 and arrives at a figure of £67,000. So the gain on the whole property after allowing for indexation is £190,000 − £67,000 = £123,000. As she let half the house for 6/12 of the time she owned it, the gain attributable to the lettings is 1/2 × 6/12 × £123,000 = £30,750. The gain attributable to her occupation of the home is £123,000 − £30,750 = £92,250. The gain attributable to the letting (£30,750) is a lot less than the gain attributable to her occupation (£92,250). But it is more than £20,000. The taxable gain on which she is liable to pay capital gains tax is therefore the excess over £20,000 ie £30,750 − £20,000 = £10,750.

The first £6,600 of gains made in the 1987–88 tax year is exempt from capital gains tax. But Elizabeth will have to pay tax on £10,750 − £6,600 = £4,150. Capital gains tax is charged at 30%, so the tax bill is 30% × £4,150 = £1,245. She will also have to pay tax on any other capital gains she makes in that tax year, as her annual exemption has been used up on the house sale.

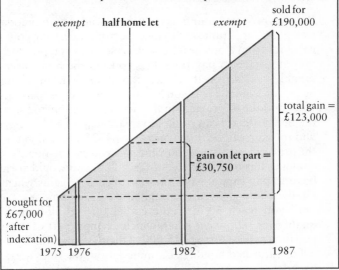

exempt   **half home let**   *exempt*   sold for £190,000

total gain = £123,000

gain on let part = £30,750

bought for £67,000 (after indexation)

1975 1976 1982 1987

home you've let at any time. If you haven't, the gain on the part you let will not be exempt from capital gains tax. The taxable gain will normally be based on the number of rooms you let or the floor area of the part you let, but could alternatively be based on the rateable value of the part you let (if it's separately rated), or on its market value. It's up to you and the taxman to agree which method to use; if you don't agree, you can appeal to the General or Special Commissioners (see p457).

If you haven't ever lived in the part of the home you've let out it will be well worth your doing so (even if only for a short period) before you sell the home. In this case the gain on the let part is apportioned according to the period you've let it. In addition, this gain (after allowing for indexation – see p419) will remain exempt from capital gains tax if it's no more than the (exempt) gain attributable to your occupation of the home (after allowing for indexation), *and* if it's no more than £20,000 (£10,000 before 6 April 1983). If either limit is exceeded, the excess (the larger excess if both limits are exceeded) is liable to capital gains tax – see Example 16, on the previous page. To get this exemption, the let part must be lived in by someone, but must not be a completely separate home (eg not a self-contained flat with its own access from the street) and you should not have had more than minor alterations made to the home.

CGTA 1979 s102; FA 1980 s80; SP14/80; SPD15.

If the letting counts as a business

If the let property counts as furnished holiday accommodation (see p259) or if (unusually) income from the letting counts as earnings from a business because of services you provide, you may not have to pay tax when you sell the home even if a taxable gain arises. If you use the proceeds from selling the home (or from the part you let) to buy another property where you continue to provide similar accommodation and services, the new property can count as replacement of a business asset and the gain can be *rolled over* (see p432). If you don't use all the proceeds in this way, only the part you use can qualify.

Doing this only defers your tax bill, as you would normally have to pay capital gains tax on rolled-over gains when you finally sell up and cease letting. However, if you don't do this until you reach 60 (or retire earlier through ill-health) you qualify for *retirement relief*, which exempts part of the gains you then make – up to £125,000 of them (see p434).

For furnished holiday accommodation, the rules above are backdated to 6 April 1982, and if you have paid too much CGT on accommodation you've disposed of since that date you can claim back the excess.

CGTA 1979 s115–121, s124; FA 1984 s50, Sch 11; FA 1985 s69–70, Sch 17.

Land with development value

Before 19 March 1985, if you disposed of land in the UK which had value partly because of its development value or which you had developed, you could have become liable to **development land tax**. This was charged at a single rate of 60% of the development value realised. Your own home, or a home built for or occupied rent-free by a dependent relative was exempt. So were certain other types of development and the first £75,000 of development value realised in any financial year.

Development land tax was abolished for all disposals made on or after 19 March 1985.

FA 1985 s93.

Tax-saving tips

● tax relief on mortgage interest and exemption from capital gains tax make buying your own home with a mortgage a very sensible investment and a tax-efficient way of acquiring a valuable asset. This applies equally to people who live in job-related accommodation

● if you have more than one home, you can keep your capital gains tax liability to a minimum by careful arrangement of your occupation of the homes and your choice of 'main' home for capital gains tax purposes

● the home you choose as your 'main' one for capital gains tax purposes doesn't have to be the one you live in most of the time, nor the one on which you get tax relief on a mortgage. It should be the one on which you think you'll make the largest taxable gain

● if you own a second home, it could be both compassionate and tax-efficient to let a 'dependent' relative live in it rent-free

● if you have used part of your home for your business or have earned income from letting part of it, it would be worth continuing to use the home (or any future homes of yours) in the same way until you reach 60 (or retire earlier through ill-health). You can then probably avoid most or all of the capital gains tax liability by claiming retirement relief on the gains you make when you sell the home and on any rolled-over gains.

21 STAMP DUTY

Stamp Duty – brought in nearly 300 years ago – has long been condemned as a confusing, complicated and ramshackle tax, with no underlying logic or social justification. More recently, it has been criticised as a tax on change, mobility, flexibility – all the qualities argued as being so desirable today.

What the tax is

Originally, Stamp Duty was a tax on *documents*, and still largely is. That's to say, what is taxed is not (for example) the actual sale of a house or shares, nor the person doing the buying or selling, but the document associated with that transaction. No document, no tax – and all quite legal too. This feature of the tax is one that, at least in theory, gives great scope for tax-avoiders. But in practice, it's usually impossible to avoid documents: the ownership of houses, for example, has to be transferred by a written document.

There are two main types of Stamp Duty:
• *ad valorem duties*, which are charged as a percentage of the price of the house, shares or whatever
• *fixed duties*, where the duty is fixed – often in pennies rather than pounds – and not related to the value of the transaction.

Transfers of houses and land

Sales or exchanges of houses, land and other property are liable for ad valorem duty of 1 per cent, with the exception that transfers up to £30,000 pay no tax. Although there is nothing in the legislation to say who should pay the tax, it is normally the buyer. The 1985 Budget scrapped ad valorem stamp duty on gifts, and on transfers of property due to the break-up of a marriage; for gifts or transfers made on or after 26 March 1985 (and gifts made on or after 19 March but not stamped until 26 March onwards), only a fixed duty of 50p is payable.

Once the price of a house goes over £30,000, Stamp Duty becomes payable on the *whole* price. To take an extreme (if unlikely) case, the tax on a purchase price of £30,000 is nil, but on a price of £30,001 the tax would be £301.

> If you're buying a house priced somewhat over £30,000, it's going to pay you handsomely if you can get the price down to £30,000. If bargaining won't do the trick, and if you are buying carpets, curtains and other fittings, try to get agreement to pay for these separately – duty is charged only on the price of the house. This could well save you some £300 in tax.

It is not possible to avoid Stamp Duty by splitting up the purchase of a house or land into two or more parts, each part for £30,000 or less. To qualify for exemption from tax, the solicitor or you (if doing-it-yourself) have to submit a certificate which says: *'It is hereby certified that the transaction hereby effected does not form part of a larger transaction or of a series of transactions in respect of which the amount or value of the consideration exceeds £30,000.'*

Council tenants buying their houses at a discounted price under the Right to Buy Scheme pay Stamp Duty on the discounted price.

FA 1985 s82–83.

Exchanges of property

These are not quite so uncommon any more since developers will sometimes buy a would-be purchaser's old house from him. With an exchange, there is no tax if no money passes hands; where there is a balancing payment, tax is charged on that balancing payment. For example, if Mr and Mrs A buy Developer B's spanking new estate house for £38,000, and if Developer B buys Mr and Mrs A's old house for £21,000, Mr and Mrs A would owe a balance of £17,000. This £17,000 is what is taxed – and since it's well below the tax-free limit of £30,000, no Stamp Duty would be payable.

Leases

What you pay for an **existing** lease on a flat or house is taxed in exactly the same way as transfers of houses and land (including the £30,000 tax-free exemption).

But **new** leases – such as a long lease on a new or refurbished flat – are treated differently, and often taxed twice over. The premium on a long lease (that is, the lump sum you are paying for the lease) is taxed in the same way as a transfer of a freehold house (except that you do not benefit from the £30,000 exemption if the yearly ground rent is over £300). But the yearly payments you have to make under the lease (excluding the service charges) are also taxed. The amount of tax depends on the length of the lease and the average amount of the yearly payments. To give one example, for new leases over 35 but not over 100 years, the once-and-for-all Stamp Duty on yearly payments between £100 and £150 would be £18.

Transfers of shares

Transfers of shares are liable for ad valorem duty of ½ per cent. This is rounded up to the nearest 50p. The stockbroker adds the tax to the cost of the shares, and it's the buyer of the shares who normally pays the tax. There is no tax-free amount – ie all of the transaction, whatever the amount, is liable for tax.

From 27 October 1986, a new tax was introduced – called stamp duty reserve tax. Under this some purchases of shares which had previously escaped stamp duty, eg shares bought and resold in the same Stock Exchange account, became subject to stamp duty reserve tax. It's charged at the same rate as stamp duty.

Life insurance policies

Duty on most life insurance policies is 50p per £1,000 of the sum insured. Since the duty is on the sum insured, and not on the amount of the premium, the tax – though not exactly swingeing – does discriminate against socially-desirable term insurance (which provides a lot of insurance for a relatively low premium). The duty is paid by the insurance company, but it would be realistic to assume that the tax is passed on to those who buy policies.

Capital duty

This is a 1 per cent ad valorem duty on the raising of share capital by companies (a requirement of the EEC). The tax doesn't apply to individuals – except, of course, that companies will tend to pass on the tax to their customers or shareholders.

22 INVESTMENTS

What counts as investment income might surprise you. For tax purposes, investment income is income which isn't *earned* – broadly, any income which isn't from a job, or business or pension. So as well as income you get from your investments, income you get from, for example, a covenant, a maintenance agreement and often from letting property will count as investment income.

There are two main taxes which apply to investments:

● **capital gains tax.** If your investment is the sort where its value can fluctuate there could be capital gains tax to pay when you sell (or give away) the investment. But for the 1987–88 tax year, the first £6,600 of net taxable gains is tax-free, the rest taxed at 30 per cent only. So if you're a higher rate taxpayer, you should consider investing for capital gains rather than income. For more details on capital gains tax, see p415

● **income tax.** Any investment income you get (such as interest or dividends) is added to your earned income. You then deduct your outgoings (see p24) and your allowances (see p22), leaving your taxable income. Income tax is charged on your taxable income at the basic rate, and at higher rates once your income is above a certain amount (£17,900 for the 1987–88 tax year).

ICTA 1970 s65, s434, s530; FA 1971 s32(3).

Example

Alan Arbor has earned income from his job of £20,000 and income from his investments of £11,000. This gives him a gross income of £31,000. From this he can deduct his outgoings of £2,500 and his allowances of £3,795. This leaves him with a taxable income of £24,705. Income tax is charged on this taxable income up to £17,900 at the basic rate of 27% and above that at higher rates, including tax at 45% on the last slice of income.

How investment income is paid

Investment income can be paid in one of four ways:
- it can be tax-free (no tax to pay) – eg the first £70 of interest from a National Savings Ordinary account. See list on p274
- it can be paid with basic rate tax (or its equivalent) already deducted – for example, share dividends. If you're a non-taxpayer, you can claim back the tax paid. See p274 for how this works
- it can be paid gross – ie before any tax has been deducted – for example, interest on a National Savings Investment account. If you are a taxpayer, you'll have to pay any basic or higher rate tax that's due. Special rules apply in the first and last few years you get interest of this type – see p276
- interest from banks, building societies, licensed deposit-takers and local authority loans is paid with no more basic rate tax to pay – but tax can't be claimed back by non-taxpayers. See pages 279 to 283 for details.

Note that if you choose to have the income added to your investment, the tax treatment is the same as if it's paid out to you.

The wife's investment income

Remember that any income which comes from the wife's investments always counts as the husband's for tax purposes – see p67. It doesn't make any difference if the couple have chosen to have the wife's earnings taxed separately. Nor does it matter if the wife bought the investment with her own money.

This doesn't apply if the husband and wife are separated.
ICTA 1970 s37, s42; FA 1971 Sch 4 para 3 (1c).

How investments are taxed – at a glance (1987–88 tax year)

investment	liable for income tax?	
alternative investments – eg antiques, gold coins	no – unless you buy and sell often, when you might count as a trader	
annuities [1]	yes – on the part which is interest	
bank investments	yes	
British Government stocks	yes	
building society investments	yes	
commodities	depends – see p281	
company loan stocks or debentures	yes	
covenants	yes	
friendly society policies	no	
income and growth bonds	yes	
let property	yes	
licensed deposit-takers	yes	
regular-premium life insurance policies	no – except possible higher rate tax if cashed in early – (see p306)	
local authority investments	yes	
maintenance payments	yes – unless voluntary	
National Savings Bank accounts	yes – but not first £70 of interest on Ordinary account	
NS Certificates and Yearly Plan	no	

[1] The *whole* of income from annuities you *have* to buy (compulsory purchase annuities) – eg as part of a personal pension plan – is taxed as earned income.

has basic rate income tax already been deducted?	liable for higher rate income tax?	liable for capital gains tax?
no (no income)	no (no income)	yes – unless value of item at time of disposal is £3,000 or less
yes, normally	yes	no
yes (in effect) – see p279	yes	no
normally yes if bought through stockbroker; not if through National Savings Stock Register	yes	not if sold after 1.7.86; liable previously if not held for at least a year or inherited
yes (in effect) – see p280	yes	no
no	depends – see p281	depends – see p281
yes	yes	yes – but not if bought after 13.3.84, and held for a year or more or sold after 1.7.86
yes – except in rare circumstances	no, not normally	no
no	no – unless policy cashed in before 7½ years	no
depends on way bond works – ask company	depends on way bond works – ask company	no – but fund pays tax on gains
no	yes	yes, if you sell the property – see p260
yes (in effect) – see p282	yes	no
no (but fund pays equivalent of basic rate tax)	no – unless cashed in early – see page 306	no – but fund pays tax on gains
yes – see pages 281 and 283	yes	yes on stocks or yearling bonds
yes – unless *small* (see p94)	yes	no
no	yes	no
no	no	no

investment	liable for income tax?	
NS Income and Deposit Bonds	yes	
SAYE scheme	no	
shares [2]	yes	
single-premium investment bonds	yes – may have to pay higher rate tax when cashing the bond	
trust income	yes	
unit trusts [2]	yes	

[2] But rules are different if held in a Personal Equity Plan – see p289.

Which investment for which investor?

Here we give some guidelines on which investment has particular advantages from a tax point of view for certain types of investors. But don't consider tax alone. Look at other aspects too – eg the after-tax return you get, risk, how long you want to invest for.

Non-taxpayers

You need to look closely at:
● investments which pay income without any tax deducted – high-income British Government stocks bought through the National Savings Stock Register, National Savings Bank accounts, National Savings Income Bonds and National Savings Deposit Bonds
● investments where income is paid with basic rate tax already deducted but where the tax can be claimed back from the taxman – company loan stock, local authority loan stock, shares, unit trusts.

Basic rate taxpayers

No particular investments stick out from a tax point of view. But if you're prepared to take a risk, you can make £6,600 in capital gains free of tax in the 1987–88 tax year.

has basic rate income tax already been deducted?	liable for higher rate income tax?	liable for capital gains tax?
no	yes	no
no	no	no
equivalent of basic rate tax deducted	yes	yes
no – but no basic rate tax to pay (fund pays tax)	yes – may have to pay higher rate tax when cashing bond	no – but fund pays tax on gains
tax already deducted, at 45% if discretionary trust, at 27% otherwise	yes – if pay tax at higher rate than deducted	no
equivalent of basic rate tax deducted	yes	yes

Higher rate taxpayers

You need to look closely at:
● investments which you hope will give a capital gain rather than income – eg low-income British Government stocks, index-linked British Government stocks, low-income local authority stock and yearling bonds, ordinary shares, ordinary shares in unquoted companies bought under the Business Expansion Scheme, unit trusts
● investments which are tax-free – eg National Savings Certificates, National Savings Yearly Plan, SAYE schemes, Personal Equity Plans.

People receiving age allowance

If your income is in the region where each extra £ of 'total income' loses you age allowance (see p104), you should consider:
● tax-free investments – eg National Savings Certificates, National Savings Yearly Plan, SAYE schemes
● investments which you hope will give a capital gain rather than income – low-income British Government stocks, index-linked British Government stocks, ordinary shares, unit trusts.

Tax-free investment income

Income or proceeds from the following investments are tax-free:

- Save-As-You-Earn (SAYE schemes)
- National Savings Certificates (and, in most cases, Ulster Savings Certificates if you live in Northern Ireland)
- National Savings Yearly Plan
- qualifying regular-premium investment-type life insurance (if held for at least 10 years, or three-quarters of the original term – whichever is shorter) – but company pays tax
- premium bonds (don't really count as income – see p19)
- first £70 interest each tax year from a National Savings Bank Ordinary account
- dividends paid by a credit union to its members
- interest on a tax rebate (see p454)
- interest to do with delayed settlement of damages for personal injury or death
- return on investments held in a Personal Equity Plan.

ICTA s340A, s375A, s394(1b), s414(1a), s415(1); ESC A31, A37 (Ulster Savings Certificates); FA 1981 s34; FA 1986 s39.

Investment income taxed before you get it

Investments taxed in this way include share dividends, unit trust distributions and interest on some British Government stocks. When you get the income, basic rate tax (or equivalent) has already been deducted. This type of income is taxed on a *current year basis* – ie your tax bill for the 1987–88 tax year is based on the income paid (or credited) to you in that tax year. From the taxman's view, you get income when it is paid out or credited, even if interest is worked out more frequently.

The Diagram opposite shows what the tax position is for different taxpayers. Income from building societies (p280), banks (p279), licensed deposit-takers (p282), local authority loans (p283), covenants (p127) and maintenance payments (p90) is treated somewhat differently.

FA 1971 s32 (1b), s36; TMA 1970 s42.

Non-taxpayers

If you don't pay tax – even allowing for income of this type – you can claim tax back. You can get the right form (R40) from your Tax Inspector.

Basic rate taxpayers

If you are liable for basic rate tax only, tax due on this income is automatically met by the tax deducted or credited.

Higher rate taxpayers

If you pay tax at higher rates, you will have to pay extra tax – worked out on the gross (before-tax) income. Any extra tax due on interest received in the 1987–88 tax year is due on 1 December 1988 (or within 30 days of the date on your Notice of Assessment, if later). Tax may be deducted under PAYE, in which case you pay some of the tax earlier – but you can choose to pay in a lump sum instead.

Your Tax Return

You should enter the gross (before-tax) amount of the interest received in your Tax Return. With share dividends and unit trust distributions, you enter the amount received and the amount of the tax credit.

Investment income taxed before you get it: what you end up with [1]

If you pay:	dividend (or interest taxed before it's paid to you)		tax credit (or tax deducted)
no tax	you can keep what you're paid AND . . .		you can claim back all the tax credited or deducted
basic rate tax only	you can keep what you're paid		the taxman keeps the tax credited or deducted [2]
higher rate tax	you can keep part of what you're paid BUT . . .		the taxman keeps the tax credited or deducted and asks for extra tax

this much if you pay tax at 50 per cent

[1] Does not apply to interest from banks, building societies, licensed deposit-takers or local authority loans
[2] But if the size of your income (including your before-tax income of this type) means that you are liable for less tax than has been credited or deducted, you can claim back the difference

Key ▮ what you end up with

☐ what the taxman ends up with

Investment income not taxed before you get it

This type of income is paid to you *gross* – ie before any tax has been deducted. Examples of income paid in this way include interest from National Savings Bank accounts and National Savings Income and Deposit Bonds, interest from deposits at non-UK branches of UK and overseas banks. Before 6 April 1984, interest from bank deposit accounts was also paid in this way – see p279 for the current position.

If you've been getting interest of this type for a few years, it will normally be taxed on a *preceding year basis* – ie your tax bill for the 1987–88 tax year will be based on the interest paid (or credited) to you in the 1986–87 tax year. This bill must normally be paid by 1 January 1988 or within 30 days of the date on the Notice of Assessment you'll get – whichever is later. But if your interest isn't very substantial and doesn't vary much from year to year, and you pay tax under PAYE, the tax on it will probably be collected along with tax on your earnings – so you'll pay some of the tax sooner.

For tax purposes you get the interest when it is paid or credited to you, even if interest is worked out on a more frequent basis.

The first and last years

Special rules apply to the first three years and last two years in which you get interest without tax being deducted. See the Charts opposite and on p278 for details.

Changes in amount of interest

If there is a big change in the amount of interest you get from a single source – eg if you greatly increase or decrease the size of your National Savings Investment account – your Tax Inspector may treat such interest as coming from a new source and apply his special rules. You won't need to worry about these rules if your interest is much the same from year to year. Note that, if you get interest from more than one source which is paid without tax deducted, your Tax Inspector will normally apply the special rules to each source separately – though, before 6 April 1984, if you got interest without tax deducted from more than one bank, your Tax Inspector could count *all* your bank interest as coming from a single source.

Working the rules

If the amount of this type of interest which you get varies from year to year, you may be able to reduce your tax bill:

• if the amount of interest in year 3 is lower than the interest you got in year 2, tell your Tax Inspector that you want your tax bill for year 3 to be based on the interest you actually got in year 3. (You can make this choice at any time within six years of the end of year 3)

● if the amount of interest in years 2 and 3 is high compared with the interest in year 4, consider closing your account (eg your National Savings Bank account) just before the end of year 4, and re-opening it a week or so later (after the start of the next tax year). That way, your tax bill for year 4 will be based on the interest you actually got in that year, rather than on the higher amount of interest you got in year 3.

ICTA s101, s109(2) Case III a–c, s119–121.

Your Tax Return

You enter in your Tax Return the amount of before-tax interest you receive in that tax year. So if you are filling in your Tax Return for income in the 1986–87 tax year, you put in the interest you get in that tax year.

Your tax bill for the first three years

	tax is initially based on:	but for some years, there's a choice:
First tax year in which you get interest from this source (year 1)	interest you get in first tax year (*current year basis*)	no choice this year
Second tax year (year 2)	interest you get in second tax year (*current year basis*)	no choice this year [1]
Third tax year (year 3)	interest you got in second tax year (*preceding year basis*)	**your choice:** you can choose to have tax based on interest you get in third tax year (current year basis). Do so if this is less than interest you got in second year [1]
Fourth and subsequent tax years . . .	interest you got in preceding tax year (*preceding year basis*)	no choice for these years

[1] But if this source of interest started on 6 April in year 1, tax for year 2 will normally be based on the interest you got in year 1 (*preceding year basis*) – and you can choose to have tax for year 2 based on interest in year 2 instead (*current year basis*). Consider doing this if interest in year 2 is lower than interest in year 1. Note, in this case, you have no further choice in year 3.

Your tax bill for the last two years

	tax is initially based on:	but for some years, there's a choice:
The last-but-one tax year in which you get interest from this source	interest you got in preceding tax year (*preceding year basis*)	**taxman's choice:** when you tell him, at the end of the next year, that you've closed your account, the taxman can revise your tax bill. He will base it on the interest you actually got in the last-but-one tax year (current year basis) if this comes to more than your original bill
last tax year in which you get interest from this source	interest you get in this tax year (*current year basis*)	no choice this year

> **Investment income surcharge**
> This extra tax applied only to investment income taxed before 6 April 1984. If your 'total investment income' was more than a certain amount (£7,100 in the 1983–84 tax year) an extra tax of 15% was payable on the excess, on top of any basic or higher rate tax. This limit of £7,100 applied to a married couple as well as a single person.
> Note that maintenance payments and covenant payments received were not liable to the surcharge. And for how investment income of trusts is treated – see p397.

How each type of investment is taxed

Alternative investments

If you invest in antiques, silver, gold coins or other tangible objects of this type, you will be hoping to make a capital gain. For how this is taxed, see p415.

Annuities

With annuities which you buy voluntarily, part of what you get back is treated as being a return of your original investment and is tax-free. The rest is taxed as investment income. For more details, see p319. The *whole* of income from annuities bought compulsorily – eg as part of a pension scheme – is taxed as earned income.

Bank interest

When you get interest from High Street banks, and the National Girobank, you don't have to pay basic rate tax on it. Instead the bank pays composite rate tax direct to the Inland Revenue in a similar way to building societies – see overleaf. But if you pay tax at higher rates, you will have to pay extra tax in the same way as for building society interest – see opposite. The composite tax rate is fixed at 24.75 per cent for the 1987–88 tax year. If you don't pay tax, you can't reclaim any of the tax that the bank has paid.

Before 6 April 1985, bank interest was taxed differently – it was paid to you without tax deducted. If you'd been receiving interest for a number of years, it was normally taxed on a preceding year basis – see p276. But in the 1984–85 tax year, under special transitional rules, bank interest was taxed on a current year basis.

FA 1984 s27, Sch 8 para 6(5); ICTA 1970 s109(2) Case III.

British Government stocks

Interest on Government stocks is paid with basic rate tax deducted, except for:
- interest on War Loan
- interest on any stock which gives you less than £2.50 gross interest each half year
- interest on stocks bought through the National Savings Stock Register (a leaflet from your post office lists these stocks)
- the discount or profit on sale or maturity of Treasury Bills.

Note that with stock issued by certain nationalised industries and stock issued by certain foreign governments which pay interest in the UK, the interest is paid with basic rate tax deducted.

Index-linked British Government stocks are treated in exactly the same way for tax purposes as other British Government stocks.

Buying British Government stocks can be a tax-efficient investment for higher rate taxpayers. If you buy at a price which is less than the price at which the stock will eventually be redeemed or sold you'll make a capital gain. The gain is free of capital gains tax for stocks sold after 1 July 1986. If you buy *low coupon* stocks – ie stocks which pay relatively low amounts of yearly interest – then you can invest for a return which is largely made up of a capital gain. But don't let tax considerations force you into investments which would otherwise be unsuitable.

ICTA 1970 s30, s93–107, s109(2) Case III; FA 1985 s67.

Building society interest

When you get interest from a building society account, you don't have to pay basic rate tax on it. This is because building societies pay tax direct to the Inland Revenue before paying out the interest to you. The rate of tax building societies pay is at a special rate which is normally worked out for each tax year. It's called the composite rate and for the 1987–88 tax year it is fixed at 24.75 per cent.

If you pay tax at higher rates, you will have to pay extra tax on your building society interest. When working out your tax bill, the Tax Inspector will include the *grossed-up* amount of interest (see p476) as part of your income. If you got £365 interest, say, from a building society, this will be grossed-up to work out your taxable income. So if the basic rate of tax is 27 per cent, the grossed-up interest is £365 ÷ 0.73 = £500. You will have to pay tax at the highest rate of tax you pay on this grossed-up amount of interest. But you are treated as having already paid basic rate tax on the interest – so you only have to hand over the difference. See the Example below.

If you don't pay tax, you can't claim back any of the tax the building society has paid. So a building society may not be the best home for your savings if your income is too low for you to pay tax. But it's always worth checking the return you can get on a building society against the return you can get on other investments – after allowing for any tax that's due. But if you're 64 or over, see p105.

When you fill in your Tax Return, you should put in the amount of building society interest you get – your Tax Inspector will work out the grossed-up amount. For the 1987–88 tax year, any higher rate tax is due on 1 December 1988 or within 30 days of the date on your Notice of Assessment if this is later.

ICTA 1970 s343(1), (3c).

Example

Charlie Carter gets £657 interest from his building society in the 1987–88 tax year. As he pays some higher rate tax, he realises he'll have to pay extra tax on this interest. He works out the grossed-up amount of interest – ie £657 ÷ 0.73 = £900.

He adds this to his other income and finds he's liable for tax at 40 per cent on the £900 grossed-up interest – ie £360 in all. But he's treated as having already paid tax on this interest at the 27 per cent basic rate (ie 27% of £900 = £243). So he has to hand over the difference of £360 − £243 = £117 to the Inland Revenue.

If Charlie had interest from a bank, licensed deposit-taker or local authority loan, the extra tax would be worked out in the same way.

Company loans and loans to individuals

Interest on company fixed-income loan stocks or debentures is paid with basic rate tax deducted. But interest on loans to private individuals will be paid without tax deducted.

For company loans bought after 13 March 1984, the proceeds are normally free of capital gains tax if you held them for a year or more, or if they are sold after 1 July 1986.

Note that if the loan is not repaid when it is due, and not likely to be repaid in future, you can set the loss off against gains for capital gains tax purposes if the loan was a loan stock or a loan or guarantee made to a UK-resident trader for use in his business. Otherwise you can't set the loss off.

ICTA 1970 s52, s242; CGTA 1979 s134, s136; FA 1984 s64; FA 1985 s67.

Commodities

How any profits you make from investing in commodities will be taxed is far from certain.

Profits from buying and selling *physical* commodities are likely to be treated as trading profits – and so taxed as earned income. A loss might count as a trading loss and you could set it off against the total of your income from all sources, but not against capital gains.

Just one isolated venture into the commodity *futures* market is likely to be treated as giving rise to a capital gain (or loss). But if you make a profit from a series of transactions, or invest as a member of a syndicate run by brokers or by a professional manager, this is likely to be treated as investment income – which means that you pay income tax at your highest rate(s).

Covenants

Payments under a deed of covenant are made with basic rate tax already deducted. If you're a non-taxpayer you can claim back the tax deducted. And normally, there's no higher rate tax to pay, even if you're a higher rate taxpayer. For more details, see p127.

Friendly society policies

Some societies have tax advantages such as paying no income tax on the fund's income or capital gains tax on any gains made in the fund. Since 1 September 1987, you have been able to

invest £100 a year in a friendly society policy of 10 years or more without paying tax on what you get back at the end. Previously, you had to pay tax on the proceeds of any friendly society policy where the amount of the life cover was more than £750. This meant that you could save only small sums for a limited period of time.
ICTA s332; FA 1980 s57; FA 1984 s73; FA 1987 s30.

Income and growth bonds

These bonds are set up in different ways, often consisting of one or more life insurance policies and one or more annuities. The tax treatment of any bond will depend on how it's set up. Bonds can include various life insurance products, such as deferred annuities with a cash option, immediate temporary annuities, single-premium endowment policies or regular-premium endowment policies.

Very briefly, the tax treatment is as follows:
● deferred annuity with cash option – proceeds are liable to tax at your highest rate on the profit you make (but you may be able to get top-slicing relief). See p302
● immediate temporary annuity – the income you get is treated as income from a voluntarily purchased annuity. The company normally deducts basic rate tax before paying it out to you. See p320
● endowment policies – at the end of the term, proceeds are taxed as a gain on a life insurance policy (if the policy is a non-qualifying one). Income from any bonuses cashed are treated as cashing-in part of a life insurance policy. See p307.

Let property

In general, income from letting property is taxed as investment income. But, in some cases, part or all of the income from furnished property can count as earnings from a business. See p254.

Licensed deposit-takers

You won't have to pay basic rate tax on the interest you get, because the company will have already paid tax to the Inland Revenue – at the same rate as banks and building societies (pages 279 and 280). If you're a higher rate taxpayer, you will have to pay more tax (see Example on p280 for how this is worked out). If you're a non-taxpayer, you won't be able to claim back the tax deducted. Since 6 April 1986, interest from foreign currency deposits at UK branches of deposit-takers has been taxed in the same way.

Before 6 April 1985, interest was normally paid with basic rate tax deducted but non-taxpayers could claim it back. *FA 1984 s27, Sch 8.*

Life insurance policies

With regular-premium policies, there is normally no tax to pay on the proceeds as long as you don't cash the policy in before ten years or the first three-quarters of the term, whichever is the shorter. For more details, see p298. And for the rules on tax relief for policies taken out before 14 March 1984, see p310. With single-premium bonds, there's no basic rate tax to pay when you cash them in, but there could be higher rate tax – see p301.

Local authority investments

Interest on local authority loans and stock, including yearling bonds, is paid with basic rate tax already deducted. Any gain you make when you dispose of stock or bonds is liable to capital gains tax – see p415. Since 6 April 1986, non-taxpayers haven't been able to claim back the tax deducted on a local authority loan issued after 18 November 1984 (as with banks and building societies – see p279).

Maintenance payments

Payments can be *voluntary* (if you can't be made to pay up) or *enforceable* (if you are legally obliged to – under a Court Order, say).

If you get voluntary payments, you don't have to pay tax on them. If enforceable payments you get are below a certain amount and are made under a UK Court Order for weekly or monthly amounts, they are *small maintenance payments*. These will be paid to you without basic rate tax deducted. If your income is high enough to pay tax, you'll have to pay some tax on the payments. For other enforceable payments, basic rate tax has already been deducted. If you pay no tax or pay less than the amount deducted, you can claim tax back. If you pay higher rate tax, you'll have to pay extra. If you've remarried, payments count as the husband's income, even if paid to the wife. For more details, see p90.

National Savings investments

With National Savings Investment and Ordinary accounts, and National Savings Income Bonds, Deposit Bonds and Index-linked Income Bonds, interest is paid without deduction of tax – and is normally taxed on a *preceding year basis* (see p276). With National Savings Certificates and Yearly Plan, index-linked SAYE and premium bonds, the proceeds are free of income tax and capital gains tax.

With National Savings Ordinary accounts, the first £70 of interest is free of tax – for husband and wife, it's £70 each. Anything more than that is taxed at basic and higher rates, if applicable. Any one person is allowed only £70 free of tax, however many National Savings Bank accounts he or she has. Note that if you and your wife have separate accounts and you have, say, £100 interest and your wife has £20, you will have to pay tax on £30 (ie £100 − £70) of your interest, even though the combined interest isn't more than 2 × £70 = £140. If you and your wife have a joint account, however, you can have £140 interest free of tax.

ICTA 1970 s109(2), s414(1a), s415(1); FA 1981 s34.

Shares

When you get dividends from UK companies there is no basic rate tax to pay. With the dividends you get a tax credit. Your gross (before-tax) income is taken to be the amount of the dividend plus the amount of tax credit. The tax credit for the 1987–88 tax year works out at 27 per cent of the gross income. So if, say, the dividend is £73, the tax credit will be £27 and the gross income £100. A basic rate taxpayer has no more tax to pay and a non-taxpayer can claim tax back. If you pay tax at higher rates, you will have to pay extra tax, but the tax credit counts as tax already paid. For the 1987–88 tax year, any higher rate tax is due on 1 December 1988 (or within 30 days of the date on your Notice of Assessment, if later). In your Tax Return you should enter both the amount of the dividend and the amount of the tax credit.

When you sell your shares, any increase in value counts as a capital gain – see p436 for more details.

If the company gives you more shares as a result of a **bonus** (or **scrip**) issue, you are not liable to income tax unless you've chosen to have the shares instead of a cash dividend (a few companies give you the choice). If this is the case, you are liable to income tax on the cash equivalent of the shares.

If you buy ordinary shares or investment trust shares in a Personal Equity Plan, you will get the gross amount of the dividend – see p289. If you buy ordinary shares in certain unquoted companies under the Business Expansion Scheme you'll get tax relief – see p292.

For details of share option or profit-sharing schemes, see p174.

ICTA 1970 s232, s242; FA 1986 s39.

> **Tax vouchers**
>
> You get a tax voucher from the company (or unit trust – see overleaf) showing the amount of the dividend (or distribution) and the amount of the tax credit.
>
> With other types of income taxed before you get it, including distributions from unit trusts which specialise in British Government stocks, you normally get a tax voucher or other document from the payer. This tells you the gross (before-tax) amount of income, the tax deducted and the actual sum you get.
>
> Keep any tax vouchers as proof that tax has been credited or deducted.

Trust income

Trusts pay tax on their income – in the 1987–88 tax year, at 45 per cent if they are discretionary trusts, at the basic rate of 27 per cent otherwise. This applies whether the income is kept by the trusts or paid out to beneficiaries. With income paid out by the trust, you get a tax credit of the amount of tax deducted.

If you are a beneficiary of a discretionary trust, and the highest rate of tax you pay is less than 45 per cent, consider asking the trustees to pay out to you as much of the trust's income as possible. You'd be able to claim tax back from the taxman. For more on trusts, see p397.
ICTA 1970 s435–444; FA 1973 s16–17.

Unit trusts

With distributions from most unit trusts, each distribution is accompanied by a tax credit. Your gross (before-tax) income is taken to be the distribution *plus* the tax credit (see *Shares* opposite).

With distributions from unit trusts which specialise in British Government stocks, tax is deducted (usually at the 27 per cent basic rate) before the income is paid to you (from the point of view of the investor, this is much the same as distributions from other unit trusts).

With the *first* distribution you get from a unit trust you're likely to get an **equalisation** payment. This is a return of part of the money you first invested, so doesn't count as income and isn't taxable.

With an **accumulation** unit trust (where income is automatically reinvested for you) the amount reinvested – apart from any equalisation payment – counts as income and is taxable.

In your Tax Return you should enter the amount of the distribution and the amount of the tax credit (or tax deducted if the unit trust invests in British Government stocks).

If you buy unit trusts within a Personal Equity Plan, the income will be tax-free – see p289.
ICTA 1970 s54, s232, s354; FA 1980 s60; FA 1986 s39.

Which schedules?

Investment income comes under the following schedules:

Schedule A – income from letting property in the UK

Schedule C – income from Government stocks, UK and foreign, paid through a UK paying agent, such as a bank

Schedule D, Case III – interest, annuities or other annual payments

Schedule D, Case IV – income from foreign securities

Schedule D, Case V – income from foreign possessions

Schedule D, Case VI – income not assessable under any other case or schedule (includes rents from letting furnished property)

Schedule F – distributions and dividends of a UK resident company.

Income regarded as yours during the administration period of a will

Any income which is regarded as yours during the administration period of a will or intestacy (ie while the details of who gets what are being worked out), will be paid to you with basic rate tax deducted.

ICTA 1970 s426(4), s427.

Tax on income from overseas investments

The tax treatment of income from abroad can be extraordinarily complicated, and if you have a substantial amount of such income you'll need to get specialist advice – and look at Inland Revenue leaflets IR6 and IR20.

In general, if you're resident and ordinarily resident in the UK (see p178), all your income is liable to UK tax, whether or not it is brought into this country. However, income from overseas investments is often taxed in the country in which it originates – so two lots of tax could be charged on one lot of income. The UK government has made agreements with a wide range of countries to limit the extent to which income may be taxed twice. Under one of these *double taxation agreements*, the amount of tax which a foreign government deducts from income before it reaches you is reduced. The tax which is actually deducted is allowed as a tax credit against the UK tax on the same income.

Suppose, for example, that you're entitled to £1,000 in dividends from the US. Tax at 30 per cent would normally be held back by the US before paying over the dividends to non-US residents. However, because of our double taxation agreement with the US, only 15 per cent is withheld – ie you get £850. If, say, you're liable for tax in the UK at 40 per cent on your £1,000 gross dividends, there'd be £400 tax to pay. But the £150 you've paid in tax to the US would be allowed as credit against the £400 of UK tax you're liable for – so you'd have to hand over to the taxman £250, not £400.

If you are liable for no UK tax (or less than has been deducted under a double taxation agreement) there'll be no further UK tax to pay – but you can't claim back the extra foreign tax you've paid.

How to get your relief

If your foreign income is paid to you through an agent (eg a bank) in the UK, who passes it on to you after deducting basic rate tax, the agent should allow for any double taxation agreement when doing his sums. But if the income is paid direct to you from abroad, you have to apply for double taxation relief yourself. To get the foreign tax reduced, get an application form from the Inland Revenue, Inspector of Foreign Dividends, Hinchley Wood, Lynwood Road, Thames Ditton, Surrey, KT7 0DP. To get a credit for the foreign tax withheld, apply to your Tax Inspector.

When UK tax is due

Your tax bill is normally based on the foreign income you get in the preceding tax year – ie your tax bill for the 1987–88 tax year would be based on the foreign income you got in the 1986–87 tax year. Special rules apply in the first three and last two years in which you get foreign income of this type – see p276. Note, however, that income from Eire is always taxed on a current year basis.

ICTA 1970 s109(2), s159, s497–498, and (for Eire) Sch 12(2); FA 1976 s49 (Eire).

Remittance basis

If this applies, you are taxed only on what income you bring into the UK. You can claim remittance basis if you're resident but not domiciled in the UK, or if you are a British subject or a citizen of the Republic of Ireland *and* you are resident but not ordinarily resident in the UK.

ICTA 1970 s122(2).

Offshore funds

Since 1 January 1984, any gain which you sell when you get an investment in an offshore fund has been liable to income tax at your highest rate, unless the fund has *distributor status*, in which case only its income is liable to income tax. An offshore fund can get distributor status if, for example, it distributes all its income.

Before 1 January 1984, any gain was liable to capital gains tax.

FA 1984 s92–98.

Tax-saving tips

• if you pay tax at higher rates, consider investing in things where the return is tax-free. Or consider investing for capital gains rather than income (the first £6,600 of net taxable gains is tax-free in the 1987–88 tax year, the remainder is taxed at 30 per cent). The higher the rate of tax you pay, the more attractive this becomes

• if you don't pay tax, a bank, building society, licensed deposit-taker or local authority loan may not be the best home for your money

• if you start getting income which is not taxed before you get it – eg National Savings accounts or bonds – you can take advantage of the special rules which apply when you start getting such income. If the amount of interest in year 3 is lower than in year 2, tell the taxman that you want your tax bill for year 3 to be based on the interest you actually got in year 3. (You can make this choice at any time within six years of the end of year 3)

• if you get investment income taxed before you get it and you don't pay tax (or pay less than has been deducted), don't forget to claim back the tax paid from the taxman

• if your income is in the region where each extra £ of taxable income loses you age allowance, investments where the return is tax-free (eg National Savings Certificates) may give you a higher after-tax return than things like a building society account where the interest is included in your 'total income'

• if you buy British Government stocks on the National Savings Stock Register you will get the interest without tax deducted and pay the tax later (if you buy through a stockbroker you get the interest with basic rate tax already deducted).

23 PERSONAL EQUITY PLANS

Personal Equity Plans (PEPs) came into operation on 1 January 1987 to encourage investment in British industry. Under a PEP, you can buy shares, unit trusts and shares in investment trust companies without paying tax on the dividend income or on any capital gain. This makes it a relatively cheap way of investing in the Stock Market – but you have to meet certain conditions:

● you can't set up your own PEP – you have to invest through a plan manager (eg a bank or unit trust manager) whose charges may be high

● there are strict rules about how much you can invest and what you can invest in

● to qualify for the tax benefits, you have to leave your money tied up in your PEP until at least 31 December of the year *after* the year in which you began your PEP.

FA 1986 s39.

The investment

The maximum you can invest in any one year (running from 1 January to 31 December) is £2,400 and with one plan manager only (though you can open another PEP the following year with another plan manager). A husband and wife can each invest the maximum in their own PEP. There is no minimum investment in theory, but in practice some plan managers may impose a minimum. If you don't invest the maximum, you can't carry your unused allowance forward to the next year. So, even if you invest only £1,400 in 1987, you can't then invest £3,400 in 1988.

To get the tax benefits, you have to leave your money invested in the PEP for the qualifying period – see overleaf. The plan manager is responsible for reclaiming tax that is normally deducted from dividends on your behalf – you don't need to enter a PEP on your Tax Return unless you withdraw money from it before the qualifying period is completed.

There are two main tax benefits:

● income tax. There is no tax to pay on any interest you may get on money within a plan waiting to be invested. Dividends are usually paid with the equivalent of basic rate tax already

deducted – the plan manager will reclaim that tax for you and reinvest it in your PEP
• capital gains tax. Any capital gain you make on your investments in the PEP is free of capital gains tax. This is on top of the normal limit for exemption from capital gains tax – £6,600 in the 1987–88 tax year.

The investor

PEPs are open to anyone aged 18 or over who is resident in the UK for tax purposes (see p178). The level of benefit you receive will depend on the rate of tax you pay:
• non-taxpayers can already reclaim the tax deducted from dividends so a PEP doesn't offer them an extra tax advantage
• basic rate taxpayers will get 27 per cent more dividend than they would have if they invested outside a PEP
• higher rate taxpayers will get 27 per cent more dividend than if they invested outside a PEP but because they won't have to pay any higher rate tax on the dividend, they save up to their top rate of tax – so the maximum tax saving is 60 per cent.

Example

Alan Avon pays tax at 50 per cent. He invests £2,000 in shares held in a PEP. In the first year he receives dividends of £100 which includes £27 tax which the plan manager reclaimed on his behalf. The reclaimed tax is reinvested in the PEP but Alan saves an additional £23 which is the extra tax he would normally have had to pay on the dividend – so his total tax saving is £27 + £23 = £50.

Length of investment

To get the full tax benefits, you have to keep your money invested in a PEP for a qualifying period of at least a full calendar year (ie 1 January to 31 December – see Diagram). After the end of the year in which you start your PEP, you can put no more cash into it. After 31 December of the year in which you started your PEP, the shares and so on which make up your PEP can carry on being bought and sold, but the proceeds of the sales and any dividends (together with the reclaimed tax) must be reinvested within the PEP within 28 days or you lose the tax benefits. If you withdraw anything from the PEP before the end of the qualifying period, you will get only the proceeds of your investments less any tax that has been reclaimed. The investments you withdraw will be treated as though you had bought and sold them in the normal way and you may have to pay higher rate tax and capital gains tax on them (see p415 for how capital gains tax is worked out).

Qualifying investments

There are certain restrictions on the type and proportion of investments you can hold in a PEP. You can include:
● shares in UK incorporated companies quoted on The Stock Exchange and shares on the Unlisted Securities Market
● authorised unit trusts and/or shares in investment trust companies but these can form only 25 per cent or £420 (whichever is larger) of your total PEP investments.

You can't transfer shares or unit trusts you already own into a PEP – you have to invest in cash.

During the first year of your PEP, you can hold as much cash in your PEP as you like, up to the maximum of £2,400. After 31 December of the year in which you began your PEP, the amount of the cash you can hold goes down to a maximum of £240 or ten per cent of your total investments (whichever is larger).

SI 1986/1948

Types of PEP

● Discretionary PEP schemes. With these you leave it to the plan manager to choose and manage your investments for you. There are also discretionary PEPs made up of unit trusts only, up to a maximum investment of £420.
● Non-discretionary or advisory PEPs. With these, you choose the investments yourself and instruct the plan manager to buy and sell for you. There may be limitations on the list of shares that the plan manager gives you to choose from.

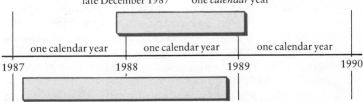

In early January 1989, Victoria decides to sell some shares and withdraw the cash from her PEP. She knows that she won't lose the tax benefits because she has completed the qualifying period of one *calendar* year

Victoria Vauxhall invests in a PEP in late December 1987

one calendar year | one calendar year | one calendar year

1987   1988   1989   1990

William Warwick invests in a PEP in February 1987

In November 1988, William wants to withdraw some cash from his PEP but is told that he will lose the tax benefits because he hasn't completed the qualifying period. Although he has held his PEP for longer than Victoria Vauxhall, he *hasn't* held it for one full *calendar* year.

24 THE BUSINESS EXPANSION SCHEME

The Business Expansion Scheme (BES) was set up to encourage investment in new or small companies, which find it difficult to raise money. Under the scheme, you buy shares in such a company and get tax relief on what you invest at your top rate of tax – ie up to 60 per cent in the 1987–88 tax year. It's a cheap way of buying shares – but there are snags:
• you are investing in the ordinary shares of unquoted companies, so it may be risky. At worst, you could lose all your money
• there are strict rules about who can invest, and about which investments qualify.
FA 1983 s26 and Sch 5; F(no2)A 1983 s5 and Sch1; IR51; FA 1984 s37; FA 1985 s44; FA 1986 s40 and Sch 9; FA 1987 s42.

Example

Ernest Ellinger invests £5,000 in a company which qualifies under the scheme. He pays tax at 50% on at least £5,000 of his income, so the cost to him after tax relief is £2,500. After five years, he sells the shares for £5,000. So he's made a gain of £2,500 (a yearly return of nearly 15%) even though the shares have not increased in value.

The investment

The maximum investment you can get tax relief on in any one tax year is £40,000. This limit applies to a married couple as well as a single person, so husband and wife can't invest more than the £40,000 between them. The minimum you can invest in any one company is £500 (but see *Investment funds*). The investment reduces your taxable income but *not* your 'total income' (see p29).

To get relief, you need a certificate from the company stating that the necessary conditions have been met – see opposite. Send this to your tax office. You'll generally get your tax relief either through your PAYE coding (see p149) or by getting a lower tax bill.

You can also get tax relief on the interest paid on a loan to buy the shares if you are buying 5 per cent or more of the share capital and the company is a *close company* – broadly, one that is owned by five or fewer people or by its directors.

In general, you get relief for the tax year in which the shares are issued. However, from 5 April 1987, if you invest in the first half of the tax year – between 6 April and 6 October – you can claim tax relief on up to half of the investment against your income in the previous year. The maximum amount you can carry back is £5,000, so this restriction will affect those who invest more than £10,000 in BES investments in the first half of the tax year. You'll generally get tax relief that's been set against the preceding year's income in the form of a cheque.

Example

John Jarvis invests a total of £12,000 in four BES companies in the first half of the 1987–88 tax year. He can carry back half of *each* investment (but only up to the £5,000 limit) to set against his income in the 1986–87 tax year. He invested just £10,000 in BES in 1986–87 so the £5,000 carried back won't take his 1986–87 BES investment total over the £40,000 limit. He can now qualify for tax relief on up to £33,000 further BES investment in 1987–88, as only £7,000 of the £12,000 invested so far counts against the £40,000 limit.

Investment funds

Investment funds spread your investment among several BES companies, which they select for you. Funds can either be 'approved' or 'non-approved'. Funds approved by the Inland Revenue can spread your investment more widely than other funds, so you can have less than £500 in shares in each company. The minimum investment in an approved fund is £2,000. Non-approved funds also select BES companies for you to invest in, but you must invest a minimum of £500 in each. The minimum investment in a non-approved fund is fixed by the fund – generally at a level of at least £1,000.

The investor

The scheme applies only to *outside investors* – ie not to people putting money into their own business. To count as an outside investor:
● you must end up owning not more than 30 per cent of the business (including what your family or business partners own). Your family includes your husband or wife, parents, grandparents, children or grandchildren. Owning 30 per cent means, say, 30 per cent of the ordinary shares *or* 30 per cent of

the share and loan capital together (excluding any bank overdraft), *or* 30% of the voting shares
- **AND** you mustn't be a *paid* director or employee of the company. You may be able to qualify for relief if you are an unpaid director (even if you get paid some expenses) or if you receive fees for providing professional services (eg legal or accountancy) to the company other than as a director or employee.

To qualify you must be resident and ordinarily resident in the UK (see p178) for the tax year in which the investment is made.

Example

David Durban invests in two unquoted companies in the 1987–88 tax year. With the first company, the share capital is to be £40,000. David invests £10,000, on which he can get full tax relief.

David invests £20,000 in the second company and the share capital is increased to £70,000. But David's parents have already invested £10,000 in the company and so David's investment brings the amount of share capital owned by his family to over 30 per cent. David can't get tax relief for *any* of his investment in the second company. If he'd invested a smaller sum – eg £5,000 – he could have got tax relief.

David's second investment
Share capital £70,000

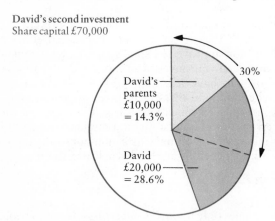

David's parents £10,000 = 14.3%

David £20,000 = 28.6%

30%

Length of investment

To get full tax relief, you've got to invest for at least five years. At the end of this time, you can sell the shares without losing any tax relief. If you sell the shares before five years are up, the relief you get is reduced by the amount of the sales proceeds – ie lost entirely if you sell the shares for the same as or more than the before-tax-relief cost to you. The relief is also completely lost if the sale is not an *arm's length* one (eg one where a proper commercial price is paid). If you get *value* from the company – eg fringe benefits or repayment of a loan – your relief is also reduced. The relief will be lost by re-opening your tax liability for the year in which relief was given.

You can also lose tax relief if, in the first three years, the company in which you invested ceases to qualify under the Scheme – eg changes its business or becomes quoted (see below). But you don't lose the relief if the company is wound up for bona fide commercial reasons.

The shares

Your investment must be in new ordinary shares and it must be genuinely additional funds – eg you and someone else can't enter into an agreement to invest in each other's company and get relief.

The company

There are several conditions which a company has to meet, including:
- it must be unquoted, so its shares can't be bought and sold on The Stock Exchange, the Unlisted Securities Market or the Third Market
- it must carry on business mainly in the UK– although it can export some or even all of its output. The company must have been formed in the UK and be resident there
- it can have subsidiaries as long as they are 100 per cent owned by the parent, and the subsidiaries are themselves qualifying companies.

A company won't qualify if:
- its business is, for example, banking, farming, insurance, leasing or hiring, share-dealing, accountancy or legal services or property development (for shares issued on or after 20 March 1985)
- it holds collectable goods (such as wine and antiques) purely as investments (for shares issued after 18 March 1986)
- more than half its net assets consist of property or land, excluding the first £50,000 of share capital issued in a year (for shares issued after 18 March 1986)
- it carries on business similar to that of another company under the control of the same person.

If it's a new company, you won't normally be able to claim tax relief on your investments until it has traded for four months, but the relief will apply to the tax year in which the shares are issued.

Capital gains tax

Shares issued on or after 18 March 1986 are free of capital gains tax the first time they are sold – ie by the original investor. For shares issued before then, the normal capital gains tax rules apply (see p415). The price you paid is taken as the *gross* amount – ie ignoring the tax relief you get. But any losses you make won't normally count as such for capital gains tax purposes.

25 LIFE INSURANCE

Life insurance at its simplest is a way of providing for your dependants when you die. But as you can see from the Table overleaf, policies have gone beyond this simplest form. Apart from insurance policies which pay out only when you die, there are policies which are mainly investments. Many of these were designed to make use of the premium subsidy available for qualifying policies – see p310. Though you can still get this subsidy on policies taken out on or before 13 March 1984, those issued after that date don't benefit. But a qualifying policy still has tax advantages when it pays out.

Tax on the proceeds

You won't have to pay income tax on the proceeds of *any* life insurance policy if (even with the policy gain added to your income) you pay tax at no more than the basic rate. And even if you're a higher rate taxpayer there'll be no tax to pay on the proceeds of a *qualifying policy* if you keep it for long enough – see opposite. Otherwise you may have to pay tax on any gain you make. How you work out the gain depends on whether the policy has come to the end of its term or you're cashing-in all or part of it early.

Note that there's normally no capital gains tax to pay on the proceeds of a life insurance policy – but see opposite and p309.

> **Basic rate taxpayers**
> Without the premium subsidy to offset high initial charges and surrender penalties on many insurance-type investments, basic rate taxpayers will often do better to choose other investments, such as unit trusts.

Qualifying policies

When a qualifying policy reaches the end of its term or pays out due to death of the person insured, the proceeds are free of income tax. So, for example, if you've kept a qualifying endowment policy till it matures there's no tax to pay. If you've kept the policy for at least 10 years (or three-quarters of the term if this is less), there won't be income tax to pay either – see p306 for more details.

Broadly, life insurance policies taken out or altered after 19 March 1968 qualify if you pay regular premiums – eg monthly or yearly. Policies issued before then qualify automatically. But there are other rules too. For example, the policy must be capable of running for at least 10 years (though for term insurance the limit is at least one year). And there are restrictions on how the premiums you pay can vary year by year and, for some policies, on the amount the policy pays out if you die during its term. The company will tell you if a policy qualifies or not.

Some types of life insurance are treated as qualifying whether or not they meet the requirements – for example, mortgage protection policies, family income benefit policies. But note that, since 18 November 1983, new policies issued by foreign companies don't qualify unless they're issued and administered by a UK branch.

Non-qualifying policies

You may have to pay tax on the proceeds of a non-qualifying policy when it matures. The gain you make counts as a taxable gain – see p302 for how to work out the gain and how it is taxed.

Tax the company pays

Though *you* get a tax-free return from a qualifying policy (or free of basic rate tax from a non-qualifying one), the insurance company has to pay tax. On profits, it pays corporation tax which is charged at the higher rate for companies – currently 35 per cent, rather than the 27 per cent paid by individuals. The 1987 Budget proposed that it pay corporation tax on capital gains too. On income from investments, it may pay corporation tax, or – more often – the equivalent of basic rate income tax. So, you have, in effect, already paid basic rate income tax.

Note that some of the business done by friendly societies is *tax-exempt*. So they don't have to pay corporation tax, or tax on investment income or capital gains which come from this business.

Finding your policy

	Term insurance	Whole-life insurance	
For investment or protection?	protection	either or both	
Qualifying policy? [1]	yes, if term one year or more	yes	
How you pay	regular premiums	regular premiums	
The benefits	**level-term** – pays out a lump sum if you die before a fixed date – if you don't die you normally get nothing. **decreasing term** – as with level term but cover decreases over the years – commonly used to pay off a mortgage if you die *(mortgage protection policy)*. **family income benefit** – pays out a tax-free income to your dependants over the remaining years of the term. Can also pay income increasing over the years. Some policies allow for some or all income to be paid as a lump sum. **flexible term insurance** – as with term insurance but you have various options – eg to increase the amount of cover each year, to continuously renew the policy at the end of each term, to convert it to an investment-type policy – without further medical checks. But watch out if you get the premium subsidy as you could lose it if you take up an option – see p312.	**whole-life** – pays out a lump sum when you die – however far in the future. Policies can be *without-profits* which guarantee a fixed sum, or *with-profits* which means that the amount which will be paid out increases over the years as the company adds bonuses. With some policies you stop paying the premiums when you reach a certain age (65, say). You can cash-in the policy before you die. **unit-linked whole-life** – your premiums buy units in funds run by the life insurance company. Some of the units are cashed each month to pay for a whole-life policy – units left are your investment. With *flexible cover plans* you can choose the amount of life cover you get and therefore how much of your premiums are used for investment. You can cash-in the policy before you die – but watch out for high surrender charges in the first few years.	

[1] Individual policies may not meet all the qualifying requirements even where we say yes – check with your insurance company.

Endowment (and friendly society) policies	Other investment-type life insurance
either or both	investment
yes, if term ten years or more	no – but see *The benefits*
regular premiums	single premium
endowment – pays out a lump sum at a fixed date or if you die before then. Policies can be with or without profits (see *whole-life*). You can cash-in the policy early – but watch out for low surrender values in the first few years. **unit-linked savings plans** – pay out a lump sum at a fixed date or if you die before then. Part of each premium goes to buy term insurance, the rest buys units in one or more investment funds. The level of life cover may be low. You can cash-in the policy early – but watch out for high surrender charges in the first few years. **friendly society savings plans** – pay out a lump sum at a fixed date or if you die before then. The level of life cover is low, and the tax-free business is limited. The limit rose slightly on 1 September 1987, to cover policies with premiums of not more than £100 a year (10 per cent of the premiums are ignored if premiums are paid more often than once a year). You can cash-in the policy early but the most you'll get back is the premiums paid (plus the premium subsidy if you got it – see p 310).	**unit-linked single-premium bonds** – pay out a lump sum when you cash them in, or if you die before then. Your premium buys units in a fund run by the insurance company. The level of life cover may be low. You can cash-in early. **income bonds** – pay out a fixed income for a set number of years, and then return your original investment. Bonds are based on *annuities* and maybe *endowment policies* (which can be qualifying). Bond will pay out if you die before a fixed date, but level of life cover is low. With some bonds you can't cash-in early. See p282 for more details. **growth bonds** – pay out a lump sum at a fixed date, or if you die before then. Bonds are based on *annuities* and/or *endowment policies* (which can be qualifying). The level of life cover is low, and with some bonds you can't cash-in early. See p282 for more details.

	Term insurance	Whole-life insurance	
What the policies are useful for	• protecting your dependants from suffering financially if you die during the term of the insurance • paying a large inheritance tax bill if death occurs within a certain time. For example, someone who has received a lifetime gift may be caught by inheritance tax if the giver dies within seven years – see p351	• protecting your dependants from suffering financially when you die – however far in the future • possibly, building up a lump sum. If for your heirs, see p316 • paying inheritance tax when you die. A husband and wife leaving everything to each other could take out *last survivor* insurance which pays out when the second person dies (ie when the tax bill is due)	

Working out the gain on a non-qualifying policy

When a policy comes to an end, the gain is normally the amount you get *less* the total premiums paid (but see p306 if you've cashed-in part of your policy earlier). If the gain arises because the person dies, the gain is the cash-in value of the policy immediately before death (if this is less than the sum insured) *less* the premiums paid.

How the proceeds are taxed

The gain (as calculated above) is added to your investment income for the year in which the policy comes to an end. You're liable for higher rate income tax on the gain (but *not* basic rate tax). So if your highest rate of tax is 50 per cent, you'd have to pay tax at $50 - 27 = 23$ per cent on the policy gain – see Example opposite. But if adding the gain to your income means that you'd be paying tax at a higher rate than you would otherwise have done – because it pushes part of your income into the next income tax bracket – the taxman should apply *top-slicing relief* to reduce your tax bill.

Top-slicing relief

Top-slicing relief, in effect, spreads the gain you make over the years that the policy has run. To work out your tax bill with top-slicing relief, first work out your *average yearly gain* by

Endowment (and friendly society) policies	Other investment-type life insurance
• building up a lump sum. If for your heirs, see p316 • paying off a mortgage	**unit-linked single premium bonds** • taking 5 per cent a year tax-free from your investment **unit-linked single-premium bonds and growth bonds** • deferring income from investments until a later date, when you are paying a lower rate of income tax **income bonds** • providing an income

dividing the total gain by the number of *complete* years that the policy ran for. Then add this average yearly gain to your income for the tax year, and work out the higher rate tax on the average yearly gain. To get your tax bill on the whole gain, multiply the tax bill on your average yearly gain by the number of complete years you have spread the gain over. See Diagram and Example overleaf. The gain counts as investment income. So for a married couple the gain is added to the husband's income, and (until 5 April 1984), there might have been *investment income surcharge* to pay as well as higher rate tax – see p278.

Qualifying policies: ICTA 1970 s393, Sch1; FA 1971 Sch3; FA 1975 Sch2; FA 1976 Sch4; FA 1984 s76 Sch15. Tax on the proceeds: ICTA 1970 s394, s395, s399, s400; FA 1975 Sch2; FA 1978 Sch2.

Example of top-slicing relief

Harris Granby bought a £20,000 single-premium bond in December 1982. He cashed it in for £30,000 in June 1987 –

The general election held on 11 June 1987 meant that the Finance Act confirming the tax rules for the 1987–88 tax year was rushed through in shortened form. Some of the Chancellor's 1987 Budget proposals were shelved, but the Conservative party has said that it would re-introduce them on being returned to power. We've marked these pre-election proposals with this symbol: 💼

making a gain of £10,000. He already has taxable income for the 1987–88 tax year of £18,400. If his tax bill was worked out in the normal way he would have to pay tax on his gain as shown below.

Tax on the gain – without top-slicing relief

rate of tax	income on which Harris pays this rate of tax	gain on bond	amount of basic and higher rate tax
27%	£17,900		£4,833
40%	£ 500		£ 200
40%		£2,000	£ 800
45%		£5,000	£2,250
50%		£3,000	£1,500
total gain on bond		£10,000	
basic and higher rate tax on gain			£4,550
subtract tax at basic rate on gain (27% of £10,000)			£2,700
total tax bill on gain			£1,850

But Harris gets top-slicing relief. With this, the *average yearly gain* of £2,500 (ie the £10,000 total gain divided by the four complete years the policy ran for) is added to his investment income for the year. His total tax bill on the gain is the higher rate tax he'd pay on this average yearly gain, times the number of complete years he held the bond. Top-slicing relief saves Harris £1,850 − £1,400 = £450.

Tax on the gain – with top-slicing relief

rate of tax	income on which Harris pays this rate of tax	gain on bond	amount of basic and higher rate tax
27%	£17,900		£4,833
40%	£ 500		£ 200
40%		£2,000	£ 800
45%		£ 500	£ 225
average yearly gain		£2,500	
basic and higher rate tax on average yearly gain			£1,025
subtract tax at basic rate on average yearly gain (27% of £2,500)			£ 675
so tax bill on average yearly gain is			£ 350
total tax bill on gain (£350 × 4)			£1,400

How top-slicing relief works

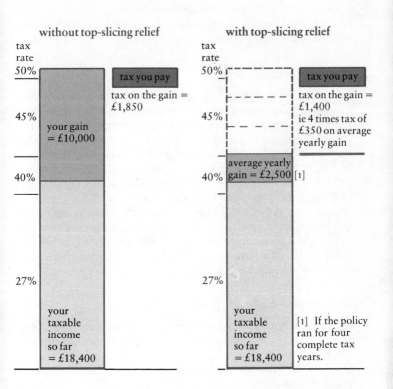

without top-slicing relief

tax rate

50% — tax you pay

your gain = £10,000

tax on the gain = £1,850

45%

40%

27%

your taxable income so far = £18,400

with top-slicing relief

tax rate

50% — tax you pay

tax on the gain = £1,400 ie 4 times tax of £350 on average yearly gain

45%

average yearly gain = £2,500 [1]

40%

27%

your taxable income so far = £18,400

[1] If the policy ran for four complete tax years.

Age allowance

Although when you cash-in all or part of a non-qualifying policy any gain is free of basic rate tax, the gain (without top-slicing relief) is counted as part of your income for the year. For most people this has no effect on their personal allowances. But if you're aged 65 or over during the tax year, increasing your income can reduce the *age allowance* (see p104) you get.

Age allowance is reduced by two-thirds of the amount by which a person's 'total income' exceeds a certain limit – £9,800 for the 1987–88 tax year. So if the gain from an insurance policy (or the excess if you cash-in part of a policy) means a reduction in your age allowance, you'll effectively pay more income tax, whether or not you're liable for higher rate tax.

ICTA 1970 s8; F(No2)A 1975 s31.

Cashing-in early

Life insurance policies with an investment element have some value – the *surrender value* – even before the policy comes to an end. How much tax you have to pay (if any) depends on whether or not the policy is a qualifying one.

Cashing-in a qualifying policy

If you've been paying regular premiums for at least three-quarters of the term of the policy, or 10 years, whichever is less, the gain you make remains tax-free. So with a 25-year term, there'd be no tax to pay if you surrendered after 10 years; with a 10-year term, there'd be no tax after 7½ years. But if you cash-in the policy before this, you'll be taxed on the gain in the same way as when a non-qualifying policy pays out. So you'll be liable for higher rate tax if it applies to you and will get top-slicing relief if this would cut your tax bill. You pay tax on the difference between the surrender value and the *gross* premiums paid (ie the premiums you've paid *plus* any premium subsidy – see p310). But you could find that some of your premium subsidy is *clawed-back*, too – see p313.

Cashing-in a non-qualifying policy

If you cash-in a non-qualifying policy before the end of its term you pay tax on the surrender value in the same way as if it had run for its full term – see p307. So you're liable for higher rate tax (but not basic rate tax) on the amount by which the cash-in value exceeds the premiums you've paid. You'll get top slicing relief if this would reduce your tax bill.

Example

Ernest Strident has a 10-year unit-linked savings plan for which the *gross* premiums (ie including the premium subsidy) are £50 a month. After five years he decides to cash-in the policy. The total gross premiums to date are £3,000 and the surrender value is £3,500, so he's made a gain of £500. His highest rate of tax for the year is 40 per cent (and the £500 gain doesn't push him into the next tax bracket, so there's no top-slicing relief). He has to pay tax at 40% − 27% = 13% on the £500 gain – ie £65 in all.

Cashing-in part of a policy

You may want to cash-in part of your policy, rather than the whole of it. Or, if bonuses are added (see Table on p300), you could surrender a bonus. This is treated in the same way as cashing-in part of your policy.

Cashing-in part of a qualifying policy

If you cash-in part of a qualifying policy after 10 years (or after three-quarters of its term if this is less), the gains you make are tax-free. But if you cash-in part of the policy before this, you'll be taxed in the same way as for non-qualifying policies – see below.

Cashing-in part of a non-qualifying policy

If you cash-in part of a policy rather than the whole of it, you may be able to avoid paying tax straight away. What happens is that you get a tax-free allowance for each *complete* year that the policy has run. So long as the allowance you're due is more than the total amount you get from the policy, there's no tax to pay at the time (though if you're 65 or over during the tax year, see *Age allowance* on p104). But when the term of the policy finally comes to an end or you cash the rest of the policy in, there may be tax to pay (see below).

For each of the first 20 years of the term of a policy the allowance is 1/20 (ie 5 per cent) of the premiums paid so far. For each year after the 20th year the allowance is 1/20 of the premiums paid in that year and the previous 19 years. So if, say, you pay £1,000 a year in premiums, your allowance after the first year will be £50, after the second £100, after the third £150, and so on. Allowances not used each year are carried forward. So, in our example, you'd have £300 of allowances by the end of the third year if you didn't use them until then.

Complete years are calculated from the date the policy is taken out – but you don't get an allowance until the first complete year starting after 13 March 1975. So if you took out a policy before then, there will be some years for which you don't get an allowance.

If you exceed your total allowances, the difference (the *excess*) is counted as a gain – see Diagram overleaf. This gain is treated in the same way as if you cash-in a whole policy – so is subject to higher rate tax but not basic rate tax . You'll get top-slicing relief if this reduces your tax bill – with the gain spread over the number of years you've had the policy, or the number of years you got allowances for if this is shorter. When an excess is added to your income, the allowances you've taken into account are cancelled, and you start building up allowances again.

How allowances and excesses work

total premiums paid so far – in this example,
a single premium paid at the start.

Year 1

Year 2

Year 3

if you cash in this much during year 4

Year 4

this amount   this amount is an excess
is tax-free   and is taxed as a gain

Key:

5% allowance for each year;
carried forward if not used in any
year.

Example

Harvey Redbridge's highest rate of tax is 50 per cent. He
bought a single-premium bond for £10,000 and wants to
withdraw as much as he can without paying tax at the moment.
For each of the first 20 years Harvey gets an allowance of 1/20
of the total premiums paid so far – ie 1/20 of £10,000 = £500.
He can cash-in £500 each year without paying tax in that year.
For the 21st year onwards his allowance is 1/20 of the
premiums paid in that year and the previous 19 years – zero
in Harvey's case as he paid for the policy all at once in the first
year. So if he uses up his allowances in the first 20 years he
won't be able to cash-in any more of his policy without paying
tax at the time (unless he's a basic rate taxpayer by then).

Paid-up policies

Making a policy paid-up means that you stop paying the premiums but don't take your money out. Making part of a policy paid-up means you can reduce your premiums.

If you make a policy paid-up the same rules apply as if you cash it in. However, you won't have to pay any tax due until the policy finally pays out. If the policy is a qualifying one (and you get the premium subsidy), and you make the policy paid-up within four years the *clawback* rules apply – see p313. Use the surrender value at the time you make the policy paid-up when you do the sums. The clawback will be deducted by the life insurance company when the policy finally pays out.
ICTA 1970 s394.

When the policy comes to an end

If you've cashed-in part of a policy before it finally comes to an end, the total gain on which you may have to pay tax is:
● the amount you get at the end *plus* any amounts you've had in the past, *less*
● the total premiums paid, any excesses you've already had (see p307) and any pre-14 March 1975 gains on the policy which the taxman was told about (either by you or the insurance company).

If after making these deductions you're left with a negative figure, you can subtract this from your 'total income' to reduce your higher rate tax bill. But you can't subtract more than the total of the excesses you've made from partial surrenders and pre-14 March 1975 gains.

Example

When Harvey's single-premium bond comes to an end, he's still paying tax at 50 per cent and so he'll have to pay tax on his gain. If Harvey used up his £500 allowance for each of the first 20 years, he'd have had 20 × £500 = £10,000 from the policy. If he got another £5,000, say, when the policy ended, his total gain would be £15,000 *minus* the £10,000 premium = £5,000, which would be added to his income for the year. Harvey would pay higher rate (but no basic rate) tax on the proceeds – but would get top-slicing relief (see p302) if it helped.
ICTA 1970 s394–395, s399; FA 1975 Sch2.

Capital gains and unit-linked policies

With a unit-linked policy, the insurance company invests your premiums in units in one or more investment funds. However, you don't own the units – the insurance company does. And so while you can get a tax-free return, the company has to pay tax on its investment income and on the capital gains it makes. In practice, the company doesn't have to sell units every time a policy is cashed-in. So, in effect, the rate at which it pays any tax on capital gains can be lower than the full percentage – say, 10 to 20 per cent. This is either deducted from the investment fund or from the proceeds of the policy when you cash it in. So if you see that a deduction has been made for tax on capital gains, it's not tax on *your* gains but on the company's. You can't claim it back as being part of your £6,600 capital gains tax limit or by setting losses against it.

Cluster policies

With some policies, instead of your premiums buying just one insurance policy, they can be used to buy several policies. For example, if your premium was £50 a month you might get a cluster of ten policies, each with a premium of £5 a month. The advantage of cluster policies is that you don't have to treat all the policies in the same way. If you're a higher rate taxpayer and you cash-in part of a non-qualifying policy, you will be taxed on any *excess* that arises (see p307). You could end up paying less tax at the time if you have a cluster of policies, and cash-in one (or more) of them. (But if you're paying tax at the same rate when you finally cash-in the rest of the proceeds, you'll pay the same amount of tax in the long run.) And if you're getting the premium subsidy there'll be less *clawback* (see p313) when you cash-in one or more of your cluster than if you cashed-in part of a single policy.

Tax relief on premiums

Qualifying policies not only have tax advantages when they pay out, but for policies issued before 14 March 1984 you may also be able to claim a subsidy from the taxman. The subsidy is worked out as 15 per cent of each premium, and you can get it if:
● the policy was issued before 14 March 1984 (see p312 if it's been varied since then)
● the policy is a qualifying one (see p299)
● the policy insures your life or that of your husband or wife
● the policy was issued by a UK company, a company legally trading in the UK, or a registered friendly society
● you are a UK resident (if you are non-resident but have UK income, you may be able to claim the subsidy – check with the taxman).

If you're eligible, you will usually pay the premiums *net* of premium subsidy – the insurance company claims the difference from the Inland Revenue (whether *you* pay tax or not). See Diagram below for how this works in practice – and how the subsidy can help investors. You can claim the subsidy on *gross* premiums you pay of up to £1,500 a year or one-sixth of your 'total income', whichever is greater. In general, your 'total income' is your before-tax income (including the taxable gains from insurance policies) *minus* your outgoings. Use the Calculator on p485 to work this out (amount *R*).

This means that if your 'total income' is £9,000 or less, the subsidy stops when your *net* premiums reach £1,275 (£1,500 *less* the 15% subsidy). (Note that premiums for a deferred annuity – see p316 – count towards this limit.) If you're married, the £9,000 limit still applies – though the 'total income' is the couple's combined 'total income'. A divorced couple get the subsidy on premiums for policies on each other's lives provided the policy was taken out before the divorce and the divorce took place after 5 April 1979.

You could also get the premium subsidy for *industrial life* and *friendly society* policies on your children's or grandchildren's lives (up to a *gross* premium of £64 per year), whether you or they paid the premiums. But for the subsidy to be available on other policies, the child had to pay the premiums and be over 12 years old (though there's no age limit for a policy taken out before 1 March 1979).
ICTA 1970 s19, s21, s27; FA 1976 Sch 4; FA 1979 Sch 4; FA 1984 s72; SP 4/79; SP 11/79.

How tax relief works

If the premium for the policy is £100 a year

The taxman pays £15 direct to the insurance company   £15

£15

£85

And you pay the remainder   +£85

= £100

£5

£95

of the £100 the company gets, it deducts £5, say, to cover the cost of life insurance, etc

The remaining £95 is invested by the insurance company   £95

So more is invested for you than you actually paid   −£85

extra invested =   £10

> **Section 226A policies**
>
> If you're self-employed or work for an employer and are not in his pension scheme, you can take out a *Section 226A* policy. This is term insurance which pays out either an income for your dependants or a lump sum if you die during the term. You can claim tax relief at your highest rate of tax on premiums of up to 5 per cent of your *net relevant earnings* – ie your taxable profits from being self-employed or your earnings from a job where you're not in the employer's pension scheme. More details on p340.

Hanging on to your subsidy

The premium subsidy continues for policies taken out before 14 March 1984. But if you have such a policy, and vary its terms so that the benefits are increased or the term is extended (whether or not this is by exercising an option already in the policy) you'll no longer get the subsidy on *any part* of the premium. However, policies which have, as part of the original contract, benefits which increase automatically will continue to get the subsidy unless the policy is varied. Below we list some of the situations in which you would lose the subsidy, and others where it won't be affected.

Alterations which will mean that you no longer get the premium subsidy

- increasing the sum insured – with an increase in premiums
- extending the term of a policy
- the substitution of one policy for another – for example, changing a whole-life policy to an endowment policy
- changing from a *without-profits* to a *with-profits* policy with the same sum insured
- shortening the term of an endowment policy with an increase in the premiums
- adding new disability or accidental death benefits
- adding a new option.

Alterations which will not affect your premium subsidy

- reducing the term of an endowment policy – with a reduced sum insured
- converting a *without-profits* policy to a *with-profits* or *unit-linked* policy – with the same premium and a reduced sum insured
- changing how often you pay the premiums (yearly to monthly, say)

- assigning the policy (but not rewriting it under the Married Women's Property Act – see p317)
- switching from one fund to another with a unit-linked policy
- surrendering a bonus
- altering the sum insured of a unit-linked policy with no increase in the premiums – so more of each premium is invested, and less goes on insuring your life
- altering the life (or lives) covered by the policy – as long as the benefits are as before, and policy is still on your, and/or your husband or wife's, life. Could apply, for example, with a joint life policy, after divorce and remarriage.

Note that if, while you were engaged, you took out a qualifying joint life policy with your fiancée (before 14 March 1984), and later get married you can claim the subsidy – even though you couldn't before. And if children reach age 12, and qualify for the subsidy, they will be able to claim it.
Inland Revenue Procedure Note 8; FA 1984 s72.

Clawback

The clawback rules are designed to prevent you making gains due to the subsidy you get on premiums – by taking away some (or all) of the subsidy you were given. The rules are applied to policies which:
- you took out after 26 March 1974 and before 14 March 1984
- qualified for tax relief
- you cashed-in or made paid-up within four years.

The amount of clawback depends on how long the policy has run for. If you cash-in the policy or make it paid-up in its first two years, all the subsidy is deducted from the surrender value; in the third year two-thirds is deducted and in the fourth year one-third. The amount deducted is paid by the life insurance company to the taxman. But there's a limit to the amount of clawback, which depends on the *gross* premiums paid so far – see below for details.

Working out the clawback

year in which the policy is cashed-in or made paid-up	first two years	third year	fourth year
Amount of clawback is **A** or **B**, whichever is less [1]	**A** 15% of the *gross* premiums paid so far	**A** 10% of the *gross* premiums paid so far	**A** 5% of the *gross* premiums paid so far
	B the surrender value *minus* 85% of the *gross* premiums paid so far	**B** the surrender value *minus* 90% of the *gross* premiums paid so far	**B** the surrender value *minus* 95% of the *gross* premiums paid so far

[1] If **B** is negative, there's no clawback to pay, and when we say *premiums paid*, this means premiums due and payable whether you've paid them or not.

Example

Bogart Fitzpatrick took out a unit-linked whole-life policy in January 1984. His *gross* premiums were £30 per month (£25.50 after the premium subsidy). In July 1987 (after 42 months) he decided to cash the policy in. The insurance company tells him that the surrender value is £1,227. To work out the clawback he works out **A** and **B** – the clawback is whichever is less.

A = 5% of the *gross* premiums paid so far
= 5% × £1,260 = £63

B = surrender value of the policy *minus* 95% of the *gross* premiums paid so far
= £1,227 − (95% of £1,260) = £1,227 − £1,197 = £30.

So the insurance company will deduct £30 from the surrender value, and will pay Bogart £1,227 − £30 = £1,197.

As the surrender value (£1,227) is less than the *gross* premiums paid, Bogart has no income tax to pay on it, even though his top rate of tax is 40 per cent.

Cashing-in part of a policy

If, within four years of taking out a policy you cash-in part of it (or make part of it paid-up – see p309), the same rules apply

– and the clawback comes to just as much as it would have done if you had cashed in the *whole* policy. But the insurance company won't deduct more than the amount cashed-in.

If, after cashing in part of your policy, you later cash in part or all of what is left, there may be more clawback. The rules for working out the clawback still apply, but:

• when working out **B**, add the value of the part you cashed-in earlier to the current surrender value of the policy
• take the smaller of **A** and **B**. From this, deduct any clawback made earlier. This gives the clawback to be made this time.

Clawback after four years

If the first time you cash-in part of a policy is more than four years after taking it out, there won't be any clawback. But if you've cashed-in part of the policy within four years, and then cash-in another part or the rest of the policy, clawback will apply. The insurance company will deduct from the surrender value (or partial surrender value) an amount equal to the *lower* of:

• the subsidy you got (15 per cent) on the last year's premiums
or
• 15 per cent of the surrender value or partial surrender value.

Example

Nathan Digby took out a qualifying unit-linked savings plan in 1977. In 1980 he wanted to buy a car and cashed-in part of his policy. Now he has to pay a large repair bill and wants to cash-in a further £400. He pays *net* premiums of £30 per month (the life insurance company collects another £5.29 a month from the taxman). The company deducts the lower of:

• the subsidy Nathan got on the last year's premiums –
ie 12 × £5.29 = £63.48
• or 15 per cent of the cash-in value –
ie 15% × £400 = £60.

So the company would pay Nathan £340, and give the taxman £60. But if Nathan then wanted to cash in another £400 in the same year, he'd only have to pay £3.48 clawback, which would remove the rest of that year's premium subsidy.
FA 1975 s7, s8, Sch 1.

Death and superannuation benefits

You can still get tax relief on certain combined sickness and life insurance policies issued by friendly societies. You'll get tax relief on the life part of your premium, at half your top rate of tax – so if you're paying tax at 50 per cent, you'll get tax relief at 25 per cent.

You can get tax relief at the same rate for the part of a trade union subscription which is for superannuation (ie pension), funeral or life insurance benefits.
FA 1978 Sch 3.

Premium subsidy for deferred annuities

You can get a 15 per cent subsidy on premiums used to buy a *deferred annuity*. You get this on gross premiums of up to £100 (ie premiums you pay of up to £85). There's also tax relief for deferred annuities which will pay an income to your dependants after your death, providing you *have* to pay the premiums either under an Act of Parliament or under the rules of your job. The tax relief you get on these compulsory payments depends on your 'total income' – see p311. And these premiums count towards the £100 limit above.

'total income'	tax relief
up to £1,000	15%
£1,001 to £2,000	22½%
over £2,000	30%

ICTA 1970 s19-21; FA 1976 Sch4; FA 1978 Sch 3.

Dealing with the proceeds

A life insurance policy will usually pay out to you, or to your estate, if you die. But you may want the proceeds to go to someone else. You could do this on your death by simply leaving them money in your will. But in that case, the proceeds of the policy will be added to your estate, and there might be inheritance tax to pay – see p351. You could instead *assign* the policy to someone else during your lifetime. You can do this by completing a *deed of assignment* and sending *notice* to the life insurance company (ask the company or a solicitor for details). You may want to assign the policy for a number of reasons:

- to make a gift
- to avoid inheritance tax by writing the policy in trust
- to raise cash
- to get a loan.

Assignment and subsidy
If you get the premium subsidy and assign your policy, you can still get the subsidy while you continue to pay the premiums. But if the premiums are paid for by someone else (other than your husband or wife) they won't qualify for the subsidy.

Gifts

If you give a policy away (by assigning it to somebody else) it counts as a gift for inheritance tax purposes. The value the taxman puts on the gift is either the market value of the policy *plus* any amounts paid out earlier, or the total amount paid in premiums up to the time you give the policy away, whichever is higher. The market value will often be close to the cash-in value. But, for example, the market value of a policy on someone close to death will be almost as high as the amount the policy would pay out on death. If you continue to pay the premiums after you've given the policy away, the amount you pay also counts as a gift. But there shouldn't be any inheritance tax to pay as the payments will normally come into one of the tax-free categories – see p356. If you die, the proceeds won't form part of your estate.

If you've been given somebody else's life insurance policy, you are liable for any tax that's due when the policy pays out or is cashed-in – see earlier for how much (if any) tax you'll have to pay.
ICTA 1970 s394; FA 1975 Sch 2.

Trusts

By getting the policy *written in trust*, you may be able to avoid inheritance tax as the proceeds of the policy are not added to your estate. The proceeds can then also be paid to the beneficiaries without waiting for probate.

If you want the policy to pay out to your wife (or husband) or children, the simplest way of setting it up in trust is to get a policy worded according to the *Married Women's Property Act 1882*. Otherwise, you'll have to get a declaration of trust written on the policy – ask the insurance company about this. As with a gift, the proceeds of policies written in trust will not form part of your estate, but the premiums may count as gifts for inheritance tax purposes unless they come into one of the tax-free categories – see p356. If the policy pays out while you're still alive (eg a growth bond), you'll have to pay any income tax that's due – though you will be able to claim it back from the trustees. For more about trusts and life insurance, see p393.
ICTA 1970 s399, s401.

Selling your policy

If you sell a non-qualifying policy, it's treated in the same way as though you had cashed it in – see p306. You'll have to pay higher rate tax on the amount that you sold the policy for *less* the premiums you've paid.

If you sell a qualifying policy you'll be taxed as above if you do so in the first 10 years or within three-quarters of its term if this is shorter (this also applies if you made it paid-up in this period and then sold it later on). And there may be clawback to pay, too – see p313. If you buy a policy, there may be capital gains tax to pay if you eventually make a gain on it (as with other assets – see Chapter 32, p415).

Note that you can't avoid paying the income tax that's due by selling your policy and buying it back – in the hope that you'd be liable for capital gains tax instead. If you've had your own policy reassigned to you, you'll have to pay income tax on the gain, not capital gains tax.

ICTA 1970 s394; FA 1983 s18 Sch 4.

Security for a loan

You may be able to use your insurance policy as security for a loan either from the life insurance company or from somewhere else – a bank, say. A loan from the insurance company is treated as a partial surrender (for the amount of the loan) if the policy was taken out after 26 March 1974 and is non-qualifying, or if it's qualifying and the money is lent at less than a commercial rate of interest. Any repayment (other than interest) of the loan you make to the life insurance company is treated as a premium when working out the tax bill at the end. If you're still alive when the policy pays out, you'll be liable for any extra tax that's due.

Note that it won't be treated as a surrender if the loan is to a person over 64 borrowing the money to buy an annuity, nor if the loan is from somewhere else – a bank or building society, say – rather than the insurance company.

ICTA 1970 s394; FA 1974 Sch 1; FA 1975 Sch 2.

Tax-saving tips

● if you get the premium subsidy (available for many policies taken out before 14 March 1984) be wary of losing it by altering the policy
● higher rate taxpayers looking for an investment giving a tax-free income could consider a single-premium bond. They can withdraw 5 per cent of the amount invested each year, tax-free; and if they pay tax at the basic rate only when the policy ends, they could avoid tax altogether
● use whole-life or term insurance to pay inheritance tax when it arises – see pages 392 and 394 for more details.

26 ANNUITIES

An annuity offers an income for life, and favourable tax treatment. But it's an offer you should refuse if you're under 75 (if a woman) or under 70 (if a man).

What is an annuity?

With an annuity, you hand over your money to an insurance company in return for a guaranteed income for the rest of your life. The older you are at the time you buy the annuity, the higher the income you can get; and a man gets a higher income than a woman of the same age (on average, men don't live as long). Note, though, that once you have handed over your money, you cannot ask for your capital back. To give an example: in return for handing over £10,000, a 75-year-old woman who paid tax at the basic rate could (in April 1987) have got an after-tax income of about £1,300 for life, however long she lived.

Type of annuity

This chapter deals with *immediate annuities*. With these, the company starts paying you the income 'immediately' – which is insurance language for six months after you buy the annuity (although it can be sooner, at a price). There are also *deferred annuities* – where you pay a lump sum now and arrange for the income to start much further in the future; deferred annuities form the basis of some personal pension plans (see p339). The most common type of immediate annuity is a *level annuity* where the income is the same each year. For a given outlay, this type gives you the largest income to start with – though, of course, inflation is likely to erode its buying-power over the years. Another type is an *increasing annuity*, where your income increases regularly by an amount you decide on when you buy.

A *single life* annuity stops when the person buying it dies. A *joint life and survivor* annuity carries on until both the person buying the annuity and someone else, usually a wife or husband, are dead.

Should you buy?

Whether or not an annuity proves to be a good buy in the long run depends on three things that no one can know the answers to:

● how long you will live; obviously an annuity will be a better buy if you live for years and years after buying it

● what happens to interest rates (and therefore annuity rates) after you have bought your annuity. If they go up, you'll be left with a relatively poor-value annuity – if they go down, you have a bargain

● the longer-term effect of inflation on the buying-power of your income.

So weighing these uncertainties, along with the one certainty that you lose control of your capital, we conclude that annuities are not a good buy for women under around 75 or men under around 70. Only for people over these ages does the extra income offered by an annuity – as compared with conventional investments – become a compelling argument. And even then think carefully before buying, be quite sure that you are willing to part with the capital you use, and shop around for the best company.

Tax treatment

If you have bought the annuity with your own money, part of the income from it is treated by the taxman as your initial outlay being returned to you, and is tax-free. The remainder of the annuity income counts as interest (ie as investment income), and is taxable.

The insurance company normally deducts tax at the basic rate from the taxable part of your income before paying you – see Diagram. If you are liable for less tax than the insurance company deducts, you can claim tax back from the taxman. If your taxable income from all sources – including from *the taxable part* of the annuity – is equal to or less than your age allowance (see p104), you can apply through the insurance company to have your annuity income paid without deduction of tax. The company will give you a form **R87** or **R88** to complete – send this to the taxman.

The amount of the tax-free part of the income – called the capital element – is worked out according to Inland Revenue rules. It is fixed in terms of £££, not as a proportion of the income from the annuity. For each type of annuity the tax-free amount is based on your age when you buy the annuity, the amount you pay for it, how often the income is paid and whether payments are guaranteed for a period even if you die. Examples are given in the Table opposite.

Tax-free income

for each £1,000 spent on a level annuity

age when you buy	woman	man
70	£72.40	£90.71
71	£76.12	£95.70
72	£80.13	£101.08
73	£84.46	£106.87
74	£89.13	£113.10
75	£94.16	£119.79
76	£99.62	£127.03
77	£105.53	£134.84
78	£111.91	£143.25
79	£118.81	£152.28
80	£126.28	£162.00

Note: all figures quoted in this chapter apply to annuities payable half-yearly in arrears, with no payment made after death. The taxman will normally round up the tax-free amount to the nearest £ – ie in your favour.

As you can see, a man gets a larger tax-free amount than a woman (corresponding to his larger income from the annuity).

With increasing annuities, the tax-free amount increases at the same rate as the income from the annuity increases. For example, for a 75-year-old woman buying an annuity that increases by 5 per cent a year, the tax-free amount in the first year would be £66.40 for each £1,000 spent on the annuity (much less than the £94.16 for a level annuity) but increasing by 5 per cent each year.

An annuity is treated in this special way only if you buy it voluntarily with your own money – not if it's bought for you by, say, a pension scheme (when the whole of the income from the annuity is taxable and counts as earned income).

ICTA 1970 s109 (taxed as interest); s230–231 (tax-free element).

A 70-year old man buys an annuity for £10,000

this gives him a before-tax income of, say, £1,500 a year

£908 is tax-free   £592 is taxed at, say, 27%

which leaves an after-tax income of £908 + £432.16 = £1,340.16

Note: the annuity is a level one, payable half-yearly in arrears, with no payment after death

Tax warning: annuities and age allowance

By and large, if you buy an annuity out of your savings or investments which had been giving you a taxable income, you don't have to worry about the possible effect on age allowance (see p104). The chances are, in a case like this, that the *taxable* part of your annuity income will be less – or in any event not much higher – than the taxable income you were getting from your savings (a large part of the income from an annuity, remember, is tax-free).

But if you buy the annuity with savings or investments that were *not* earning you a taxable income, and if you are at present getting the benefit of age allowance, you might find that your age allowance is reduced. The same could apply if, for example, the annuity is bought for you by your pension scheme (in which case the whole of the annuity income is taxable).

Example

Shirley Alpine, 75, lives alone on a state retirement pension of £2,054 for the full 1987–88 tax year. She also receives alimony from her former husband totalling £6,795 gross (before deduction of tax). She has no outgoings. Her 'total income' (see p29) works out as follows:

state retirement pension	£2,054
alimony (gross)	£6,795
'total income'	£8,849

Since her 'total income' is under £9,800, she qualifies for the maximum age allowance of £2,960. She is therefore liable for tax at 27% on £8,849 − £2,960 = £5,889.

To boost her income, she decides to cash in her National Savings Certificates and Premium Bonds (which she's had no luck with) and spend the £25,000 proceeds on an annuity, which will bring in £3,750 a year before tax. The tax-free capital element of the annuity is £2,354 (rounded up to the nearest £); so the remaining £1,396 would be taxable. Her new 'total income' works out as:

state retirement pension	£2,054
alimony (gross)	£6,795
taxable part of annuity	£1,396
'total income'	£10,245

Shirley's 'total income' is £445 over the £9,800 limit. Her age allowance would therefore be reduced by two-thirds of £445, ie £296.

So Shirley would be paying tax at 27 per cent not only on the £1,396 taxable part of the annuity income, but also on an additional £296 of income, which is the amount by which her age allowance is reduced. The annuity means £456.84 extra tax – around £80 more than she'd expected. So she thinks again – deciding to buy a smaller annuity and hang on to some of her investments.

Home income schemes

If you're elderly and own your own home, you may be able to boost your income with a home income scheme. A 75-year-old woman, for example, with a home worth £30,000, could increase her income after basic rate tax by around £1,200 a year. A man of 70 would get about the same.

How the schemes work

Whoever is running the scheme – a building society or insurance company – gives you a loan based on the security of your home, and then uses this loan to buy an annuity for you. While you live, you get the income from the annuity – after deduction of loan interest and basic rate tax (see Diagram overleaf and *Mortgage interest tax relief*, p325). When you die, the loan is repaid out of your estate (possibly, but not necessarily, from the sale of your home).

The schemes are available for freehold houses, and for leasehold property with a substantial part of the lease still to run (50 to 80 years, depending on the company). The most you can borrow is a percentage (for example, 65 or 80 per cent) of the market value of your home. There's usually a minimum and maximum loan (and certainly not more than £30,000, which is the maximum on which you can get tax relief). You may be able to take part of the loan in cash in return for a rather lower income.

Inflation will reduce the buying-power of your fixed income from these schemes, but it correspondingly reduces the value of your debt – so rising prices don't work wholly against you. And given that the value of your home is likely to continue to go up, you may be able to use the increase in value to get a further loan which could be used to buy another annuity.
FA 1974 Sch 1 para 24; IR 11.

How a home income scheme works

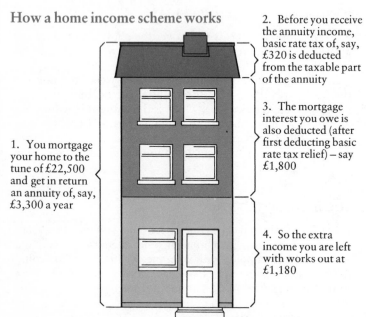

1. You mortgage your home to the tune of £22,500 and get in return an annuity of, say, £3,300 a year

2. Before you receive the annuity income, basic rate tax of, say, £320 is deducted from the taxable part of the annuity

3. The mortgage interest you owe is also deducted (after first deducting basic rate tax relief) – say £1,800

4. So the extra income you are left with works out at £1,180

Note: You qualify for tax relief on the mortgage interest, whether or not you pay tax. If you are a higher rate taxpayer, you will be able to claim from the taxman extra tax relief on the mortgage interest; but you will be liable for extra tax on the taxable part of the annuity. If you don't pay tax, you can reclaim the tax deducted from the annuity.

Should you buy?

It makes very good sense that an elderly person should be able to continue to live in their own home, while spending some of the accumulated value of that home. But the financial arguments may be less favourable. It would be realistic to assume that the elderly person concerned may not always be able to cope on their own, and may, say, sell up and move in with relatives. In this situation, someone who has taken out a home income scheme could lose out (particularly if left with a rather poor-value annuity).

All in all, a useful last resort – but try other ways of increasing your income first.

The sell-your-home version

Some versions of home income schemes involve you in selling your home to the company running the scheme. Among other drawbacks, you may not benefit from the increasing value of your home. Not recommended.

Mortgage interest tax relief

Most of the schemes involve getting a mortgage on your home, and using the loan to buy an annuity. You are entitled to tax relief on up to £30,000 of loans secured on your only or main home provided you are 65 or over and use the money to buy an annuity.

Basic rate tax relief is given to you under the MIRAS scheme – which means that the building society or insurance company will allow for tax relief at 27 per cent on the loan interest when working out how much income to hand over to you. You get the benefit of this 'tax relief' in full, even if you pay little or no tax. Higher rate taxpayers can claim extra tax relief from the taxman – see overleaf.

Age allowance

If, before taking out a home income scheme, you were getting the benefit of age allowance (see p104), the chances are that you will continue to benefit. And if age allowance was in your case restricted (because your 'total income' was over £9,800) you may well find that your age allowance will be *increased*. This welcome, but rather unexpected state of affairs comes about because the gross mortgage interest is deducted from your gross income in working out your 'total income'.

Example

Before taking out a home income scheme, Mrs Anna Smythe, a 75-year-old widow, who has no outgoings, had a 'total income' of:

state retirement pension	£2,054
pension from former employer	£8,500
'total income'	£10,554

Mrs Smythe's 'total income' was therefore £754 over the £9,800 limit. Her age allowance was cut by two-thirds of £754, ie £502 was deducted from the maximum allowance of £2,960 – leaving £2,458 of age allowance (a mere £33 over the single person's allowance).

But Mrs Smythe's tax situation looked very different after taking out the home income scheme. Her 'total income' now works out as:

state retirement pension	£2,054
pension from former employer	£8,500
taxable part of annuity	£855
gross income	£11,409
less outgoings: mortgage interest	£1,270
'total income'	£10,139

Her 'total income' is now only £339 over the £9,800 limit. Her age allowance will therefore be reduced by two-thirds of £339, ie £226. This leaves Mrs Smythe with £2,734 of age allowance – which is £276 *more* than she had before taking out the home income scheme. Her after-tax income goes up by not just the money from the home income scheme (about £850 a year), but by a further 27 per cent of £276 – ie £74 – because of her increased age allowance.

If you pay higher rate tax

You'll qualify for extra tax relief on the mortgage interest (you'll already have been given tax relief at the basic rate). Claim from the taxman. And he, in turn, will charge you with the extra tax due on the interest element of the annuity.

If you don't pay tax

You still get the benefit of the basic rate 'tax relief' on the mortgage. And you should claim back from the taxman the basic rate tax deducted from the interest element of the annuity. You may be able to arrange for this tax not to be deducted in the first place – see p320.

27 BUILDING UP A PENSION

During your working life, you will probably be building up an income from various sources for your retirement. National Insurance contributions you pay can mean you qualify for state retirement pension. You'll get pensions from employers' pension schemes you've belonged to, and if you've been self-employed or in a job but not a member of a pension scheme, you may have paid into your own personal pension plans, usually with an insurance company (but see below). You may also have some income from savings and investments, or perhaps you'll have created some ready cash by moving to a smaller home or selling a business.

Although a state retirement pension provides a basic income which is currently kept in line with inflation, few people would want to have no other income. The real advantage of pension schemes and personal pension plans over other forms of saving is the tax concessions they get. You get full tax relief on the contributions you make into the scheme up to certain limits. No tax is charged on investment income or capital gains made by a pension fund. And you can normally swop part of your pension for a tax-free lump sum.

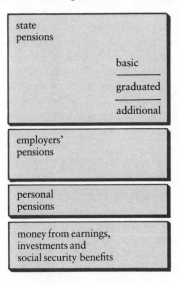

state
pensions

basic
graduated
additional

employers'
pensions

personal
pensions

money from earnings,
investments and
social security benefits

Details of how income from pensions is taxed are given in Chapter 9. In this chapter we deal with contributions to the different kinds of pension, and the rules governing the schemes themselves.

The Government proposes to allow anyone – even those presently in an employer's pension scheme – to take out their own personal pension plan. The Finance Bill following the March 1987 Budget fixed the starting date for the new personal plans as January 1988 (April 1988 for those still in an employer's scheme) and contained a number of provisions on how these would work (although detailed regulations had still to be issued). The whole of this part of the Finance Bill was lost when the government called a June election. Following the election, the Government re-introduced the pensions section of the Bill (see bookmark for the latest news). We describe how these proposals could affect your pension planning in the sections marked with this symbol:

The state pension scheme

Basic retirement pension

You qualify for a basic state retirement pension by paying (or being credited with) enough National Insurance contributions of certain types during your working life. The contributions which count are:

- Class 1 contributions (paid by people who work for an employer; but reduced rate contributions paid by some married women and widows don't count towards a pension)
- Class 2 contributions (paid by the self-employed)
- Class 3 contributions (which are voluntary payments to make up any gaps in your contribution record)
- Flat rate contributions made before 6 April 1975 (the predecessors of Class 1 and Class 2 contributions).

Class 4 contributions paid by the self-employed don't carry any entitlement to a pension.

Additional pension

Since 1975, during periods spent working for an employer, you can build up the right to an additional state pension related to your earnings. But many employers' pensions schemes are 'contracted-out' of the additional state pension scheme. This means you make lower National Insurance contributions, but you don't build up any additional state pension; instead, your employers' scheme has to provide a better package of benefits, and has to guarantee that your pension is broadly equivalent to (or better than) the additional state pension you would have earned during the same period.

Before the June 1987 election, the Government proposed that, from April 1988, it should be possible for employers to offer 'simplified' occupational schemes which could be contracted-out of the additional state pension *without* having to offer this guarantee (see p332). And, from January 1988, new personal pensions could be available to employees, which would also be contracted-out without offering this guarantee (see p340).

Graduated pension

Graduated pensions are a relic of the state scheme which existed from 1961 to 1975. They were built up by people who earned more than £9 a week. The Department of Health and Social Security keeps records of how many units of pension each person has earned, and you'll get a small pension based on these at retirement age. In the year to April 1988, the most you can normally get is £4.44 a week for a man, £3.72 for a woman.

How state pensions are taxed

State pensions are paid without any tax being deducted, and are treated as earnings. Any tax due is often collected under PAYE from any employer's pension you get – see p110 for details.

If a married woman gets a state retirement pension it counts as her earnings if it's based on her own National Insurance contributions – so wife's earned income allowance can be set against it. If a wife gets a pension based on her husband's contributions, her pension normally counts as her husband's earnings, and the allowance can't be set against it – see example below. If a wife is entitled to a pension of her own but chooses to get a pension based on her husband's contributions because this is higher, she can count as her earnings the amount of pension she was entitled to on her own contributions.
ICTA 1970 s219(1).

Example 1

Jean Austin gets a basic pension of £1,142 a year based on her husband's contributions, but this counts as *his* income for tax purposes. In 1987–88, she also gets £1,200 pension from her former employer. This counts as *her* earnings, so she can set the wife's earned income allowance against it.

National Insurance contributions from 6.4.87 to 5.4.88

National Insurance contributions are worked out on your weekly or monthly earnings *before* deducting payments to an employer's pension scheme or personal pension plan. You don't pay contributions on fringe benefits or expense payments you get.

Some married women and widows earning £39 a week or more may have chosen to pay reduced rate Class 1 contributions. For the 1987–88 tax year, these are 3.85% on all earnings up to £295 a week. If they are self-employed, they can choose to pay no Class 2 contributions. Reduced rate contributions don't carry any entitlement to a state pension.

You don't need a 100% contribution record to get a full pension, but it may be worth filling gaps by making voluntary Class 3 contributions (£3.75 a week for the 1987–88 tax year).

Class 1 contributions for employees

- Earnings of £100 a week or more
Contracted-out: 9% on first £39 a week plus 6.85% on excess up to £295 a week
Not contracted-out: 9% on all earnings up to £295 a week
- Earnings between £65 and £99.99 a week
Contracted-out: 7% on first £39 a week plus 4.85% on excess
Not contracted-out: 7% on all earnings
- Earnings between £39 a week and £64.99 a week
Contracted-out: 5% on first £39 a week plus 2.85% on excess
Not contracted-out: 5% on all earnings
- Earnings below £39 a week
No contributions payable.

Contributions for the self-employed

- *Class 2:* £3.85 a week if earnings from self-employment in 1987–88 tax year are more than £2,125.

Employers' pension schemes

An employer's pension scheme which is approved as *exempt* by the Inland Revenue can be an effective way of saving for retirement. The employer normally pays most or all of the cost, and can deduct his contributions when working out his taxable business profits. The contributions he pays are a valuable tax-free fringe benefit for you. If the scheme is contributory, you get full tax relief on your own contributions, so the cost to you is very small compared with the amount invested each year in the fund – see Diagram. Each time you're paid, your employer

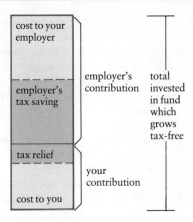

subtracts the amount of your pension contributions (including any additional voluntary contributions you make – see p336) from your gross pay. He then uses the PAYE system to work out the tax that's due on the 'net' pay that's left – see p146 for more details.

In addition, the pension fund doesn't have to pay any tax on its investment income or capital gains, so the return on its investments is likely to be higher than with other ways of saving. At retirement, you are allowed to receive a substantial tax-free lump sum. The pension you get is taxed as earned income, not investment income.

ICTA 1970 s208; FA 1970 s21.

Conditions for approval

To qualify for these tax concessions, a pension scheme must either be set up under an Act of Parliament (as many schemes for public employees are), or must be 'exempt approved' by the Inland Revenue. Approval is automatic if the scheme meets all the statutory conditions, but the Inland Revenue have the power to approve schemes which don't entirely conform – see overleaf.

The main statutory conditions for approval are:
● the scheme is set up in connection with a business or undertaking carried on in the UK by someone resident in the UK
● the scheme is set up with the genuine aim of providing benefits for employees. These may be paid to the employee, his widow, children, dependants or personal representatives
● the employer must contribute to the scheme and give details about it to every employee entitled to join
● there is someone resident in the UK who will be responsible for administering the scheme

- the only benefit of the scheme for an employee is a pension on retirement at a fixed age between 60 and 70 (55 and 70 for a woman). The pension mustn't be more than one-sixtieth of the employee's final pay for each year of service (up to 40 years' service). But the scheme may allow you to exchange part of your pension for a tax-free lump sum of up to three-eightieths of your final pay for each year of service (up to 40 years' service)
- if any pension is payable to an employee's widow if he dies after retirement, the amount mustn't be more than two-thirds of the pension he was entitled to
- no other benefits can be paid, no contributions can be refunded, and your pension entitlement can't be paid to you in any other way.

FA 1970 s19; FA 1971 s21(3).

Discretionary approval

Very few employers' pension schemes conform to all the conditions above, but are approved under the Inland Revenue's discretionary powers. In particular, they may approve schemes which:
- give higher benefits to people with less than 40 years' service (opposite we list the maximum amounts which are allowed)
- give a lump sum of up to four times yearly salary, and pensions for your widow, children or dependants if you die before retirement
- allow you to retire early, as long as you're at least 50 (or at

---

Simplified schemes

Before the 1987 election the Government intended to allow employers to set up simplified pension schemes which qualify for Inland Revenue approval. There would be two types:
- a scheme based on final pay, to provide a pension of not more than 1/80 of final pay for each year's service, part of which could be exchanged for a tax-free lump sum of up to 3/120 of final pay for each year of service. If you or your employer paid in extra, the maximum pension could be brought up to 1/60 of final pay, and the lump sum to 3/80 of final pay for each year of service
- a 'money purchase' scheme, where the pension received depends on what you and your employer invest, and how it grows. An employee could contribute up to 17.5% of earnings and there would be no fixed limit to the amount of pension received. The maximum lump sum would be 25% of the value of the plan on retirement. The schemes would be 'contracted-out' of the additional state pension scheme, but *wouldn't* have to guarantee to provide a broadly equivalent pension to the additional state pension you could have earned.

any age if you're too ill to work again) and still receive benefits
- allow contributions to be repaid in certain circumstances
- are connected with a business which is carried on partly abroad, or by a person not resident in the UK.

The Inland Revenue can approve schemes giving even wider benefits than these (eg pensions for widowers). The main factors they take into account when considering schemes for approval are given below. More details in *IR12 Occupational Pension Schemes*, from the Superannuation Funds Office, Lynwood Road, Thames Ditton, Surrey KT7 0DP.
FA 1970 s20; FA 1971 s21(4).

Maximum benefits

Pension

This depends on the number of years you've worked for the employer before normal retirement age, and on your 'final salary':

years of service before retirement age	proportion of 'final salary'
1 to 5	$\frac{1}{60}$ for each year
6	$\frac{8}{60}$
7	$\frac{16}{60}$
8	$\frac{24}{60}$
9	$\frac{32}{60}$
10 or more	$\frac{40}{60}$

If you have worked for the employer for at least ten years before normal retirement age, you can ask him to pay in extra contributions for you (if the scheme's rules allow it) to give you a pension of up to two-thirds your 'final salary'. These proportions are *before* you exchange any pension for a lump sum. But if you're entitled to other pensions from previous jobs or from personal pension plans, these will be taken into account in working out the maximum you can get.

The scheme can define 'final salary' in any way it chooses, so long as it's not more favourable than either:
- your pay in any of the five years before normal retirement date, or

● your average pay for any three or more consecutive years in the thirteen years before normal retirement date.

Note that a controlling director's 'final salary' must not be more than would be allowed by the second definition.

'Pay' can mean your salary plus bonuses, commission, directors' fees and the taxable value of any fringe benefits. If the first definition is used, payments apart from salary must be averaged over at least three years. If the pension is based on the amount you earned in years before the final one, the scheme is allowed to increase the figure in line with any increase in the cost of living from the end of that earlier year until your retirement (known as 'dynamisation').

These rules apply to your pension in the first year of retirement, but the scheme can provide for your pension to be increased within limits each year to compensate for inflation.

Lump sum

Scheme rules may allow part of the maximum pension, worked out as above, to be exchanged for a tax-free lump sum. The maximum lump sum allowed depends on the number of years

years of service before retirement age	proportion of 'final salary'
1 to 8	$\frac{3}{80}$ for each year
9	$\frac{30}{80}$
10	$\frac{36}{80}$
11	$\frac{42}{80}$
12	$\frac{48}{80}$
13	$\frac{54}{80}$
14	$\frac{63}{80}$
15	$\frac{72}{80}$
16	$\frac{81}{80}$
17	$\frac{90}{80}$
18	$\frac{99}{80}$
19	$\frac{108}{80}$
20 or more	$\frac{120}{80}$

you've worked for the employer before normal retirement age, and on your 'final salary'. So if you have been in the job for twenty years or more, the maximum tax-free lump sum you're allowed is 1½ times your 'final salary'.

Pre-election proposals

In the 1987 Budget, the Government proposed certain changes to the way benefits from an employer's scheme would be taxed. These would have come into effect from the date of the Budget, 17 March 1987. If the government is re-elected the date the proposals come into effect may be changed.

The proposals are that, for anyone joining an employer's pension scheme on or after 17 March 1987:

● the maximum tax-free lump sum on retirement should be £150,000

● the definition of 'final salary' for company directors or those earning more than £100,000 should be the second of the two definitions given at the bottom of p333 and top of p334

● the maximum pension of two-thirds salary should only be allowed if you've worked for the employer for at least twenty years. The maximum pension permitted, if your employer is willing to make extra contributions, should be one-thirtieth of final salary for every year of service.

Who can join?

An employer who runs his own pension scheme can decide whether it is for all the company's employees or only certain of them, and whether membership is compulsory or voluntary. And he can operate different schemes for different employees – eg 'executive' schemes for directors and favoured employees (see p338).

However, from 6 April 1988 no employer's scheme would be compulsory.

Contributions

The employer must contribute more than a token amount to the pension scheme. There is no set limit on an employer's contributions, as long as they are reasonable compared with the benefits provided. An employer can also make special payments to provide additional benefits for selected members (eg an employee who joined the company late in life and hasn't earned much pension entitlement).

Basically it's the employer who decides whether he will pay the full cost of the scheme or if the scheme is to be contributory. If it's contributory, he decides how much employees will pay, but to satisfy Inland Revenue rules this can't be more than 15% of their earnings.

Additional voluntary contributions (AVCs)

In addition to any regular contributions he has to pay, an employee may make additional voluntary contributions (AVCs) to the scheme. This is particularly useful in the years before retirement if the total benefits you'll get from your employer's pension scheme fall short of the maximum allowed by the Inland Revenue. You get full tax relief on these contributions, and there is no tax charged on income or capital gains your money earns from being invested, so AVCs are a very tax-efficient investment. At retirement, you can normally decide which of the possible retirement benefits you want your AVCs to top up – eg your pension (or increases to it to compensate for inflation), your tax-free lump sum, your dependants' pensions, or a combination of these. But you must keep within the individual limit for each benefit. Consult your pensions manager if you want to make AVCs. Things you'll need to check are:

• what benefits the scheme would provide in return for your AVCs. There is no point in paying contributions which would earn you more pension or other benefits than the maximum you're allowed

• you're not allowed to pay more than 15% of your earnings in any tax year in pension contributions (*including* any voluntary ones).

In his 1987 Budget, the Chancellor proposed that an employee should be allowed to make AVCs to a completely separate AVC scheme of his or her choice. However, he also proposed that from 7 April 1987, you should only be able to use your AVCs to improve pension benefits – on retirement you wouldn't be able to take any part of the fund as a lump sum.

Example 2

John Friar is 62 and due to retire when he's 65. Because he's changed jobs several times in his working life, his total pension will be a lot less than the maximum allowed. So he arranges to pay £100 a month in additional voluntary contributions. As he's a basic rate taxpayer, he gets tax relief at 27% on each £100 he pays in – so the cost to him is only £73 a month. The money is paid into a special AVC account currently paying 12% interest tax-free. When he retires three years later there is £4,300 in the account. This is equivalent to a yearly return on his contributions (after allowing for tax-relief) of almost 35%.

Leaving a scheme

When you leave a job, the money or pension rights that have built up for you may be *preserved*, so that you get a pension based on them when you retire. Pension rights built up since 1 January 1985 must be increased by 5% a year or in line with price inflation whichever is lower. Alternatively, they can be *transferred* to your new employer's scheme, or you can buy an insurance policy (known as a Section 32 policy) which will provide retirement benefits. From April 1988 you may also be able to transfer your pension rights into a personal pension plan (see p340).

If you have been a member of a contributory scheme for less than 5 years (2 years from April 1988), you may be able to withdraw your contributions (but not your employer's) if the scheme's rules allow it. Schemes can also allow you to withdraw any contributions you made before 6 April 1975. Normally 10% tax will be deducted by the trustees from contributions you withdraw, but there's no further tax to pay.

This means that an employer's pension scheme can be a useful means of short-term savings, especially for someone who is confident they won't be in the job long and would only get a small preserved pension if they left their contributions in the scheme. If, for example, the scheme pays interest of 4% a year on refunded contributions (which is fairly typical of schemes which pay interest) the after-tax return to a basic rate taxpayer who left the job two years after joining the scheme would be around 26%. Even if no interest is paid, the return is over 21%. This return comes from the tax relief on your contributions and the low rate of tax on the refund. But beware:

● if the scheme is *contracted-out*, there will almost always be a deduction from your refund to buy you back into the state scheme

● getting a refund means that you forfeit the right to a preserved pension from the scheme – something you might regret later in life.

The pension you get

The pension you get from an employer's pension scheme counts as earned income – so a married woman can set the wife's earned income allowance against a pension she gets from a former employer. Tax is normally deducted under PAYE, but if the pension is paid by an insurance company tax may be deducted at the basic rate – see p136.

You can, of course, swop part of your pension for a tax-free lump sum. Even if you only want an income this can be worth doing, as the initial after-tax income you'd get from buying an annuity with the money may well be higher than the pension you'd forgone. This is partly because an annuity you buy voluntarily is taxed differently from the pension: part of each payment is regarded as return of your capital and is tax-free. The rest is regarded as investment income (so for a married woman, it counts as her husband's income and wife's earned income allowance can't be set against it).

But don't overlook the fact that your pension may be increased from time to time to keep pace with inflation. If your pension scheme guarantees increases of, say, 5% a year, you should compare the initial income from an annuity increasing by the same amount. If your pension scheme gives substantial discretionary increases to pensions, remember that an annuity you've bought voluntarily will miss out on these, so you could lose out in the long term.

FA 1970 Sch 5 Part II para I (taxation of pensions).

Selected employees and controlling directors

An employer who wants to make special arrangements for selected employees or directors (including controlling directors) can do so:

● by running a separate scheme to provide all their pension benefits

● by arranging a scheme for them which tops up the benefits they get under the firm's standard scheme

● by making them special members of the firm's scheme, getting a different scale of benefits.

If it is to qualify for the tax concessions, each scheme must be approved by the Inland Revenue. The same rules apply as with other employers' schemes.

A scheme of this kind can be arranged through an insurance company, or the employer can administer the investment of the funds himself. For a family company, where the employer and the directors are the same people, this can have two possible advantages: the pension fund can provide the capital for buying company assets, such as business premises; and up to half of the pension fund can be loaned back to the company. Any scheme with fewer than 12 or so members which invests any of its funds directly will normally have to conform to the requirements in the Inland Revenue's Memorandum No.58 (February 1979) if it is to qualify for approval.
FA 1970 s21.

Personal pension plans

The National Insurance contributions paid by self-employed people (including partners in a partnership) qualify them for the basic state pension but no additional pension. Most self-employed people therefore need to make additional provision for their retirement. A personal pension plan (often called a *self-employed retirement annuity*) makes it possible for them to do so, with full tax relief on their contributions (up to certain limits) and with the money invested in a tax-free fund. These tax concessions mean that personal pension plans are likely to be much more tax-efficient for these people than any other way of saving for retirement – see Diagram.

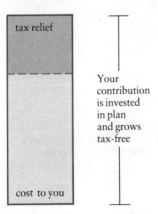

tax relief

cost to you

Your contribution is invested in plan and grows tax-free

If you are in a job but not a member of the employer's scheme (either because there isn't one, or because you aren't eligible, or because membership is voluntary and you've chosen not to join), you can take advantage of a personal pension plan to top up your basic and additional state pensions. Anyone with freelance earnings can also contribute to one of these plans (and see Box below). Note that your earnings from work which makes you qualify for a personal pension plan are known as *non-pensionable earnings*.

You're not disqualified just because your employer provides you with some life insurance cover which will pay out a lump sum if you die while employed by him or only provides a pension for your spouse or dependants. You'll still be entitled to take out a personal pension as well.

If you take out a personal pension plan, you can also get tax relief at your top rate of tax on premiums (up to set limits – see p343) for certain life insurance policies which provide a lump sum or an income for your widow(er) or dependants after

---

New personal pension plans

Before the June 1987 election the Government proposed that, from 4 January 1988, personal pension plans should be available to all employees, not just the self-employed or people with non-pensionable earnings. However, employees who are already members of an employer's pension scheme would have to wait until 6 April 1988 before they leave their employer's scheme and take out a personal plan. The new plans would be 'contracted-out' of the state additional pension for employees but wouldn't have to guarantee to provide a pension at least equal to the additional state pension you would otherwise have earned. You'd have to pay a minimum contribution to your plan each year – the part of your own and your employer's National Insurance contributions which would otherwise have gone towards your state additional pension. The DHSS would pay this into your plan for you, some time after the end of the tax year to which it applies. You could pay extra into your plan if you wished, or take out other plans – you could have as many plans as you like, provided you don't pay in more than 17.5% of your earnings each year. If you're an employee, your employer could pay into your plan if he wishes (he doesn't have to), but his contributions would be counted towards the overall limit.

To encourage employees to take out the new personal plans, the Government proposed to pay an extra incentive of 2% of your earnings into your plan each year until 1993. If you took out a plan between 4 January and 6 April 1988, you could have the incentive backdated to 6 April 1987. However, if you'd been a member of an employer's contracted-out scheme for two years or more on 6 April 1988 and left it to take out a personal plan, you wouldn't get the 2% incentive.

With the new personal pension plans, you would be allowed to take a pension from age 50.

your death (known as *Section 226A* policies). These policies can be written in trust for your dependants, so that there's no inheritance tax to pay on the benefits.
ICTA 1970 s226 – 226A; ESC A41; FA 1971 Sch 2.

The benefits you can get

You can decide when you want to start receiving the benefits of the plan. This doesn't have to be when you actually retire, but must be sometime between your 60th and 75th birthday (but see Box opposite). People in occupations where it is normal to retire earlier (eg pilots, certain sportsmen, female nurses) can start taking the benefits earlier, as can anyone who becomes too ill to carry on working.

With nearly all plans, you don't have to take your pension from the company (or companies) you've been saving with. The 'open-market option' allows you to shop around to see if you can use the money that's built up for you to get a higher pension from another company.

The pension doesn't have to be a level amount. You can choose one which starts off lower but increases each year to help compensate for inflation. You can also choose a joint-life pension – payable as long as either of two people is alive – which will, of course, be lower than a pension on one life only.

The pension you get is treated as earned income, so a married woman can set wife's earned income allowance against it. The insurance company normally deducts basic rate tax from each payment before paying it out. If your income is too low for you to pay as much tax as has been deducted, you can claim back the excess.

You can normally choose to take a lower amount of pension and get a tax-free lump sum. The maximum lump sum the Inland Revenue will allow is three times the biggest remaining pension the company could pay you – though the plan may be more restrictive. If you take a lump sum, you may find the annuity you can buy with it is higher than the pension you've given up – see p337.

With the new personal pensions (see opposite) the maximum tax-free lump sum you can take would be 25 per cent of the value of your plan(s) on retirement, or £150,000 if lower.

If you die before you start receiving the benefits of the plan, all the premiums you've paid can be refunded with or without interest, depending on the plan (though some plans provide a higher pension and no refund). If a refund is made to your personal representatives it becomes part of your estate and may be liable to inheritance tax. But if the policy is arranged so that any payment is made direct to your widow or widower, or arranged under a trust, there will be no inheritance tax liability on your estate.

ICTA 1970 s226; FA 1971 s20; FA 1976 s30; FA 1980 s33; FA 1983 s19.

Borrowing back from the plan

Many personal pension plans allow you to get a loan on the strength of the money you've paid in. You can often pay only interest on the loan and can repay the loan from the lump sum you get when you retire if it's large enough.

Some insurance companies have schemes for using the 'loanback' to buy your own home. This is a cheap way of getting a mortgage. But repaying the loan will eat heavily into your lump sum at retirement and, if your non-pensionable earnings fall, you may need a different kind of mortgage.

How much can you pay in?

The rules about how much you can pay into personal pension plans each year are complicated and depend partly on how much you have paid in previous years. Companies may refuse to accept premiums which are above the Inland Revenue limits. If you do exceed the limits, you won't get tax relief on the excess, and the pension that comes from it will be taxed as investment income rather than earned income.

If you pay too much into one of the new personal pension plans (see Box on p340) your contributions must be refunded – you won't be allowed to leave them invested.

ICTA 1970 s227 – 227A.

Net relevant earnings

The maximum you can pay into personal pension plans in a tax year depends on your *net relevant earnings* for the tax year. A husband and wife each have their own net relevant earnings. If you're self-employed, these are your *taxable profits* (see p192) being assessed for the tax year. This will normally mean your business takings (including money owed to you) for your accounting year ending in the previous tax year, less allowable business expenses, capital allowances, stock relief and any losses from earlier years of the business which haven't been set off against other income. If you're in a job, your net relevant earnings for the tax year are your salary, plus the taxable value of fringe benefits, less any allowable expenses. For freelance work, net relevant earnings are the fees you've received less any allowable expenses. The Table opposite shows what your net relevant earnings are for the 1987–88 tax year.

	income taxed on	net relevant earnings for 1987–88 tax year
if you're in a job	current year basis	pay from that job in 1987–88 tax year
if you have freelance earnings	current year basis [1]	taxable profits in 1987–88 tax year
if you're self-employed	preceding year basis [2]	taxable profits [3] in accounting year ending in 1986–87 tax year

[1] If a substantial part of your income comes from freelance work, you may be taxed on a preceding year basis as if you were self-employed.

[2] In the first two and last three years of a business, there are special rules about what income your tax bill is based on – see p188.

[3] If your business makes certain payments (patent royalties, covenant payments, annuities), they must be deducted from your taxable profits when working out your net relevant earnings.

Example 3

David Lloyd has been self-employed for some years, and in his accounting year which ended on 31 December 1986 (ie in the 1986–87 tax year) his taxable profits were £12,500. David also has a part-time job lecturing in evening classes. There's no pension from this job, and in the 1987–88 tax year he earns £1,700. David's net relevant earnings for 1987–88 are £12,500 + £1,700 = £14,200.

How much tax relief?

You get tax relief at your highest rate of tax on personal pension premiums of up to 17½ per cent of your net relevant earnings for that year. Husband and wife each have their own 17½ per cent limit worked out on their own net relevant earnings. Tax relief on Section 226A life insurance policies (see p340) is limited to premiums of not more than 5% of net relevant earnings. This limit is part of the overall 17½ per cent limit, not additional to it.

If you're an employee taking out one of the new personal plans, the minimum contribution paid by the DHSS (and the 2% incentive, if you qualify – see p340) will not count towards the overall 17.5% limit.

People aged over 50 at the start of the tax year can pay more than 17½ per cent of their earnings in pension premiums and still get full tax relief. See first two columns of the Table on p345 for the limits for the 1987–88 tax year.

If you're self-employed, premiums you pay in, say, the 1987–88 tax year will normally reduce your tax bill for that year, even if you're using up unused relief from earlier years (see below). But if you backdate a premium (see p346), you reduce the tax bill for the year it's backdated to – so you get a tax rebate if you have already paid tax for that year.

If you were an employee taking out one of the new personal pension plans (see Box on p340), you would pay your premium for the current year with basic rate tax deducted – so for every £100 you wished to invest, you would hand over only £73. The Inland Revenue would pay the balance directly to your plan. Higher rate taxpayers would then claim the balance of their tax relief from the Inland Revenue.

Example 4

David Lloyd's net relevant earnings for the 1987–88 tax year are £14,200. He is not aged over 50, so can get tax relief on up to 17½% of £14,200 = £2,485 of premiums he pays in 1987–88. Up to 5% of £14,200 = £710 of this can be premiums for Section 226A life insurance policies.

Unused relief from the last six years

You can get tax relief on premiums above the 17½ per cent allowance (up to the whole of your net relevant earnings for the year) if you didn't pay the maximum premiums allowed in any of the previous six tax years. You have to use up the earliest unused relief first.

Arnold Chippendale is a self-employed cabinet-maker who has been contributing to a personal pension plan for ten years. But now that retirement is drawing closer he's worried about the size of his pension and wants to invest more. For how he juggles his contributions to get full tax relief, see Example 5 on p346 and Example 8 on p348.

With the new personal pensions you would only get tax relief for a previous year if you were not a member of an occupational pension scheme in that year.

To work out if you've got any unused relief, you have to use the limits that applied in the relevant tax year – see Table below.

ICTA 1970 s227A; FA 1980 s32.

Table: maximum premiums qualifying for tax relief in different tax years

limit for pension premiums [1]

Age at start of tax year	1987–88	born [2]	1982–83 to 1986–87	1980–81 and 1981–82	1977–78 to 1979–80 [4]
50 or less	17½%	after 1933	17½%	17½%	15% or £3,000
51 to 55	20%	1916 to 1933	20%	17½%	15% or £3,000
56 to 60	22½%	1914 or 1915	21%	20½%	18% or £3,600
61 or more	27½%	1912 or 1913	24%	23½%	21% or £4,200
		1910 or 1911	26½%	26½%	24% or £4,800
		1908 or 1909	29½% [3]	29½%	27% or £5,400
		1907 or earlier	32½% [3]	32½%	30% or £6,000

limit for life insurance premiums

whenever born	5%		5%	5%	5% or £1,000

[1] Until (and including) the 1981–82 tax year, the higher limits for people born before 1916 did not apply if you were getting a pension from a former full-time job or were entitled to receive such a pension in the future. This was repealed by *FA 1982 s38*.

[2] The higher limits for older contributors were based on year of birth up to (and including) the 1986–87 tax year. From the 1987–88 tax year onward, the higher limits are based on your age at the start of the tax year.

[3] But you can't get tax relief on any premiums you pay after your 75th birthday.

[4] Before 6 April 1980, if you paid more in premiums than the *per cent* limit for a tax year, you could be allowed tax relief on these extra premiums (up to £££ limit for that year) in your tax bill for either the 1980–81 or 1981–82 tax years – but not later irrespective of your other payments. If this applies to you, check whether you've been given the tax relief in one of those years.

The general election held on 11 June 1987 meant that the Finance Act confirming the tax rules for the 1987–88 tax year was rushed through in shortened form. Some of the Chancellor's 1987 Budget proposals were shelved, but the Government has said that it will re-introduce them. We've marked these pre-election proposals with this symbol:

Example 5

Arnold Chippendale is a self-employed furniture maker, who has paid £1,000 a year into a personal pension plan for ten years. He has paid only basic rate tax in these years. He checks what his net relevant earnings have been for the last six years to see if he has any unused relief, and sets the figures out in the Table below.

In 1987–88, Arnold's net relevant earnings are £18,000, so his 17½ per cent limit for premiums is £3,150. But he can afford to pay £5,500 in premiums this year. Unless he backdates some of his total premium (see below), the first £3,150 of this must go on paying his maximum premiums for 1987–88, but the remaining £2,350 can use up the £925 unused relief from 1981–82, the £1,275 from 1982–83 and £150 of the £1,100 unused relief from 1983–84. This leaves £950 unused relief from 1983–84 to carry forward, along with the unused relief from 1984–85, 1985–86 and 1986–87 which is untouched.

Arnold's taxable income for 1987–88 will be reduced by £5,500.

If Arnold's plan was one with a loanback arrangement, he could borrow enough from his plan to pay further premiums to use up the remaining unused relief. This could be worth doing if he thought there was little chance of paying enough to use up the unused relief in the next few years – eg if he was winding up his business and taking a job with a pension.

tax year	net relevant earnings £	maximum premium £	premium paid £	unused relief £	premiums paid in 1987–88 £	unused relief to carry forward £
1981–82	11,000	1,925	1,000	925	925	0
1982–83	13,000	2,275	1,000	1,275	1,275	0
1983–84	12,000	2,100	1,000	1,100	150	950
1984–85	10,000	1,750	1,000	750	0	750
1985–86	14,000	2,450	1,000	1,450	0	1,450
1986–87	12,000	2,100	1,000	1,100	0	1,100
Totals so far:				6,600	2,350	4,250
1987–88	18,000	3,150			3,150	0
Total paid in 1987–88					5,500	
Total unused relief to carry forward						4,250

Backdating premiums

You can ask in any tax year to have all or part of the premiums you pay in that year treated for tax purposes as if you'd paid them in the previous tax year (as long as you have sufficient unused relief for that year). And if you didn't have *any* net relevant earnings in the previous tax year, you'll be able to get the premiums treated as if you'd paid them in the year before that.

This means that if you can't afford to make payments this year to use up all the tax relief available to you (including any unused relief from previous years) you may be able to catch up next year. It also means that if your top rate of tax was higher last year, it will be worthwhile asking for some of the premiums you have paid this year to be treated as if you'd paid them in the previous year in order to equalise your top rate in the two tax years. That way you'll get more tax relief (and you'll get part of your tax relief sooner).

Lloyd's underwriters can ask for a premium they have paid in the tax year to be treated as though it was paid up to three tax years before, as long as in that year they have sufficient unused relief resulting from Lloyd's underwriting activities. *ICTA 1970 s227(1BB); FA 1980 s33(2); FA 1982 s37.*

Example 6

David Lloyd's net relevant earnings in 1986–87 were £20,000, and he paid tax at 40% on the top £2,000 of his taxable income. He could have paid up to 17½% of £20,000 = £3,500 in premiums, but only paid £1,500, so has £2,000 unused relief. In 1987–88, David's income is not liable for any higher rate tax. But he can ask for the first £2,000 of his premiums to be treated as if he'd paid them in 1986–87. He'll then get relief on the £2,000 at 40% instead of 27% and the net cost to him will be £1,200 instead of £1,460. He'll also get an immediate rebate rather than waiting for a lower tax bill.

Making the most of available relief

Backdating premiums and using up unused relief from past tax years can be combined to give even greater benefit. If, say, you have £1,000 of unused relief from seven years ago, you can ask to have £1,000 of the premiums you pay this year treated as though you'd paid them last year. As long as you've used all last year's available relief, the premiums can then use the relief from six years earlier.

If you had no net relevant earnings last year, you can backdate part of this year's premium to the year before and use up unused relief from six years before that – ie eight years ago. See Examples 5 and 6.

The two facilities can also be usefully combined for someone approaching retirement (or even after retirement as long as they're under 75) who has had non-pensionable earnings for a number of years. As Example 7 shows, it can be very worthwhile withdrawing other savings in order to pay the maximum contributions into a personal pension plan in order to use up all the available relief.

Example 7

Harry Grey is 64 and due to retire in 1988–89 when he's 65. He has saved up £10,000 in his building society and was intending using this to buy an annuity – he would have got around £1,163 a year after tax for life. But as Harry has not been a member of an employer's pension scheme for many years, nor has he contributed to a personal pension plan, he would do much better to take advantage of his unused relief.

His earnings and unused relief are shown in the Table below.

If Harry were to withdraw the £10,000 from his building society and pay it into a single-premium personal pension plan he could use the current year's available relief of £2,750, most of the £8,262 unused relief from the previous six tax years, and the £875 relief from 1980–81. He does it like this.

tax year	net relevant earnings £	unused relief £		how his 1987–88 premium is allocated £
1980–81	5,000		875	0
1981–82	5,500	962		0
1982–83	6,000	1,200		0
1983–84	6,500	1,300	8,262	0
1984–85	7,000	1,400		0
1985–86	8,000	1,600		0
1986–87	9,000	1,800		5,345
1987–88	10,000		2,750	4,655
totals			11,012	10,000

In order to use any of his available relief from the 1980–81 tax year (seven years ago), Harry has to ask the taxman to treat some of his premium as though he paid it in 1986–87. In that tax year,

Example 8

Arnold Chippendale (see Example 5 on p346) realises he has some unused relief from the 1980–81 tax year. His net relevant earnings for that year were £10,000, and the maximum premium he could pay was £1,500. As he only paid £1,000 in premiums that year, he has £500 unused relief. He can claim it by asking for £500 of the total premium he pays in 1987–88 to be treated as if it had actually been paid in 1986–87.

Unless Arnold paid an extra £500 in premiums, £500 of his total premium would, in effect, be reallocated from 1983–84 and 1982–83 to 1980–81. As Arnold only pays basic rate tax in the 1987–88 and 1986–87 tax years, this won't affect the amount of tax he pays, but it will mean an extra £500 unused relief from 1983–84 to use up in the future.

he earned £9,000, got the married man's allowance of £3,655, and paid tax under PAYE of £1,550.05. If Harry asks for £1,550.05 ÷ 0.29 = £5,345 of his total £10,000 premium to be treated as if he paid it in 1986–87, he'll get tax relief on the full amount and will get all that £1,550.05 tax repaid to him.

Harry gets tax relief on the rest of his £10,000 premium (ie on £10,000 − £5,345 = £4,655 of it) in the 1987–88 tax year – a tax saving of £1,256.85. So his total tax rebate is £2,806.90.

Harry's tax position for the last two tax years is shown in the Table below.

In return for his £10,000 premium, the pension plan will pay him an income of around £685 a year after tax. In addition, Harry will get a tax-free lump sum from the plan of around £2,500. If he uses this and his £2,806.90 tax rebates to buy an annuity, this would give him an additional after-tax income of around £590. So Harry's net income from doing things this way would be £685 + £590 = £1,275 for life. This is £112 more a year than if he'd just bought an annuity with the whole £10,000.

Note that, as long as Harry has sufficient net relevant earnings in 1988–89 when he retires, he will be able to switch more money from his savings into personal pension plans.

	1986–87 £	1987–88 £
Harry's earnings	9,000	10,000
minus pension premiums	5,345	4,655
	3,655	5,345
minus married man's allowance	3,655	3,795
	0	1,550
tax at 29% (1986–7) and 27% (1987–8)	0	418.50

Unused tax relief from longer ago

If an assessment becomes final for a tax year more than six years ago, and means that there's some unused tax relief, you can use it as long as you pay the premium within six months of the assessment becoming final, *and* you pay the maximum amount allowable for the current tax year.
ICTA 1970 s227A; FA 1980 s32; SP 9/80.

How to claim your tax relief

When you take out a plan, the insurance company will send you a *Self-Employed Premium Certificate* (SEPC). Send this to your tax office. Each year, enter the premiums you've paid in your

Tax Return, and get *form 43* from the taxman to give details of your payments, and to tell him in which tax year you want them to qualify for tax relief.

Tax-saving tips

- a pension scheme of one type or another is likely to be your most tax efficient way of saving for retirement

- if you are in a firm's pension scheme, you can boost your pension considerably by making additional voluntary contributions. Tax concessions mean you get a very high overall return on these contributions. It can be particularly worthwhile making these in the years immediately before retirement

- contributions paid by your employer into a pension scheme are a valuable tax-free fringe benefit. If the pension you have earned is less than the maximum allowed, it is worth trying to persuade your employer to make extra contributions for you individually

- a company can have its own pension scheme for its controlling directors. Full tax relief is given on contributions, and it may be possible for the company to borrow back from the fund

- if you are self-employed, or in a job but not a member of the employer's pension scheme, you can take advantage of the tax concessions on personal pension plans. To get a healthy pension, you'll need to pay into schemes for a large part of your working life. But if you have failed to make contributions in the past, you can catch up to some extent by making use of unused relief from the past and by backdating premiums. In the last few years before retirement, this can be particularly valuable, as can withdrawing other savings (and even borrowing back from the fund) to pay the premiums.

28 INHERITANCE TAX

You may have got your money in many ways: by gift or inheritance, by earning, or by investment. Along the way, you, or someone else, has probably paid tax on what you now own.

When you come to pass your money on – whether as a gift in your lifetime or as a legacy when you die – there could well be a bill for inheritance tax (IHT). And this can be true even if you don't think of yourself as being rich.

In this chapter, and in the two chapters that come after, we take you, in stages, into the rules for inheritance tax:

● this chapter explains the basic rules, and tells you how to work out an IHT bill. It explains the straightforward ways of saving tax; and gives a hint of more complex tax-saving schemes

● chapter 29 goes into detail on tax planning techniques

● chapter 30 explains the tax rules for trusts.

Domicile
We're assuming that everyone who reads this is domiciled in the United Kingdom. Your domicile is, broadly, the country where you've chosen to end your days. It can be quite different from the country where you're living – though if you've been resident in the UK for 17 out of the last 20 tax years you'll have UK domicile (so far as IHT is concerned) whether you like it or not. If you're not domiciled in the UK, rules are different. For example, if you *are* domiciled in the UK, gifts to a non-UK domiciled husband or wife are exempt only up to £55,000.
IHTA 1984 s267.

> **A voluntary tax?**
> Don't be misled. Careful planning can greatly reduce – or even
> wipe out – any liability to IHT. No planning at all can mean a heavy
> bill. But remember that, if you don't plan, you yourself aren't any
> worse off. It just means that there's less for your heirs. So don't
> gamble with your own financial security just to save tax for others.

How the tax works

Inheritance tax replaced capital transfer tax with effect from
18 March 1986. Although many of the capital transfer tax
(CTT) rules were retained, many new rules, rather similar to
those for estate duty which was itself replaced by CTT in 1974,
were introduced. Under the new rules, there are two types of
gift you can make during your lifetime:

● *potentially exempt transfers (PETs)* – IHT is only charged on
these gifts if you do not survive for seven years after making
the gift. PETs include gifts to other individuals (eg from parents
to children), or gifts to accumulation and maintenance trusts
and trusts for disabled people (see p398).

In his 1987 Budget, the Chancellor proposed treating
'interest in possession' trusts as PETs too.

● *chargeable transfers* – broadly, any gift which does not
qualify as a PET, such as a gift to a discretionary trust, or gifts
involving companies. This type of gift is immediately liable to
IHT and counts towards the giver's *running total* (see below).
If the running total is above a set amount, IHT is payable (but,
if the gift is made during the giver's lifetime, only half the full
rate of tax is payable).

On your death, the whole of your estate, ie, roughly
speaking, what you own when you die, is liable to IHT, as are
any PETs made in the seven years before your death.

However, some gifts are free from IHT whenever they are
made, for example gifts between husband and wife. So if a wife
gives her husband a million pounds there's no tax to pay. But
if she gives the same amount to her children or friends, it won't
count as a tax-free gift and there may be IHT to pay. For a list
of tax-free gifts, see p356 onwards.

IHTA 1984 s2–4, s18; FA 1986 s100–101.

Running total, nil rate band

Under the CTT rules, all gifts you made within the previous 10
years, other than exempt gifts, counted towards your *running
total* of chargeable gifts. If you had a running total at 17 March
1986 this will still be relevant in calculating your IHT bill for

gifts made after that date, except that gifts made more than seven years ago (rather than 10 years) will now be knocked off your running total. If you make chargeable transfers which push your running total above a set figure (£90,000 in the 1987–88 tax year) there will be tax to pay. The first £90,000 of gifts you make is known as your *nil-rate band*, in other words it's the part of your running total on which you pay tax at a rate of zero.

IHTA 1984 s7, Sch 1.

Example 1

On 31 December 1985 Marian Jones gave £60,000 to her son Walter. None of this counted as a tax-free gift, and as she had made no taxable gifts in the previous 10 years her running total became £60,000. Marian wants to give her daughter Julie £60,000 on her eighteenth birthday in November 1987. But because Julie is still quite young, she is not sure that she wants her to have access to the money immediately, although she is happy for her to have the income from it. Marian has another daughter, Rebecca, who is now 16, and she is considering making part of the £60,000 available to Rebecca as well. The various choices open to Marian are:

● she could give the £60,000 to Julie and Rebecca equally as an outright gift. This would count as a PET, and no IHT would be payable unless Marian died within seven years of the gift

● she could put the £60,000 into an accumulation and maintenance trust for Julie and Rebecca (see p403). This would also count as a PET with no tax payable immediately

● she could put the £60,000 into a trust for Julie and Rebecca in equal shares, with them having an immediate right to the income from it – ie an interest in possession trust (see p399). If the Chancellor's Budget proposal becomes law, (see opposite) this would also be treated as a PET with no tax payable immediately. Otherwise, it would be treated as a chargeable transfer

● she could put the money into a discretionary trust of which Julie and Rebecca are the beneficiaries. This would count as a chargeable transfer, so the £60,000 would be added to her

---

The general election held on 11 June 1987 meant that the Finance Act confirming the tax rules for the 1987–88 tax year was rushed through in shortened form. Some of the Chancellor's 1987 Budget proposals were shelved, but the Government has said that it will re-introduce them. We've marked these pre-election proposals with this symbol:

existing running total to give a new running total of £60,000 + £60,000 = £120,000. IHT of £4,500 would be payable on this amount immediately, (assuming the tax is paid out of the £60,000). However, if Marian were to limit the gift to just £30,000, no IHT would be payable because her running total would only be £60,000 + £30,000 = £90,000, the amount of the nil-rate band.

In the end Marian decides to set up the accumulation and maintenance trust, as this passes the maximum amount of money over to Julie and Rebecca, with no immediate tax bill, and with the safeguard that they can't spend all the money at once.

How large is the gift?

IHT is charged on the **loss to the giver**, not on what the getter ends up with. So if *you* pay the tax on the gift, the loss to you includes the tax you pay – and the tax bill is worked out on this *grossed-up* value. Starting on p367, we show you how to calculate the tax, no matter who pays it.

Warning: if you own shares in a family company – 51 per cent, say – and give some away, so that you lose your controlling interest, the loss to you (on which tax is charged) can be many times more than the benefit to the getter.

Which of you should pay the tax?

There's no tax advantage either way. Suppose you are making a gift and want the recipient to end up with £10,000. After taking your running total into account, the tax due is £1,764.71. You can either hand over £10,000 and pay the tax (£1,764.71) yourself, or hand over £11,764.71, and let the recipient pay the tax (£1,764.71).

Tax rates

Under CTT there were two sets of tax rates – one for lifetime gifts and one for gifts on death. Under IHT there is only one table of tax rates (shown on p371) starting at 30 per cent (for running totals between £90,000 and £140,000) and going up to 60 per cent (for a running total above £330,000). However:
• gifts on death, or in the three years before death, are charged at the full rate
• tax payable on chargeable transfers during your lifetime is charged at only 50 per cent of the full rates (but tax may have to be recalculated at the full rates if the giver dies within seven years of the chargeable transfer – see p370)

● on gifts made more than three years before death you only have to pay a percentage of the full amount of tax, worked out at the full rates (see Table below).

Years between gift and death	Percentage of the full tax payable
Up to 3 years	100%
More than 3 but less than 4	80%
More than 4 but less than 5	60%
More than 5 but less than 6	40%
More than 6 but less than 7	20%
More than 7	00%

Remember, it is the tax which is reduced, not the value of the gift, so if the tax would be nil, no relief can be claimed to set against other gifts.
IHTA 1984 s7, FA 1986 s100–101, Sch 19.

Tax on death

When you die, you are considered to make a taxable gift of all the property you own at the time, *plus:*
● the value of any insurance policies paid into your estate
● the value of any PETs made in the seven years before death
● the value of any chargeable transfers made in the seven years before death
and *minus*:
● tax-free gifts – eg to a husband or wife, or to a charity (see overleaf)
● debts and reasonable funeral expenses (but debts may be restricted if they arise from gifts you made previously).
If the total comes to more than the amount of the nil-rate band (£90,000 in the 1987–88 tax year), IHT is payable.

Unlike a lifetime gift, the value of the total gift you make on death is not grossed-up. But the values of individual legacies (eg '£20,000 to my daughter Sara') may be grossed-up (see Example 10 on p376) and the tax due comes out of the *residue* – ie what's left when all the legacies have been paid. This can mean that much (or all) of the residue is swallowed up in tax. You can avoid this by saying specifically in your will that individual legacies bear their own tax.
IHTA 1984 s4–5.

When a gift is made

It's usually easy to decide when a gift is made. For example, if you give your son £10,000 by cheque, it will be the date on which the cheque is cleared by your bank and your account is debited. For some gifts, however, it may not be quite so straightforward. If you make a gift with some strings attached, (known as a *gift with reservation*) the gift will not be made, for IHT purposes, until it becomes a completely free gift (ie the benefit ceases to be reserved). For example, if you gave your home to your son, but continued to live there, this would be treated as a gift with 'reservation of benefit' and, if you were still living there on your death the house would be counted as part of your estate, even though it would actually belong to your son. You could avoid the problem if you paid your son a full market rent for the property, but this would not normally be sensible as your son might have to pay tax on the rent.

The rules for gifts with reservation of benefit only apply for gifts made after 17 March 1986, so a gift made before then is unaffected. The rules are complicated: if you are considering a gift with reservation of benefit, get professional advice.
FA 1986 s102, Sch 20.

Tax-free gifts

Tax-free gifts are ignored by the taxman. If a gift is tax-free:
- there's no tax to pay on it – either by you or by anyone else
- the gift isn't added to your running total – so it doesn't eat up your nil-rate band.

If you're going to make gifts, it's clearly sensible to use the opportunities you have to make gifts tax-free. Tax-free gifts fall into three types:
- gifts which are tax-free whenever they are made – ie regardless of whether they're made during life or on death
- gifts which are tax-free only if made on death
- gifts which are tax-free only if made during life.

Gifts tax-free whenever they are made

- gifts between husband and wife of any amount. These can be in cash, property, or anything else. There's no limit at all – even if you're separated. (For divorce, see p100.) If the person who receives the gift isn't domiciled in the UK but the donor is, gifts above a total of £55,000 will count as a PET. (For IHT planning between husband and wife see p360)
- gifts to UK charities of any amount. Special anti-avoidance rules can apply if you give part of a property (eg a share in land

or a business) to a charity and keep the rest yourself
- gifts of any amount to British political parties. (But if made on, or in the year before, death, only the first £100,000 is tax-free)
- gifts of any amount to certain public institutions – eg the National Gallery, the British Museum, the Victoria and Albert Museum, local authorities and universities
- gifts of heritage property to a non-profit-making body, provided Treasury approval is obtained. *Heritage property* is outstanding land or buildings, and books, manuscripts or works of art of special interest
- gifts of shares or securities to a trust for the benefit of all or most of the employees of a company provided that the trustees hold more than half of the ordinary shares in the company and have voting control.

IHTA 1984 s18, s23–26, s28.

Gifts tax-free on death only

- the estate of a person whose death was caused or hastened by active military service in war or of a warlike nature. This would include the estates of servicemen killed in Northern Ireland or the Falkland Islands. It can also include people wounded in earlier conflicts who die earlier than they otherwise would have done
- a lump sum paid under your occupational pension scheme to your dependants if you die before reaching retirement age, *provided the trustees have a discretion as to who gets the money* (they usually do). Because they have a discretion, the lump sum never forms part of your estate – so there's no gift for tax purposes. Within set limits you can say who you want to get the money – and your wishes will normally be respected. The total lump sum can be up to four times your salary at the time of your death together with a return of your contributions to the scheme
- a lump sum paid to your dependants on your death at the discretion of the trustees of your personal pension plan if you are self-employed or if you are an employee who is not in an employer's pension scheme.

IHTA 1984 s154, s151, s58.

Gifts tax-free in life only

- wedding gifts. Each parent of the bride or groom can give up to £5,000 tax-free (it doesn't have to be to their own child). A gift by either the bride or the groom to the other in anticipation of the marriage is tax-free up to £2,500 – though

once they are married they can normally make tax-free gifts of any amount to each other. A grandparent or remoter ancestor can give up to £2,500 tax-free. Anyone else can give up to £1,000. Gifts don't need to be in cash. Strictly speaking, wedding gifts have to be made *in consideration of the marriage,* and *conditionally on the marriage taking place*

● gifts made as normal expenditure out of income. This allows you to give money away year after year without an IHT liability. The gifts must be part of a consistent pattern – though not necessarily to the same person each time. If your giving has just begun, the first gift will be covered by the exemption if it's clear a pattern of gifts will follow – eg you start to pay regular premiums on a life insurance policy for someone's benefit. Because gifts must come out of income, a gift of anything other than cash won't usually be covered. Your gifts must leave you with sufficient income to maintain your normal standard of living. If you find you have to resort to capital, eg selling shares, in order to live in your usual way, you will lose the exemption unless you make up the lost capital out of income in a later year

● after divorce, transfers of property to an ex-husband (or ex-wife) will usually be exempt from tax. This is because there won't usually be any 'donative intent' – ie any intention to make a gift. In other words, the transfer is made as part of the divorce settlement

● gifts for the maintenance of your family. A gift for the maintenance of your spouse or ex-spouse is tax-free. So is a gift for the maintenance of a child of one or both of you (including an adopted child) if the child is under 18 or is still in full-time education or training. The exemption also covers gifts for the maintenance of a child you have been taking care of for some time in place of either of his parents

● gifts to meet the regular needs of a relative of either you or your spouse are tax-free if the relative is unable to support himself or herself owing to age or infirmity. Gifts to your mother or mother-in-law are covered even if she is able to support herself, provided she is widowed, separated or divorced

● small gifts. You can give an unlimited number of people

gifts of up to £250 (each) a year. You won't need to use this exemption if the gift is tax-free for another reason. If you give more than £250 to anyone the exemption (for that person) is lost *even for the first £250*

● any gifts of up to £3,000 in a single tax year which aren't tax-free for any other reason. These gifts don't have to be in cash. If you don't use up the exemption in one year, you can use the rest of it in the following year, provided you've used up that year's exemption first. Any part of the £3,000 still unused at the end of the following year is lost– ie it can't be carried forward.

IHTA 1984 s10–11, s19–22.

Example 2

In the 1986–87 tax year, Simon used up £1,000 of his £3,000 exemption. In the 1987–88 tax year, he makes gifts of £4,500 which aren't tax-free for any other reason. The taxman will say that the first £3,000 (of the £4,500) came out of the 1987–88 allowance. The other £1,500 of the gift comes out of the unused 1986–87 allowance. But the remaining £500 unused allowance from 1986–87 can't be carried forward to 1988–89.

Basic tax planning

There are no universal rules of IHT planning which dictate what everyone should do and should not do. It all depends on your personal circumstances. IHT is not just a rich man's tax. On the other hand, many people who are no more than comfortably off – worth up to £150,000, for example – worry too much.

If you don't plan for IHT, it's no skin off your nose. It simply means that there's less for your heirs. So don't dive into complicated schemes just to give your children slightly more than they would otherwise get. Above all, don't risk your own – or your spouse's – financial security by giving away more than you can afford while you're still alive.

Having said all that, it does of course make a lot of sense to take account of the IHT rules when you're planning your gifts. You may not necessarily go for the biggest tax-saving: IHT planning is a mixture of knowing the rules and applying common sense. Overleaf we tell you how.

First principles

● make use of your exemptions – in particular the annual exemption of £3,000, and the *normal expenditure out of income* exemption

- try to make gifts which will be treated as PETs rather than chargeable transfers, so that if you live seven years the gift will be completely free of tax
- if you can afford to, use up your nil rate band – then in seven years' time you can use the band again
- if you have a stable marriage, make gifts to your spouse so that he or she can make tax-free gifts to other people. (The gift to your spouse must be genuine. If he or she must hand it on, the husband and wife exemption won't apply, and the whole gift may be treated as a PET).

Estate spreading

Estate spreading means giving away wealth now. The idea is to reduce the amount you're worth – so that there will be less tax to pay when you die. Estate spreading can make sense if:
- it doesn't destroy your financial independence *and*
- IHT on death would be substantial *or*
- the person receiving the gift needs it now.

But hesitate if the gift will be chargeable to IHT immediately, ie it will not be a PET (see p352). Although chargeable transfers are chargeable at half the full rates, more tax may have to be paid if you die within seven years of making the gift. The nil rate band is normally increased each year so your liability to IHT may turn out to be less than expected. If the gift you propose to make will be a PET there will be no immediate liability to tax but if you die within seven years the person to whom you made the gift may be called upon to pay some tax. This may mean that they will finish up with less than you had intended them to receive. It is possible to state in your will that the IHT payable on gifts made within seven years of your death should be met out of the residue of your estate and not by the individuals who received the gifts.

Equalisation of estates

For a married couple the first step in estate spreading is often said to be the equalisation of their estates – ie their total wealth is divided equally between them. Because gifts between husband and wife are exempt, this can usually be done tax-free (but see Box on p351).

This can have a number of advantages, particularly if one spouse had little personal wealth before. For example, both may be able to make use of the annual exemption, the small gifts exemption, and gifts made as normal expenditure out of income (see p357), whereas, if the family wealth had remained largely in the hands of one spouse it would have been possible for that spouse alone to make use of these exemptions. If the joint wealth is fairly substantial it may be possible for each spouse to make gifts of more than the exemptions available. These will count as PETs and will be totally tax-free after seven years.

The other major advantage is in the amount of IHT payable on death. As each spouse now has wealth in their own right, each can leave part at least of their estate to the children or grandchildren. Without equalisation, there might be no tax at all to pay on the first death, but a very high bill on the second. *IHTA 1984 s18.*

Example 3: equalisation

Jonathan and Sally are married. Sally is worth £300,000; Jonathan is worth nothing. In their wills, they have left everything to each other. This means that there will be no tax to pay on the first death (because of the husband and wife exemption). But on the second death, the tax (at the current rates) will be £87,000. They decide to equalise their estates. Sally gives Jonathan £150,000 (no tax to pay). And they redraw their wills so that all their property goes to their children. This means that, on each death, tax will be charged on £150,000. Tax on £150,000 is £19,000. So in total the tax bill will be twice this: ie £38,000. Equalisation seems to have saved £49,000. But a less drastic solution might be better.

Sally's estate includes their home, worth £100,000. Suppose Sally still gives Jonathan half her estate, including a half share of the property, but when redrawing their wills they each leave their half share in the property to the survivor, with the residue to the children. This means that, whoever dies first, the children get £100,000 (less tax) and the survivor gets £200,000 including the house. It may be possible for the survivor to reduce the £200,000 further, eg by making use of their exemptions. Even if this doesn't happen, the tax at current rates will be £3,000 on the first death (a lot less than £19,000) and £39,000 on the second – a total of £42,000. This is only £4,000 more than the tax bill if they leave half of their joint wealth to their children on the first death. It also gives the survivor the security of owning the whole home instead of relying on the children's goodwill to continue living there, or the freedom to sell it and buy something smaller.

Warning: it's easy to be far too enthusiastic about equalisation. It's important to make sure that the survivor will have enough income to maintain their usual standard of living. In the Example above, whether Jonathan or Sally dies first, the survivor will be left with their home, worth £100,000, and other assets also worth £100,000. It's only those other assets which will provide an income for the survivor. So when working out how much to leave to the children, it's vital to consider what level of income the survivor will need, how much they can get from other sources, eg pensions, and how much income they are likely to get from their capital. If either Jonathan or Sally gets a pension from their former employer, what will happen to it on their death? Will the survivor get a widow's or widower's pension or does the pension stop? What happens if they split up? This sort of question must be answered before they go ahead and equalise their estate.

Estate freezing

Estate freezing is the slow but sure way of passing your money on – so it's more suitable for people in middle life than late life. You don't actually make a gift. What you do is to 'freeze' the value of part of your estate at its present level, and allow the increase in value (which would otherwise have come to you) to benefit someone else. More details on p388. (But note that you will be liable to income tax on the income from the investments.)
IHTA 1984 s2–3.

Using trusts

If you put money or other property into an accumulation and maintenance settlement for your children or grandchildren (see p403), you reduce the value of your estate straightaway, yet the children don't get the gift until they're adults. Meanwhile the trust fund grows outside your estate.
IHTA 1984 s71.

Using your will

Your will can be a very important step in planning (see p376). Consider leaving some property direct to your family rather than to your surviving spouse. You can also give your executors flexibility without an additional tax charge by setting up a discretionary trust in your will to allow them to juggle gifts between different possible beneficiaries within a period of two years of your death.
IHTA 1984 s144.

Life insurance

Life insurance provides a simple way of setting up a trust for your children or grandchildren, which you can build up by regular contributions, generally exempt under the *normal expenditure* rule. Make sure the proceeds don't form part of your estate – see p317.

You could also consider putting unit trusts into trust for your children or grandchildren using regular savings. Some unit trust managers offer this facility.

Splitting the house

Your house may be the single most valuable asset you own – and it is not exempt from IHT. So you could consider sharing its ownership with your children or grandchildren (see p386). But this will now work only if you both live in the property and share the expenses.

Valuing a gift

The next few pages deal with how to value (for IHT purposes) something which is given away. This is the first step in working out the tax on the gift. Remember that, if it's a PET, it's the value of the gift at the date it's made on which IHT will be charged if you do not survive seven years. If you are going to make a gift of land, antiques, paintings, a business, or unquoted shares or securities, get a professional valuation first:

- it's useful evidence when you're negotiating a value with the taxman
- you're less likely to get an unexpectedly high IHT bill.

'Market value'

In the normal case, *value* equals *open market value*. This means that the value of an asset is taken to be the price which it would fetch if it was sold in the open market at the time of the gift. *(IHTA 1984 s160.)*

For gifts of money, there's no problem. The value of the asset is the amount of money itself. For a gift of a car or furniture, the value is what you could expect to have sold it for. (This means that, when you're valuing an estate on death, you should use the *second-hand* value of furniture, fridges, etc.)

The rest of this section deals with exceptions to the normal rule.

Value of property on death

The taxman assumes that any piece of property – eg land, or a holding of shares, is sold in one lump. So he won't speculate as to whether your property could have been broken up for sale in parts to get a higher or a lower price, unless the division would have been a natural and easy thing to do.

The taxman won't take account of the difficulty (or impossibility) of putting the property on the market at one time. He'll assume that there's a ready market, and that the sale itself won't affect the market value. This can cause severe problems where shares in a private company are involved: the value, for tax purposes, can be higher than the price you could get.

IHTA 1984 s160.

Favoured property

Certain types of *favoured property* – farms, businesses – have the benefit of a statutory discount from their actual value (see p394): ie the value of the gift, for tax purposes, is reduced.

Joint interests in land

If you have a joint interest in land – eg you're a co-owner of a house – the starting point is to take the open market value of the land as a whole, and allocate to you your share of that value. Your share is then discounted (ie reduced in value for IHT valuation purposes – by 10 per cent say).

Life insurance policies
For how these are valued, see p317.

Unit trusts

Units in a unit trust scheme authorised by the Department of Trade are valued at the managers' buying ('bid') price on the day concerned, or the most recent day before that on which prices were published.

Quoted shares and securities

The market value of shares and securities quoted on The Stock Exchange, excluding shares on the Unlisted Securities or Third Markets (USM), is the lower of *either*:
• the lower closing price on the day of the gift plus a quarter of the difference between the lower and higher closing prices for those shares for the day (known as the 'quarter-up' rule), *or*
• half-way between the highest and lowest recorded bargains in those shares for the day.

Example 4

You hold £1 Ordinary shares in XYZ plc whose ordinary shares are listed on The Stock Exchange. You need to know their market value on 1 June 1987. The Stock Exchange Official Daily List which is published after that day but which records prices on that day shows that a £1 Ordinary share in XYZ plc was quoted at 175–181 with bargains marked at 176, 176½ and 179. The 'quarter-up' valuation gives 176½ and the mid-way valuation gives 177½. So the market value is taken to be 176½ a share.

Unquoted shares and securities

Valuing these can get you into murky waters. It's very much a matter for negotiation with the taxman. Some clues:

● bargains in shares on the Unlisted Securities Market (USM) or Third Market are shown in The Stock Exchange List, but the taxman won't accept the price of these bargains as final

● if the taxman has recently decided for someone else what your particular type of shares are worth, he will probably apply that value to your holding

● the fictional 'purchaser' of the shares will be assumed to know information about the company confidential to the directors at the time of the gift. This could put the value up or down

● the taxman will probably try to compare your unquoted shares with quoted shares in a company of equivalent size in the same line of business (if there is one)

● if you own 75% of the ordinary shares you will usually have the power to put the company into liquidation. This could mean your holding is worth 75% of the underlying assets of the company

● if you have a bare majority of the ordinary shares, you will be able to decide what dividends are paid – so the after-tax earnings of the company may be a better guide to the value of your shares. The value of the assets will probably still be the starting point – *less* a discount because you can't put the company into liquidation

● if you are a minority shareholder (and not director), the dividends paid will be a good guide to the value of your shares

● for securities other than shares, eg loan stock, the rate of interest and the likelihood of its being paid are important. If you have a right to repayment of your principal at any time and the company is in a position to repay you, the value of your securities should be increased.

IHTA 1984 s168.

Life interests and reversions

If you give someone, eg your widow, the right for life to all the income from particular property or the exclusive right to occupy or enjoy certain property, for IHT you will put her in the same position as if she owned the property. So there is no tax advantage in giving your widow just a life interest. However, from a practical point of view you may wish to give a person no more than a life interest so that you can be sure that your capital will find its way to your children or grandchildren, for example, once the 'life-tenant' has died.

But make sure that your trustees have a wide power to apply capital for the benefit of the life-tenant in case of emergencies.

Because the person with the life interest is treated as owning the whole property, a gift of the reversion (ie rights to the property when the life interest ends) is normally valued at *nil* – provided it's never been bought or sold.

IHTA 1984 s4–5, s48–49.

Related property

Property is 'related', for tax purposes, if it is owned by your spouse (either directly or through trustees), or if it is now, or has been in the previous five years, owned by a charity to which you or your spouse gave it.

Where property is related to other property, and its value as part of the combined properties is greater than its value on its own, the higher value may be taken as the actual value.

IHTA 1984 s161.

Example 5

Suppose you own 55% of the Ordinary Shares in XYZ Ltd and your wife owns 45%. The value of your holding on its own is £70,000 and the value of your wife's is £40,000. Suppose the value of a 100% holding is £160,000. The value of your holding for IHT is 55% of £160,000, ie £88,000, and not £70,000.

Related property disposed of after your death

Suppose that on your death you own 45% of the ordinary shares of a family company, your wife owns 35% and your son 20%. Your 45% will be valued as 45/80ths of an 80 per cent holding (ie your share of your and your wife's combined holding). However, if your executors make an actual sale of your 45%, and your wife does not sell at the same time, and if the sale is to a complete outsider – at a price which is less than the holding's related value – within 3 years of your death, your executors can claim that the valuation on your death should be

readjusted to a valuation on an unrelated basis.
IHTA 1984 s176.

Other sales after death: quoted shares or securities; interests in land

● if quoted shares or securities, or units in an authorised unit trust, are part of your estate on death and the person who is liable to pay the IHT on the property sells them within a year of your death for less than their value immediately before your death, the later (lower) value may be substituted to re-calculate the IHT liability

● if your estate on death includes an interest in land which is later sold – by the person liable to pay the IHT on the property – within three years of your death, and the sale price is less than the value at the date of your death (*less* by at least 5% or £1,000), that later value may be substituted for the value on your death and the IHT re-calculated.
IHTA 1984 s178–198.

How IHT is calculated

The amount of tax depends on four things:

● **the size of the gift** The gift, for tax purposes, is the *loss to the giver* – including any tax paid by the giver. This can be far more than the getter ends up with

● **whether the gift is a PET or a chargeable transfer** (see p352). If the gift is a PET (and most gifts you are likely to make will be), there is no tax to pay at the time, but there may be if you die within seven years of making the gift. If the gift is a chargeable transfer, then tax may have to be paid now (but the tax will be recalculated, and extra may have to be paid, if you die within seven years)

● **the size of your running total** Your running total is the total of all chargeable transfers made by you in the seven years before the gift you are now making, including any tax you've paid. Remember that it includes gifts made before 18 March 1986 under the capital transfer tax rules, and only chargeable transfers (but *not* PETs) made after 17 March 1986

● **whether the gift is made during life or on death** Chargeable transfers made during your lifetime are taxed at half the normal rates. For gifts on death, or within seven years of death, the tax is charged at the full rates, but with relief on a sliding scale for gifts made more than three years before death. PETs made within seven years of death become taxable, and these must be taken into account when working out IHT (or recalculating the tax on chargeable transfers).
IHTA 1984 s7.

How to use the calculator

The calculator on p370 and tables on p371 allow you to work out the tax on a gift using either of two starting points:
● **the total cost to you** (ie the **gross gift** you're making) This is the amount you're worse off by, assuming the recipient pays any tax. Use this starting point if you've decided the exact size of gift you can afford
● **the net benefit to the recipient** (ie the **net gift** you're making) This is the amount the recipient ends up with, after any tax has been paid. Use this starting point if, for example, you want to give away an object – eg a picture – or if you know the exact sum of money you want the recipient to end up with.

The calculator is simple to use, but you must make sure, at each stage, that you use the correct line of the correct tax rates table. The calculator and Examples tell you what to do but do remember to knock off any available exemptions first.

Calculating IHT on death

On death, a number of separate calculations have to be done:
● the tax due on any PETs made in the seven years before your death has to be worked out. In order to do this, it's necessary to look back at any gifts made in the seven years before that PET – ie up to 14 years before death
● any extra IHT due on chargeable transfers made in the seven years before death has to be calculated
● only then can the tax due on the estate be worked out.
These calculations can be extremely complicated when looked at as a whole, but in fact it is possible to break them down into a number of relatively simple calculations which can all be done using the calculator on p370 – see Examples 9 and 10.

The calculations also depend on whether;
● all the gifts you make are tax-free. This will be the case if everything goes to your wife (or husband), or to charity
● all the gifts you make are taxable. This will be the case if everything goes to your children or to your friends
● some gifts are tax-free, others are taxable. This will be the case if, for example, you divide your property between your wife (or husband) and your children.

We give examples of all three cases. In the third case (some gifts tax-free, others not) we've assumed that all the residue is a tax-free gift. If part of the residue is tax-free, and part is taxable (eg you divide the residue in equal shares between your wife and your children), the calculation of tax is horribly complicated. Unless you get clear professional advice to split the residue in this way, it's best to avoid it.

Example 6: a lifetime gift where you know the total cost to you
(a gross gift)

Stephen has a running total of £90,000 and wants to set up a discretionary trust for the benefit of his nephew and niece. He is prepared to give the trustees £60,000, but he expects them to pay any tax out of this sum. Because it is a lifetime gift, Stephen uses Table 1 overleaf to check the tax owing

- **Step one – tax on £90,000** Looking along *line X* of Table 1, Stephen finds that the tax on £90,000 is nil
- **Step two – for gifts where you know the total cost to you.** The gift (£60,000) plus the running total (£90,000) = £150,000. This is amount *F* in the Calculator overleaf
- **Step three – tax on amount F** Since it's a gross gift, Stephen sticks with *line X*. The nearest amount below *F* is £140,000, and the tax on this is £7,500 (amount *G*). Tax at 20% on the remaining £10,000 is £2,000 (amount *H*) – making £9,500 at *J*
- **Step four – subtract D from J** £9,500 (amount *J*) minus nil (amount *D*) = £9,500. This is the amount of tax on Stephen's gift which will be payable by the trustees.

Let's suppose that Stephen was feeling more generous and decided that the trustees should have the whole of the £60,000 and he would pay any tax due. The tax payable would be as follows:

- **Step one – tax on £90,000** Looking along *line X* of Table 1 Stephen finds that the tax on £90,000 is nil
- **Step two – for gifts where you know the net benefit to the recipient** Subtracting nil from £90,000 leaves £90,000 which is amount *Q*. Adding in the net amount of the present gift, £60,000, makes £150,000. This is amount *F*
- **Step three – tax on amount F** Since this is a net gift Stephen looks along *line Y* of Table 1. The nearest amount below *F* is £132,500. Tax on this is £7,500. Tax at 1/4 of the balance of £17,500 amounts to £4,375 making £11,875 in total
- **Step four – subtract D from J** £11,875 (amount *J*) less nil (amount *D*) = £11,875. This is the tax on Stephen's gift.

Stephen's new running total is his old running total of £90,000 plus the gift to the trustees (£60,000) plus the tax on the gift (£11,875) – ie £161,875.

Inheritance tax calculator

You can use this calculator, with the tax rates, opposite, for any gift made on or after 6 April 1987. The tax thresholds are likely to be raised in the 1988 Budget. When this happens, unless major changes are made to the tax, you should still be able to use the calculator, but you'll have to use the new figures.

Step one: work out tax on your existing running total [1] Enter your running total of chargeable transfers before making the gift in question, including any tax paid by you	A
Look along *line X* in the Table opposite [2] to the nearest amount below A, and read off the tax due, using the *tax so far* line	B
Work out the tax due on the remainder of your running total, using the relevant percentage from the *tax rate* line [3]	C
Add B to C D is the tax on your existing running total [4]	D
Step two: for gross gifts (where you know the total cost to you): Enter the gift you're giving now	E
Add E to A	F
OR Step two: for net gifts (where you know the net benefit to the recipient): Subtract amount D from amount A	Q
Enter the gift you're giving now	E
Add E to Q	F
Step three: work out the tax on amount F Look along the correct line [5] of the correct Table [2] to the nearest amount below F, and read off the tax due on this amount, using the *tax so far* line	G
Work out the tax due on the remainder of F, using the relevant percentage or fraction from the *tax rate* line [3]	H
Add G to H	J
Step four: subtract D from J Amount K is the tax on the gift. Your new running total if you started knowing the total cost to you is amount F. Your new running total if you started knowing the net benefit to the getter is amount F plus amount J	K

[1] If A is £90,000 or less, amounts B, C and D will be nil.   [2] Use *Table 1* if it's a lifetime gift; use *Table 2* for gifts made on death (or within seven years of death).   [3] For examples of how to do this, see p369.   [4] This may be different from the tax actually paid on your running total. *Ignore this, and enter the amount as instructed.*   [5] Use *Line X* for gifts where you know the total cost to you; *Line Y* where you know the net benefit to the getter.

Table 1: Rates of inheritance tax on chargeable gifts made during life

X Gross gifts [1] tax rate	nil	15%	20%	25%	30%	
running total [3]	£0	£90,000	£140,000	£220,000	£330,000	or more
tax so far	nil	nil	£7,500	£23,500	£51,000	
Y Net gifts [2] running total [4]	£0	£90,000	£132,500	£196,500	£279,000	or more
tax rate	nil	3/17	1/4	1/3	3/7	

Table 2: Rates of inheritance tax on gifts made on death (or in the seven years before) [5]

X Gross gifts [1] tax rate	nil	30%	40%	50%	60%	
running total [3]	£0	£90,000	£140,000	£220,000	£330,000	or more
tax so far	nil	nil	£15,000	£47,000	£102,000	
Y Net gifts [2] running total [4]	£0	£90,000	£125,000	£173,000	£228,000	or more
tax rate	nil	3/7	2/3	×1	3/2	

[1] Use *Line X* if you know the *total cost to you* (ie the amount of the gift including any tax paid by you)
[2] Use *Line Y* if you know the *net benefit to the recipient* (ie the amount he or she ends up with after deducting any tax which he or she pays)
[3] This is what the taxman calls your running total (ie the gifts you've made including any tax paid by you)
[4] This is your running total not including any tax paid on your gifts
[5] The tax on gifts made more than three years before death is reduced in line with the sliding scale shown on p355.

Your annual exemption – a warning

While working out the possible IHT due on your death, watch out for your annual exemption. During your lifetime, any PET you make is ignored and your £3,000 annual exemption (including any amount carried over from the previous year) is set off against any chargeable transfers you make. When a PET becomes chargeable on your death it is treated, for the purpose of allocating the annual exemption, as if it had been made *after* any chargeable transfer in that year. This can mean that if the only gift you made in one particular year was a PET, and you carried forward your annual exemption for that year, if that PET does become chargeable because of your death, your annual exemption will have to be set against that PET, and it couldn't be carried forward after all.

Who pays the tax?

As we said on p355, tax on gifts left in your will comes out of the residue, unless you specifically say that gifts bear their own tax. This can eat up the residue – as Example 10 on p376 shows. For the difference between *tax-free* and *free of tax*, see Box on p376.

Any IHT (or extra IHT) due on your death on PETs or chargeable transfers made in your lifetime has to be paid by the recipient, unless you say otherwise in your will.

Your estate on death

The taxman treats you as making a gift *just before you die* of everything which belongs to you (with a few exceptions). In this way the taxman is able to catch property which ceases to belong to you on your death such as:

● land which you and someone else own as joint tenants. (On death, the property automatically passes to the other joint tenant)

● a right to the income from trust property (under IHT rules you're treated as owning the property which produces the income) if that right ends or passes to someone else on your death.

IHT also catches increases in the value of your estate which take place because of your death such as:

● the proceeds of a life insurance policy on your own life payable to your estate on your death

● lump sum benefits under a superannuation scheme to which your estate is entitled on your death.

A drop in value of your estate owing to your death may also be taken into account so long as it is not because of the termination or transfer of a legally recognised interest of yours in an item of property: therefore the taxman would allow for:

- a drop in the value of your business if its goodwill is very dependent on you
- the termination of an annuity payable only during your life, and which you had purchased from an insurance company.

The property which forms part of your estate on death for IHT purposes will generally be given its open market value (for more about value, see p363).

You can deduct from the value of your estate any debts, and the cost of reasonable funeral expenses – this doesn't include the cost of a tombstone. Debts include any tax due before you died, but don't include any IHT bill caused by your death, and watch for the type of debts mentioned on p355.

IHTA 1984 s4–5, s171–177.

Example 7: only tax-free gifts

Gerald has a running total of £75,000. The value of his estate on death is £250,000. He leaves £150,000 to his wife and the rest to charity. There is no IHT on his estate on death.

Example 8: no tax-free gifts

Susan has a running total of £93,000. She dies on 1 August 1987. The net value of her estate is £200,000. She leaves £75,000 free of tax to her son Tom and the residue to her other son Jim. Tax on Tom's £75,000 comes out of the residue (see opposite).

Tom and Jim use the calculator to find out the tax due. Because it's a gift on death, they use Table 2 throughout.

Step one:
- **Amount A** (running total at the date of death) is £93,000
- The nearest amount below £93,000 is £90,000 so **Amount B** (tax on this amount) is NIL
- **Amount C** (tax at 30% on the remaining £3,000 is £900)
- **Amount D** (£900 plus NIL) is £900.

Step two:
Where you make no tax-free gifts on death the whole value of your estate is subject to IHT. This value is *not* grossed-up – see p355, so in effect, the value of the estate is the *total cost to you*. Tom and Jim therefore continue to use *Line X* of Table 2.
- **Amount E** (the gift being given now) is £200,000
- **Amount F** (*E* plus *A*) is £293,000.

Step three: tax on amount F
- The nearest figure below £293,000 is £220,000, so **Amount G** (tax on this amount) is £47,000
- **Amount H** (tax at 50% on the remaining £73,000) is £36,500
- **Amount J** (*G* plus *H*) is £83,500
- **Amount K** (*J* minus *D*) is £82,600.

This is the tax on Susan's estate. All the tax comes out of the residue – so Tom ends up with £75,000, and Jim ends up with the residue (£125,000) *less* the tax (£82,600) = £42,400.

Quick succession relief

If you die within 5 years of receiving a gift on which IHT has been paid, some of that tax can be subtracted from the IHT due on your estate. The amount subtracted is worked out by two simple formulae:

• divide the net value of the gift to you by the gross value of the gift, and multiply the result by the tax paid on the gift
• deduct 20% of the answer for each *complete* year since the gift.

You get this tax credit whether or not you still own the gift at your death.

There is a similar relief for IHT on the termination of your interest in settled property, whether or not the termination takes place on your death.

IHTA 1984 s141.

Example

Joe gave Bruce £30,000 in January 1986. He also paid the IHT which came to £8,000. Bruce dies 18 months later. His estate is given an IHT credit of:

$$\frac{(30,000)}{(38,000)} \times £8,000 \times 80\% = £5,052.63.$$

Example 9: IHT payable on your death on PETs and chargeable transfers

Roger makes the following gifts and dies in March 1994:

April 1987	Gift to his son Arthur	£60,000
May 1989	Gift to a discretionary trust	£100,000
July 1992	Gift to his daughter Emma	£80,000

In each case, the recipients have agreed to pay any tax due, and Roger has used up all his exemptions.

To work out the IHT, we need to look first at whether any tax was paid in Roger's lifetime (we'll assume that the tax rates stay at 1987–88 levels). As the gifts in 1987 and 1992 to Arthur and Emma were gifts to individuals, they were treated as PETs and no IHT was payable at the time. However the 1989 gift to the discretionary trust was a chargeable transfer, not a PET, and so was liable to IHT immediately. We can use the calculator to find out how much tax, using Table 1 on p371 because the IHT is due in Roger's lifetime.

• **step one – tax on Roger's running total.** The running total is nil as Roger's earlier PET to Arthur is ignored during his lifetime.
• **step two – for gifts where you know the total cost to you.** The chargeable transfer (£100,000) plus the running total (nil) comes to £100,000. This is amount *F*.
• **step three – tax on amount F.** Looking along *line X* of Table 1, the nearest figure below £100,000 is £90,000, on which no tax is due. Tax at 15% on the excess of £10,000 is £1,500.

So during Roger's lifetime the only tax he has to pay is £1,500. On his death in March 1994, we need to look back at the gifts made in the seven years before the death to see what IHT (or extra IHT) is payable. Any tax due has to be paid by the recipient, no matter who paid the tax on the original gift.

Gift to Arthur in April 1987
This was made within seven years of Roger's death so has become taxable. As its value is below £90,000 (the nil-rate band) no IHT is payable, but on his death, it will form part of Roger's running total, which is now £60,000.

Gift to discretionary trust in May 1989
The trustees have already paid tax of £1,500 on this gift. As the tax was calculated at half the full rates, the trustees could expect to pay a further £1,500 tax. They are in for a nasty shock, as the calculator shows.

● **step one – tax on the running total, now £60,000.** This is less than £90,000 so *line X* of Table 2 shows that no tax is due.

● **step two – for gifts where you know the total cost to you.** The gift (£100,000) plus the running total (£60,000) = £160,000. This is amount *F*.

● **step three – tax on amount F.** Looking along *line X* in Table 2 the nearest amount below *F* is £140,000 on which the tax is £15,000. Tax at 40% on the excess of £20,000 = £8,000. £8,000 + £15,000 gives a total tax bill of £23,000.

● **step four – subtract D from J.** Amount *J* (£23,000) minus amount *D* (nil) = £23,000. This is the amount of tax due, but as Roger died more than four but less than five years after he made the gift, only 60% of that tax actually has to be paid (see table on p355). 60% of £23,000 is £13,800, but the trustees have already paid £1,500. So the amount they have to pay now is £13,800 − £1,500 = £12,300 – considerably more than they expected.

Gift to Emma in July 1992
As a PET, no tax was due at the time it was made, but we have to use the calculator to find the tax due now that Roger has died.

● **step one – tax on running total, now £160,000.** In the previous step this was worked out as £23,000 (you don't use the reduced tax of £13,800, as this would make the tax payable on the new gift more than it should be).

● **step two – for gifts where you know the total cost to you.** The new gift (£80,000) plus the running total (£160,000) = £240,000. This is amount *F*.

● **step three – tax on amount F.** Looking along *line X* in Table 2, we find the nearest amount below *F* is £220,000, on which the tax is £47,000. Tax at 50% of the excess of £20,000 = £10,000. £47,000 + £10,000 gives a total tax bill of £57,000.

● **step four – subtract D from J.** Amount *J* (£57,000) minus amount *D* (£23,000) = £34,000. This is the tax due on Roger's £80,000 gift to Emma. As he died within three years of making the gift, the full amount of tax is due.

Note that, although Emma was given £20,000 more than Arthur, she will actually finish up with less as she has to pay £34,000 in tax whereas her brother has no tax to pay. This sort of problem could have been avoided by saying in Roger's will that the tax should be paid out of his estate.

We've now found out how much tax is due on PETs and chargeable transfers made in Roger's lifetime. The next step is to work out the tax on Roger's estate. We show you how in Example 10 overleaf.

Example 10: a mixture of tax-free and taxable gifts on death
When Roger dies in 1994 he is a widower with an estate of £250,000. From Example 9 we know that his running total of gifts made before death is £240,000 (amount F) and the tax due on this amount is £57,000 (amount J).

In his will Roger leaves his son Arthur and his daughter Emma £50,000 each, *free of tax*. He leaves the residue of his estate to charity. Using the calculator on p370 we can now work out the IHT on his estate. Because it's the tax on death, we use Table 2.

Step one:
• **Amount A** (the running total) is £240,000, and tax on this (amount D) is £57,000

Step two:
£50,000 is what Arthur and Emma should each end up with, so it's a gift where you know the benefit to the recipient (a net gift)
• **Amount Q** (A minus D) is £183,000
• **Amount E** (the total of gifts to Emma and Arthur) is £100,000
• **Amount F** is £283,000

Step three:
Because it's a new gift, you need from now on to use *line Y*.
• The nearest amount below £283,000 is £228,000. Tax on this amount (amount G) is £102,000
• **Amount H** (tax at 3/2 on the remaining £55,000) is £82,500
• **Amount J** (G plus H) is £184,500.

Step four:
• **Amount K** (J minus D) is £127,500. This is the IHT on Roger's estate. So Roger's estate will be distributed as follows:

Value of estate	£250,000
less gifts to Arthur and Emma	£100,000
less IHT payable to Inland Revenue	£127,000
Amount left for charity	£22,500

In the end little will reach the charity, possibly far less than Roger had hoped. If Roger had left a specific amount, say £30,000, to the charity in his will with the residue split equally between Arthur and Emma, the IHT payable would have been £123,000, a tax saving of £4,500.

Tax-free and free of tax

A *tax-free* gift is an exempt gift – ie no tax is charged on that gift. A *free of tax* gift is taxable – 'free of tax' means that the giver wants the getter to end up with a gift of that size after any tax has been paid. So – in Example 10 – the free of tax gifts to Emma and Arthur are taxable; the gift to charity is tax-free.
IHTA 1984 s36–42.

Making your will

If you are concerned about IHT on your death, your will is an important step in co-ordinating IHT planning in your lifetime.

Tax apart, it is wise to make a will to avoid unnecessary uncertainty on your death – and to reduce the likelihood of disagreements amongst your relatives and friends. Also, you might be surprised by what happens to your property if you don't leave a will. For example, if you live with someone without being married, the *Intestacy rules* (see overleaf) give them nothing.

Basic points

• if you're married, make sure you leave your wife (or husband) enough to live on. Remember that old age can be expensive – so, if you can, leave a large safety margin. It's only when you've done this that you should look at ways of cutting down the IHT bill

• consider making enough taxable gifts on your death to use up your nil rate band (see p352 for what this is). You can do this by making gifts direct to your children or grandchildren

• although gifts between husband and wife are exempt, gifts to children *aren't* exempt

• unless you say specifically that gifts bear their own tax, the tax on them will normally come out of the residue. If you've left the residue to your wife or husband, much (or all) of it could be swallowed up in paying the tax on other gifts – see Example 10 opposite.

Tax subtleties

*(A **free-of-tax** gift is a taxable gift, but the tax on it comes out of the residue; an **after-tax** gift is a taxable gift which bears its own tax; an **exempt** gift is a gift covered by an exemption – eg a gift to your wife or husband)*

• gifts in your will to your spouse or someone you live with should be subject to a condition that the other person survives you for 30 days. Otherwise, if, say, you are killed in an accident and the other person dies a few days later, your property will be channelled through the other person's estate – increasing IHT on that estate to no purpose. (The IHT rules actually permit you to stipulate a 'survivorship' period of up to six months) *IHTA 1984 s92.*

• if you are making free-of-tax gifts there may be a lower tax bill if all the free-of-tax gifts you make are specific gifts rather than gifts of residue

● there is no tax advantage in making after-tax gifts in your will if none of your gifts of residue are exempt

● if *part* of the residue is left as an exempt gift, there may, in some cases, be less tax to pay if some of your specific gifts are tax-free and some are after-tax. The calculations are nightmarish, and you'll need professional advice. Not worth doing for most people.
IHTA 1984 s36–42.

● if you own a business or a farm, there can be a tax saving if you give your wife or husband a cash legacy in the will with the residue to the children.

Joint tenancies

A joint tenancy has nothing to do with being a tenant. It's one way in which two (or more) people can share the ownership of land, including freehold land and houses.

Property belonging to you on a joint tenancy passes automatically to the survivor when you die. You cannot give it to someone else under your will – even though it forms part of the value of your estate on death for IHT.

If this isn't what you want, you can *sever* the joint tenancy and convert it into a tenancy in common – which *can* be left to someone else under your will (see p386). Your solicitor will be able to advise on this.

Discretionary trust

If you are uncertain what to do with the whole or part of your estate, you can set up a discretionary trust in your will, under which the trustees have two years in which to give away the property. (Discuss your wishes with the trustees before making your will so that you know that they are willing to act and that they understand the position.)

If they make the gifts within two years of your death, for IHT it is as if you made the gifts yourself. It is normal to say in your will who will get the property if it's not disposed of within two years.

Intestacy

If you die without leaving a will, statutory rules, shown below, say how your estate will be divided up (there are different rules in Scotland and Northern Ireland). These rules can be overriden by an order under the Inheritance (Provision for Family and Dependants) Act 1975, or by a disclaimer or re-arrangement by your beneficiaries – see opposite. Normally, the arrangements under an intestacy are treated, for IHT purposes, as though you had made those gifts yourself.

If you leave a surviving spouse

Your surviving spouse is always entitled to all your household effects – eg car, furniture. If there are children (or remoter issue), she also gets the first £40,000 plus the income for life from half the rest. The other half goes straight to the children in equal shares. When she dies, her life interest is divided equally among the children. However she can (if she chooses) redeem her life interest in return for a capital sum (which depends on her age) and she can require the family home to be transferred to her in return for giving up some other interest in the estate.

If there are no children, she gets the first £85,000, plus half the rest. The other half goes to your parents if they have survived you, to your brothers and sisters (or their children) if they have not.

If you leave no children or remoter issue, no parents and no brothers, sisters, nephews, or nieces, your surviving spouse gets the lot.

If you leave no surviving spouse

If you leave no surviving spouse your whole estate goes to your children. If you leave no children either, your estate is split up among your relations.

After you've gone

Re-arrangement of your estate by agreement – basics

After your death the gifts you made on death can be re-arranged – the revised gifts take effect for IHT just as if they had actually been made by you. (The same is true of arrangements

made between your relatives if you die without leaving a will.)
Various rules apply:
● the new arrangements must take effect within two years of
your death
● the arrangements must have the consent of all beneficiaries
under your will who are affected by them
● the parties to the arrangement must give their consent in
return for what they get under the arrangements (or for no
return at all) – not in return for anything else.

To get the relief, it has to be claimed, generally within six
months of re-arrangement. The relief can be claimed even if:
● the effect is to make someone a beneficiary of your estate
who was not one under your will
● the people concerned have already received their gifts.

If someone refuses a gift (or disclaims it within two years)
your estate is taxed as if the gift to that person was never made.
No claim needs to be made in this case.
IHTA 1984 s142.

There is a separate and more limited relief for settled
property: if someone refuses an interest in settled property and
the disclaimer is not made in return for anything, for IHT it is
as if the interest was never given. Before implementing a
rearrangement you should get professional advice: the Inland
Revenue have been known to deny IHT relief on slight grounds.

Rearrangement – worth it?

A re-arrangement of your gifts is a good idea if you haven't left
enough for your surviving spouse, and have given more than
enough to other members of your family. They can re-direct
their gifts without a further IHT charge. (Such a re-arrangement
could mean a *refund* of IHT – because more of the revised gift
would be tax-free.)

Alternatively, if your surviving spouse has far more than will
be needed, he or she can direct gifts to other members of your
family. And if, for example, you have given property to your
wife for life and after her death to your son, they could (if your
son is over 18) agree to split the property between them now.
This might reduce the tax when your wife dies.

However:
● the arrangements can't retrospectively alter the income tax
position. If someone has been receiving income from a gift
which he subsequently gives up, he is taxed on the income he
received
● if a parent redirects an income-producing legacy to his or
her unmarried child under 18, the parent will be taxed on that
income until the child reaches 18 or marries

● there is a special stamp duty relief for deeds used to implement rearrangements on or after 26 March 1985. Each deed is liable only for 50p duty. The conditions for relief are similar to those for IHT relief

● there is a similar rule for CGT. Variations and disclaimers within 2 years of your death can be treated as if you had made the revised gifts yourself and as if the original gifts had not been made. The CGT relief does not have to be claimed just because the IHT relief is.

A re-arrangement by the court

If you are domiciled in England and Wales, or in Northern Ireland (but not Scotland) certain people can apply to the court under the *Inheritance (Provision for Family and Dependants) Act 1975* (or corresponding provisions) for 'reasonable financial provision' from your estate. These people are:

● your surviving spouse
● a former spouse of yours who has not remarried
● any child of yours (including an illegitimate or adopted child)
● any other person who has been treated as a child of the family in relation to any marriage of yours
● any other person whom you were maintaining, either wholly or in part, immediately before your death, eg a cohabitee.

The court can order:

● periodical payments
● a payment of a lump sum
● the transfer or settlement of property in your estate
● the transfer or settlement of property which your estate is directed to acquire
● the variation of an existing marriage settlement under which you were a beneficiary by reason of being a party to a marriage.

For IHT, property transferred under an order is treated as having passed on your death.

An order can be made in respect of property held jointly by you which passes automatically on your death to the surviving joint owner. Moreover, if the court thinks you gave away property within the 6 years before your death so as to defeat an application for financial provision, the court can reverse the gift. (Your running total is then recalculated and reduced – which may lead to a repayment of IHT to your estate. However, the value of your estate on death will go up by the amount of the gift plus any tax repaid.)

IHTA 1984 s146.

382   The Which? Book of Tax

Paying IHT

Who has to pay

The taxman looks first to the giver for tax on a lifetime gift – so if you want the other person to pay the tax, get his promise that he will. If you don't pay the tax the taxman can get it from the other person anyway. If he has given the property to someone else, the taxman can recover the tax from that person.

If you die within seven years of making a gift, the tax, if any, is due from the person you made the gift to – see p368.

For IHT on your death, your personal representatives – or the trustees of settled property if you died having an *interest in possession* in settled property – are liable for the tax. So are the beneficiaries if they have received the property.

IHTA 1984 s199–205.

When to tell the taxman

When you make a taxable gift you have to tell the taxman if:
- your total of taxable gifts for the current tax year exceeds £10,000, or if
- your running total – including the current gift – exceeds £40,000.

You tell the taxman about lifetime gifts on **form C–5** which you get from the Capital Taxes Office (address on p508).

Always keep accurate records of the gifts you've made, and the tax – if any – you've paid on them.

For IHT on your death your personal representatives must deliver an account to the Probate registry – see *Tax for executors*, p407.

IHTA 1984 s216–217.

When to pay the tax

Tax on lifetime gifts is normally due six months after the end of the month in which you make the gift. But if you make the gift after 5 April and before 1 October, tax is due on 30 April in the following year.

IHT on your death is payable six months after the end of the month in which you die but your personal representatives will usually want to get probate (or letters of administration) before then – see p407. To do so they will have to deliver the accounts and pay the tax first.

Interest is charged on unpaid tax from the time it was payable. Current rates are 6% for IHT on death (or for additional tax at death rates on a lifetime gift) and for IHT due on chargeable gifts made during your lifetime.

IHTA 1984 s226, s233.

Payment by instalments

Sometimes IHT can be paid in instalments and in some cases the instalments do not attract interest – see opposite. The instalment option is available for lifetime gifts (if the other person pays the tax) and for gifts on death of:

● land and buildings, wherever situated
● a business or an interest in a business
● timber, where a lifetime gift has triggered IHT deferred from a previous owner's death
● a controlling holding of shares or securities – whether quoted or unquoted – in a company
● a non-controlling holding of unquoted shares or securities in a company, if certain conditions are specified.

If you want to pay by instalments you should tell the taxman by the normal due date for paying tax. This is six months from the end of the month of the gift. (For lifetime gifts made between 6 April and 30 October, it's 30 April of the following year). The tax has to be paid in 10 equal yearly instalments. The first instalment is due on the normal due date for paying the tax. Normally interest is due on the outstanding tax. But in the following cases, interest is only due if instalments are not paid on time for:

● agricultural land
● a business, or an interest in a business
● many holdings of unquoted shares or securities.

IHTA 1984 s227–229, s234.

29 INHERITANCE TAX PLANNING

Now that inheritance tax (IHT) has replaced capital transfer tax (CTT), you need to look at planning from a different point of view. Some of the ideas which worked for CTT will still be useful for IHT – particularly the very basic step of making your will.

How much should you be worth before you start taking action to avoid IHT? Although the nil rate band has been increased substantially, to £90,000, above that tax starts at 30 per cent. If you died tomorrow leaving an estate of £250,000, the taxman would want £62,000 (assuming none of the gifts you make are tax-free). So thinking about IHT is still worthwhile even with a modest estate. But some people worry too much about IHT. It's even more important to avoid jeopardising your own future. Make sure that what's left is enough to support you, or your surviving partner. You may need an increasing income as you grow older.

There are two basic ways of easing the effect of IHT:
- by reducing the tax bill
- by finding ways to pay the bill.

Reducing the tax bill

Basic points

- If you're married, it's possible to avoid all IHT when the first partner dies by leaving everything to the husband or wife. But this could result in a much larger tax bill on the second death unless the surviving partner can reduce their estate somehow.

● Although most gifts you make will count as Potentially Exempt Transfers (PETs – see p352), and so will only be taxable if you die within seven years of making them, it's still a good idea to make use of your exemptions and tax-free gifts. These will never produce a tax bill. In particular, remember the £3,000 annual exemption (which can be carried forward for one year); the small gifts exemption of £250 to each individual each year (but you can't give £3,000 plus £250 to the same person tax-free); and gifts made as normal expenditure out of income. If one of your children or grandchildren gets married, see if you can make the maximum tax-free gift allowed at that time (see p358).

● If you are married, consider dividing your total wealth between you, not necessarily in equal shares, so that each of you can make use of your exemptions, and each of you can leave at least part of your estate directly to your children or grandchildren – see *Estate spreading* on p360.

● If you're very wealthy, and can really afford to make substantial gifts, make them sooner rather than later. If you survive for three years after making the gift the tax is reduced on a sliding scale (see p355), and if you survive seven years there is no tax at all. So if you make a PET of £90,000 today and died in four years time, the gift would become a taxable gift. Assuming you'd made no other gifts there would be no tax to pay (because £90,000 is in the nil-rate band), but the £90,000 would count towards your running total when working out the IHT on your estate at death.

● It can be a good idea to skip a generation. If your children have no need for your money themselves, pass your assets to your grandchildren, either directly or through an accumulation and maintenance trust (see p387).

● Do you hold a reversionary interest in a trust – ie someone (the 'life tenant') has a life interest in the trust and you will be entitled to all the assets in the trust when they die? If you don't need the trust assets, consider giving your interest away before the life tenant dies. A reversionary interest is completely exempt from IHT, but if you take the property on the death of the life tenant, all of the property will then form part of your estate for IHT purposes.

● Do you hold *favoured property* such as business, or agricultural property (see p394) – or can you acquire some in preference to less favourably taxed property? If you do own some, think before leaving it to your spouse. The gift would be tax-free anyway and the advantage of the favourable tax treatment would be lost. It might be better to leave it to someone else.

● Don't forget that capital gains tax may have to be paid if you make a lifetime gift. You can normally hold-over any CGT bill (see p427), but tax will have to be paid when the recipient parts with the property. There's no CGT on death, so it might be better to hang on to property which would produce a large CGT bill until you die – you need to do your sums quite carefully to find out whether it's better to pay CGT now, or risk an IHT bill on your death. But it's not normally sensible to pay tax now in order to save a possible tax bill later.

● Tread very carefully with any gift which the taxman might regard as a *gift with reservation* (eg if you give your house away but continue to live there – see p356). The new rules mean that if you make a gift, but reserve some benefit from it for yourself, no matter how small, it doesn't count as a gift until your possible benefit stops. As the rules are so new, it's not always possible to say exactly how they will be interpreted.

The family home

This is many people's largest single asset, and can, on its own, push you over the nil rate band. Under the CTT rules it was often possible to give away at least part of your interest in the property during your lifetime, but still continue living there.

This isn't possible under IHT, except in certain situations. For example, if your daughter and son-in-law are living with you and you give them half of the house, then provided you each contribute your fair share of the running expenses, this will not be treated as a gift with reservation but as a proper gift made at that time. This would not be true if they did not live with you, or you did not pay your fair share of the running expenses.

If you own your home jointly with someone else, it makes a difference how ownership is set up (in England and Wales):

● joint tenants each own their own respective shares of the house, but when the first person dies, their share passes to the survivor automatically

● tenants in common each own a completely separate share of the house, which they can leave to whoever they wish. This has the advantage over a joint tenancy that you can leave your share to your children rather than your partner if you prefer, so reducing the value of the surviving partner's estate. This won't count as a gift with reservation as the person who dies first will not be reserving any benefit for themselves.

If you want to own your home as tenants in common, your solicitor can draw up a simple document to do this. But before doing so, you want to make sure that whoever you leave your share to will honour the wishes of the surviving partner, eg as far as selling the house goes.

Accumulation and maintenance settlements

These are a very good way of estate spreading – though you'll need professional advice before setting one up. You can use them to pass on any sort of property to your children or grandchildren provided that you accept that when they get to 25, at the latest, they will own the property, or at least the income from the property. More details in *Trusts*, p403.

Discretionary trusts

With a discretionary trust you can make a gift now which need not be received by anyone for a long time. The trust can be for a wide range of possible beneficiaries, and you can exercise some control over the property. A discretionary trust can be particularly useful if you wish to make a gift now, but you do not think the beneficiaries are ready to have control of the money you want to pass over. If you make a gift to the trust which does not result in a tax bill, eg because the amount is not more than the nil rate band (£90,000), no IHT will be payable if the trust's capital is passed on to the beneficiaries before the tenth anniversary of the trust, whatever the value of the property at the time. More details in *Trusts*, p401.

Benefits which are not gifts

Not everything you do which benefits your heirs constitutes a gift for IHT. If you provide services free of charge to a company which your children own, this is not a taxable gift. Or if you have information about a promising opportunity for investment you could pass that on (for example to the trustees of your children's accumulation and maintenance settlement) without making a taxable gift.

Back-to-Back Scheme

Under this scheme you invest a lump sum in a life annuity. This would usually have the effect of reducing the value of your estate for IHT by the whole of the lump sum. The annuity gives you a regular income, part of which represents a return of capital and part actual income (see *Annuities*, p319). Out of the income you buy a qualifying life policy written in trust for the named beneficiaries to whom you want to pass on your money. Provided that the life policy is issued on the basis of a full medical examination and is issued on the same terms as if the annuity had not been purchased (the taxman requires all this) the annual premiums will be tax-free gifts for IHT if they are regular, come out of income and leave you with enough to maintain your standard of living. The proceeds of the policy should be tax-free for the beneficiaries. The annuity won't form part of your estate on death.
IHTA 1984 s21, s263.

Estate freezing

Estate freezing is the steady but sure way of passing your money on. You freeze the value of an asset in your estate by giving away the growth in value but keeping the present value.

● A simple example of estate freezing is making an interest-free loan to your son who invests it in unit trusts. If the loan is repayable on demand, there's no gift for IHT. But if you can't effectively call in your loan quickly, you could be regarded as making a gift equal to the value of the opportunity you have lost of earning interest on that money during the time it took to repay it – or conceivably the income from the unit trust could be taxed as though it was yours

● You can also allow the free use of things other than cash – eg furniture or a boat. There is no gift unless it's clear, when you allow the use, that there will be problems getting the property back

● Be careful if the asset you lend actually earns income itself. If you allow your son free use of land, and he receives rent from

the land, the taxman would probably try to treat the rent as your income, not your son's.
IHTA 1984 s2–3.

Freezing the family business

There are two schemes. Use the first scheme if a private company ('X Co') you own has become quite valuable and is expected to continue growing. You want to retain the growth so far and pass the rest on. Here's one way in which it can be done (and see diagram on p391):

- your children (or their trustees, if the children are still under 18) subscribe for ordinary shares in a new company, 'New Co', formed to take over X Co

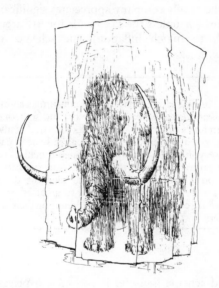

- you exchange your shares in X Co for *non-cumulative redeemable preference shares* in New Co of a total value equal to the current market value of X Co. (You could also use this method where your existing business is unincorporated. You simply exchange your business itself for the preference shares)
- the preference shares carry the right to procure a liquidation of New Co at any time – so you can get back the value of what you put in (your shares should not have voting rights on anything other than a liquidation).
    Here's the effect of doing this:
- the exchange doesn't reduce the value of your estate – so there's no gift for IHT purposes

• the preference shares have no right to share in the capital profits which X Co makes in the future: these will belong to New Co, and will be reflected in the value of New Co's ordinary shares. Provided New Co pays no dividend, the most the preference shares can be worth is their face value – so the future growth in the value of X Co belongs to your children.

Clearly before setting up a scheme like this you need professional advice. You may be able to retain effective control of the company through a trust (for your children) of the ordinary shares in New Co.

A point to watch is business property relief (see *Favoured Property*, p394). If you are currently entitled to 50% business property relief, that may drop to 30% if the preference shares will not give you control of more than 25% of the company. So unless the family company appreciates significantly in value in real terms (or unless the tax bands for IHT aren't increased by enough to match inflation), the scheme may not be worthwhile.

Waivers

For IHT the omission to exercise a right constitutes a gift if the effect of the omission is to leave you worse off and someone else better off. Certain types of waiver are not gifts for IHT. A waiver of wages or salary is not a gift, even if you have already been paid – though in this case you should repay the money quickly. You can also waive, for up to 12 months in advance, your right to share in the dividends on a company's shares, provided the dividend hasn't become payable yet. This can be used to great advantage to shift value in family companies if your children – or their trustees – are shareholders.

Scheme two

The second scheme is useful if you have a private company which is not valuable at the moment but which is likely to become valuable. You want to benefit your children, but want to retain control for the moment. One option would be an accumulation and maintenance settlement, but let's assume you don't want this – because, for example, you don't want to pass the company on to your children or grandchildren until after they are 25.

Suppose the existing share capital of the company consists of 1000 Ordinary £1 shares. What you do is this:
• reorganise the share capital so that there are 100 'A' Ordinary shares and 900 'B' Ordinary shares
• the 'A' shares have full voting rights but no other rights. The 'B' shares have the exclusive right to the assets of the company

on liquidation, but have no material voting rights until a specified future date. This is the date you intend your heirs to take over control of the company. At that date all the shares become shares of the same class

● you give the 'B' shares to your children or to a trust for their benefit. The value of the gift, for IHT purposes, will be small – even though eventually the shares could be very valuable.

It is not a good idea to do this scheme with a company which is already worth a lot.

Freezing the family business

Scheme one

You own

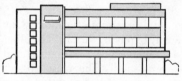

X Co worth £300,000

Your children own the shares in

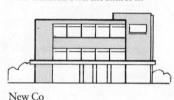

New Co

You swap X Co for £300,000 of non-cumulative redeemable preference shares in New Co.

Ten years later, New Co is worth, say, £700,000, but your shares are still worth £300,000.

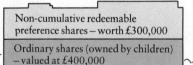

Non-cumulative redeemable preference shares – worth £300,000

Ordinary shares (owned by children) – valued at £400,000

Scheme two

You own Z Co worth £10,000

Z Co has 1,000 ordinary shares

You split the shares

| Voting (kept by you) | 10% |
| Non-voting (given to your children) – taxable gift of £9,000 | 90% |

Ten years later, the shares merge.

Your share is worth 10% of the new value of the company. If, say, the company is worth £100,000, your children will own £90,000 worth of shares.

Paying the tax bill

Once you've looked at all the ways of reducing the IHT bill, it's time to find ways of paying the tax itself – for example, if you have made a gift which you hope will reduce your possible tax bill, but only if you survive another seven years. Life insurance has an important role to play here.

Life insurance

Life insurance policies feature prominently in IHT planning. Under the CTT rules, life insurance companies could design special 'inheritance trusts' for passing on your money, but these trusts lost their usefulness when IHT was introduced. However, inheritance trusts set up before 18 March 1986 are unaffected by the new rules.

Life insurance policies are still a useful weapon. One attraction is that they provide a way of paying the tax. The other attraction is that they offer a simple way of setting up and running trusts. Paperwork is very small. The trust doesn't receive anything until the policy pays out – so there aren't accounts to file every year.

Insurance policies are also a good way of saving regularly, and, of course, of insuring against a risk – eg your sudden death.

Keep the proceeds out of your estate

The proceeds of a life insurance policy aren't exempt from IHT. So if your policy pays out to your estate, this will increase the size of your estate for IHT purposes – which could mean a higher tax bill. The answer is to write your policy in trust for your beneficiaries.

Example

If you take out a whole life policy on your own life for your own benefit, the proceeds on your death will form part of your estate on death. But if the policy is written in trust for the benefit of your wife and children, the proceeds on your death go straight to them.

The policy can be for a stated term, or for the whole of your life. If the policy is in trust for someone other than your wife or husband, the premiums paid will count as a gift each year, but these will be covered by the exemption for normal expenditure out of your income (see p357). If the premiums paid are fairly substantial, you may need to use your annual exemption instead.

> **Gift of a policy**
> If you give away a life policy, the value of the gift is normally either the market value of the policy or the premiums you've paid (whichever is higher). Market value is normally close to the surrender value – but a policy given away by someone close to death would be worth almost as much as it would pay out.

Trusts and life insurance

Generally, you can have a policy written on any sort of trust permitted by law. There are four standard types:

• **a fixed gift.** You specify the gift – eg 'to my sons Larry and Phil in equal shares', or 'to my wife Pauline absolutely'

• **a group gift.** This provides for a group of beneficiaries – who need not all have been born at the time of the gift. You can also impose conditions on the gift. For example a policy for 'each of my children Caroline, Tom, Chris and any other children of mine who shall attain 21 or marry under that age, and if more than one then in equal shares'. Your trustees could also be given a limited power to switch shares so that not every one of your children shared equally

• **a flexible trust.** This is an *interest in possession settlement* (see p399) with named beneficiaries. The trustees have broad powers to change the shares of the beneficiaries or even give their shares to a brand new beneficiary (for example you or your wife). There is no IHT if the gift is switched to you or your wife in your lifetime, or to your widow within two years of your death. But there could be IHT if shares are switched between your children – this would depend on their running totals for IHT. Under an accumulation and maintenance settlement, switching between children can normally be done without an IHT charge: but with that type of settlement it would not be possible to benefit your spouse

• **discretionary trusts.** A policy can be written on discretionary trusts. This allows the trustees to distribute the proceeds of the life policy in such shares as they choose to whoever they want (out of a specified class of beneficiaries) – eg 'to those of my grandchildren living at my death as my trustees shall decide, in such shares as they decide'.

There should be no IHT liability, except to the extent that the life insurance company's investment fund outperforms inflation, provided your running total is within the nil rate band when you set up the policy, *and* (if the policy is a single premium policy) the single premium doesn't take you above the nil rate band, *and* (if you pay regular premiums) the premiums are normal expenditure out of income.

This sort of trust gives a great deal of flexibility, but it is more common to use a flexible trust – see above. You would use a discretionary trust if you were totally in doubt about what shares, if any, you wanted your possible beneficiaries to take, or if those beneficiaries had significant running totals of their own so that there would be IHT on switching shares in a flexible trust.

Joint lives

A life policy can be taken out on joint lives – usually your wife and yourself, although the other person could be your child – with the proceeds payable on the first death or the second. For a couple this can be a cheaper way of getting life cover than separate policies. So you can provide for the survivor by making the policy pay out on the first death to the survivor. There will be no IHT if the survivor is your spouse because it will be a tax-free gift. Alternatively, you could provide that the policy only pays out on the death of the survivor. In that case it should be written in trust for your children or whoever you are passing your money on to. That way it won't form part of the survivor's estate.

Term insurance

Term insurance is often used by relatively young people to provide for their dependants in the event of their premature death. It can also be a useful way of providing against the extra IHT in case you die within seven years of making a PET. The policy should be written in trust for the person you make the gift to.

Favoured property

Business property

If certain conditions are met, gifts of business property – in life or on death – are valued at less than the cost to you. A 'smaller' gift equals less tax on the gift. Property which qualifies:
- **an unincorporated business** – eg a solicitor's practice, a corner shop, a share in a partnership. Discount of 50% – ie a gift worth £100,000 is taxed as though it was a gift of £50,000
- **shares or loan stock with a controlling interest** (ie you have a majority of the general voting rights). Discount of 50%. The shares can be either quoted or unquoted
- **unquoted shares** not quoted on *any* recognised stock exchange (eg a minority holding in a family company). Discount of 30%. From 17 March 1987, substantial minority

holdings (more than 25% but not more than 50%) get a 50% discount. Note that from 17 March 1987, shares and securities quoted on the Unlisted Securities Market will be treated in the same way as those for quoted companies and no business relief will be available for minority holdings in USM companies. *FA 1987 s58 and Sch 8.*

• **land, buildings or equipment** *owned by you yourself,* and used wholly or mainly by a business carried on by a company which you control or by a partnership of which you are a partner. Discount of 30%. (Rules are complicated, and you'll need advice)

• **land, business or equipment which is settled property** – if you have the *interest in possession* **and** you use it wholly or mainly for the purposes of a business which you carry on. Discount of 30%.

In all these cases, to get the discount you must have owned the property for at least two years immediately before the gift (or your death). If you've owned it for a shorter time, you may still qualify if the property replaces other property which you acquired more than two years before the gift (or before death).

You won't, in any case, get the discount if the business consists wholly or mainly of:
• dealing in securities; stocks or shares; land or buildings
• the making or holding of investments.

Property for personal use doesn't qualify for the discount – so if, for example, you control a company which owns cars used mainly for private purposes, the discount on the value of your controlling interest won't apply to the cars.

For gifts of both business and agricultural property which count as PETs when made, the appropriate relief is only available if the recipient still owns the property, or a qualifying replacement property, at the time of the donor's death (or the recipient's death if earlier). If the donor survives seven years from the date of the gift, then it is tax-free anyway. *FA 1987 s58 and Sch 8.*

Other favoured property

• **agricultural property.** If the land is tenanted, the discount is 30%. If you have vacant possession, or the right to get it within 12 months, the discount is 50%. You need to have either owned the land for 7 years while someone else has used it for agricultural purposes or to have actually occupied the land yourself for agricultural purposes for 2 years

• **timber.** The value of timber (but not the land underneath) in your estate on death may be entirely ignored for IHT purposes if you were given it, or had owned it for at least 5 years. IHT at death rates will be due if the beneficiary sells or gives it away in his lifetime. If he hangs on until he dies, IHT on *your* death will be permanently waived

● **heritage property** (historic houses, works of art, etc). If strict conditions are met, tax may be deferred – perhaps for ever. Undertakings have to be given to the Treasury concerning maintenance, preservation, and public access.

30 TRUSTS

Trusts are not only for the rich. Even if you're no more than comfortably off, one type of trust – the *accumulation and maintenance trust* – can be worth considering for your children, grandchildren, or other infants for whom you've got a soft spot. And many people who are not rich at all set up trusts in their wills.

In this chapter, we tell you:
- what a trust is and how it pays tax
- what use it can be in tax planning.

Cast of characters

There are three sorts of characters for nearly all trusts:
- **a settlor.** This is the person who sets up the trust, and puts money (or property) into it
- **trustees.** These are the people who 'own' the trust property. But unlike a normal owner, they can't do what they like with it. They have to follow the instructions of the 'instrument' – often a deed or a will – which sets up the trust. There are also legal rules about what they must (and must not) do
- **beneficiaries.** These lucky people are the ones who will – or in some cases may – be given money, or property, or the use of property, from the trust – see Example, below.

Example

Ned Settlor sets up a trust in his will. He wants his wife Gladys to have all his money, but he wants the house to go to their children after her death. So he leaves the money direct to Gladys, but he leaves the house to trustees 'in trust for my wife Gladys for her life and afterwards to my children in equal shares'. Gladys and the children are the beneficiaries.

Note: Ned is careful to take competent legal advice. As a result, the trust is worded so that:
- if Gladys is short of money, the trustees can 'advance' money to her – ie they can raise capital on the security of the house, and give it to Gladys. (If they do this, the children will get less)
- if Gladys wants to move, she can sell the house and buy another.

Trusts and tax – a bird's eye view

Income tax

- Trusts with an *interest in possession* (see opposite) pay tax at the basic rate (27 per cent in the 1987–88 tax year) on all their income
- *Discretionary trusts* (see p400) normally pay tax at a combined rate of 45 per cent on all their income – ie the basic rate of tax, plus an additional rate sufficient to bring the total rate up to 45 per cent. So for the 1987–88 tax year, when the basic rate is 27 per cent, the additional rate is 18 per cent. Although basic rate tax is paid on all the trust's income, the additional rate is paid on the income *after* deducting the allowable expenses of the trustees
- When the trustees pay income to a beneficiary, they normally subtract tax – at 27 per cent (for trusts with an interest in possession) or 45 per cent (for discretionary trusts) – before making the payment. If the beneficiary pays tax at a lower rate, he or she can claim back the difference from the Inland Revenue
- *Warning*: if the settlor (or his wife) can be paid income from the trust (even if none is actually paid), any undistributed income is taxed as though it's his. If he can revoke the trust, *all* income is taxed as though it's his.

ICTA 1970 s446, s447; FA 1973 s16, s17.

Capital gains tax

Rules for trusts are exactly the same as for individuals, except that whereas individuals can make net taxable gains (in the 1987–88 tax year) of £6,600 before there's tax to pay, the limit for most trusts is only half as much (£3,300). Settlors can claim hold-over relief (see p427) on gifts they make to a trust. Trustees can claim hold-over relief on gifts they make to beneficiaries.

CGTA 1979 s52, Sch 1 para 5, 6; FA 1980 s79; FA 1982 s82.

Inheritance tax

Until 17 March 1986, gifts *into* trusts were liable to capital transfer tax in the same way as most other gifts, except for gifts to charitable trusts which were exempt. From 18 March 1986 capital transfer tax was abolished and replaced by inheritance tax (IHT), and the following rules now apply:

- gifts to discretionary trusts are chargeable to IHT at 50 per cent of the normal rates, depending on the total of other gifts already made by the settlor at the time of the gift
- gifts to accumulation and maintenance trusts and trusts for

the disabled are treated as *potentially exempt transfers (PETs)* and so may become liable to IHT on a sliding scale, if the settlor dies within seven years of making the gift – see p352

● gifts to interest in possession trusts are treated in the same way as discretionary trusts, but the Government has proposed that they should be treated as PETs

● gifts to charitable trusts are exempt from IHT.

For gifts out of a trust:

● if someone has a life interest (or some other *interest in possession*), see below for the tax rules

● if there isn't a life interest (or interest in possession), the trust is called a *discretionary trust*, and tax is worked out under a complicated formula which we explain on p401

● *accumulation and maintenance trusts* have special rules – see p403.

Trusts with an interest in possession

The simplest example is a trust with a life interest – eg a gift 'to Gladys for life, and then to my children in equal shares'. Another simple example is a gift for a fixed number of years – eg 'to Fred for 20 years, and then to Jim'. In these examples, Gladys and Fred have an *interest in possession*, and the children and Jim have what's called *reversionary interests* – ie they are entitled to the trust property when the interest in possession comes to an end.

If you have an interest in possession in trust property, you are treated, for IHT purposes, as owning the whole of the trust property. So when the interest in possession ends, there is a gift, for IHT purposes, of the whole property. The whole of the trust property in which you had an interest is liable to IHT, depending on *your* running total of previous gifts, although the tax is actually payable by the trustees. *But:*

● the Government has proposed that the ending of your interest in possession should be treated as a PET if the property passes to another individual absolutely, or another individual becomes entitled to an interest in possession, or the property becomes subject to an accumulation and maintenance trust or a trust for the disabled

● if the interest comes to an end on your death, the full value of the trust property will be liable to IHT in the same way as if it formed part of your estate

● if more than one person shares an interest in possession, they'll be treated as owning the proportion of the property which corresponds with their share

- because the people with an interest in possession in effect own the whole property for IHT purposes, the *reversionary interest* (ie the interest next in line) is ignored. This doesn't apply if the reversion has ever been bought or sold (there are other technical exceptions)
- if you have an interest in possession in trust property, and then become 'absolutely entitled' to the property – ie you genuinely own it – there's no IHT charge when your interest in possession ends
- there's also no charge to IHT if, when an interest in possession ends, the property goes back to the settlor (or to his wife, provided he hasn't been dead for longer than two years). *IHTA 1984 s48–50, s52, s53.*

Example

Boris Settlor owns a large (and valuable) house. In his will, he leaves it to his son Reuben for 20 years, and then (as an absolute gift) to his 4 year old grandson Amos.

There may be IHT to pay on the following two occasions:
- when Boris dies and the property passes to the trustees in trust for Reuben. The value of the property when Boris dies will be taken into account when working out any IHT payable on his estate, plus his running total of previous gifts before his death
- at the end of Reuben's 20 years when the property passes to Amos.

Discretionary trusts

These are trusts where the trustees can decide who gets the money. For example, you could set up a trust under which the trustees could pay income (or capital) 'in such proportions as they in their absolute discretion shall decide, to all or any of my children David, Maureen, Alison, any of their children, grandchildren or remoter issue, with any income or capital remaining on 1 August 2067 to be given to charitable purposes'.

The reason for the gift at the end is that trusts *must* come to an end (unless they're charitable). There are various ways of making sure that they do, and the one we've chosen above is to end the trust on a certain date within 80 years. Sometimes it's not clear whether a trust is discretionary or not. A trust to pay income 'in equal shares to my children David and Maureen' is *not* discretionary, since David and Maureen can insist on getting their shares. But suppose the trustees could vary those shares. Broadly:

- if they can vary the shares in which income is paid *after it's arisen* (eg bank interest already received by the trust), the trust is discretionary
- if they can vary the shares *only for income which has yet to arise* (eg next year's bank interest), the trust is one with interests in possession.

Tax on gifts from discretionary trusts

There may be an IHT bill:
- when gifts of capital are made from a discretionary trust (there's no IHT on a gift which is income of the person who receives it)
- (whether gifts are made or not) every 10th anniversary from the time the trust was set up. This charge is called the *periodic charge*.

Tax is normally charged at a single rate (called the *effective rate*) on all gifts of capital made from the trust in the first 10 years. The effective rate is different for each trust. The actual tax charged is a fraction of the effective rate – see below. It's quite possible for the effective rate to be nil. The effective rate is recalculated at each periodic charge, and the new rate normally lasts for 10 years.
IHTA 1984 s58, s64–66, s68, s69.

How much tax on gifts of capital in the first 10 years?

step 1: take the amount the trust was worth at the time it was set up, *plus* the value of any property added to the trust after it was set up, using its value at the time it was put in to the trust. (If the settlor set up other trusts on the same day as this trust, you must also add the amount they were worth at the time they were set up)

step 2: work out tax on a *gross gift* of the total *step 1* amount, using the settlor's running total on the day before he set up the trust but at the rates of tax in force at the date of the gift out of the settlement

step 3: divide the tax on this gift by the *step 1* value of the trust, and multiply by 100. This gives you the *effective rate of tax*

step 4: multiply the result by 0.3

step 5: multiply the result by the number of complete periods of three months for which the property in the gift has been in the trust

step 6: divide the result by 40

step 7: multiply the result by the amount of the gift made by the trustees. This gives you the tax due on the gift.

> **Technical points**
> ● If the gift is of property which has been in the trust for differing amounts of time, steps 5–7 have to be done separately for each bit
> ● If you make a second gift to the trust of substantial value (broadly 5% of the trust value or more), your running total at the time of the second gift may be used in the calculations, if it's higher than your original running total
> ● It's a good idea to set up a trust when your running total is as low as possible
> ● There are slightly different rules for trusts created before 27 March 1974.

Example

On 11 June 1987, Simon, with a running total of £89,000, set up a discretionary trust with a gift of £40,000. This was the only trust he set up on that day.

On 12 September 1990, the trust makes a gift (of capital) of £30,000 to Philip. Let's assume that IHT rates haven't changed between now and 1990 – that means you can use the Calculator on p368.

step 1: value of the trust at the time it was set up   £40,000
step 2: Simon's running total when the trust was set up
                                                                £89,000
         tax on a gross gift of £40,000 by someone with
         a running total of £89,000   £5,850
step 3: divide £5,850 by £40,000 and multiply by 100[1]
                                                              14.625%
step 4: multiply the result by 0.3   4.387%
step 5: multiply the result by the number of complete
         periods the property has been in the trust (13)
                                                              57.031%
step 6: divide by 40   1.426%
step 7: multiply by the gift (£30,000) to find **tax due** £427.80

[1] all percentages must be rounded to three decimal places

Note: if the trust paid the tax on the gift (ie so that Philip gets £30,000 after tax), the before-tax gift is:

$$£30,000 \times \frac{100}{100 - 1.426} = £30,433.99.$$ Tax on this is £433.99.

The periodic charge

This is calculated in exactly the same way as a gift in the first 10 years, except that:
● the gift of the trust (step 1) is the amount the trust was worth immediately before its tenth anniversary, *plus* the initial value

of any other trusts set up by the settlor on the same day as this trust was set up
● the running total is the settlor's running total on the day before he set up the trust *plus* the total pre-tax amounts of any gifts made by the trust in the previous ten years
● if the settlor has put more property into the trust since he set it up, use his running total immediately before he made the additional gift, if this is higher. Some transfers can be knocked off this total – consult the capital taxes office (address on p508).
● if property has been put into the trust in the previous ten years, the periodic charge on that property is reduced by one fortieth for every complete period of three months from the previous ten-year anniversary *before* that property went in.

Accumulation and maintenance trusts

These are a special type of discretionary trust. If you stick to the rules, there is no IHT charge when the capital from the trust is paid to the beneficiaries, and there is no periodic charge.

Who they're for

They're commonly used as a way of putting money into trust for your children. Overleaf we tell you, broadly, how it works:

- while your children are still young, you set up the trust and put some capital in it
- income made by the trust is accumulated (ie kept in the trust). Any income which isn't accumulated must be used for the 'maintenance, education or benefit' of your children
- some time after your children reach 18, and by the time they reach 25, the trust comes to an end and the property is shared among them. If you don't want the trust to hand out the capital, you can give the children the right to the income instead. You can give the capital later.

If you set up a trust for your children, you'll be taxed at your top rate of tax on any income paid out for them while they're under 18 (unless they're married) – see Box opposite for rules. The money will count as *your* income, not your children's.

If the trust *isn't* for your children, or they're over 18 or married, income paid out for them will count as *their* income. Any child, no matter how young, is entitled to the full single person's allowance of £2,425. So if, say, a child has no other income, and is paid income of £2,400 (gross), the trustees deduct tax at 45% (£1,080), and hand over £1,320. The child can claim back the £1,080.
ICTA 1970 s437; FA 1973 s16, s17.

The rules in detail

rule 1: at least one of the beneficiaries must be alive when the trust is set up. So a trust 'for my son Alan's children' is no good unless Alan already has a child. Children of Alan's born later are added to the list of beneficiaries. If all the beneficiaries die, but others could be born, the trust still keeps going.

rule 2: at least one of the beneficiaries must get an *interest in possession* in at least part of the trust property before he or she reaches the age of 25. A right to the income of part (or all) of the property is an interest in possession. So is the right to a share of the trust capital.

rule 3: there can be no entitlement to trust property until a beneficiary has acquired an interest in possession. (This doesn't contradict rule 2: to get an interest in possession you must have a *right* to income or capital. If trustees merely decide to hand out income or capital to you there's no right to it, and no interest in possession)

rule 4: the trust must come to an end within 25 years, unless *rule 5* applies

rule 5: the trust can last for more than 25 years if all the beneficiaries have one grandparent in common. Illegitimate and adopted children count in the same way as legitimate children. If one of the beneficiaries dies before getting an

interest in possession, his or her share can go (if the trust deed says so) to his or her widow, widower, or children.
IHTA 1984 s58, s71.

Income paid to your children

Income paid (from a trust set up by you or your wife) to children of yours who are under 18 and unmarried is taxed as your income (and at your top rate of tax). You get a tax credit equal to the tax which the trustees have to deduct before they pay out the income.

Normally, the trustees deduct tax at the 27% basic rate, *plus* an additional rate of 18% – making 45% in all.

If you have to pay *more* tax than the trustees deduct, you can claim back this extra tax from the trustees (or – though you probably wouldn't want to – from the child who receives the income). If you receive a repayment of some of the tax deducted you must pay this to the trustees or your child.

The general election held on 11 June 1987 meant that the Finance Act confirming the tax rules for the 1987–88 tax year was rushed through in shortened form. Some of the Chancellor's 1987 Budget proposals were shelved, but the Government has said that it will re-introduce them. We've marked these pre-election proposals with this symbol:

31 TAX FOR EXECUTORS

The people who deal with what you own when you die are your *personal representatives*. Popularly, they tend to be called 'executors' (hence the title of this chapter) though, correctly, the term *executors* applies only to personal representatives appointed by a valid will. Where there is no valid will (an intestacy) the personal representatives are *administrators*. So far as tax is concerned, however, there is no difference between the two kinds of personal representatives – both have virtually the same responsibilities.

The time between when a person dies and when the property in that person's estate is finally distributed is called the *period of administration*. During the period of administration, the personal representatives are concerned with three main taxes:

- **inheritance tax**
- **capital gains tax**
- **income tax**.

In this chapter, we take each of these taxes in turn, and look at the particular points that concern personal representatives.

Inheritance Tax (IHT)

The Inland Revenue account, and payment of IHT

The *Inland Revenue account* has to be signed by the personal representatives. It lists the value of every asset (shares, house, or whatever) owned or jointly owned by the person who has died, and the amounts of any debts.

The IHT bill (if any) must be paid by the personal representatives when they apply for probate – or, if it's an intestacy, when they apply for letters of administration. In some cases, the IHT can be paid in instalments – see below.

Broadly, there will be IHT to pay unless

- the value of the estate at death (less any debts)
- plus any taxable gifts in the 7 years before death
- minus anything left to the deceased's wife or husband

comes to £90,000 (from 17 March 1987) or less. (For a fuller explanation, see p351).

If the total comes to less than £70,000 (including the *total* value of any property jointly owned by the person who has died), *and* the application for probate or letters of administration is made by a solicitor, there's no need for an Inland Revenue account. If you're making a personal application, you'll need to complete a form listing all the assets and liabilities of the estate, so that the *personal application department* of the Probate Registry can check that an Inland Revenue account is not needed.

IHTA 1984 s216.

Tax by instalments

If the estate includes buildings, land, or certain agricultural or business property or private company shares, the personal representatives can opt to pay the tax on that part of the estate in 10 annual instalments, starting at the end of the month six months after the date of death. This will usually help, because until probate (or letters of administration) is obtained, the money in the estate is 'frozen', and can't be used – even to pay an IHT bill. Many building societies have an arrangement with the Inland Revenue which allows them to release money in their accounts before probate. Even so, personal representatives will often need to borrow to pay the IHT.

If you choose to pay by instalments, you'll usually have to pay interest –currently at 6 per cent – on the money still owing (but see p383 for exceptions). 6 per cent is almost certainly less than the cost of borrowing to pay the IHT.

If the property is sold, all the tax outstanding must be paid at once. Even if the property isn't sold, it may be that – after probate has been obtained – there will be enough money in the estate to pay the IHT in full. In this case the IHT should be paid off, if the 6 per cent interest charged by the Inland Revenue is likely to be more than could be earned (after tax) by investing the money elsewhere.

IHTA 1984 s226–229, s233–234.

Example

When Mrs Bognor died, the value of her estate was £100,000. Her house was worth £80,000; the other £20,000 was made up of money, furniture, pictures, and personal effects. The tax bill was £3,000. The rules allow four-fifths of this to be paid by instalments – ie the same proportion as the value of the house bears to the total value of the estate.

Probate values: lowest not always best

The lower the probate value, the lower the IHT bill. But, especially if there's no IHT to pay, it can make sense to declare the probate values as high as realistically possible. This is because the probate value is also the beneficiary's base cost when it comes to working out capital gains tax on any future disposal of that asset.

CGTA 1979 s49.

Example

Stanley Wood left his flat (worth between £30,000 and £40,000) to his daughter Julie, who already had a house of her own. In June 1987, Julie sold the flat for £43,900 (after subtracting the selling costs). Her gain, for tax purposes (ignoring indexation allowance), is £43,900 *less* the probate value. She hasn't used any of her annual £6,600 exemption (see overleaf), so her tax bill will be anything from nil (if the probate value was £37,300 or more) to £2,190 (if the probate value was £30,000). (£43,900 − £30,000 = £13,900. £13,900 − £6,600 = £7,300. Tax at 30% on £7,300 = £2,190.)

Stock market slump protection

The probate value of quoted stocks and shares is based on stock market prices at the date of death. If the stocks and shares are sold within one year of the date of death, and if the *total proceeds* before the expenses of selling of all those sold is less than the probate value, the personal representatives can ask to have IHT based on these lower sale prices, not the original probate value.

IHTA 1984 s178–180.

Form 30 – and after

When it seems that no more assets or debts will come to light, the personal representatives complete *form 30*. Once the second copy of this is returned to them – with the certificate signed and stamped – personal representatives are secure in the knowledge that no more IHT will be demanded of them. Form 30 fixes the value of assets conclusively as at the date of death. If a sale, for example of a house, is expected to raise a much larger figure than that declared (or agreed with the district valuer – an Inland Revenue official), it may be wise to delay the sale until form 30 is signed and stamped. Until this is done, the question of value can be re-opened.   *(IHTA 1984 s239.)*

Capital Gains Tax (CGT)

CGT and the £6,600 exemption

When someone dies, there is no CGT to pay on what that person leaves. The personal representatives acquire the assets at the probate value, and if they sell any of those assets during the administration period (ie before distributing them) they will be liable for CGT in much the same way as an individual. All disposals of taxable assets must be included in the personal representatives' annual Tax Return (see opposite). A beneficiary who inherits an asset must take the probate value as the base value for working out CGT on any future sale.

Currently, an individual can make £6,600 of *net taxable gains* (ie gains minus losses) in a tax year before any CGT is due. Personal representatives also have the £6,600 exemption – independently of the beneficiaries – in the tax year of death and for each of the two following tax years.
CGTA 1979 s2, s49, Sch 1 para 4; TMA 1970 s12.

Personal representatives to distribute? Or sell and then distribute?

The fact that the personal representatives *and* each beneficiary have a £6,600 exemption from CGT (see above) offers great scope for reducing tax. Much will depend on the tax situation of the beneficiaries; so the personal representatives should work out with them how best to make use of all the £6,600 exemptions available.   *(CGTA 1979 Sch 1 para 4.)*

Tax Return

All disposals of taxable assets must be included in the personal representatives' annual Tax Return – see opposite.
TMA 1970 s12.

Example

Mr Potts owned lots of shares when he died, and he left them equally to his three children. The inheritance tax on the shares comes out of the residue – so there's no tax for the children to pay. The shares have a probate value of £100,000 – but when the time comes to hand over the shares to the children, their value has risen to £121,000.

- The children haven't used up any of their £6,600 exemptions, and nor have the personal representatives (PRs)
- If the PRs sell the shares before handing them over, they can subtract £6,600 from the £21,000 gain, leaving capital gains tax to pay on £21,000 *minus* £6,600 = £14,400. Tax at 30% = £4,320
- If the PRs hand each child £40,000 worth of shares, each child will have made a gain of £7,000 (ie a third of £21,000). Each child will have a capital gains tax bill of 30% of £400 (£7,000 − £6,600) = £120
- If the PRs sell enough shares to realise a gain of £6,600, and distribute the rest as shares – which are then sold by each of the beneficiaries – tax on the £21,000 gain can be avoided altogether. Care must be exercised in order to be able to show that the shares sold by the PRs were sold in the course of administering the estate.

Charities

Broadly, charities don't have to pay CGT. If a charity is left money, it can be worthwhile to give it an equivalent gift of property which has risen in value between probate and the time of the gift. There's no CGT to pay when the property is handed over, and the charity doesn't suffer (since it doesn't pay CGT), and the PRs' £6,600 exemption can be used elsewhere.

CGTA 1979 s195.

Income Tax

It is up to the personal representatives to sort out, with the deceased person's tax office, his tax affairs up to the date of death. The normal tax rules for individuals apply; tax allowances are granted for a full year, even if death took place early in the tax year. If a tax refund is due, this counts as an asset in the dead person's estate; if extra tax is due, this counts as a debt.

Quite separately from this, the personal representatives are responsible for paying income tax on income arising from assets in the estate during the administration period. Personal representatives are treated as a separate entity for income tax purposes, and special rules apply – spelt out overleaf.

Tax rate

Personal representatives pay tax at the basic rate, but not at higher rates – however large the income of the estate may be. They are not entitled to any income tax allowances.
ICTA 1970 s3.

Tax Return

The personal representatives must complete a Tax Return for each tax year (or part of a tax year) until the administration of the estate is complete. The Tax Return is usually issued by the deceased person's tax office; but occasionally it may be dealt with by the tax office in the personal representatives' area.
TMA 1970 s7.

Types of income and how taxed

Examples of income received during the administration of an estate (ie between death and the distribution of the estate) are:
● dividends from UK companies and distributions from most unit trusts: these come with a tax credit which meets the basic rate tax due. Personal representatives therefore have no extra tax to pay
● interest from building societies, banks, licensed deposit-takers and local authority loans: basic rate tax is deemed to have been paid on this, so personal representatives have no tax to pay or claim back
● interest from National Savings Investment account: interest is paid gross (without deduction of tax), so personal representatives will be liable for tax at the basic rate on this interest.

Allowable interest payments

Personal representatives can claim tax relief (on behalf of the estate) for up to 12 months if, in order to pay IHT before the grant of probate or letters of administration, they've borrowed money. The tax relief is the amount of interest paid on a separately identified loan account for the purpose of paying IHT. They can also deduct any interest paid on legacies where the legacies are paid more than one year after the date of death (though in this case the interest counts as taxable income of the beneficiary who receives it).
FA 1974 Sch 1 para 17; ICTA 1970 s428, s432.

Form R185 (and how to avoid it if you can)

The personal representatives distribute the income during the period of administration (after deducting administration expenses that can properly be deducted from the income). Before handing over the income, they will have paid tax at the basic rate. The person who receives the money has to declare the *grossed-up amount* in his tax return (ie if he gets £730 he has to gross this up to £1,000 – see p29). If he pays tax at the basic rate only, there'll be no more tax to pay. If he pays tax at higher rates, there'll be extra tax to pay. If his income, including the grossed-up amount, is too low to pay tax (or to pay as much as has been deducted), he can claim tax back.

The personal representatives have to give each beneficiary a *form R185* showing the actual amount of income handed over, and the grossed-up amount.

Where the administration of an estate is simple and there is just one person, eg a widow, wholly entitled to the estate (or perhaps two or three people equally entitled, such as children) the Inspector of Taxes of the deceased person may agree that the income of the estate may be dealt with directly in each beneficiary's own Tax Return. This avoids the need for form R185: the personal representatives simply tell each beneficiary what they are entitled to, and the beneficiaries include this in their own Tax Returns.
ICTA 1970 s55, s427(3).

Example

The income from the late Mrs Eastbourne's estate is £1,100. Tax of £297 is paid by the personal representatives; and they can also deduct administration expenses of £91. The beneficiary – a distant relative – therefore receives £1,100 *minus* £297 *minus* £91 = £712. The personal representatives give the beneficiary form R185 showing the amount handed over (£712) and the grossed-up amount. To find the grossed-up amount they divide £712 by 0.73 (= £975).

32 CAPITAL GAINS TAX

For CGT and your home, see Homes and land p242.

Note: nearly all statutory references are to the Capital Gains Tax Act 1979. We haven't, in all cases, given the full reference – so *s101* = *CGTA 1979 s101*. Other statutes are mentioned individually.

The simplest example of making a capital gain is *selling something you own at a profit*. For example, you buy a Rembrandt etching for £10,000, and sell it a couple of months later for £12,000. Your capital gain (ignoring any allowance for inflation) is £2,000, or a bit less if you can claim some expenses of buying and selling.

But you can make a capital gain even though no buying or selling is involved – for example, if you give away something which you've inherited. So here are the basic rules:

• you can make a capital gain (or loss) whenever you *dispose of an asset*, no matter how you come to own it

• broadly, anything you own (whether in the UK or not) counts as an asset – for example, houses, jewellery, shares, antiques

• you dispose of an asset not only if you sell it, but also if you give it away, exchange it, or lose it. You also dispose of an asset

if you sell rights to it (eg grant a lease), or if it is destroyed or becomes worthless, or if you get compensation for damage to it (eg insurance money) and don't spend all the money on restoring it
- not every gain you make will be taxable, nor will every loss be recognised by the taxman
- there is no CGT to pay when you die
- special rules apply to gifts between husband and wife (see p430), and can apply if you dispose of a business (see p432)
- for nearly any gift, you can avoid an immediate tax bill (see p427).

CGTA 1979 s1,s2,s4,s19–21,s28.

What is a taxable gain?

To work out your taxable gain, this is what you do:

Step one: take the **final value** of the asset. This will be the *disposal proceeds* (if you sold it); its *market value* (if you gave it away); or, if it is destroyed, the *insurance proceeds* (if any). For damaged assets, see p445.

Step two: subtract your **allowable expenses** on the asset. These are:
- the **initial value** of the asset. This is *what you paid for it* (if you bought it); its *market value at the time of the gift* (if you were given it – though see p427 for special rules about gifts); its *market value at the date of death* (if you inherited it)
- costs of acquiring the asset – eg legal fees, stamp duty, commission
- money spent on increasing the value of the asset if the increase in value still shows at the time of disposal, but not money spent on normal repairs or maintenance
- costs of disposing of the asset, eg legal fees, agents' commission, cost of valuing the asset for CGT purposes
- costs (eg legal costs) of confirming your title to the asset.

Domicile

If you're neither resident nor ordinarily resident (see p178 for definitions) you won't be liable for UK capital gains tax on disposals from the day after you leave the UK until 5 April before you come back. And if you've been away for at least three years this exemption continues until the day before you return. You can take advantage of this by disposing of assets that would produce chargeable gains, or by selling and then buying back the asset while you're away, so realising the gain when there's no tax to pay. If you're dealing with shares make sure that you buy them back the day after you sold them, or later.

CGTA 197 s2, s155.

Important note: you may also be able to subtract an **indexation allowance** (see p419). This helps to protect you against being taxed on 'gains' which are simply the result of inflation.
CGTA 1979 s1, s29A, s31–33; FA 1980 s79; FA 1982 s86.

Example 1

Larry bought a second home in January 1987 for £35,000. He paid legal fees of £350 and stamp duty of £350. In July 1987 he built an extension with materials costing £500. He sold the home in October 1987 for £38,500. His agent's fees were £965 and his legal fees were £300. He works out his taxable gain (before any indexation allowance):

	£
Sale proceeds	38,500
less **allowable expenses:**	
Purchase price	35,000
Costs of acquisition	700
Costs of improvements	500
Expenses of disposal	1,265
Taxable gain	1,035

Larry gets no allowance for his own labour, because he did not pay for it.

Tax-free gains

Gains on some assets are free from capital gains tax. (The other side of the coin is that *losses* on these assets can't normally be used to reduce your taxable gains for tax purposes.)

The main assets on which gains are tax-free are:
- your own home – see p242 *(s101)*
- private motor cars. This rule normally favours the taxman, since you usually sell your car for a loss. But if you sell a vintage or classic car at a gain, that will be tax-free unless you make a habit of doing this – in which case you could be taxed as though you were trading in cars *(s130)*
- National Savings Certificates, National Savings Yearly Plan, Premium bonds and SAYE deposits
- British money including post-1837 gold sovereigns *(s19)*
- currency for personal use abroad. Normally, foreign currency is an asset for CGT purposes. But gains on currency for the use of your family and yourself abroad, eg on holiday or to maintain a home abroad, are tax-free *(s133)*
- betting winnings *(s19)*
- British Government stocks (or options in them) disposed of after 1 July 1986 (though income tax might be due on any accrued interest). Before 2 July 1986, gains were only tax-free

if the stock was held for a year or more or inherited. This exemption now extends to many types of corporate bond, so long as you acquired them after 13 March 1984.
CGTA 1979 s67; FA 1984 s64; FA 1986 s59.

- shares, unit trusts and investment trusts held in a Personal Equity Plan (see p289)
- shares issued after 18 March 1986 under the Business Expansion Scheme – on their first disposal only
- life insurance policies. The proceeds – whether on maturity, surrender or sale – are tax-free provided that you did not buy the policy from a previous holder *(s143)*
- damages for any wrong or injury suffered by you in your private or professional life, eg damages for assault or defamation *(s19)*
- settled property. If you have been given an interest under a UK settlement (but not the underlying property), the proceeds if you sell it are tax-free *(s58)*
- timber. A gain on the disposal of timber – whether growing or felled – is tax-free provided that you're not taxed as carrying on a forestry trade (in which case the disposal will be liable for income tax as a trading transaction). The exemption does not apply to the land on which the timber was growing *(s113)*
- decorations for valour. A gain on the disposal of an award for valour or gallant conduct is tax-free, eg your father's VC or George Cross, provided that you did not buy the award *(s131)*
- gifts to charities or certain national institutions *(s146)*
- a gift of *heritage property* is tax-free if it satisfies certain conditions (for what *heritage property* is, see p357). *(s147)*
- any chattel which had a predictable useful life of no more than 50 years when you first acquired it, eg electronic equipment, yachts and race-horses, provided that you have not used the asset in your business so that it qualified for capital allowances *(s127)*
- for chattels with a predictable life of more than 50 years, gains may be partly tax-free – broadly, the rules are as follows:

If the *disposal proceeds* are less than £3,000, any gain is tax-free. So if you buy a watercolour for £1,500 and sell it for £2,750 the gain is tax-free.

If the *disposal proceeds* are more than £3,000, your taxable gain is *either* your actual gain *or* 5/3 of the excess over £3,000, whichever is the lower.

If the disposal proceeds are less than £3,000, and you've made a loss, you're assumed to have received £3,000. So if you buy a picture for £4,000 and sell it for £2,000, your loss, for tax purposes, is £1,000.

If you sell a set of articles (eg a set of matching chairs), separately, but in effect to the same person, the taxman is likely to treat the sales as a single sale. So if you sold 6 chairs for £2,000 each, you'd be taxed as though you'd made a single sale of £12,000, not six sales of £2,000. *(s128)*

Indexation allowance

The *indexation allowance* gives some protection against being taxed on paper profits. It works like this: your allowable expenses are linked to the Retail Prices Index (RPI) and increased in line with the index. The effect is that your taxable gain is reduced. See p498 for a list of the RPI figures from March 1982, when indexation started.
FA 1982 s86; FA 1985 s68.

How to use the indexation rules

Step one: work out your gain or loss in the normal way, taking no account of the indexation rules. So you take the asset's **final value** (see p416), and subtract your **allowable expenses** (see p416).

Step two: work out the total of your indexation allowances (see below), and *subtract* them from your unindexed gain on the asset.
- if the result is still a gain, this is your gain for tax purposes
- if the result is a loss, this is your loss for tax purposes
- if the result of **Step one** was a loss, your loss for tax purposes is the *Step one* figure increased by your indexation allowances.

Working out your indexation allowances

For assets which you first owned on or after 31 March 1982:
- link the initial value (and acquisition costs) to the Retail Prices Index from the month in which you acquired the asset
- link any subsequent allowable expense to the RPI from the month in which the expense becomes 'due and payable'. The same applies to the costs of defending your title to the asset.

For assets which you first owned before 31 March 1982:
Indexation only applies from March 1982. So:
- link any allowable expense made *after* 31 March 1982 to the RPI from the month in which the expense becomes 'due and payable'
- for the initial value plus any other expenses made before 31 March 1982, you have a choice: EITHER link any allowable expenses made before 31 March 1982 to the RPI from March 1982 OR don't index-link any pre-March 1982 expenses. Instead, link the asset's value on 31 March 1982 to the RPI from March 1982.

You should choose to index whichever figure is higher. If

you want to choose the March 1982 value, tell the taxman within two years of the end of the tax year in which you dispose of the asset.

Calculating the indexation allowance

The taxman uses this formula:

$$\textbf{allowance} = allowable\ expense \times \frac{(\text{RD} - \text{RI})}{\text{RI}}$$

The step $\frac{(\text{RD} - \text{RI})}{\text{RI}}$ is worked out to 3 decimal places.

RD = the RPI for the month in which the asset is disposed of
RI = the RPI for the month in which the expense is linked to the RPI. RPI figures from March 1982 are shown on p498.

So if, for example, you buy something for £5,000, and the RPI for the month in which you buy it is 400, and the RPI for the month in which you sell it is 500, your indexation allowance for the initial value is worked out like this:
allowable expense = £5,000; RD = 500; RI= 400; (RD − RI) = 100.

So the calculation is £5,000 × $\frac{100}{400}$ = £1,250.

How to use the calculators

The two calculators, overleaf, allow you to calculate your gain on any asset disposed of since 5 April 1985. (Don't use them for assets on which a gain is tax-free. If *hold-over relief* has been claimed, see p427. For shares and unit trusts, see p436.)

The calculators are simple to use. They take you step by step through the stages of working out your gain. Below, we give an Example of using the calculators.

Example 2

Setting the scene

Peter bought a weekend place by the sea in 1971 for £20,000. He paid £2,000 in May 1971 on exchange of contracts. The balance of £18,000 and stamp duty of £200 were paid on completion in June 1971. In July he paid his solicitor's fees of £300. In August 1983 he paid a builder £2,000 to construct a patio. It was completed in September 1983.

Peter exchanged contracts in January 1987 for the sale of the bungalow at a price of £61,000. The sale was completed in March when he paid his solicitor's fees of £800 and his estate agent's commission of £1,525.

Working through the calculators

First, Peter finds out his gain, *without allowing for indexation*.
Amount A is £20,000 (initial value) + £200 (stamp duty) + £300 (solicitor's fees) = £20,500.
Amount B is £2,000 (builder's costs) + £800 (solicitor's fees) + £1,525 (estate agent's commission) = £4,325.
Amount C is (£20,500 + £4,325) = £24,825.
Amount D is £61,000.
Amount E (£61,000 − £24,825) = £36,175.

Next, Peter moves on to *Step two* to calculate his indexation allowances. He uses the table on p498 to find out RPI figures for the relevant months.

First, he takes the initial value of the asset, plus the costs of acquiring it, which comes to £20,500. However, he can instead take the market value of the asset on 31 March 1982. Peter gets a written estimate from his estate agent that the value on 31 March 1982 would probably have been £45,000. So Peter elects to take this figure instead of the actual amount spent.
Amount Q is £45,000.
Amount H is the RPI figure for the month in which Peter disposes of the bungalow, ie on exchange of contracts. For January 1987 the RPI figure was 100.00.
Amount J is the RPI figure for March 1982 which was 79.4.
Amount K is 100.0 − 79.4 = 20.6
Amount L is 20.6 ÷ 79.4 = 0.259
Amount M is 0.259 × £45,000 = £11,655.

This is the indexation allowance for the deemed initial value of the bungalow.

The calculation must be done again for the improvement costs. Note that, if you take the market value of an asset on 31 March 1982 instead of its initial value, you must ignore any additional costs (eg for improvements) incurred before then.
Improvement costs:
Amount Q is £2,000.
Amount H is 100.0.
Amount J is the RPI figure for the month in which the expenditure was incurred, ie, August 1983, and is 85.7.
Amount K is 100.0 − 85.7 = 14.3
Amount L is 14.3 ÷ 85.7 = 0.167.
Amount M is 0.167 × £2,000 = £334 which is the indexation allowance for the allowable expenditure on improvements.

The incidental costs of disposal are not indexed because they were incurred after the bungalow was disposed of. Therefore, **Amount E** is £11,655 + £334 = £11,989
Amount G (£36,175 − £11,989) = £24,186.
This is Peter's taxable gain on the disposal.

Capital gains tax calculator

Use this calculator to work out your taxable gain or allowable loss on an asset you've disposed of. Don't use it if your gain was tax-free. For shares and unit trusts read p436 first. If you've disposed of an asset since 5 April 1982 you may also be entitled to an indexation allowance.

Step one Enter the **initial value** plus acquisition expenses of an asset **Initial value** means the *purchase price* if you bought the asset. It means its *market value at the time of the gift* if you were given it. It means its *market value at the date of death* if you inherited it	A
Enter the total of your subsequent allowable expenditure including expenses of disposal	B
Add A to B	C
Enter the **final value** of the asset. This will be the **sale price** if you sold it or its **market value at the time of the gift** if you gave it away	D
Subtract C from D	E
Use the calculator opposite to see whether you're entitled to any indexation allowances. If you are, enter them at F in this calculator, even if E is a minus figure	
Step two Enter your total **indexation allowances** which you find using the calculator opposite	F
Subtract F from E, or add F to E if E is a minus figure	G
G is your **taxable gain** on the asset. If G is a minus number, you have no taxable gain, but an **allowable loss** instead	

Assets first owned before 6 April 1965

CGT was introduced to tax gains arising after 5 April 1965. Gains and losses arising before then are exempt from CGT. The exemption is given in one of two ways – both of which we explain here. If you make no choice, the taxman will apply the first method. If you want to use the second method, you must tell the taxman within two years from the end of the tax year in which you dispose of the asset.

Once you've chosen the second method, the taxman won't let you change your mind. So you should work out your gain using *both* methods to see which is better for you.
CGTA 1979 s28, Sch5.

Indexation allowance calculator

You may need to work through this calculator several times: once to find the allowance for the asset's initial value plus allowable expenses of acquisition; and then again for each subsequent item of allowable expenditure. There's no indexation allowance for disposal costs. See p498 for a list of RPI figures.

Enter the expense on which you want to work out the indexation allowance; this could be the initial value plus incidental expenses of acquisition, a subsequent item of allowable expenditure, or the market value on 31 March 1982	Q
Enter the Retail Price Index (RPI) figure for the month in which you disposed of the asset	H
Enter the RPI figure for the month in which indexation begins. For the initial value plus the allowable expenses of acquisition this will be the RPI figure for the month in which you acquired the asset *or* the RPI figure for March 1982, whichever is the later. For expenditure after acquisition this will be the RPI figure for the month in which the expense became due and payable *or* the RPI figure for March 1982, whichever is later	J
Subtract J from H	K
Divide K by J (work out the result to three decimal places)	L
Multiply L by Q	M
M is the indexation allowance for the relevant expense. Add together the indexation allowances for the various items of expenditure and enter the grand total at F in the main calculator opposite	

You must use *method 2* for:
 • shares or securities you owned on 6 April 1965 which were then quoted on The Stock Exchange
 • units in unit trusts which you owned on 6 April 1965
 • land acquired before 6 April 1965 which you've since disposed of for a figure which reflects development potential.

Method 1

You work out your gain – using the indexation rules, if they apply, just as if CGT had been in force for the whole period of your ownership. If you've still got a gain, you find out your taxable gain in the following way (the *Method 1 rules*):

- divide the gain (ie after indexation, if any) by the number of complete months you've held the asset. Count only the period since 6 April 1945 if you acquired the asset before then
- multiply the result by the number of complete months between 6 April 1965 and the date of disposal
- the result is your taxable gain. An allowable loss is calculated in the same way as a taxable gain.

If you have spent money on improving the asset, Method 1 gets a little more complicated.

Step one: split the allowable expenses into separate blocks. *Use the actual money values*, not increased by indexation:

- block one is the initial value *plus* acquisition costs
- block two is the first expense of improving the asset or defending title to the asset
- block three is the second expense of improving the asset or defending title to the asset (and so on for blocks four, five etc)
- blocks of expenses for improving or defending your title to the asset can be grouped as one block (see Step five)
- expenses of disposing of the asset are ignored.

Step two: take the amount of the gain, after allowing for indexation, but before applying the *Method 1 rules* above.

Step three: spread the gain proportionately among the blocks of allowable expenses. For example, if *block one* is £6,000, *block two* is £2,000, and *block three* is £4,000, a gain of £36,000 would be spread as follows: £18,000 to block one; £6,000 to block two; £12,000 to block three.

Step four: apply the *Method 1 rules* to block one.

Step five: for blocks two, three, etc, if the expense was first reflected in the asset's value *after* 6 April 1965, the taxable gain for the block will be the amount apportioned under Step three (ie £12,000 for block three). If this doesn't apply, move to Step six.

Step six: take the date on which the expense was first reflected in the asset's value (or 6 April 1945 if this is *later*); divide by the number of complete months from then to the date of disposal; and multiply by the number of complete months between 6 April 1965 and the date of disposal.

Step seven: add up the results to Steps four to six. This is your taxable gain.

This method can have distorting results if you acquire an asset for a small sum, and then spend a larger sum on it later. In this case, the taxman will try to attribute a fairer amount of the gain to the cost of acquisition.

Method 2

Work out your gain as though you acquired the asset on 6 April 1965 *for its market value at that time* (see p436 for more about

Example 3: which method to choose?

Roger purchased a block of flats on 1 June 1947 for £30,000. On 1 April 1958 he paid a contractor £20,000 to carry out improvements to the building. On 1 January 1970 he paid a contractor £40,000 to add a floor to the building. Roger sold the block for £170,000 on 6 March 1977.

Method 1

	£	£
Disposal proceeds		170,000
less Cost of the building	30,000	
Improvements	20,000	
New floor	40,000	90,000
Gain		£80,000

Apportion gain to expenditure:

£

block one
Cost of building $\dfrac{30,000}{90,000} \times 80,000 =$ 26,667

block two
Cost of improvements $\dfrac{20,000}{90,000} \times 80,000 =$ 17,778

block three
Cost of new floor $\dfrac{40,000}{90,000} \times 80,000 =$ 35,555

Step four (for block one)   £
$\dfrac{26,667 \times 143^{**}}{357^{*}} =$ 10,682

*   complete months from 1.6.47 to 6.3.77
** complete months from 6.4.65 to 6.3.77

Step six (for block two)
$\dfrac{17,778 \times 143^{**}}{227^{*}} =$ 11,199

*   complete months from 1.4.58 to 6.3.77
** complete months from 6.4.65 to 6.3.77

Step five (for block three)

Gain attributable to new floor (in full)	35,555
Taxable gain	£57,436

Now try method 2

Suppose the market value of the building on 6 April 1965 was £70,000.

	£	£
Disposal proceeds		170,000
less Value on 6.4.65	70,000	
New floor	40,000	110,000
Gain		£60,000

Therefore, Method 1 is preferable for Roger.

the market value of shares).

Generally, this will reduce your taxable gain if more of the rise in value of the asset is attributable to your period of ownership before 6 April 1965 than after.

Method 2 can't be used to create (or increase) a loss. If, for example, you bought a second home for £2,000 in 1960, and its April 1965 value was £4,000, and you sold it for £3,000, so that Method 2 would give you a loss and Method 1, a gain, you are treated as making neither a gain nor a loss, ie as if you sold for £2,000.

How much tax?

Some gains are free of CGT – see **Tax-free gains**, p417. And there's no tax on the first slice of your net taxable gains. This is index-linked and rises year-by-year with inflation unless Parliament decides otherwise: for the 1987–88 tax year it is £6,600. A settlement which you have set up is also entitled to relief from tax on its first slice of taxable gains – but in this case the slice is £3,300. If you have created more than one settlement the relief is divided between them equally, but with a minimum relief for each settlement of £330.

You pay tax at 30 per cent on all net taxable gains above £6,600. To arrive at your net taxable gains for the year:

Step 1 Subtract losses on assets disposed of during the year from your taxable gains for the year. Ignore gains and losses on assets where a gain is tax-free – see p417.

Step 2 If the answer to Step 1 is a minus number, your net taxable gains for the year are zero, and there's no tax to pay. You can carry the minus amount forward to future tax years, together with any losses left over from previous years.

Example 4

In the 1987–88 tax year Larry lost £3,000 on some shares he had sold. In the same year he made a gain of £11,750 on a picture. He has £3,000 of unrelieved allowable losses from previous years.

Step 1 Subtracting his allowable loss for the year from his taxable gain for the year leaves £11,750 – £3,000 = £8,750.

Step 2 The answer at Step 1 comes to more than £6,600, so the allowable losses brought forward from earlier years will be used to reduce his net taxable gains to £6,600. £8,750 – £6,600 = £2,150, so Larry will use £2,150 of his losses from previous years to reduce his net taxable gains to the exempt slice, leaving him with £3,000 – £2,150 = £850 to carry forward to 1988–89 and later years.

If the answer comes to more than £6,600, any allowable losses you have left from previous years will be used to reduce your net taxable gains, but *not* to below the £6,600 level. This saves the losses being wasted. If you still have allowable losses left, these can be carried forward to future years.
CGTA 1979 s3–5, s29, Sch 1 para 6.

Gifts

When you give something away, you're usually treated as disposing of it for what it is worth, even though you get nothing for it. So if you buy a picture for £20,000 and give it away a few months later when it's worth £25,000, you'll make a taxable gain of £5,000.

The person who receives the gift is treated as having paid what the property is worth. So – in the Example below – if the person receiving the picture sells it later on for £28,000, his taxable gain (ignoring indexation) is £28,000 minus £25,000 = £3,000.

If the asset is one which is exempt from CGT – see list starting on p417 – there is no tax liability if you give it away.
CGTA 1979 s29A.

Hold-over relief

The giver and recipient can jointly claim this relief (provided the recipient is resident or ordinarily resident in the UK). This avoids a CGT bill at the time of the gift. But – on a later disposal by the recipient – there can be more tax to pay.
FA 1980 s79; FA 1981 s78; FA 1982 s82.

Example 5
John buys a picture for £20,000 in March 1987. He gives it to Susan in July 1987 when the picture is worth £25,000. Susan sells it later for £28,000. They jointly claim hold-over relief. The effect (ignoring indexation) is that Susan takes over John's 'base value' of £20,000 – ie the *initial value* of the picture when John acquired it. So when she sells the picture, her gain is £28,000 (disposal proceeds) *less* £20,000 (John's base value) = £8,000. For cases where the giver has other allowable expenses, or indexation allowances, read on.

Other points

- if hold-over relief is claimed, the recipient gets the benefit of the giver's allowable expenses (if any) and of his indexation allowances (if any) up to the time of the gift. So the recipient's *base value* is the *total* of the deductions which the giver could make from the disposal proceeds if hold-over relief weren't being claimed. For instance if Peter, in Example 2 on p420, had given away the bungalow by the sea, and hold-over relief had been claimed, the recipient's base value would be £36,814

• indexation: the recipient's base value (see above) is linked to the RPI from the month of the gift

• hold-over relief can be claimed again on a subsequent gift

• if the ultimate recipient keeps the gift until death, there will be no CGT to pay, since there is no CGT charge on death (see p431)

• it's pointless to claim hold-over relief if (without claiming the relief) your net taxable gains for the year are no more than £6,600. You won't pay tax either way, and the recipient could pay more

• hold-over relief can be claimed on gifts into (and out of) a trust. For gifts into trust, the relief can be claimed by the giver alone

• if you part with something for less than its full worth, you can still claim hold-over relief. But if the amount you actually get for it is higher than your allowable expenses, you will have to pay capital gains tax on the sum received less expenses at the time (assuming it is more than your annual exemption) and only the gain that is left after that can be held-over.

If the recipient emigrates within six tax years of the year in which he received the gift from you, and hasn't, by then, disposed of the property, he will become liable to CGT on the held-over gain. If he does not pay the CGT it can be collected from you.

FA 1980 s79; FA 1982 s82.

Gifts: think about inheritance tax

If you make a gift of property and there is no decision to hold-over the gain (with the result that you have to pay CGT), your CGT liability will neither increase nor reduce the inheritance tax (IHT) – if any – on the gift.

If the recipient pays the CGT for you that will reduce any IHT there may be – not surprising since you will have given him less.

If you make a gift and hold-over relief is claimed, any IHT on the gift will reduce the CGT when the recipient comes to dispose of the property.

CGT and the family

If you dispose of an asset to a *connected person*, you are treated by the taxman as disposing of the asset for its market value at the time of the gift. A *connected person* includes your wife or husband, *and*:

• a relative. *Relative* means brother, sister, ancestor or lineal descendant (but not uncle, aunt, cousin, nephew or niece)
• the wife or husband of a relative
• your wife or husband's relative
• the trustees of a settlement which you have set up
• a company which you control
• a person with whom you are in partnership or their wife or husband or relative.

So if you don't sell for the proper commercial price, you'll be taxed as if you had, even if you didn't intend to make a gift. You can, though, claim hold-over relief – see p417.

More important still is that if you make a loss on a disposal to a connected person, you can only set that loss off against a gain from another disposal by you to that person. This is the case even though your loss is a proper commercial one – ie owing to the market value rule. So if you sell shares at a loss to your son, the loss cannot be used to reduce your general taxable gains for the year.

CGTA 1979 s62–63.

Husband and wife

Gains of husband and wife

A husband and wife who are not separated are entitled to only one tax-free slice of gains (ie £6,600 in the 1987–88 tax year).

A husband and wife who are married before the start of the tax year (or on the first day of the tax year) normally have their gains taxed jointly – ie wife's gains are set off against husband's losses, and vice versa. But if one of you has made net losses, and the other's net gains are less than £6,600, the one who has made the losses should ask for them to be carried forward and set against his or her own gains in the future. This saves you 'wasting' the losses.

To do this, one of you must tell the taxman within 3 months of the end of the tax year concerned. The arrangement will continue for subsequent tax years unless you revoke it.

A husband and wife living together as UK residents are entitled to only one main residence exemption and only one dependent relative's residence exemption – see pages 242 and 243.

CGTA 1979 s45, s101, s105, Sch 1 para 2.

Gifts between husband and wife who are not separated

- Whether or not any money changes hands, there is no tax to pay at the time of the disposal, and there is no gain or loss for tax purposes
- The recipient gets the benefit of the giver's base value, plus the giver's allowable expenses, plus any indexation allowances up to the time of the gift. (The same as the rules for hold-over relief)
- The recipient's base value (ie giver's base value plus giver's allowable expenses, plus giver's indexation allowances) is linked to the RPI from the month of acquisition.

CGTA 1979 s44 FA 1982 Sch 13 par 3.

Example 6

Graham makes a taxable gain of £5,000 in 1987–88. His wife Susan has an allowable loss of £2,750 in the same year. She made no taxable gains. If normal rules apply, Susan's loss will be set against Graham's gain to give him a net taxable gain of £2,250. This is a waste of these losses – they don't save any tax, because Graham's gains are anyway well below the £6,600 tax-free slice.

So Sue asks the taxman to set her loss against her own gains from future years.

Example 7

The taxable gains for Stephen and Marian (who are married) for the 1987–88 tax year are as follows:

	Stephen	Marian
	£	£
taxable gains	8,000	700
allowable losses	200	nil
losses from earlier years	4,500	nil
taxable amount	3,300	700

The normal rule is that the £6,600 slice of tax-free gains is split between husband and wife in proportion to their *taxable amount* (see above).

If this were done, the split would be:

for Stephen $\frac{3,300}{4,000} \times 6,600 = £5,445$

for Marian $\frac{700}{4,000} \times 6,600 = £1,155$

Although there would be no tax to pay, part of Marian's tax-free slice would be wasted and Stephen would be using losses from earlier years to cover his taxable gains. Instead, they agree to vary the way the tax-free slice is split. Stephen takes £5,600 and Marian takes £700.

Stephen	£
taxable gains for the year	8,000
less allowable losses for year	200
	7,800
less losses brought forward	2,200
taxable amount	£5,600
CGT **payable**	£ nil
Marian	£
Taxable amount	700
CGT **payable**	£ nil

Note: Stephen and Marian couldn't have varied the split if their combined taxable amounts had been more than £6,600.
CGTA 1979 Sch 1 para 2 (1) (b).

Death

There is no CGT to pay on death. This has profound implications on whether you should make gifts in your lifetime, or wait until you die. This is because:

● rates of *inheritance tax* (IHT) for gifts made on death are higher than for gifts made more than 3 years prior to death (see Chapter 28)

● for *capital gains tax* (CGT) there is often a tax liability on gifts made during life. Even if hold-over relief is claimed, the eventual tax bill for the recipient can be substantial

● so there's often a 'trade-off' between the two taxes.

Depending on your wealth (and potential liability to IHT), it may be worth giving now – paying CGT and cutting down IHT on your death – or hanging on – risking a higher IHT bill, and avoiding CGT altogether
- in general, the less well-off you are, the better it is to hang on to things until you die
- either way, remember that you can pass property gradually from your estate without tax – by making use of the £6,600 tax-free slice of CGT, and by using the exemptions for IHT.
CGTA 1979 s49.

CGT **and executors**

On death, your estate passes to your personal representatives – see *Tax for executors* on p407. The taxman regards them as acquiring the property at its *market value at the date of your death*. The effect is that the value of everything you own is given a 'free uplift' to its value at the date of death. The beneficiaries of your estate acquire the assets at the market value as from the date of death. Indexation applies from the date of death.

Allowable losses in the tax year of your death (made before your death) are set off first against your taxable gains for that period. Any losses which are left over can be set off against taxable gains of your widow or widower for the whole year, unless the survivor elects against this. If there are still losses left over they can be set against your taxable gains for the three tax years before the tax year of death, taking later years first (but the losses are only needed to reduce the taxable gains to the level of the annual exemption – see Example 4 on p426). This is the only time when allowable losses can be carried back.

CGT **and business**

Replacing business assets

If you dispose of a *qualifying business asset* and invest an amount equal to the disposal proceeds in another qualifying business asset during the period of one year *before* the disposal or within three years *after* the disposal, you can claim *roll-over relief* on your taxable gain on the disposal of the old asset. Qualifying assets are:
- land and buildings occupied and used for the purpose of your trade
- plant or machinery which is fixed but which does not actually form part of a building – eg heavy engineering

equipment bolted to the floor of a workshop
- ships, aircraft and hovercraft – but not vehicles
- goodwill.

CGTA 1979 s115–121.

Other points

- Any indexation allowance available on the old asset is taken into account in determining the size of the gain held over
- If you have more than one business, the reinvestment need not be in the same business as the one in which the old asset was used
- If the asset you disposed of was used for private purposes as well as business purposes, or if you do not spend an amount equal to the whole of the disposal proceeds on the new asset, only a proportionate part of your taxable gain is deferred
- You may even be able to claim roll-over relief if you dispose of an asset which you own personally but which is used for the purposes of the trade carried on by your "family company" (see page 435) if you then purchase a new qualifying asset which is used for the purposes of the trade carried on by the same family company. Roll-over relief is available in this situation even if you charge the company a full market rent for the asset.

How it works

The gain is usually held over by reducing (for tax purposes) your acquisition cost for the new asset. So when you dispose of the new asset, the amount you can subtract (in working out your taxable gain) is reduced. (You can hold over your tax liability again by investing in another qualifying asset.)

If you reinvest in a *wasting asset*, ie in an asset with a predictable life not exceeding 50 years when you acquire it, or in an asset which will become a wasting asset in the next 10 years, your gain is deferred until the earliest of the following:

- you cease to use the new asset for the purposes of your trade
- the tenth anniversary of your acquisition of the asset
- you dispose of the new asset without reinvesting the proceeds in a new qualifying asset. If you *do* reinvest (in a non-wasting asset), the original gain is rolled over into the new asset, and the deferred gain is cancelled.

Turning your business into a company

The usual tax reason for incorporating a business is to take advantage of corporation tax rates – which can be much lower than income tax on trading profits.

But capital gains made by a company may be taxed *twice*, first when the company makes them, and again when you take the money out of the company. So get professional advice before going ahead.

If you do decide to incorporate your business, you can get CGT relief when you exchange the assets of the business for shares in the company. To get the relief, you must transfer your business as a whole to a company (as a going concern) in exchange, wholly or partly, for shares. The company can be one you have just set up, or it can be one which is already in business. So far as you exchange the business for shares, any taxable gain is deferred until you dispose of the shares. The relief applies automatically.
CGTA 1979 s123.

Example 8

Tom has set up a company to take over his business. Some of his business assets stand at a capital loss and some at a capital gain. Setting off allowable losses against taxable gains, his net taxable gain in transferring the whole business to the company entirely for shares was £85,000.

The business is the only asset of the new company, so the market value of the shares which Tom acquired was the same as the value of his business – ie £250,000.

There is no taxable gain for Tom now. But – for tax purposes, the acquisition cost of the shares (ie £250,000 – the value of the business), is *reduced* by the amount of the held-over gain: £250,000 − £85,000 = £165,000.

The acquisition cost of the business (for the new company) is £250,000.

Retirement relief

If you are aged 60 or over or have to retire before then due to ill-health, and you dispose of a business (or shares in it), part or all of your gain may be tax-free. This relief is available for any kind of disposal including sale, gift and selling off assets after the business has ceased. You don't actually have to retire to get the relief, providing that:
● you are 60 or over, *or*
● you are retiring due to ill-health. You'll need to satisfy the taxman that you are incapable of carrying on your work and that your incapacity is likely to be permanent.

The disposal requirements are:
● you must be disposing of the whole or part of a business which you have owned for at least one year, *or*
● you must be disposing of shares which you have owned for at least one year in a family trading company or a holding

company for the business you worked in. To satisfy this condition, you must be entitled to at least 25 per cent of the voting rights (or at least 5 per cent if you and your family have more than 50 per cent of the voting rights) *and* you must be a *full time working director* in the company or a subsidiary. 'Full time' generally means that you spend substantially the whole of your working hours in the directorship.

Relief is also available where trustees dispose of shares or assets in which you have an interest (though not if your interest is only for a fixed period of time).

FA 1985 s73–74, Sch 23.

How much tax relief?

You get the maximum relief (of £125,000 after 5 April 1987) if you have owned the business or shares for 10 years. (This doesn't mean that you must have owned every asset of the business for 10 years.)

If your period of ownership is one year or more, you get 10 per cent of the maximum relief for every year of ownership.

If you dispose of a business, you only get relief on the permanent capital assets of that business; the relief doesn't apply to the disposal of trading stock. Similarly if you dispose of shares, you only get relief so far as the value of those shares represents chargeable business assets.

You only get one lot of retirement relief, ie one exemption of £125,000, but you need not use it on one disposal.

FA 1985 s65–66, Sch 20; FA 1987 s47.

Example 9

Bill bought a newsagent's shop in 1979 when he took early retirement from a company. In 1982 he was able to buy a second shop because his business had been doing well. In July 1987 he sold the business as a whole as a going concern. He was 64 at the time. His gain on selling the business was £35,000.

Bill has owned the business for 8 years so he is entitled to 80% of the maximum relief, ie 80% of £125,000 = £100,000. So his whole gain is exempt.

Gifts of business assets

If you give business assets (or sell them at an undervalue) to an individual or trust you can claim hold-over relief (see p427) so long as the recipient isn't resident overseas.

There is a special hold-over relief for a gift of business assets by an individual to a company resident in the UK. The relief applies to the disposal of a business asset which you have used in your business for the period you have owned it. It also applies to shares in your family trading company.

If you claim the relief, the gain you make on the disposal is held over and deducted from the acquisition cost of the asset for the company. If you charged the company a special low price for the asset but still made some gain, that gain is taxable. But the rest of the gain is held over.
CGTA 1979 s126.

Retirement relief or hold-over relief?

Ideally, you should go for retirement relief, rather than for hold-over relief, because hold-over is only a deferral of tax – not exemption from tax.

But if retirement relief is not available, or is insufficient, the general hold-over relief for gifts or the special relief for gifts of business assets can be very useful in passing on your business in your lifetime. But bear in mind that holding over your gain will reduce the other person's acquisition cost.

Shares and unit trusts

Special rules for shares are necessary because of their uniform nature. One share of a particular class in a given company is just the same as another share of the same class in that company: eg one Ordinary Share of £1 in ICI is worth just as much as any other £1 Ordinary Share in ICI.

Rules are straightforward if all the shares you own of a particular type were acquired by you at the same time, and disposed of all together. In this case, you calculate CGT in the same way as for any other asset. (Though if you acquired the shares before 6 April 1965 and they were quoted at that date, special rules apply – see p444.)

Problems begin if you have acquired shares of the same description at different times. When you come to dispose of the shares, special rules decide *how much the shares cost you*; *which shares you've disposed of*; and *what your indexation allowance is* (if any). The (very complicated) rules are explained on the following three pages.

Investment trusts and unit trusts

The taxman applies the same rules to shares in an investment trust as for quoted shares in any other type of company. The rules for shares also apply to units in a unit trust.

Example 10

Don has a holding of 2,500 £1 Ordinary Shares and 500 7% £1 Preference Shares in European Plastics PLC. He acquired the Ordinary Shares for £2,100 in June 1982 and he acquired the Preference Shares for £250 in May 1973.

In June 1988 he disposes of all the Ordinary Shares for £5,250 and all the Preference Shares for £350. The gross gain on each disposal, ignoring incidental costs, is:

Ordinary Shares	£	**Preference Shares**	£
Proceeds	5,250	Proceeds	350
less: Cost	2,100	less: Cost	250
Gross gain	3,150	Gross gain	100

In each case Don is entitled to an indexation allowance:
RPI for month of disposal – June 1988 – is assumed to be 105.8.
RPI for March 1982 is 79.4.
RPI for June 1982 is 81.9

The indexation allowance is:

Ordinary shares	**Preference Shares**
$\dfrac{105.8 - 81.9}{81.9}$ *	$\dfrac{105.8 - 79.4}{79.4}$ *
$\times \text{£}2,100 = \text{£}613.20$	$\times \text{£}250 = \text{£}83$

The taxable gain on the Ordinary Shares = £3,150 – £613.20 = £2,536.80

The taxable gain on the Preference shares = £100 – £83 = £17.

If Don had sold only half of his holding of Ordinary Shares and only half of his holding of Preference Shares, his allowable costs for each disposal would have been half the allowable costs shown in the example.

*calculated to the third decimal place

Which shares did you sell?

If you have acquired shares of *the same class* in *the same company* at different times, the taxman has special rules for deciding which shares you've disposed of. These rules decide:

• the price you paid for the shares (or their *initial value* if you didn't buy them)
• when you acquired the shares
• how much indexation allowance you're entitled to (if any).

Example 11, starting on p440, shows how the rules work in practice.

These rules apply to all shares disposed of on or after 6 April

1985, whether or not they're listed on The Stock Exchange or dealt in on the Unlisted Securities Market (USM). For the rules before that date see example 11.

Shares bought after 5 April 1985 are valued at the *lower* of:
- the lower of the two quoted closing prices shown in The Stock Exchange Daily Official List for that day, plus *one-quarter* of the difference between the lower and the higher closing price
- half-way between the highest and lowest recorded prices for the day of valuation. See p444 for how shares bought before 6 April 1965 are valued.

If you dispose of shares in stages, the taxman looks at an earlier disposal before a later disposal in seeing which shares you have disposed of.

The taxman will say that you have disposed of the shares in the following order:

Batch one: shares acquired on the same day as disposal

If you acquire and dispose of (or vice versa) shares of the same type on the same day, the disposal will be matched to the acquisition made on that day.

Batch two: shares disposed of within 10 days of acquisition

Next, the taxman looks at all the shares of the same type which you acquired at any time within 10 days before the disposal. There is no indexation allowance for shares owned for 10 days or less. This is to prevent you buying shares at the end of one month and selling them at the beginning of the next to get one month's indexation allowance.

Batch three: shares acquired after 5 April 1982

Shares acquired after 5 April 1982 but before 6 April 1985 which have not been disposed of on the same day or within ten days are pooled. The cost of each share is taken to be your average cost of acquiring the shares in the pool. So if you bought 2,000 shares for £5,000, then another 2,000 for £6,000, then another 2,000 for £7,000, the average cost would be £18,000 divided by 6,000 = £3 a share. You have a separate pool for each type of share you hold in a company. This pool (the 1985 pool) is separate from the 1982 pool (see Batch four). Any more shares of that type which you acquire after 5 April 1985 are added to the pool, unless you disposed of them on the same day or within 10 days. The total acquisition costs of pooled shares are treated as expenditure on a single asset. (However, the indexation allowances for the 1982 pool and the 1985 pool are calculated differently – see Example 11, starting on p440.)

FA 1982, s88 and Sch13; FA 1985 s68 and Sch 19.

Batch four: shares acquired after 5 April 1965 and before 6 April 1982

If you bought several lots of the same share at different times in this period, they are put into a pool (the 1982 pool). As with the 1985 pool, the cost of each share in the pool is taken to be your average cost of acquiring the shares.

Nothing can be added to this pool after 5 April 1982 (though see *Rights and bonus issues* below).

Indexation runs from March 1982.

Note: if you added to the pool in the twelve months before 6 April 1982, the pool may be frozen at 5 April 1981 instead of 5 April 1982. This will happen if the total of pooled expenditure at 6 April 1982 is greater than the total at 6 April 1981. In this case, the taxman will start off by keeping each of those acquisitions out of the pool. Looking at those shares and all the shares of the same type which you bought after 5 April 1982 and before 6 April 1985, he will match them with shares disposed of during that same period to see if any shares acquired during that period are still left at 6 April 1985. If any shares acquired during 1981–2 are left, they will become part of Batch 4. The rules used to identify shares disposed of before 6 April 1985 are summarised overleaf.

Batch five: shares acquired before 6 April 1965

The taxman will match the shares you dispose of with shares bought later rather than earlier. However, you can elect to pool them with your Batch four shares instead. (Remember that in calculating the indexation allowance for property owned on 31 March 1982 you can index the market value of the property at that time.) *(FA 1985 s68 and Sch 19.)*

Rights and bonus issues

Extra shares you get under a rights or bonus issue count as belonging to the same batch as the original shares to which they relate.

Rights issues give you the right to buy new shares in proportion to your existing shareholding. When you come to sell shares, you take the cost of the original shareholding *plus* the cost of the rights issue, apply the index-linking rules to them separately, divide by the number of shares in the whole shareholding, and multiply by the number of shares you've sold. This is your acquisition cost for the shares you've sold.

Bonus issues give you free shares to tack on to an existing shareholding. Because the shares are free, your acquisition cost (or your pool cost, if this applies), will be affected. Eg if you buy 2,500 shares for £5,000, and are given a bonus issue of 1,500 shares, your cost per share falls from £2 to £1.25. This adjusted cost is indexed from the same day as the original shareholding was indexed.

CGTA 1979 s78–79; FA 1982 Sch 13 para 5.

Example 11

Sue has built up a holding of Worldwide Pharmaceuticals 50p Ordinary Shares – listed on The Stock Exchange.

She has bought

1 August 1962	1,500 shares for £1,250
1 May 1964	500 shares for £ 375
1 January 1965	2,000 shares for £1,600
1 May 1969	750 shares for £ 450
1 July 1975	1,000 shares for £ 800
1 February 1981	1,750 shares for £1,600
1 June 1983	2,500 shares for £2,400
1 April 1985	1,250 shares for £1,500
4 March 1986	3,000 shares for £4,500

She has sold

1 February 1978	1,000 shares for £ 850
1 March 1981	500 shares for £ 460
2 April 1984	2,000 shares for £2,300
1 August 1985	2,500 shares for £3,250
3 March 1986	3,000 shares for £4,500
3 June 1987	1,500 shares for £2,400

Notes: 1. Market value of the shares on 6 April 1985 was 80p, and on 31 March 1982 was 94p.
2. The relevant RPI figures are: March 1982 (79.4), June 1983 (84.8), April 1985 (94.8), August 1985 (95.5), March 1986 (96.7) – see p498. The June 1987 figure is assumed to be 101.7.

The rules described on pages 438 and 439 apply only to disposals on or after 6 April 1985. First Sue has to work out which shares she still owns on 6 April 1985 because she has made some disposals before then. There are two sets of rules she must use.

Sales after 5 April 1965 and before 6 April 1982

Shares sold are matched with shares bought in the following order:
● shares bought on the same day
● shares bought before 6 April 1965 taken in the order of buying
● shares bought after 5 April 1965 and before 6 April 1982 – these form a pool.

Using these rules, the sale of 1,000 shares on 1 February 1978 is matched with 1,000 of the 1,500 shares bought on 1 August 1962. The sale of 500 shares on 1 March 1981 is matched to the remaining shares bought on 1 August 1962.

Sales after 5 April 1982 and before 6 April 1985

Shares sold are matched with shares bought in the following order:
● shares bought in the same Stock Exchange account – assuming they are listed
● shares bought within the 12 months before the sale taken in the order of purchase
● shares bought more than 12 months before the sale but before 6 April 1982 unless they are in the following pool
● shares bought after 5 April 1965 and before 6 April 1982 which are pooled

- shares bought before 6 April 1965 taken in *reverse* order of purchase.

Using these rules, Sue matches the 2,000 shares sold on 2 April 1984 with 2,000 of the 2,500 shares bought on 1 June 1983.

Holding on 6 April 1985

So on 6 April 1985, Sue's holding of shares is as follows:
- purchased before 6 April 1965 (Batch 5 shares): 2500 shares remain
- purchased after 5 April 1965 and before 6 April 1982 (Batch 4 shares): a pool of 3,500 shares; total cost was £2,850
- purchased after 5 April 1982 and before 6 April 1985 (Batch 3 shares): a pool of 1,750 shares remains; total cost was £1,980.

Sale on 1 August 1985

As Sue made no purchases on the same day (Batch 1) or within the previous 10 days (Batch 2), the taxman looks to see what shares are within Batch 3. There are 1,750 shares in that Batch, so the 2,500 shares Sue is selling now are matched with the 1,750 shares in Batch 3, and with 750 of the shares in Batch 4.

First the taxman needs to work out the indexation allowance to the date of the disposal. He takes the shares owned on 6 April 1985 and works out the indexation allowance so far. Then, each time shares are added to, or withdrawn from, the pool, the indexation allowance is calculated again. On a disposal of shares from the pool, the initial value and the indexation allowance for these shares is a proportion of the initial value and indexation allowance for the whole pool.

The taxman's calculations will look something like this:

Batch 3 shares

	No. of shares	Unindexed value of pool	Indexed value of pool
		£	£
Purchase 1 June 1983			
Balance after sale on 2 April 1984	500	480	480
Indexation allowance to April 1985			
$£480 \times \dfrac{94.8 - 84.8}{84.8}$			56
	500	480	536
Purchase 1 April 1985	1,250	1,500	1,500
	1,750	1,980	2,036
Indexation allowance to 1 August 1985			
$£2,036 \times \dfrac{95.5 - 94.8}{94.8}$			15
	1,750	1,980	2,051
Sale 1 August 1985	*minus*(1,750)	(1,980)	(2,051)
Shares left in Batch 3	0	0	0

Example 11 continued
The taxman works out the capital gain on Sue's Batch 3 shares as follows:

	£
Sale proceeds $\frac{1,750}{2,500} \times £3,250$	= 2,275
Less allowable expenses (purchase price)	1,980
Unindexed gain	295
Less indexation allowance (£2,051 − £1,980)	71
leaves a chargeable gain of	£ 224

Batch 4 shares
Next the taxman moves on to work out the tax on Sue's Batch 4 shares. Because she's only parting with 750 out of the 3,500 shares in this pool, the sale proceeds and the initial value are a proportion of the value for the whole pool:

	£
Sale proceeds $\frac{750}{2,500} \times £3,250$	= 975
Less allowable expenses (purchase price) $\frac{750}{3,500} \times £2,850$	= 611
leaves an unindexed gain of	364

Because these shares were acquired before March 1982, Sue has a choice of working out the indexation allowance by reference to either the actual cost of the shares, or their market value on 31 March 1982 (see p419) – although the indexation allowance itself only runs from March 1982. She does the sums:
Using the actual cost
$$£611 \times \frac{95.5 - 79.4}{79.4} = £123$$

Using the March 1982 value
750 shares @ 94p each = £705
$$£705 \times \frac{95.5 - 79.4}{79.4} = £143.$$

The March 1982 value provides the highest allowance of £142, which Sue deducts from the £364 unindexed gain to end up with a chargeable gain of £364 − £143 = £221 for her Batch 4 shares.

Sue's total chargeable gain from the shares she sold on 1 August 1985 is £224 + £221 = £445.

Sale on 3 March 1986
Sue sold 3,000 shares on 3 March and bought them again on 4 March as a 'bed-and-breakfast' deal (see p445) – done to create a gain and use up some of her annual CGT exemption for the 1985–86 tax year. There are no shares in Batches 1 or 2, and all the shares in Batch 3 were used in working out the gain on the 1 August 1985 sale. But there are 2,750 left in Batch 4 and these will be used first. The other 250 shares will be taken from Batch 5.

Batch 4 shares
The taxman works out the chargeable gain for the Batch 4 shares in the same way as for those in the 1 August 1985 sale above.

Sale proceeds $\frac{2,750}{3,000} \times £4,500$ 　　　　　　　　 = 　£ 4,125

Less allowable expenses (purchase price) £2,850 − £611 = 　2,239

Unindexed gain 　　　　　　　　　　　　　　　　　 　1,886

Less indexation allowance (using March 1982 value)
2,750 shares @ 94p each = £2,585

$£2,585 \times \dfrac{96.7 - 79.4}{79.4}$ 　　　　　　　　　 = 　　564

leaves a chargeable gain of 　　　　　　　　　　　 　£1,322

Batch 5 shares

Sue bought three lots of Worldwide shares before 6 April 1965, so the taxman matches up the shares she's selling now to the Batch 5 shares bought nearest to that date. She bought 2,000 shares on 1 January 1965, and she can choose either the price she actually paid for them or their market value on 6 April 1965. She does the sums and finds out that there would be no difference between the two methods, so the taxman uses the price she paid:

Sale proceeds $\frac{250}{3,000} \times £4,500$ 　　　　　　　 = 　£ 375

less allowable expenses (purchase price) $\frac{250}{2,000} \times £1,600$ = 　200

Unindexed gain 　　　　　　　　　　　　　　　　　 　175

less indexation allowance (using March 1982 value)
250 shares @ 94p each = £235

$£235 \times \dfrac{96.7 - 79.4}{79.4}$ 　　　　　　　　　 = 　　51

leaves a chargeable gain of 　　　　　　　　　　　 　£124

Sue's total chargeable gain from the shares she sold on 3 March 1986 is £1,332 + £124 = £1,446.

Sale on 3 June 1987

As more shares were bought on 4 March 1986, Sue now has some Batch 3 shares. There are no shares in Batches 1 or 2, so the 1,500 shares she is selling will be matched with 1,500 of these Batch 3 shares. The taxman calculates the pool of shares in Batch 3 on 3 June 1987 to work out initial value and indexation allowance.

	No. of shares	Unindexed value of pool (£)	Indexed value of pool (£)
Purchase 4 March 1986	3,000	4,500	4,500
Indexation allowance to June 1987			
$£4,500 \times \dfrac{101.7 - 96.7}{96.7}$			234
	3,000	4,500	4,734
Sale 3 June 1987　*minus*	(1,500)	(2,250)	(2,376)
Balance remaining in pool	1,500	2,250	2,376

Example 11 continued
Then the taxman works out the chargeable gain as follows:

		£
Sale proceeds		2,400
Less allowable expenses (purchase price)		2,250
Unindexed gain		150
less indexation allowance (£2,367 − £2,250)	=	117
leaves a chargeable gain for Sue of		£ 33

Sue's chargeable gain from the sale on 3 June 1987 is £33.

Takeovers, mergers and reconstructions

If you exchange your existing shares for new shares on a takeover or merger, or if the company is being reconstructed, the exchange will not normally give rise to a disposal. As far as *time of acquisition* and *cost* are concerned, the new shares will be in the position of the old.

But if you exchange your old shares for new shares and cash, you are taken to have disposed of a proportion of your old shares. The gain or loss which you make on the disposal is a proportion of the gain or loss you would have made if you had disposed of the shares entirely for cash. That proportion is the percentage of the exchange represented by cash. So if the exchange is ¼ cash, ¾ new shares, your gain or loss will be ¼ what it would have been if you had taken all cash.
CGTA 1979 s77–88.

Quoted shares acquired before 6 April 1965

The taxman assumes that these shares were disposed of by you on 6 April 1965 and immediately re-acquired by you for what they were worth on that date. The normal rule for calculating the market value of quoted shares (see p438) is *not* used. Instead, the taxman makes a calculation which is more favourable to you. He uses the greater of:
• the lower of the two quoted prices shown in The Stock Exchange Official Daily List for that day, plus half the difference between them
• the price halfway between the highest and lowest prices at which bargains were recorded on that day, excluding bargains at special prices.

A similar calculation should be done for shares quoted on a stock exchange other than London.

These shares are *not* pooled with shares of the same type which you acquired after 5 April 1965. Instead, your taxable gain (or loss) on a disposal of the shares is the difference between market value at 6 April 1965 and the disposal proceeds (less any indexation allowance).

This calculation is then compared with the 'truth' – ie the taxman sees whether you would have made a gain, or a loss, using the initial value of the shares when you first acquired them (ie – in most cases – what you actually paid for them).

If the first calculation would have the effect of increasing a real loss (or gain), the taxman takes the actual loss (or gain) instead.

If one calculation shows a gain, and the other shows a loss, you are treated as having made neither a gain nor a loss for tax purposes.

CGTA 1979 s28, Sch 5 para 1.

Bed-and-breakfasting

You 'bed-and-breakfast' shares by selling them, and then buying them back the following day. The purpose is as follows:
• if you have made a gain on the shares, and your net taxable gains for the year are below the £6,600 exempt slice, you could sell enough shares to bring your gains for the year up to, but not beyond, the exempt slice. This would create a higher acquisition cost for the shares, so your taxable gain on a later disposal would be reduced
• if your taxable gains for the year look like being more than the exempt slice, and you own shares which are standing at a loss, you could sell enough shares to bring your gains for the year down to the exempt slice.

Insurance policies

If you receive insurance proceeds for damage to, or the loss of, an asset, you may have a CGT liability unless the proceeds of disposal of that asset are tax-free. So if you receive insurance money in compensation for theft of your jewellery, you may have a CGT liability – but not if you get insurance money when your main home burns down.

However, there's no liability on the proceeds if you spend them in restoring or (generally within one year of the loss) replacing the asset. The rules work like this. For restorations:
• the proceeds are deducted from your allowable costs for the asset
• if you spend the money on restoring or replacing the asset, and if this is an allowable expense for CGT (it normally is) the figures balance: ie what you spend is added back to your allowable expenses.

For replacements:
- the proceeds are deemed to be equal to your allowable costs for the original asset including any indexation allowance
- any excess of the proceeds (plus any remaining value in the original asset), is deducted from the allowable cost of the replacement asset.

The taxman may be difficult where insurance proceeds are spent restoring a damaged item which was badly in need of repair at the time of the damage, since part of the expense will be for repair (not allowable) rather than for restoration (allowable). You also have to be a little careful about what constitutes replacement: if you 'replace' your stolen necklace with a watercolour, the taxman is unlikely to be co-operative.
CGTA 1979 s21.

Paying CGT

If, in the tax year ending 5 April 1987, all the points listed below apply, enter *gains not exceeding £6,600, disposals not exceeding £13,200* in the **Chargeable assets disposed of** section of the 11P Tax Return (for form P1 leave the capital gains section blank):
- you made taxable gains of no more than £6,600
- the total value of the assets liable to CGT which you disposed of was no more than £13,200
- if you are married, you and your husband or wife do not have your capital gains assessed separately, and neither wants his or her own losses to be set only against his or her own future gains.

In any other case – or if, overall, you made a loss for the year – enter a description of all the taxable assets disposed of in the year, and figures for taxable gains and allowable losses. Include gains and losses on all homes, even though a gain on your main home is normally tax-free. When entering a loss, don't forget to write *loss*. Attach details of how you worked out your gains and losses.

If you disagree with the assessment of CGT which the taxman makes, you must make a written appeal to your tax office within 30 days of the issue of the assessment. If you don't appeal, the CGT is due either on 1 December after the end of the tax year in which the taxable gains were made, or 30 days after the assessment is issued if that gives a later date for payment.
CGTA 1979 s5.

33 YOU AND THE INLAND REVENUE

How your tax office is organised

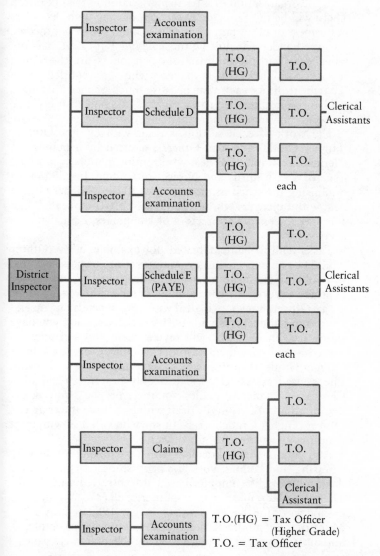

T.O.(HG) = Tax Officer (Higher Grade)
T.O. = Tax Officer

When you write to or telephone your tax office, who will you be dealing with? And where does he or she stand in the pecking order?

The Diagram overleaf shows a typical tax office structure. The District Inspector is the person in charge. He will be assisted by several Tax Inspectors – how many, will depend on the size of the district. Some of these Inspectors will be concerned solely with examining business accounts and making enquiries. Other Inspectors will be concerned mainly with the organisation of a particular section in the tax office. There will be the *Schedule D section*, dealing with taxpayers in business or other taxpayers whose main sources of income are taxed under Schedule D; the *Schedule E (or PAYE) section*, which deals with all employees and pensioners; and the *Claims section*, dealing with taxpayers who are entitled to a repayment of tax each year because much of their income is paid to them after deduction of tax. In small districts, one Inspector may manage more than one section.

The work of each section is dealt with by Tax Officers (Higher Grade) and Tax Officers, assisted by a number of Clerical Assistants who deal with routine matters such as the issue of Tax Returns and Notices of Coding. In addition to organising the work of others, Tax Officers (Higher Grade) deal with taxpayers whose affairs are more complicated than average, for example directors of companies, or higher rate taxpayers.

Tasks tend to be demarcated: for example, a Tax Officer would not be expected to examine a set of business accounts – a job for an Inspector. And an Inspector would not be expected to revise the code number of an employee – a job for a Tax Officer. So who will deal with you, depends on you and the job in hand. If it is your business accounts that you have submitted, an Inspector will review them and – if they are agreed – will pass them to the Tax Officer, or Tax Officer (Higher Grade) if appropriate, to, say, revise your assessment. The revised assessment will probably be written out by a Clerical Assistant. All grades can, therefore, be involved, but if your affairs are primarily dealt with by a Tax Officer or Tax Officer (Higher Grade) it is he or she who will deal with most enquiries you make to the tax office.

And your chances of dealing with a computer? All the PAYE assessing and coding work for Scottish-based employees is dealt with by the computer based at Centre 1, East Kilbride. The Inland Revenue aim to computerise all PAYE assessing and coding work for the rest of the UK by late 1987 or early 1988. Much of the computerisation of PAYE has now been completed, and most Notices of Coding and many Schedule E assessments are now prepared by computer. The new computer-based forms look different to the previous forms, but provide all the same information.

The tax office is not concerned with the *collection* of tax – this is the responsibility of the Collector of Taxes. With the introduction of computerised assessment and collection records, most of the collection of tax charged by assessments will be dealt with centrally; but local collection offices will still be involved in collecting tax from defaulters.

Taxpayer's charter

In July 1986 the Inland Revenue and HM Customs and Excise issued a **taxpayer's charter** setting out what taxpayers have the right to expect from them – in particular:

● help and information (and, in return, taxpayers are expected to provide full facts)

● courtesy and consideration

● fairness

● privacy and confidentiality

● recognition of the need to keep to the minimum necessary the costs taxpayers incur in complying with the law

● the right to independent appeal and review of your case.

Copies of the charter are available from local tax and VAT offices.

Which tax office deals with your affairs

Not necessarily the tax office closest to where you live. Your tax office will depend on your circumstances:

● **Employees** As a general rule, your affairs will be dealt with by the tax office dealing with the area where you work, more particularly the place from which you are paid. However, if you work for a large organisation, your tax office may be one of the very large ones known as London Provincial districts – mainly in the north of England (eg Bradford, Manchester, Salford) – which deal solely with the tax affairs of employees. If you are a Government employee – eg civil servant or member of HM forces – your affairs will be dealt with by one of the Public Departments offices in Cardiff. Your employer will be able to tell you which tax office deals with your affairs, and your reference number. Your reference number will be the one that applies to your employer: so all employees at the same place will have the same reference number. If you change your job, your reference number will change; your tax office may also change if your new employer is in a different area.

● **Self-employed** If you are in business on your own account, or in partnership, your place of business will determine which tax office deals with your affairs.

● **Income mainly from pension or investments** If you are getting a pension from a former employer, your tax affairs may well be dealt with by the tax office dealing with the area in which the pension fund paying your pension has its office. But if the pension from your former employer is fairly small, or your only pension is the state retirement pension or widow's pension, your affairs will be dealt with by the tax office dealing with the area in which you live.

● **Unemployed** You stay with the tax office of your last employer.

● **Special cases** If you have to fill in a Tax Return in your capacity as trustee, the tax office will be one of the limited number which deal with the affairs of trusts and settlements.

Local PAYE enquiry offices

As the affairs of many taxpayers are dealt with by tax offices a hundred or more miles away, the Inland Revenue have set up local PAYE enquiry offices, so that you can call in and discuss any tax problems. A full list with addresses and telephone numbers is in *IR52* – available free from any tax office (or try the phone book under *Inland Revenue*).

When you contact the Revenue, always give your tax reference number (if you know it). This speeds things up.

Tax forms

Tax Returns

There are several different types of Tax Return, designed for different types of taxpayer:

● **Form P1** This is the most straightforward Tax Return and is issued to the majority of employees. If you are an employee and your affairs are not complicated, this is the Tax Return you will probably be sent. It is also likely that you will *not* be asked to complete one each year (although this does not absolve you of the need to tell your tax office of any new source of income, see opposite).

● **Form 11P** This Tax Return also goes to employees, but is issued to those with more complicated affairs – for example directors of companies, or people who pay higher rates of tax.

● **Form 11** This is for people who are in business on their own account, or in partnership, or whose main sources of income are chargeable to tax under Schedule D.

● **Form 1** This form is issued to partnerships, for completion on behalf of the partnership – and shows the partnership income for the tax year and how that income has been shared between the partners. It is sent out *in addition* to Form 11 which will be sent to the individual partners. Form 1 is also issued to the personal representatives of someone who has died, so that they can report the income arising during the period of administration of the estate. Form 1 also goes to trustees of a settlement. But Form 1 only asks for information about sources of income which have not had tax deducted before payment – so further forms are issued to trustees, which ask for information about income which has been paid after deduction of tax, including dividends from UK companies.

● **Form R40** This is the form sent to people who claim a repayment of tax each year. Unlike all the previous Tax Returns – which are normally issued in April – form R40 will be sent to you at the same time as the repayment for the previous year is dealt with and the cheque sent to you.

● **Form R232** This form is issued to you if you have to make a return on behalf of someone who cannot do so themselves. For example, if your child receives payments under a Deed of Covenant from your parents – or from some other relative – you will be sent form R232 so that you can claim on behalf of your child any repayment due.

If you are sent a Tax Return, you are required to complete it, sign and date the declaration, and send it back to the tax office within the time limit shown on the Tax Return. This is normally 30 days. In practice, the Inland Revenue will not penalise you if your Tax Return is not completed and returned within the time limit. But if you are very late in sending in your Tax Return, ie after the end of the tax year in which the Tax Return was issued to you, the Inland Revenue can impose penalties (see p461).

If you are not sent a Tax Return but are receiving income which the Inland Revenue are not aware of, you must notify your tax office of this income. Failure to do so within one year of the end of the tax year in which the income arose can result in a penalty not exceeding £100.
TMA 1970 s7, s8.

Notice of Coding

Form P2 If you are an employee, you will be sent a Notice of Coding – usually a Form P2 – which shows the code number that your employer will use to calculate the tax to be deducted from your pay. On the reverse of the form, the tax office will show how your code number has been arrived at. The computer version of form P2 is form P2(T). On this form, the calculation of the code number appears on the front, not the reverse. More details in Chapter 12 (p136).

Notices of Assessment

These are forms on which the taxman works out how much you owe. In Chapter 34, we give examples of a **Notice of Assessment**.

Correspondence and disputes

This section is about writing to – and talking to – the taxman, and solving problems that way. For the more formal procedures of an *appeal*, see p455.

Your move

There may well be times when you will need to take the initiative and write to your tax office – eg if you become entitled to a new allowance. In such a case, write a brief letter giving all the relevant information. For example, if you get married and want to claim the extra allowance due, the tax office will need to know: the wife's name and maiden name, date of marriage, and her employer; her tax office and reference number would also be helpful.

It is essential when writing to your tax office that you quote your reference number. This will be shown on any Notice of Coding, Notice of Assessment or Tax Return which you have received. Your papers are filed under your reference number, not under your name, and your Inspector may not be able to trace your papers without your reference number. If the Inspector cannot immediately trace your papers this will add to the delay in dealing with your letter.

Do not expect a lightning-quick reply from your tax office. Delays in dealing with correspondence are not uncommon – how long will vary from tax office to tax office. Certain matters are given priority, for example, repayments. So if you consider that you are entitled to a repayment, write *repayment claim* (preferably in red) at the top of your letter – your claim is then more likely to get priority.

. . . and theirs

After you have sent in your Tax Return, the tax office may write to you and ask for further infomation about the income shown or expenses claimed. Although such a letter will probably be signed by an Inspector or Tax Officer (Higher Grade), the person actually dealing with your affairs may well be a Tax Officer (see *How your tax office is organised*, on p447). Your reply should be addressed to 'HM Inspector of Taxes', but it will probably go straight to the person dealing with you. If the letter is about your business accounts, your correspondent is the Inspector responsible for the examination of your accounts.

When replying to any letters from your tax office, give the information requested if this is possible (and try to see the request as reasonable).

Problem-solving

If you are convinced that the Inspector is being *un*reasonable in his request for further information, a telephone conversation or meeting with the Inspector may succeed in sorting things out. A meeting should present no problem if your tax office is a local one. But if it's not, you can arrange with the local tax office for your file to be passed to them for a short period so that you can discuss your affairs with a local Inspector.

If (in your view) the person you are dealing with continues to be unreasonable, you could write a personal letter to the District Inspector – his name will appear at the head of any letter you receive, also on your Tax Return and any Notice of Assessment. Mark the envelope and letter for his personal attention, and ask him to review all the correspondence; you should summarise the main points in your argument again. The District Inspector should reply personally, and he will either agree with you or set out fully the reasons why your argument is not accepted.

If you are still unable to get any satisfaction from your tax office, write to the Regional Controller who deals with your tax office (names and addresses of Regional Controllers can be got from any tax office). In your letter to the Regional Controller, set out concisely and clearly your grounds for complaint against your tax office, and ask him to investigate on your behalf.

Claiming tax back

It's quite common for people to pay too much tax. For example:
● too much tax has been deducted under PAYE (see p146)
● you've paid too much tax on income you've received (see overleaf)
● you've paid too much tax in previous years – eg you've forgotten to claim an allowance or an outgoing. If this has happened in your case, you can claim back the tax overpaid in the six tax years before the tax year you're now in. So if you claim before 6 April 1988, you can recover tax overpaid as far back as the 1981–82 tax year.

> If you receive covenant or maintenance payments, they will usually have had basic rate tax deducted before the money is paid to you. (The same applies to some types of investment income – see p274.)
>
> If your income, including the grossed-up amount of the payments, is too low to pay tax, you can claim back all the tax deducted. If you should pay *some* tax, but less than the amount deducted, you can claim back the difference. (You can't claim back tax deducted from building society or most bank interest – see p280.)

What to do

- Write to your tax office, saying why you're making a claim, and (if you know) how much you're claiming.
- If you're sending back a Tax Return at the same time, write *REPAYMENT CLAIM* at the top (preferably in red).

If your rebate is £25 or more, you may be entitled to some interest. But the rebate doesn't start to earn interest until 12 months after the end of the tax year for which it is due, or until the end of the tax year in which you actually paid too much tax – whichever is later.

Mistake by the taxman

The staff in your tax office are not infallible, and mistakes do happen from time to time. It is therefore important to check all correspondence received from your tax office, such as a Notice of Assessment or Notice of Coding.

If the taxman is after you for tax you owe due to a mistake on *his* part (eg if he has overlooked part of your income which you've told him about) from tax years further back than the previous one, you may not have to pay all (or any) of the tax you owe. But this will apply only if you've taken reasonable care to keep your tax affairs in order and up-to-date, and if, as far as you're aware, you don't owe the taxman money. You'll be let off paying all of the tax you owe if your gross (before-tax) income in the tax year in which you get the assessment is no more than £8,500. If it's between £8,501 and £10,500, you'll pay a quarter of what you owe; between £10,501 and £13,500 you'll pay a half; between £13,501 and £16,000 you'll pay three quarters; and between £16,001 and £23,000 you'll pay nine tenths. Above £23,000 you pay the lot.

If you're 65 or over, or receiving the state retirement or widow's pension, all the limits above are increased by £2,500 – so, for example, there would be no tax to repay if your income was £11,000 or less.

These limits apply if you were first told about the mistake

on 23 July 1985 or later. If you were told before then the limits were lower.
ESC A19.

Mistakes by you

You may perhaps discover that a mistake in past Tax Returns has resulted in your paying more tax than is actually due from you. If this has happened, it is possible to make a claim to have the appropriate assessment corrected and any tax overpaid repaid to you. The time limit for such a claim is six years from the end of the tax year in which the assessment giving rise to the overcharge was made. But you cannot get a repayment of tax overcharged as a result of an assessment determined by the Commissioners in the absence of the appropriate accounts or Tax Return (see *Appeals*, below). Nor can you claim tax back if your Tax Return was completed on the basis of the law as it was then understood to be, which has since been changed following a decision in a case before the Courts.

Appeals

When you are sent any kind of tax assessment, it is important that you check it straight away. You are allowed 30 days from the date of the assessment in which to appeal against a Notice of Assessment if you consider it is incorrect. If you do not appeal within this period, the assessment becomes *'final and conclusive'* and cannot be altered. The appeal, which must be in writing, is sent to the Inspector who issued the Notice of Assessment, and must state the grounds of the appeal. Your tax office will send you, with the Notice of Assessment, a pink appeal form which you can use to make your appeal. Although you could write your appeal in a letter, it helps your tax office if you use the appeal form provided, perhaps accompanied by a letter if appropriate.

If you are unable to appeal within the 30 days allowed – for example, you are away on holiday or business or in hospital when the Notice of Assessment is issued – send in your appeal, as soon as you can, with an explanation for the delay, and the Inspector will probably accept your appeal. If the Inspector is reluctant to accept a late appeal, you may request that your application for a late appeal be heard by the General Commissioners – see p457.

Within the same time limit for appealing against the assessment, you should also apply to the Inspector for the postponement of any tax charged which you consider to be in excess of your true liability. The pink appeal form includes

space for your postponement application. You must also state why you consider that tax should be postponed. If you do not make an application to postpone the tax which you consider is not due, the whole of the tax charged on the assessment will be payable by the normal due date, and the Collector of Taxes will keep chasing you until it is paid.

If you make an application to postpone part of the tax charged and this is accepted by the Inspector, the tax not postponed becomes payable 30 days after the Inspector's agreement to your application if this is later than the normal due date.

If you do not pay the tax agreed as payable by the time it is due, the Collector of Taxes can charge you interest – currently at the rate of 8.25 per cent – from the due date until the date of payment. If you are self-employed or run a business, note that the interest on overdue tax is not allowable as a business expense.

Settling the appeal

The vast majority of appeals against assessments are settled by agreement with the Inspector. It is quite likely, therefore, that after discussion or correspondence with your tax office you will reach an agreement on the correct amount of income chargeable, or the correct amount of relief or deduction due, and the Inspector will then revise the assessment in line with the figures agreed. Any further tax then due as a result of the issue of that revised assessment is due for payment 30 days after the issue of the revised assessment, or the normal due date if later.

Any further tax found to be due following the issue of a revised assessment may attract interest. The rules about the charging of interest are fairly complicated; but broadly, if the Notice of Assessment has been issued at the correct time, ie before the normal due dates for payment, interest will start no later than six months after the normal due date (for Schedule D Assessments, it will always be 1 July following the year of assessment). If the assessment is issued late, ie more than six months after the normal due date, interest will start from 30 days after the date of issue of the Notice of Assessment.

The Revenue has power not to charge interest if it comes to less than £30 (and normally does not do so).
TMA 1970 s31, s46, s49, s55, s86.

Appeals before the Commissioners

If you are unable to reach agreement with the Inspector, two possible courses of action are open to you. You can give up – ie accept the Inspector's point of view, and pay the tax due on the basis of his figures. Or you can ask for your appeal to be heard before the Commissioners.

You appeal to the *General Commissioners* or the *Special Commissioners*. The Special Commissioners are tax experts. The General Commissioners are unpaid local people who hear appeals in your area; they aren't usually tax experts, but have a paid Clerk to advise them on legal matters.

In some cases you have no choice about whether to go to the General Commissioners or the Special Commissioners. For example, the Special Commissioners must consider your appeal in certain specified (and usually complex) circumstances, or if you're claiming because you made a mistake filling in the *Income* section of your Tax Return and the taxman has refused your claim.

If on the other hand, your appeal is about your PAYE code, or you're claiming tax back because you've failed to claim a personal allowance, it's the General Commissioners who must deal with it.

Other appeals normally go automatically to the General Commissioners, too. But if your appeal depends on some fine point of law (as opposed to a matter of fact, or common sense) you can elect to have your appeal heard by the Special Commissioners. You must make this choice within 30 days of the date of the Notice of Assessment. The General Commissioners have the power to direct that your election be disregarded.

TMA 1970 s31, s33, s46; FA 1984 Sch 22.

At the Commissioners

Taking an appeal before the Commissioners will certainly be time-consuming, and may be expensive if you engage someone to appear on your behalf. You can appear on your own behalf, and the Commissioners are required to hear any barrister, solicitor, or qualified accountant who appears for you.

The preparation and presentation of your case before the Commissioners is extremely important. As appellant, it is up to you to prove that, say, the assessment which you are appealing against is excessive. Although the proceedings before the Commissioners are not as formal as in Court, the normal rules of evidence will apply. You, as appellant, will open the proceedings and will put your case. The Inspector then responds by putting the view of the Inland Revenue; and you then have a final opportunity to stress the important points in your own case and deal with any points raised by the Inspector which you had not previously covered. Any witnesses produced by either you or the Inspector can be cross-examined; and the Commissioners can summon anybody to appear before them.

When preparing your case, bear in mind that the Commissioners will know nothing about you or your affairs until the day of the appeal hearing. So introduce yourself, and the facts of the matter under dispute, as clearly and briefly as you can. If you want to show documents in support of your case, make sure you have enough copies for the Commissioners (there are usually three of them at a General Commissioners' hearing) and the Clerk. The Inspector will probably have copies on his file already, but if not have copies for him too. You may want to refer to previous decided tax cases: the Clerk will almost certainly have copies of these available, but it would be as well to take copies of these too.

It may be possible, before the hearing and in conjunction with the Inspector, to prepare an agreed statement of facts – supported by appropriate documents – which can be presented to the Commissioners. This will save time on the day of the hearing. However, it will still be necessary to explain the facts to the Commissioners, and provide the Commissioners and

Clerk with a copy of the agreed statement of facts and documents.

It is a good idea to have your own presentation typed out in full, with copies for the Commissioners and Clerk. Take the Commissioners carefully through the arguments, both for and against your case. Do not ignore the points you know the Inspector will make. If you deal with his points at the same time as you deal with your own, you are likely to strengthen your own case while at the same time reducing the impact of what the Inspector will say later. You will also give the impression of being a reasonable person — there is almost certainly something in the Inspector's argument, and it is just as well if you are seen to recognise this.

If, in spite of all your efforts, the Commissioners decide in favour of the Inspector, and you don't agree, you must immediately register your dissatisfaction with the decision. If you don't do this immediately, you lose the right to take the case further. Do this verbally at the end of the hearing, or (if the decision is communicated by letter) by an immediate written reply. You may then, by giving notice in writing to the Clerk within 30 days, require the Commissioners to state and sign a case for the opinion of the High Court (see below). You must also pay the fee of £25.

TMA 1970 s50, s56; FA 1984 Sch 22.

. . . and after

The tax payable as a result of the decision of the Commissioners must be paid, regardless of any request for the opinion of the High Court.

The decision of the Commissioners on a question of fact is final, and can only be overturned if the decision was such that no reasonable body of Commissioners could have reached that decision on hearing the evidence.

Otherwise, an appeal against the decision of the Commissioners can only be made on a point of law. The appeal is normally to the High Court, then to the Court of Appeal and ultimately to the House of Lords. From 1 January 1985, certain appeals against the decision of the Special Commissioners may be referred direct to the Court of Appeal, missing out the High Court. Some appeals may skip the Court of Appeal and go straight to the House of Lords. In Scotland, the equivalent of the High Court is the Court of Session, and an appeal from the Court of Session is direct to the House of Lords.

The taking of an appeal through the procedure outlined above can be very expensive. At the Commissioners' hearing each party pays his own costs. However, after that stage it is usual for the costs of both sides to be awarded against the unsuccessful litigant – and you could be faced with a bill running to many thousands of pounds. So consider very carefully before you start on this road.

TMA 1970 s50, s56; FA 1984 Sch 22.

Investigations

The Inland Revenue may start an investigation, or enquiry, into your affairs. These fall broadly into three categories:

● an enquiry into an omission of a source, or sources, of income from your Tax Return, or an understatement of the income declared

● an enquiry into your business accounts

● a more serious investigation into your affairs when the Inland Revenue suspect fraud or wilful default.

An investigation in the last category may well be conducted by one of the Inland Revenue Enquiry Branch Offices and not your local tax office. If you find that the Enquiry Branch is investigating your affairs, you would be well advised to seek professional advice.

The Inland Revenue receive information from a variety of sources. For example, banks are required to make a return of interest credited to their customers of more than £400 in one year. Information such as this is compared with the taxpayer's return – and if the income is not shown, the Inspector will write to the taxpayer suggesting that the Tax Return submitted is incomplete and ask him to reconsider the entries made. If you receive such a letter, go over your Tax Return carefully (you should always keep a copy of what you fill in). If you find that you have omitted something from your Tax Return, make a full report of all income omitted for all years concerned as soon as possible. If the amount of tax involved is not too substantial it should be possible to agree a settlement fairly quickly.

In reaching a settlement with your Inspector he will take into account a number of factors. First, he will calculate the amount of tax which is due on the income or capital gain previously omitted from your Tax Return. Secondly, he will add to the tax an amount of interest at the appropriate rate, calculated from the date the tax ought to have been paid, assuming it had been declared at the proper time. Finally, he will add to the tax and interest a penalty.

TMA 1970 s88, s95.

Maximum penalty

If you fail to send back your Tax Return within 30 days, your Tax Inspector can charge you £50, plus £10 for each further day. In practice he will rarely do this (see p451).

If the Inland Revenue loses tax, either because you didn't send back your Tax Return, or because you sent it back but filled it in wrongly, the maximum penalties are:
● the amount of the tax lost, if due to negligence
● twice the amount of tax lost, in the case of fraud.

The £50 applies to *each* Tax Return. So if income had been omitted from three Tax Returns (but not as a result of fraud) the maximum penalty would be £150 plus the amount of tax.

New tax penalties?

The Keith Committee in its report suggested that a new system of working out penalties for tax offences should be introduced. Based on these proposals, the Government introduced changes to the system for dealing with VAT offences from the 1985–86 tax year. So far, the present system for income tax offences has not been changed.

FA 1985 s11–29, s32.

The Inland Revenue also have power to charge interest and penalties if you submit your Tax Return so late that the Inspector is unable to make an assessment on income or gains shown on that Return at the proper time. While the Inspector may seek to charge interest from the normal due date for the payment of the tax due, he is less likely to impose penalties unless your Tax Return is very late. *(TMA 1970 s93, s95.)*

Mitigation of penalties

It is most unlikely that your Inspector will apply the maximum penalty – unless the amount of tax involved was very substantial, the omission had continued over many years, and you had denied all knowledge of the income when challenged. The Inspector takes all these factors into account and if, for example, you had reported all previously omitted income when first challenged, or better still reported the omission voluntarily before the Inspector challenged you, the amount of income and tax involved is fairly small, and you co-operated fully with the Inspector to bring the matter to a speedy conclusion, the amount of the penalty is likely to be fairly small. In any case, the amount of penalty is something you may be able to negotiate with the Inspector (see below).

The offer in settlement

At the end of the enquiry the Inspector will ask you for two documents. First, he will ask you to sign a *Certificate of full disclosure*. The declarations previously signed on your Tax Return have been proved to be incorrect, and this new Certificate confirms that, taking into account the income disclosed in the enquiry, you have now made a full return of all your income for the years covered by the enquiry. He will also ask you to make a formal offer in settlement of the tax lost, interest, and penalties. The Inspector's letter will normally suggest the amount of the offer which he considers the Board of Inland Revenue will accept. By deducting the tax and interest from the amount of the offer suggested by the Inspector, you can calculate the amount of penalty which he considers is due. If you feel this is unreasonable, it is open to you to make a reduced offer in settlement. This will be considered by the Inland Revenue Head Office, in the light of the recommendation of the local Inspector, and may well be accepted if reasonable. Once the offer has been accepted, the tax is payable direct to the Collector, within a period agreed in advance with the Inspector, and no formal assessments will be made.

It was announced on 29 August 1986 that offers in settlement will include provisions for the charging of interest if the amount due under the settlement is not paid by the agreed date. Previously it was not possible for the Inland Revenue to charge interest if the amount due was paid late.
SP6/86

Enquiry into your business accounts

Under the current procedure, the Inspector will review all accounts submitted and, using his local knowledge and experience, will select certain accounts for detailed examination. One factor which the Inspector will take into account will be the gross profit percentage. The Inspector will know the average for similar businesses in the area, and if accounts reach him showing a gross profit percentage well removed from the average, this may well prompt him to select these.

The first you'll know about it may be when the Inspector writes and asks some detailed questions about your accounts. If you have an accountant acting on your behalf, and in particular in the preparation of your accounts, the Inspector will probably first direct these questions to your accountant. It is possible that the enquiry will be settled by correspondence, but it is more usual for the Inspector to request an interview with you, and your accountant if you have one.

The interview with the Inspector

This can be a daunting experience, particularly for first-timers. The Inspector will want to establish why the pattern of your business is different from others of the same type in his area (there may be perfectly good reasons for this, of course); and he will also want to ensure that any adjustments made for tax purposes – for example, private use of a car – have been worked out correctly. He will therefore ask you a lot of searching questions about your business: eg how you run it, how frequently you make up your books, how purchases and sales are recorded, how frequently you bank your takings, whether you bank all your takings and pay for all purchases by cheque, or whether you keep cash to pay for purchases or wages. He will also probably enquire into your lifestyle to see if the amount shown for drawings is adequate. It is usual to try to establish an approximate total for your living expenses – including such items as the cost of clothes, holidays, entertainment, general household expenses, and so on. From this information, the Inspector will form a view about the accuracy of your accounts and the need to continue the enquiry. If he is satisfied with your explanations, and if your business accounts reflect all your takings and only business expenses, this will probably be the end of the enquiry. The Inspector may suggest some adjustments to the private proportion of any expenses, but these are likely to be minor.

If, however, the Inspector is not satisfied with your explanations, or the drawings shown do not reflect accurately your total living expenses, he will seek to increase your profit for tax purposes to reflect the adjustments which he considers are due. If the adjustment is of a fairly minor amount, the Inspector may not suggest any adjustments to previous years' accounts. But if the adjustment for the current year is more substantial, the Inspector may well seek to adjust the profits for previous years.

The Inspector will make full notes of the interview, and will forward copies to you or your accountant for approval. It is important to review these notes carefully and report any inaccuracies you find to the Inspector immediately so that corrections can be made and the revised notes agreed between you. This can be important if you fail to reach agreement with the Inspector and the matter has to be taken before the Commissioners, when the notes of the meeting will probably be introduced as evidence.

Settling the enquiry

If you are able to agree with the Inspector the amount of any adjustment to your business profits for tax purposes, the enquiry can be settled. If the adjustments are fairly minor, the Inspector will probably simply revise the assessments and you will be asked to pay the tax to the Collector in the usual way. If, however, the adjustments are more substantial and cover a number of years, the Inspector will probably seek a settlement on the lines described above, to include interest and penalties.

34 CHECKING YOUR INCOME TAX

Why check your income tax?

Because the taxman might get it wrong. Every year, *Which?* gets letters from members who have received substantial tax rebates because they found something wrong with their assessment and queried it. Using the Calculator and other information in this Chapter should ensure that you pay no more tax than you legally have to.

How your income tax is worked out

Your income tax bill for the tax year is based on your 'gross income'. This is basically the total of all your income which is assessable for the tax year. It doesn't include income which is tax-free. If you are married, it includes both husband's and wife's income, unless you got married during the tax year – see p72. (If the wife's earned income is taxed separately, see p74.) There are special rules for certain types of income – see overleaf. And with some types of income, this year's tax bill is based on the amount you received in the previous tax year (this mainly applies to business profits and certain investment income not taxed before you got it).

You are allowed to make certain deductions from your gross income. For example, contributions to your employer's pension scheme can be deducted from your earnings from a job (see p331), and certain expenses can be deducted from income from being self-employed or letting property.

Taxable income

You won't have to pay tax on all your gross income as individuals and married couples are allowed a certain amount of income free of tax – called a Personal Allowance. In certain circumstances you may qualify for additional allowances – see p124. You also get 'tax relief' on certain payments you make – called 'outgoings'. What this means is that you're not charged tax on the amount of income you use to make these payments. When you have subtracted your allowances and outgoings from your gross income, what you have left is the amount on which income tax will actually be charged – often called *taxable income*.

If the income chargeable to tax is no more than £17,900, it will normally all be taxed at the basic rate (which, in the 1987–88 tax year, is 27 per cent).

If you have more than £17,900 chargeable to tax, the first £17,900 is taxed at the basic rate. This 'basic rate band' will be extended if you have outgoings (like mortgage interest) on which you have already had basic rate tax relief (by making lower payments) but on which you are also entitled to relief from higher rate tax. After that, any further income you have is taxed at a series of higher rates – see Diagram below.

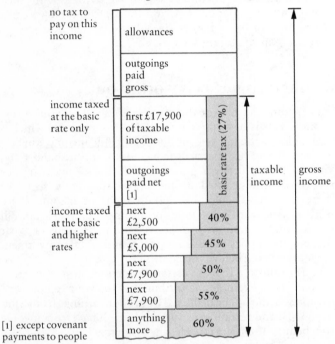

Special rules for certain types of income and outgoings

Building society and bank interest

Basic rate tax is deemed to have been paid on building society interest and most interest from banks, deposit-takers and local authority loans (see pages 279–283 for details) before it is paid out to you. Because of this you don't have to pay basic rate tax on the interest (nor can you reclaim tax if your income is too low to pay tax). But the grossed-up amount of interest you receive is included in your gross income. If your taxable income (including the grossed-up amount of the interest), is high enough for you to pay tax at higher rates, higher rate tax is charged on the interest at the difference between the higher rate and the basic rate. For example, if your highest rate of tax is 40%, tax will be charged at 40% − 27% = 13% on the grossed-up amount of the interest.

Golden handshakes

If you receive over £25,000 when you leave a job, there are special values for calculating the tax on the excess. See p158.

Taxable gains on life insurance policies

These are free of basic rate tax, but the gain is included in your income and, if you are liable to higher rate tax, you will have to pay tax on the gain at the difference between the higher rate and the basic rate (as with building society interest). But *top-slicing relief* can reduce your tax bill on the gain – see p303.

Covenant payments you receive

Covenant payments you receive are liable to basic rate tax (which should have been deducted by the payer) but they aren't liable to higher rate tax.

If you have made outgoings net of basic rate tax

You have given yourself basic rate tax relief on these when you made the payments. With covenant payments to people this is all the tax relief you're entitled to. But with mortgage interest under MIRAS, payments into personal pensions, maintenance payments and covenant payments to charities, you're entitled to higher rate tax relief on the gross amount of the payments. The taxman usually gives you this relief by ignoring the payments when he works out your basic rate tax and by deducting the gross amount from your income liable to tax at higher rates. See p471 for an example.

Notices of Assessment

The Inland Revenue use Notices of Assessment to tell you your total tax bill for the year and to show how it has been worked out. If you pay tax under PAYE and your affairs are straightforward, you may not be sent a Notice of Assessment – though you can ask for one if you wish. (This isn't always a good idea, as the taxman might then ask you to pay small amounts of tax unpaid because of roundings in the PAYE system.) If most of your income comes from earnings and pensions, you'll be sent a Schedule E Notice of Assessment like the one on p472. Small amounts of investment income or freelance earnings taxed under Schedule D and property income taxed under Schedule A may also be shown on this Notice. But if you have substantial amounts of these, you'll get a separate Schedule A and D Notice of Assessment like the one opposite. If you have several sources of income and are liable to higher rate tax, you may also get a higher rate Notice of Assessment (Form 900) showing how it's been worked out.

Computerisation

The Inland Revenue is steadily altering their forms so that they can be printed out by computer. At the moment, some districts are computerised (ie Wales and the Eastern Counties) while others are not. All the forms contain the same information, but the computerised forms will only print out what's relevant to you, while forms designed to be filled in by hand include a number of pre-printed headings.

Checking a Notice of Assessment

If the Assessment covers all your income, the simplest way to check it may be to work out your tax bill using our Income Tax Calculator (page 475). A Notice of Assessment does not list your income, outgoings and allowances in the way we do. For example, if you have received income from which basic rate tax has been deducted, such as share dividends, and you are liable for tax at the basic rate only, the taxman may leave out both the income and the tax deducted from his calculation. But the final figure you get – the difference between the tax you have paid and the tax you should have paid – should work out the same whichever method is used.

Appealing against a Notice of Assessment

If you get a Notice of Assessment, check it at once. If you think any of the figures on it is wrong, you must normally appeal within 30 days of the date on it. If it's a Schedule A or D assessment, you must still pay all the tax demanded, unless you also apply for a postponement of part or all of the tax. See p455 for details.

Income Tax (Schedule A or D) and Class 4 National Insurance Contributions	**1 Net amount payable**		
Inland Revenue		**First instalment**	**Second instalment**
Year 1987-88 ending 5 April 1988	Income tax	£ 2,520.72	£ 1,348.65
Assessment No. File No.	Class 4 NIC	£ 213.26	£ 213.25
D	Total	£ 2,733.98	£ 1,561.90

In any reply give assessment and/or file no. (if any)

Where tax is payable a notice to pay is attached

Roger Burns
14 Twintrees Avenue
Swinside

Class 4 NIC

Profit	£ 11,360
Lower limit	£ 4,690
Charge at 6.3% on	£ 6,770
Amount payable added to 1	£ 426.51

Date of issue

15 Nov. 1987

Notes

General
By law, this notice is addressed to you personally but if you have a professional adviser or agent please let him see this **Notice of assessment** at once. The enclosed form 64D supplements the notes below.

Estimated assessments
An E before any amount indicates that it has been estimated.

Payment
Payment of any tax and/or Class 4 NIC shown in the **first instalment** box in part 1 above should comply with the directions for payment on the attached **notice to pay** without further request.
Any amount shown in the **Second instalment** box in Part 1 is due on 1 July 1988.
See also note 2 on form 64D.

Appeals and postponement applications
If you disagree with the assessment then appeal in writing within 30 days from the date of issue above. Also, if you consider that the amount charged is excessive you may apply to postpone payment of some or all of the tax etc.
See notes 1 and 2 on form 64D.

Interest on tax payments
Interest is chargeable on tax paid late and may accrue before the amount of tax payable has been agreed.
See note 3 on form 64D.

2 Notice of assessment

Source of profits or income	£	£
Roger's Joke Shop	13,200	
Property Rents		5,400
Investment Income		1,740
Balancing charge		
Deductions Retirement annuity paymts 1,370		
Capital allowances 1,840		
Class 4 NIC (50%) 214		
Losses		
Interest, unless paid net of tax 160		
Allowances		
Personal/Wife's earned income 2,425		
Housekeeper/Additional personal		
Dependent relative		
Total allowances 6,009		
Less amount allowed in part 3		
Balance given in this assessment 6,009	3,210	2,799
Net amount chargeable to tax	9,990	4,341
Tax chargeable		
Basic rate 27% on £ 14,331	2,697 30	1,172 07
Higher rate(s) on £		
Additional rate £ at %		
Net tax payable	2697 30	1,172 07

HM Inspector of Taxes

District stamp

3 Allowances etc allocated

	Allow-ances	Income charged at					
		27%	%	%	%	%	%
Totals							
This assessment		14,331					

300B(Z)

How to read a Schedule A or D Notice of Assessment

You'll get one of these assessments if you let property or work for yourself (full-time or spare-time), or have investment income not on your Schedule E Notice of Assessment. It usually comes with a demand to pay the tax you owe. In the description which follows, we refer you to Roger Burns' Notice of Assessment for 1987–88, on p469.

At the top of Part 2, the taxman enters the main sources of Roger's income. In his accounting year ending in the 1986–87 tax year, Roger Burns made a profit, after deducting allowable business expenses, of £13,200 in his Joke Shop. Roger also gets rents from unfurnished property which, after deducting allowable expenses, are expected to be £5,400. He also got £1,740 untaxed investment income in the 1986–87 tax year.

In his business, Roger claims capital allowances of £1,840. He has also paid £1,370 in retirement annuity premiums. He can claim relief against half the Class 4 National Insurance contributions that he pays in the 1987–88 tax year (see below for how these are worked out).

Roger paid interest of £160 on a home improvement loan from a finance company, and gets single person's allowance of £2,425.

His *Total Allowances* come to £6,009. His retirement annuity payments and capital allowances can only be set off against his business profits. But setting the interest payment, relief against National Insurance contributions and personal allowance against his investment income (tax on which is due on 1 January) helps to keep down the amount of tax payable in the first instalment. The income remaining comes to £14,331, not high enough for Roger to be liable to any higher rate tax.

The £2,697.30 tax on Roger's business profits is due in two instalments of £1,348.65 on 1 January 1988 and 1 July 1988. The £1,172.07 tax on his property rents and investment income is also due on 1 January 1988, making total tax of £2,520.72 due on that date.

The taxman also uses the form to work out Roger's Class 4 National Insurance contributions. His £1,840 capital allowances are subtracted from his £13,200 business profits, leaving £11,360. There are no contributions on the first £4,590 of this, but 6.3% on the remaining £6,770 = £426.51. Half of this amount is added to each of Roger's tax instalments, so the total he has to pay the taxman is £2,733.98 in January and £1,561.90 in July.

How to read a Schedule E Notice of Assessment

The main calculations are done in Sections 1 and 2. Section 3 shows subsidiary calculations and adjustments, while Section 4 explains what the taxman has done in Section 3. In the following description we refer to Dan Tucker's Notice of Assessment for the 1987–88 tax year – shown overleaf. For how Dan checks on the taxman by working out his tax for himself, see p492.

Section 1

Section 1 deals with earned income – wages, salary, fringe benefits, pensions, and so on. These are all entered in the middle column (£29,180 in our example). If you've paid allowable expenses which you can deduct from your earnings, these are entered in the first column. The amount of tax you've already paid on earned income (eg under PAYE) is entered in the third column. Your income less deductions is entered in the *Amount of assessment* Box. If the taxman has estimated any figure, he'll put an E in front of it.

In certain circumstances, there may be no mention of a wife's earnings – for example, if you pay tax at the basic rate only, and her earnings are taxed under PAYE. (This is because – if the PAYE system has worked correctly – the correct amount of tax due on her income will have been collected.)

Section 2

This starts with the figure for *Allowances given in this assessment* (£6,170 in our example), which is worked out in Section 3 (see below). This figure is subtracted from the *Amount of assessment* figure (£28,760), and the result is the *Amount chargeable to tax* (£22,590). The taxman works out the tax due on this amount, and enters the result in the *Tax assessed for* line (£6,674.50). (In Section 2, the taxman tells you what slices of your income are being taxed at what rates. These slices should tie up with the *Given in this assessment* figures in Section 3.) Next, he adjusts the *Tax assessed for* figure (if need be) to take account of any tax overpaid or underpaid in previous years. Lastly he subtracts the total of *Tax deducted* from Section 1, leaving you with the amount of tax still to pay or to claim back – £103.50 to claim back in our example.

In Dan's case, he has overpaid tax by £103.50. This is because the taxman made no allowance in Dan's PAYE coding for the interest on his home improvement loan which qualifies for relief at his top rate of tax – 45%. 45% of £230 = £103.50 too much tax deducted. So Dan will get a cheque for this amount from the taxman.

Section 3

This starts by listing your personal allowances. After that, there's a space for any outgoings you've made which you've

Inland Revenue
Income Tax - Schedule E
Assessment notice and statement
of tax unpaid or overpaid

- This assessment notice for the year shown below gi
details of
  –your earnings, pensions, benefits etc.
  –the allowances given
  –the tax deducted during the year
  –the tax unpaid or overpaid at the end of the year.
- If you do not understand any part of the assessm
please ask me. My address is shown at the left.

Issued by
H.M. Inspector of Taxes

Please use this reference if you wi
or call. It will help to avoid delay.

**Year to
5 April
1988**

Date
of
issue

See Note	SECTION 1 Income from employment, pension, benefit etc.	Deductions £	Amounts £	Tax deducted or refunded (R = tax refunded)
	TH Marshall & Co		18,080	4,739-50
	Expenses & benefits	420	2,100	
	Slagthorpes		9,000	2,038-50
			29,180	6,778-00
	less deductions		420	

Amount of assessment	28,760	
SECTION 2		
Allowances given in this assessment (see Section 3)	6,170	
Amount chargeable to tax	22,590	
	£	p
Chargeable at:		
Basic rate 27% on £ 18,700	5,049	00
Higher rates 40% on first £ 2,500	1,000	00
45% on £ 1,390	625	50
less (see Section 4)		
TAX ASSESSED FOR	6,674	50
Add underpayment for earlier years		
Deduct overpayment for earlier years		
less tax deducted	6,778	00
Net tax unpaid at 5 April		
Net tax overpaid at 5 April 1988	103	50

P70(T)
Part 2

How to appeal

If you think the assessment is wrong

- send me a written appeal within 30 days of the date shown below
- say what you think is wrong with the assessment
- give the correct facts or say when you expect to have them
- return this notice to be revised

More advice on appeals is given in Note 29 of the enclosed notes.

Dan Tucker
23 Railway Cuttings
Slagthorpe

- I must by law send this notice to you personally, but if you have a professional adviser/agent you should show it to him/her at once.

How to check this notice

Some general notes are attached.

Section 1 shows the sources of income, the amounts assessed and any tax deducted during the year. An "E" before any figure means I do not know the correct amount and have estimated it. If you do not agree with any estimate you should appeal and tell me the correct figure.

Section 2 shows the allowances given against this income, the charge to tax and the net tax unpaid or overpaid at the end of the year.

Section 3 gives details of the allowances due and, if the total is not given in this assessment, how the rest has been given. If you are chargeable at more than one rate of tax the chart shows how the rates have been used.

Section 4 explains any unusual points.

SECTION 3 Allowances etc.

See Note

Personal allowance 3,795

Wife's earned income allowance 2,425

Loan interest 230

		Basic rate % 27	Higher rates % 40	45		
Total allowances and rates	6,450	20,200	2,500	1,390		
Given elsewhere:						
Interest	280					
Taxed income			800			
Building society interest			700			
Given in this assessment →	6,170	18,700	2,500	1,390		

SECTION 4 Explanation

TAXED INCOME IN SECTION 3 IS DIVIDENDS PLUS TAX CREDITS

MAXIMUM OF BASIC RATE BAND £17,900

ADD HOME LOAN INTEREST
- see note 25 overleaf £ 2,300

TOTAL CHARGE AT 27% IN SECTION 3 £ 20,200

paid in full (eg loan interest not paid under MIRAS). The taxman puts down £230 for interest which Dan paid on a home improvement loan. These allowances and outgoings are added together, and entered in the first Box on the left. If you've received any gross investment income (ie without tax being deducted), the amount of this income will be subtracted from the figure in the Box. This is the way the taxman collects tax on this income: ie by subtracting this amount from your allowances, an equivalent amount will be subject to tax. In Dan's case, interest of £280 from his National Savings Investment account is subtracted from the figure in the Box. The result is shown on the line below the Box, and the same figure (£6,170) reappears in Section 2.

The other main purpose of Section 3 is to explain how much of your income is being taxed at the basic rate. The basic rate band is £17,900. But in the Notice of Assessment the taxman may adjust this figure as a way of giving you tax relief or collecting tax:

● if you've paid outgoings net of basic rate tax (eg mortgage interest paid under MIRAS), the taxman will add the gross amount to your basic rate band. This is a neat way of giving you any higher rate tax relief due to you on these outgoings. This won't be done for covenant payments, other than amounts you covenant to charities, because you don't get higher rate tax relief on them. In Dan's case, the taxman adds £2,300 grossed-up interest that Dan pays under MIRAS increasing the total amount charged at basic rate tax to £20,200

● if you've received income which has been taxed before you get it (eg, as in Dan Tucker's case, dividends or building society interest) the taxman will subtract this figure from your basic rate band. This is a neat way of collecting any higher rate tax which may be due on this income. The taxman won't do this for covenant payments you receive – because they're only rarely liable to higher rate tax.

Section 4

Explains what the taxman has done in Section 3.

Using the Calculator

Over the next few pages you will find Boxes to fill in with details of your income, outgoings and allowances. The instructions in the Boxes tell you how to check exactly how much income tax you should pay for the 1987–88 tax year. If, at the end, the amount of tax you should pay (amount Z) is different from the amount you have paid (amount C) by more than a few pounds, you should raise it with the taxman.

If the Calculator looks long and complicated, do not be deterred. We've split it into a number of steps, and most people will only have to fill in Boxes 1, 2, 5 and 7. At the end of each

Box you are told where to go next. You will be diverted via Boxes 3, 4 or 6 only if they are relevant to your tax situation. There are a number of figures (amounts *A* to *L*, and *Q* to *U*) which you need to carry through from Box to Box. It's a good idea to jot these down on a separate piece of paper as you complete the Calculator, in order to avoid having to look back to previous Boxes. There is additional help before each Box to guide you through.

Your marital status on 6 April 1987

This is important in deciding whether or not you should enter your spouse's income in the Calculator as well as your own:
• If you were single, widowed, separated or divorced on 6 April 1987, only include your own income in the Calculator. If you got married during the tax year, see below.
• If, on 6 April 1987, you were married, you must include your husband's or wife's income, outgoings and allowances as well as your own. The Calculator assumes your incomes are taxed jointly – for how to work out what your tax would be if you had the wife's earnings taxed separately, see p74.
• However, if you are a woman who was widowed or separated from your husband during the 1987–88 tax year, you should only enter your own income, outgoings and allowances from the date of death or separation up to 5 April 1988.

Special cases

There are a few circumstances not fully covered by the Calculator where you will have to do some extra sums:
• If you got married after 6 April 1987 and before 6 April 1988, husband and wife each count as single and will each need to fill in their own Calculator. But the husband gets all or part of the married man's allowance, and either of you may be able to transfer unused allowances to the other (see p73).
• If you are a married couple with the wife's earnings taxed separately (see p74), husband and wife will each have to fill in their own Calculator as if single, but with the wife's investment income (see p67) entered in the husband's Calculator. At the end, add up the 'Total tax you're liable for' on each Calculator to get the combined tax bill.
• If you received over £25,000 when you left a job, there are special rules which may reduce the tax on the excess (see p158).
• If you have losses from self-employment, the rules for setting these off against other income are complicated (see p204). Take professional advice.

'Gross' and 'Net'

With certain types of payment, the payer deducts tax at the basic rate from each payment made – eg from each £100 (the gross amount) he will deduct £27 tax and hand over only £73 (the net amount).

If you know only the net amount actually paid over and you need to know the gross amount, you can either add back the tax deducted (eg £73 + £27 = £100), or you can divide the net amount by 0.73 (eg £73 divided by 0.73 is £100).

These rules do not apply to income taxed under PAYE.

What to enter in Box 1

Enter in the spaces provided on p480 the gross amounts of your income assessable to tax in the 1987–88 tax year – see below for details. If any tax has been deducted by the payer you must include it in the amount of income you enter, *and* enter the amount of tax in the 'Tax already paid' column. If you have already paid some tax for 1987–88, enter this also in the 'Tax already paid' column.

You need only enter whole £££ in the income column, but enter pounds and pence in the 'Tax already paid' column.

Earnings from employment

The basic figure to enter is your total earnings in the tax year, after deducting any contributions you paid to your employer's pension scheme. This figure will normally be on the P60 form your employer gives you at the end of the tax year. Include in the figure you enter the taxable value of any fringe benefits you had (see p161) and any expense allowances you got which you did not spend on allowable expenses (see p137).

If you have received any commission, bonus, tips, taxable sick pay, maternity pay, holiday pay or other additions to your salary, include these in the figure you enter. But if you received any profit-related pay under a registered PRP scheme (see p141), include only half the amount of PRP (the rest is tax-free).

Deduct from the total you enter anything you spent on allowable expenses out of your earnings, and fees you paid to qualifying professional bodies, which were not reimbursed by your employer (see p143).

Enter the total tax deducted by your employer in the 'Tax already paid' column.

Earnings from self-employment and freelance work

Enter the taxable profits from your business, trade or profession (see p186). Also enter any money you've received from freelance or sparetime work, after deducting any allowable expenses (see p222). In each case make sure that you enter the figures on which the taxman is basing your 1987–88 tax bill (see p187).

Pensions, social security benefits

Enter the taxable pensions and benefits you received in the 1987–88 tax year (see pages 117 and 118). If you got a pension from abroad, see p111.

If you got any unemployment or supplementary benefit because you were unemployed, on short time or on strike, enter the taxable amount shown on the statement from your benefit office. But don't include any amount paid to you by your employer and included on your P60 form (which you should already have entered under 'Earnings from employment').

Maintenance or alimony received

Enter the gross amount of enforceable payments (eg under a court order) in the 1987–88 tax year which were payable to you or *for* children in your care. Don't enter any voluntary payments, nor payments *to* your children (see p91).

Income from property

Enter the total rents received, *plus* any profits you made on gas or electricity supplies, *less* any allowable expenses (see p258) and *less* any qualifying interest you paid in full on a loan to buy or improve the property. (But if you paid the interest net of tax under the MIRAS system, don't deduct it here but enter it in Box 3 on p485 instead, if you are directed there.)

Interest not taxed before you get it

This includes interest from:
● National Savings Bank investments
● certain British Government stocks (see p279)
● Co-operative Society deposits.
See pages 270 to 273 for a full list. The interest is normally taxed on a *preceding year basis* (see p276), in which case enter the income you got in the 1986–87 tax year.

Dividends from UK shares, unit trusts

Add the tax credits (or the amount of tax deducted, shown on the tax vouchers) to the amount of dividends you received in the 1987–88 tax year, and enter the result.

With unit trusts (see p285), don't enter any equalisation

payment you have received, but with accumulation unit trusts include the gross amount of income re-invested during the tax year.

Enter the total tax credits and deductions in the 'Tax already paid' column.

Investment income taxed before you get it

This includes income from certain British Government stocks, company loan stocks and debentures, and income from trusts and settlements (see p274). Enter the *gross* amount paid or credited to you in the 1987–88 tax year, and the total tax deducted.

Covenant payments received

Enter the gross amount of the payments you received in the 1987–88 tax year, and the tax deducted by the payer.

Interest from banks, building societies, deposit-takers and local authority loans

Enter at D the total amount of interest paid out to you (or credited to your accounts) in the 1987–88 tax year. Then divide amount D by 0.73 to obtain the *grossed-up* amount and enter this at E. You don't need to enter anything in the 'Tax already paid' column for this income.

Gains on life insurance policies

The proceeds of most life insurance policies are tax-free and should not be entered – see p298. But if you have made any *taxable* gains, or an *excess* from cashing in part of a policy (see p306), enter the total in Box 1 overleaf. You may also have to enter this again in Box 6 on p489.

Annuities, income and growth bonds

Check with the insurance company how much is taxable and how it is taxed, and enter it in the appropriate line of Box 1.

Finally . . .

Add up the income shown to get amount A, and the 'tax already paid' column to find amount C. If you received any covenant payments, add them to amount A to find amount B (otherwise B is the same as A). Add any taxable gains on life insurance policies to amount E to find amount F, and then go to Box 2 on p483.

Income and tax already paid (Box 1)

Enter the gross amount of income you have received from the sources listed opposite which is being taxed in the 1987–88 tax year. Also enter in the right-hand column the amount of tax that has been deducted or which you have already paid, and the amount of any tax credits you have received. Do not enter any income which is tax-free. See pages 477 to 479 for more help.

Then add up the income shown to get amount *A*, and the 'tax already paid' column to find amount *C*. If you received any covenant payments, add them to amount *A* to find amount *B* (otherwise *B* is the same as *A*). Add any taxable gains on life insurance policies to amount *E* to find amount *F*, and then go to Box 2 on p483.

[1] Your 1987–88 tax bill may be based on income you received in the 1986–87 tax year (see pages 187 and 270).
[2] But not tax-free interest – see p273.

Box 1 – Income and tax already paid

	gross amount £££	tax already paid £ p
Earnings from jobs, after deducting pension contributions and allowable expenses. Include taxable value of fringe benefits. Also enter tax deducted for 1987–88		
Taxable profits from business. Fees from freelance work. [1] Also enter any tax for 1987–88 already paid		
Before-tax income from pensions. Also enter any tax deducted		
Social security benefits (taxable amount)		
Maintenance or alimony payments received. Enter gross amount and any tax deducted		
Income from property (after deducting allowable expenses and qualifying interest paid gross) [1]		
Interest not taxed before you get it [1] [2]		
UK share dividends and unit trust distributions (add tax credits to amount received and enter total). Also enter tax credits and tax deducted in the 'tax already paid' column		
Other interest and dividends already taxed (enter before-tax amount). Also enter tax deducted		
Add up income above	**A**	
Covenant payments received. Enter gross amount and tax deducted by the payer		
Add covenant payments received to amount A	**B**	
Add up tax already paid in far column		**C**
Interest from banks, building societies, deposit-takers and local authority loans. Enter at D the total interest paid out to you or credited to your accounts in the 1987–88 tax year	**D**	
Divide amount D by 0.73 to obtain the grossed-up amount, and enter this at E	**E**	
Enter any taxable gains or excesses on life insurance policies		
Add up amounts in previous two lines	**F**	

GO TO BOX 2 ▷

Outgoings paid in full (Box 2)

Enter in Box 2 opposite the amounts of the outgoings listed, rounding the figures *up* to the next whole pound.

Self-employed pensions and life insurance

Enter any personal pension plan premiums you paid which qualify for tax relief in the 1987–88 tax year. Include payments which qualify because you didn't pay the maximum premiums in an earlier year, but *not* premiums that you have asked to be treated as having been paid in an earlier tax year (see p346).

Include any premiums you paid for special life insurance policies which qualify for tax relief (known as Section 226A policies – see p341).

Interest you pay gross

Only enter here interest which you paid in 1987–88 which qualifies for tax relief and which you paid in full, ie without deducting any tax (see p26).

Most mortgage interest should *not* be entered here because it is paid net of tax under the MIRAS system (enter it in Box 3 if directed there).

Small maintenance payments

Enter here only payments made under a court order which qualify as small maintenance payments (see p94) and which you paid without deducting any tax.

Class 4 National Insurance contributions

If you have to pay Class 4 contributions on your income from self-employment, enter half the total paid (or due) for the 1987–88 tax year.

Finally . . .

Do the additions and subtractions in Box 2 to get amounts *G, H, I* and *J*. Then check the four statements at the bottom of the Box. If any of them applies to you go to Box 3 on p485. If not, you can go straight to Box 5 on p487.

Box 2 – Outgoings paid in full

	£
Enter certain outgoings you have paid which qualify for tax relief in the 1987–88 tax year (rounded up to the next whole £)	
Payments into pension and life insurance policies for the self-employed which qualify for tax relief in the 1987–88 tax year	
Interest which qualifies for tax relief but which you have paid without deducting tax	
Small maintenance payments, from which you have not deducted any tax	
Half amount paid in Class 4 NI contributions for 1987–88 (if self-employed)	
Add up the outgoings above	**G**

Now work out the following:	
Subtract amount G from amount B in Box 1	**H**
Add amounts A and F in Box 1 and subtract amount G	**I**
Add amounts B and F in Box 1 and subtract amount G	**J**

WHERE NEXT?

DO ANY OF THESE APPLY TO YOU?

- you were single on 6 April 1987 and amount I is more than £20,325
- you were married on 6 April 1987 and amount I is more than £21,695
- you (or your spouse) were born before 6 April 1923 and amount J is more than £9,800
- you (or your spouse) made any covenant payments or maintenance payments from which you deducted tax.

IF ANY OF THESE APPLIES TO YOU, GO TO BOX 3 OVERLEAF.

IF NONE OF THESE APPLIES, GO STRAIGHT TO BOX 5 ON p487.

Outgoings paid after deducting tax (Box 3)

You need only complete Box 3 if directed to it from Box 2.

In each case, check how much you have actually paid in the 1987–88 tax year and enter this in the 'Amount actually paid' column. Then divide the amount by 0.73 and enter the answer in the 'Gross amount' column.

Mortgage interest paid under MIRAS

Most mortgage interest should be entered here, and also loans for improving property which come under the MIRAS system (see p241). If you have a MIRAS loan on property you let, the gross amount of interest you enter cannot be more than your net income from let property (see p256).

Personal pensions and 'free-standing' AVCs

Enter any payments you have made into a personal pension since 4 January 1988, and any payments you have made since October 1987 which count as 'free-standing' additional pension contributions.

Maintenance paid net of tax

Enter only enforceable payments you made in the 1987–88 tax year from which you have deducted tax (see p94).

Covenant payments

Enter the payments you made in the 1987–88 tax year under deeds of covenant to charities and individuals.

Finally . . .

Add the two pairs of gross amounts to find amounts K and L, then add up K, L and M to find amount N. If you made any maintenance or covenant payments, follow the instructions to work out amounts P and Q. Most people will go to Box 5 on p488 next. But if you (or your spouse) were born before 6 April 1923, work out amount R and go to Box 4 on p486 first.

Box 3 – Outgoings paid after deducting tax

In each case, enter the amount you actually paid, then divide it by 0.73 to get the gross amount to enter in the far column	Amount actually paid £	Gross amount £
Mortgage interest paid net of tax under MIRAS		
Payments into personal pensions and 'free-standing' additional pension contributions (see p340)		
Add the two gross amounts above		**K**
Maintenance paid after deducting tax		
Covenant payments to charities		
Add the two gross amounts above		**L**
Covenant payments to people		**M**
Add up amounts K, L and M and enter the total at N		**N**

IF YOU MADE ANY MAINTENANCE
OR COVENANT PAYMENTS:
Add up amounts
L and M above   **P**

Then, compare amount P with
amount D in Box 1:
If amount P is less than
amount D, enter zero at Q.
If D is less than P,
subtract D from P and enter
the result at Q   **Q**

WHERE NEXT?

WERE YOU (OR YOUR SPOUSE)
BORN BEFORE 6 APRIL 1923?

IF YES, subtract amount N
from amount J (in Box 2),
enter the result at R
and GO TO BOX 4.   **R**

IF NO, GO STRAIGHT TO BOX 5

Age Allowance (Box 4)

If you were (or your spouse) were born before 6 April 1923, you may be entitled to some age allowance (see p104). How much depends on your 'total income' (amount R from Box 3) and your age. Follow the instructions in Box 4 to work out exactly how much age allowance you are entitled to (if any). Then go to Box 5 and enter your age allowance (or personal allowance) in the top space.

Box 4 – Age allowance

First, look in the Table below to find amounts a and b and write them in the Boxes below.

If you are:		amount a is:	amount b is:
a single person (including widowed, separated and divorced)	born before 6 April 1908	£3,070	£10,767
	born between 6 April 1908 and 5 April 1923	£2,960	£10,602
a married couple	either or both born before 6 April 1908	£4,845	£11,374
	others	£4,675	£11,119

Fill in amounts a and b here: [**a**] [**b**]

Now look back to Box 3 for amount R.

If amount R is £9,800 or less, your age allowance is amount a. Go straight to Box 5 on p488, and fill in your age allowance.

If amount R is more than amount b, you do not qualify for age allowance. Instead, you get the ordinary single person's allowance (£2,425) or married man's allowance (£3,795). Go straight to Box 5 on p488 and fill in your allowance.

If amount R is between £9,800 and amount b, carry on:

Subtract £9,800 from amount R	
Multiply the amount in the previous line by 2	
Divide the amount in the previous line by 3	
Subtract amount in previous line from amount a	**c**

Your age allowance is amount c.

GO TO BOX 5 ON p488 AND FILL IN YOUR AGE ALLOWANCE.

Allowances and Business Expansion Scheme (Box 5)

Personal allowance or age allowance

Married couples normally get the married man's allowance and the wife's earned income allowance (see below), except in the year of marriage or if the wife's earnings are taxed separately (see p74). Everyone else gets the single person's allowance.

But people over 64 may get a higher age allowance (see opposite). If you were not diverted via Boxes 3 and 4, you get the full amount of age allowance (amount *a* shown in the Table in Box 4).

Wife's earned income allowance

This is normally £2,425. But it cannot be more than the wife's earned income (see p67).

Other allowances

If you or your spouse qualified for any other allowances in the 1987–88 tax year, enter the total here (see page 22).

Business Expansion Scheme

If you've made investments under the Business Expansion scheme (BES), enter at *S* the amount which qualifies for tax relief in the 1987–88 tax year (which may include investments made up to 6 October 1988 – see p293).

Finally . . .

Add up your allowances and BES investments and subtract the total, *T*, from amount *H* (in Box 2) to find amount *U*.

If you have made any covenant payments or maintenance from which you have deducted tax, and amount *Q* is more than amount *U*, replace amount *U* with the figure at *Q*.

Most people then go straight to Box 7 on p490. But if amount *I* in Box 2 is more than £20,325 (£21,695 if you were married before 6 April 1987), there may be some higher rate tax to pay so you will have first to go to Box 6 on p489.

488 The Which? Book of Tax

Box 5 – Allowances and Business Expansion Scheme

	£
Allowances: Enter the amounts of allowances you qualified for in the 1987–88 tax year:	
Personal allowance (£2,425 single, £3,795 married) or age allowance (worked out in Box 4) [1]	
Wife's earned income allowance (up to £2,425) (see p64)	
Other allowances (see p22)	
Business Expansion Scheme (BES): amount invested which qualifies for relief in the 1987–88 tax year (see p292)	**S**
Total allowances and BES: add the amounts entered above	**T**
To find your taxable income: subtract amount *T* from amount *H* in Box 2 (if amount *T* is more than *H*, amount *U* is zero)	**U**

If you made any covenant or maintenance payments from which you deducted tax and amount *Q* (in Box 3) is more than amount *U*, cross out the figure you have written at *U* and insert amount *Q*.

WHERE NEXT?

Look back at amount *I* in Box 2.

IS AMOUNT *I* MORE THAN £20,325 (MORE than £21,695 IF MARRIED)?   IF YES, GO TO BOX 6 ⟶

IF NO GO STRAIGHT TO BOX 7 ⟶

[1] If you or your spouse are over 64 and you did not have to go to Box 3 or Box 4, you get the full amount of age allowance (amount *a* in Box 4)

Higher rate tax (Box 6)

If your income is high, this Box checks whether any higher rate tax is due on it and, if so, how much.

Follow the instructions to work out amounts *V* and *W*. Compare them to work out amount *Y*.

If amount *W* is lower than amount *V*, you will need to use the 'Higher Rate Tax Table' opposite to work out amount *Y*. For example, if amount *X* is £5,000, amount *Y* is £5,000 × 0.18 − £125 = £775. Amount *Y* is the higher rate tax due on all your income. It doesn't include any basic rate tax, as this will be worked out separately, in Box 7.

If you have made any taxable gains or excesses on life insurance policies, your higher rate tax may be reduced by **top-slicing relief** (see p302). The rest of Box 6 will work this out for you. Deduct the relief from amount *Y* before going on to Box 7 on p490.

Box 6 Higher rate tax

Add amounts A and F from Box 1 and enter the total	**V**
Add up amounts G, K, L and T from Boxes 2, 3 and 5	
Add £17,900 to figure in previous line	**W**

Compare amounts V and W:

IF V IS LOWER – There is no higher rate tax to pay.

> GO STRAIGHT TO BOX 7 OVERLEAF

IF W IS LOWER, carry on:

Subtract amount W from amount V	**X**
Then use the 'Higher Rate Tax Table' below to work out what the higher rate tax would be on amount X and enter this at Y	**Y**

Higher Rate Tax Table

If the amount is:	to work out the higher rate tax:
up to £2,500:	multiply the amount by 0.13
£2,501 to £7,500:	multiply the amount by 0.18 and subtract £125
£7,501 to £15,400:	multiply the amount by 0.23 and subtract £500
£15,401 to £23,300:	multiply the amount by 0.28 and subtract £1,270
over £23,300:	multiply the amount by 0.33 and subtract £2,435

HAVE YOU MADE A TAXABLE GAIN ON A LIFE INSURANCE POLICY (or an excess from cashing in part of a policy) which you have had for two complete years or more?

> IF NO – GO STRAIGHT TO BOX 7

IF YES – carry on, as you may be entitled to some top-slicing relief. Work this out here and deduct it from amount Y before going to Box 7.

Top-slicing relief	
Enter taxable gain or excess	**d**
Enter number of complete years you had policy for [1]	**e**
Divide amount d by e	**f**
Add up amounts A, E and S from Boxes 1 and 5	**g**
Add up amounts f and g	
Subtract amount W from amount in previous line	**h**

IS AMOUNT h A MINUS FIGURE?

> IF YES – top-slicing relief has cancelled out your higher rate tax. GO TO BOX 7, entering zero in the 'Higher rate tax' line.

IF NO, carry on working out your top-slicing relief overleaf:

[1] If you have made an excess at some time in the past, enter the number of complete years since you made the last excess.

Top-slicing relief

Subtract amount W from amount g (if a minus figure, enter zero)		**j**
Use Table opposite to work out what the higher rate tax would be on amount h and enter here		**k**
Use Table opposite to work out what the higher rate tax would be on amount j and enter here		**m**
Subtract amount m from amount k		**n**
Multiply amount n by e		**p**
Add amount X to amount S (from Box 5)		
Use Table below to work out what the higher rate tax would be on amount in line above and enter here		**q**
Add amount m to amount p		**r**
Subtract amount r from amount q		**t**

Amount t is your top-slicing relief. Deduct it from amount Y and enter the result in the 'Higher rate tax' line of Box 7.
(If the result is a minus figure, enter zero.)

GO TO BOX 7

Total tax you're liable for (Box 7)

Your basic rate tax is 27% of amount U from Box 5. If you went to Box 6, add on the higher rate tax (amount Y) to find your total tax bill for the 1987–88 tax year (amount Z).

Compare this with amount C in Box 1 (tax already paid) to find out if you still owe any tax or if you are due for a rebate.

Box 7 – Higher rate tax

	£	p
Basic rate tax: Enter 27% of amount U from Box 5		
Higher rate tax: If you went to Box 6, enter any higher rate tax due (after deducting any top-slicing relief on life insurance gains)		
Total tax you're liable for: Add the two amounts above [1]		**Z**

Compare amount Z with amount C in Box 1
(the total tax you have paid) and write
the difference in this Box:

If amount Z is more than amount C, you still owe this much tax.

If amount C is more than amount Z, you can claim back this much tax.

But you may need to make an adjustment if you owe (or are owed) tax from a previous year.

[1] In this Calculator, amount C 'Tax already paid' and amount Z 'Total tax you're liable for' do not include the notional basic rate tax deemed to have been paid on interest from banks, building societies, deposit-takers and local authority loans.

Higher rate tax table

If the amount is:	to work out the higher rate tax:
up to £2,500:	multiply the amount by 0.13
£2,501 to £7,500:	multiply the amount by 0.18 and subtract £125
£7,501 to £15,400:	multiply the amount by 0.23 and subtract £500
£15,401 to £23,300:	multiply the amount by 0.28 and subtract £1,270
over £23,300:	multiply the amount by 0.33 and subtract £2,435

Example: Nellie Dean uses the Tax Calculator

Box 1: Income

Nellie Dean is a widow, aged 67. She is a self-employed fortune-teller, and in her accounting year ending in the 1986–87 tax year her taxable profits were £4,200 (her 1987–88 tax bill is based on the previous tax year's profits). She also received a total of £6,100 in pensions, from which tax of £2,188.62 had been deducted.

She adds together £4,200 and £6,100 and enters the result, £10,300, at A. Since she has no income from covenants, the same figure is carried forward to B. The only other income that Nellie had was £73 from a building society account which she enters at D. This already has the equivalent of basic rate tax deducted and Nellie 'grosses up' the interest by dividing amount D by 0.73. This comes to £100 which Nellie enters at E and carries forward to F.

Box 2: Outgoings paid in full

Nellie has no outgoings in this list – her profits in 1987–88 were too low for her to have paid Class 4 National Insurance. She enters zero at G, so amount H is the same as B (£10,300). She puts £10,400 at I, and also at J. She checks the *Where next?* questions and finds that the third one applies to her so she moves on to Box 3.

Box 3: Outgoings paid after deducting tax

Nellie paid £146 mortgage interest under the MIRAS system in the 1987–88 tax year. Grossed up, this comes to £200. She enters both amounts. She has none of the other outgoings listed, so amount N is £200. The *Where next?* question applies, so Nellie subtracts N from J (£10,400 − £200) which leaves £10,200 to enter at R.

Box 4: Age allowance

Nellie finds amount *a*, £2,960, and amount *b*, £10,602, in the Table. Next she finds that amount R is greater than £9,800 but less than amount *b*. Subtracting £9,800 from R leaves £400.

Nellie follows the rest of the instructions and works out amount *c* as £2,694.

Box 5: Allowances and BES

Nellie's only entry is her age allowance of £2,694 which she carries down to *T*. She subtracts this from *H* (£10,300) which gives a value for *U* of £7,606. Looking back at *I*, Nellie finds that she can move straight on to Box 7.

Total tax you're liable for

27% of amount *U* is £2,053.62 which Nellie carries down to *Z*. Comparing this with the £2,188.62 tax she entered at *C*, Nellie finds that she is owed £135 by the taxman. The reason for this is that the taxman estimated Nellie's business profits for last year at £4,500. This meant not only that she paid tax at 27% on the extra £300 profit but also that she lost £200 age allowance, so she has been charged basic rate tax on an extra £500 income.

Example: Dan Tucker uses the Tax Calculator

Box 1: Income

In the 1987–88 tax year, Dan Tucker earned £18,080, after deducting contributions to his employer's pension scheme. He also got fringe benefits worth £1,680 and was paid expenses of £420. Doris, his wife earned £9,000 from her job. He adds all these together, except the allowable expenses, and enters the grand total of £28,760 in Box 1. He adds together the tax paid by him and Doris, which comes to £6,778.00, and enters this in the '*Tax already paid*' column.

Under *Interest not taxed before you get it*, he enters the £280 interest from their National Savings Investment account that they received in the 1986–87 tax year and on which no tax has yet been paid. Next, he enters £800 share dividends plus tax credits, and puts the amount of the credits, £216.00, in the *tax already paid column*. He adds up all the income entered so far and enters the total, £29,840, at *A*. They have no income from covenants, so Dan enters £29,840 again at *B* and moves on to add up the tax already paid, £6,994.00. He enters this at *C*. Finally, Dan enters £511 interest from their building society account at *D*, 'grosses it up' by dividing by 0.73, and enters the result, £700, at *E*. They have no life insurance gains, so £700 is carried forward to *F*.

Box 2: Outgoings paid in full

The only thing Dan has to enter here is £230 interest which he pays on a home improvement loan that falls outside the MIRAS system. This amount is carried forward to *G*. Dan works out *H* as £29,610 and both *I* and *J* as £30,310. Then he looks at the *Where next?* questions and finds that the second one applies to him, so he moves to Box 3.

Box 3: Outgoings paid after deducting tax

Dan paid £1,679 mortgage interest under MIRAS in the 1987–88 tax year. 'Grossed up', this comes to £2,300. He has none of the other outgoings listed. K is £2,300 and so is N. The *Where next?* question does not apply to Dan or Doris, so he moves to Box 5.

Box 5: Allowances and BES

Dan enters the married man's allowance of £3,795 and the wife's earned income allowance of £2,425. They have no other allowances nor any BES investments, so T is £6,220. Subtracting this from H (£29,610) gives a value for U of £23,390. Dan looks back to find amount I (£30,310); this is more than £21,695, so he moves on to Box 6.

Box 6: Higher rate tax

Dan works out amount V as £30,540. Following the instructions, he adds £8,750 to £17,900 to get a figure of £26,650 for W. Since W is lower than V, Dan carries on working through the Box. X is £3,890. He multiplies this by 0.18 and subtracts £125 and enters the result, £575.20 at Y. Dan can move straight on to Box 7.

Box 7: Total tax you're liable for

27% of amount U is £6,315.30. Adding on amount Y, Dan gets £6,890.50 for amount Z. He compares this with the tax he has already paid (C) which is £6,994, and finds that the taxman owes him £103.50. Dan compares his completed Calculator with the Schedule E Notice of Assessment that the taxman sent him (see p472). The amount of tax he's owed agrees with the taxman's calculation, and most of the other figures correspond. But note that the taxman didn't include the share dividends in the income taxable at the basic rate, and didn't add the tax credits on them to the tax already paid – so the entry at *Tax deducted* on the Notice of Assessment is £6,778.00 rather than £6,994.00.

35 TAX FACTS

This chapter to gives you information you will need for checking your tax liability in past years. Remember that you can go back for up to six tax years before the current tax year: ie back to the 1981–82 tax year if you get your claim in before 6 April 1988. This chapter gives you the tax rates that applied for all these years, together with the personal allowances, the taxable values for company cars, and lots more. We give the rates of inheritance tax from 1986 when the tax was introduced, and the rates of its predecessor, capital transfer tax, back to 1980. We go back six tax years for capital gains tax. Later on in the chapter, we give a list of the Inland Revenue leaflets you're most likely to come across, and we take you through the Inland Revenue concessions – which can reduce the tax which, technically, you ought to pay.

Rates of tax charged on each slice of taxable income over the last seven tax years

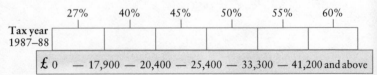

	27%	40%	45%	50%	55%	60%
Tax year 1987–88						

£ 0 — 17,900 — 20,400 — 25,400 — 33,300 — 41,200 and above

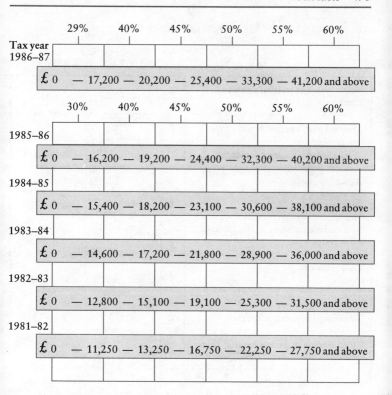

Tax year 1986–87	29%	40%	45%	50%	55%	60%
£ 0	— 17,200	— 20,200	— 25,400	— 33,300	— 41,200 and above	

	30%	40%	45%	50%	55%	60%
1985–86	£ 0 — 16,200	— 19,200	— 24,400	— 32,300	— 40,200 and above	
1984–85	£ 0 — 15,400	— 18,200	— 23,100	— 30,600	— 38,100 and above	
1983–84	£ 0 — 14,600	— 17,200	— 21,800	— 28,900	— 36,000 and above	
1982–83	£ 0 — 12,800	— 15,100	— 19,100	— 25,300	— 31,500 and above	
1981–82	£ 0 — 11,250	— 13,250	— 16,750	— 22,250	— 27,750 and above	

Capital gains tax rates for the last seven tax years

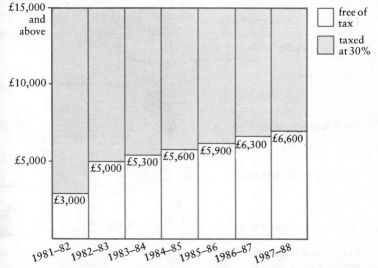

Tax years running from 6 April in one year to 5 April in the next

Allowances for the last seven tax years

		1987–88	1986–87
Single man's or woman's personal allowance	£	2,425	2,335
Married man's personal allowance	£	3,795	3,655
Wife's earned income allowance	£	up to 2,425	up to 2,335
Age allowance Single man or woman Married man Single man or woman aged 80 or more Married man if he, or his wife, is aged 80 or more	£	up to 2,960 up to 4,675 up to 3,070 up to 4,845	up to 2,850 up to 4,505 — —
Child allowance	£	—	—
Additional personal allowance	£	1,370	1,320
Housekeeper or person looking after children allowance	£	100	100
Dependent relative allowance single woman claiming (or wife with earned income taxed separately) other person claiming	£	145 100	145 100
Son's or daughter's services allowance	£	55	55
Blind person's allowance	£	540	360
Life insurance		←	
Death & superannuation benefits	£	←	
Personal pension payments	£	←	
Widow's bereavement allowance	£	1,370	1,320
Contribution to most employers' pension schemes	£	←	

1985–86	1984–85	1983–84	1982–83	1981–82
2,205	2,005	1,785	1,565	1,375
3,455	3,155	2,795	2,445	2,145
up to 2,205	up to 2,005	up to 1,785	up to 1,565	up to 1,375
up to 2,690 up to 4,255 — —	up to 2,490 up to 3,955 — —	up to 2,360 up to 3,755 — —	up to 2,070 up to 3,295 — —	up to 1,820 up to 2,895 — —
—	—	—	—	up to 165 per child
1,250	1,150	1,010	880	770
100	100	100	100	100
145	145	145	145	145
100	100	100	100	100
55	55	55	55	55
360	360	360	360	360
15% of gross premiums for policies taken out before 14 March 1984 →				
You get tax relief on part of trade union subscription which goes towards pension, funeral or life insurance benefits, and on some friendly society premiums →				
normally up to 17.5 per cent of 'net relevant earnings' →				
1,250	1,150	1,010	880	770
up to 15 per cent of earnings →				

Retail prices index (RPI)

Use these figures for working out your indexation allowances for capital gains tax. The RPI was rebased in January 1987 – in other words, went back to 100. We've reworked the index figures for months before January 1987 so that they are easily comparable with figures for later months. Index figures for months after this book goes to press will be announced by the Department of Employment, usually in the middle of the month following that for which they apply, and published in the Department's monthly Employment Gazette (try your local reference library).

	1982	1983	1984	1985	1986	1987
January	[1]	82.6	86.8	91.2	96.2	100.0
February	[1]	83.0	87.2	91.9	96.6	100.4
March	79.4	83.1	87.5	92.8	96.7	100.6
April	81.0	84.3	88.6	94.8	97.7	101.8
May	81.6	84.6	89.0	95.2	97.8	101.9
June	81.9	84.8	89.2	95.4	97.8	
July	81.9	85.3	89.1	95.2	97.5	
August	81.9	85.7	89.9	95.5	97.8	
September	81.9	86.1	90.1	95.4	98.3	
October	82.3	86.4	90.7	95.6	98.5	
November	82.7	86.7	91.0	95.9	99.3	
December	82.5	86.9	90.9	96.0	99.6	

[1] Indexation allowance only runs from March 1982.

Car fuel benefit

This Table shows the charges for free petrol for 'higher-paid' taxpayers from the 1983–84 tax year. These apply if you receive any petrol for private use from your employer, regardless of how much or little. If you don't count as 'higher-paid', see p169.

size of engine	1988–89	1987–88
up to 1,400cc	£480	£480
1,401–2,000cc	£600	£600
2,000cc +	£900	£900

size of engine	1986–87	1985–86	1984–85	1983–84	1982–83
up to 1300cc	£450	£410	£375	£325	£325
1301–1800cc	£575	£525	£480	£425	£425
1800cc +	£900	£825	£750	£650	£650

'Higher-paid'
The £8,500 limit (see p163) has remained unchanged since 6 April 1979.

Tax calendar

(dates when tax for the 1987–88 tax year is due)

Type of income or gain	Date tax due
Wages or salary Most pensions from employers	Deducted when you get the income (eg monthly, weekly) under PAYE
Investment income already taxed Share dividends and unit trust distributions Building society interest. Interest from banks and licensed deposit-takers. Interest on most local authority loans.	Tax at basic rate deducted (or deemed to have been deducted) before you get the income. Any higher rate tax is due on 1 December 1988 [1]
Investment income not taxed before you get it [2]	1 January 1988 [1]
Rents which count as investment income [3]	1 January 1988 [1]
Profits from being self-employed [4]	Normally two equal lump sums: 1 January 1988 and 1 July 1988 [1]
Capital gains	1 December 1988 [1]

[1] Or 30 days after date on the Notice of Assessment, if this is later.
[2] Tax normally based on income received in 1986–87 tax year.
   But special rules for opening and closing years (see p276).
[3] For how rents from property are taxed, see p254.
[4] Tax normally based on profits for accounting year ending in 1986–87 tax year (see p187). Special rules for opening and closing years.

Note: If most of your income comes from employment or an employer's pension, any tax due on income from other sources – provided it doesn't vary much from year to year – may in practice be deducted under PAYE from your earnings so you will not be paying tax at dates shown in *Date tax due* column.

Scale charges for company cars

If you're 'higher-paid' and have a company car, you'll have to pay tax at the rates shown in the Table below. If you don't count as higher-paid, the taxable value of a company car is nil. For further details, see p169.

*Market value of car when new

Tax year from 6 April in one year to 5 April in the next	Size of engine	
1988–89		
	up to 1,400cc 1,401cc – 2,000cc 2,000cc +	
1987–88		
	up to 1,400cc 1,401cc – 2,000cc 2,000cc +	
1986–87		
	up to 1,300cc 1,301cc – 1,800cc 1,800cc +	
1985–86		
	up to 1,300cc 1,301cc – 1,800cc 1,800cc +	
1984–85		
	up to 1,300cc 1,301cc – 1,800cc 1,800cc +	
1983–84		
	up to 1,300cc 1,301cc – 1,800cc 1,800cc +	
1982–83		
	up to 1,300cc 1,301cc – 1,800cc 1,800cc +	
1981–82		
	up to 1,300cc 1,301cc – 1,800cc 1,800cc +	

Age of car at the end of the tax year					
Under 4 years	4 years or more	Under 4 years	4 years or more	Under 4 years	4 years or more
*up to £19,250		*£19,250 – £29,000		*more than £29,000	
£580	£380				
£770	£520	£1,595	£1,070	£2,530	£1,685
£1,210	£800				
*up to £19,250		*£19,250 – £29,000		*more than £29,000	
£525	£350				
£700	£470	£1,450	£970	£2,300	£1,530
£1,100	£725				
*up to £19,250		*£19,250 – £29,000		*more than £29,000	
£450	£300				
£575	£380	£1,320	£875	£2,100	£1,400
£900	£600				
*up to £17,500		*£17,500 – £26,500		*more than £26,500	
£410	£275				
£525	£350	£1,200	£800	£1,900	£1,270
£825	£550				
*up to £16,000		*£16,001 – £24,000		£24,001 +	
£375	£250				
£480	£320	£1,100	£740	£1,725	£1,150
£750	£500				
*up to £14,000		*£14,001 – £21,000		£21,100 +	
£325	£225				
£425	£300	£950	£650	£1,500	£1,000
£650	£450				
*up to £11,500		*£11,501 – £17,300		£17,100 +	
£270	£180				
£360	£240	£780	£528	£1,260	£840
£540	£360				
*up to £9,600		*£9,601 – £14,400		£14,401 +	
£230	£155				
£300	£200	£660	£440	£1,050	£700
£450	£700				

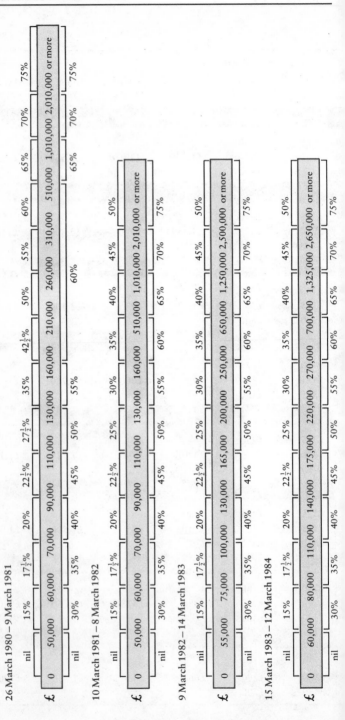

Capital transfer tax rates from 26 March 1980 to 17 March 1986

Capital transfer tax and inheritance tax rates

The tables on these two pages give tax rates for capital transfer tax (CTT) and inheritance tax (IHT). The top set of figures gives the rates of tax for gifts made during life. The bottom set of figures gives the tax rates for gifts made on death (or within three years of death). Under IHT, gifts to individuals (and to certain trusts) are liable to tax only if made on death or in the seven years before death. The tax on gifts made between three and seven years of death is reduced on a sliding scale (see p355).

The figures in the coloured lines are running totals of gifts. For CTT these are gifts made up to 10 years before a particular gift on which you want to work out the tax; for IHT they are the running total of chargeable transfers made up to seven years before a particular gift.

Chapter 28 shows you how to work out tax on a gift or estate on which there's inheritance tax to pay because of the donor's death in the 1987–88 tax year.

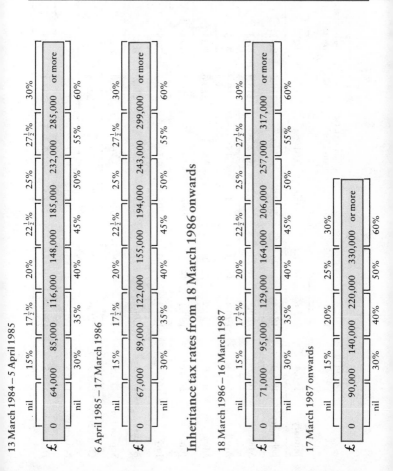

13 March 1984 – 5 April 1985

£	0	64,000	85,000	116,000	148,000	185,000	232,000	285,000 or more
	nil	15%	17½%	20%	22½%	25%	27½%	30%
	nil	30%	35%	40%	45%	50%	55%	60%

6 April 1985 – 17 March 1986

£	0	67,000	89,000	122,000	155,000	194,000	243,000	299,000 or more
	nil	15%	17½%	20%	22½%	25%	27½%	30%
	nil	30%	35%	40%	45%	50%	55%	60%

Inheritance tax rates from 18 March 1986 onwards

18 March 1986 – 16 March 1987

£	0	71,000	95,000	129,000	164,000	206,000	257,000	317,000 or more
	nil	15%	17½%	20%	22½%	25%	27½%	30%
	nil	30%	35%	40%	45%	50%	55%	60%

17 March 1987 onwards

£	0	90,000	140,000	220,000	330,000 or more
	nil	15%	20%	25%	30%
	nil	30%	40%	50%	60%

All stocks index

	began in 1979	1980	% increase on 1979	1981	% increase on 1980	1982	% increase on 1981	1983	% increase on 1982	1984	% increase on 1983
January	156.4	185.6	18.68	198.6	7.01	217.0	9.27	229.1	5.58	242.6	5.90
February	158.0	188.4	19.25	199.8	6.06	218.6	9.41	230.5	5.45	243.6	5.69
March	160.6	189.9	18.25	201.7	6.22	218.9	8.53	231.4	5.72	246.1	6.36
April	163.4	190.4	16.53	204.0	7.15	219.7	7.70	233.4	6.24	Stock relief is abolished for accounting periods starting after 13 March 1984. For accounting periods which straddle this date, stock relief is worked out on the rise in the all stocks index from the start of the accounting period until March 1984.	
May	165.0	190.9	15.70	205.5	7.65	220.6	7.35	234.4	6.26		
June	167.1	192.1	14.97	206.4	7.45	220.5	6.84	235.2	6.67		
July	169.5	193.9	14.40	206.5	6.50	221.1	7.08	235.5	6.52		
August	171.3	194.1	13.31	208.6	7.48	221.7	6.28	237.3	7.04		
September	173.2	194.8	12.48	209.9	7.76	223.0	6.25	238.7	7.05		
October	175.9	195.6	11.20	211.8	8.29	224.3	5.91	238.9	6.51		
November	177.5	196.2	10.54	213.1	8.62	225.3	5.73	239.1	6.13		
December	179.5	196.5	9.48	214.5	9.17	227.1	5.88	240.3	5.82		

Tax forms you might come across

In this section, we list and explain briefly the more common Inland Revenue forms:

Tax returns

P1	The tax return for people with fairly simple tax affairs
11P	The tax return which is intended for people with above average incomes and who work for an employer
11	Mainly for the self-employed
1	For partnerships, trustees, executors and personal representatives

Reclaiming tax

P50	If you're out of work for more than 4 weeks and are not claiming unemployment or supplementary benefit, use this form to claim back tax you've overpaid
R40	If you're a non-taxpayer, but tax has been deducted from any income you receive from certain investments, or alimony or maintenance payments, use this form to claim back tax
R185(AP)	Use this form to claim back tax on covenant payments you've received
R232	Use this form to claim back tax for your child (or for an incapacitated person)

Employment

P45	Your employer will give you this when you leave a job
P46	Your employer will give you this to fill in when you start your first job
P15	Coding claim – you should fill this form in at the same time as P46 and send it to the taxman immediately to get your PAYE code
P38(s)	For students who get holiday jobs, if their total income doesn't exceed the single person's allowance (£2,425 in the 1987–88 tax year)
P60	Your employer gives you this (or an equivalent certificate) at the end of the tax year – it tells you how much you've earned during that year and how much tax has been deducted
P11D	Your employer uses this form to declare to the taxman how much he's paid you during the tax year in the way of expenses, fringe benefits etc

Payments you make

R185   Use this form to certify that you've deducted tax from a payment you're making

IR47   The standard form supplied by the Inland Revenue if you want to make covenant payments to an adult son or daughter

43   Use this form if you need to provide the taxman with details of personal pension payments

C–5   Use this form if you need to tell the taxman about any chargeable transfers for inheritance tax purposes

R111   This is the certificate of non-reciprocity you may have to sign to declare that a covenant is above board, if you are making payments to a child under 18

R110   The certificate of non-reciprocity you sign if you are making covenant payments to anyone else

Income

14   If you are married and want to have the husband's and wife's earnings *taxed separately*, you can choose to do this up to a year after the end of the relevant tax year. So if you decide to opt for this for the 1987–88 tax year, send this form to the *husband's* tax office before 6 April 1989

14–1   Husband's and wife's earnings will continue to be taxed separately until you cancel form **14** by signing this form

11S   Fill in this form if you want husband's and wife's income to be *separately assessed*

11S–1   Sign this form to cancel form IIS

P2   This is the **Notice of Coding** the taxman will send you to tell you what your PAYE code is

Notices of Assessment

300   **Schedule A or D Notice of Assessment**
You'll get this form if you let property or are self employed

P70   **Schedule E Notice of Assessment**
You may be sent this form if most of your income comes from a job

900   Notice of Assessment for higher rate taxpayers

CG4   Capital gains tax assessment

Inland Revenue leaflets

Here we list the main explanatory leaflets available from the Inland Revenue. You can get most of them from your local tax or PAYE Enquiry office. The others are available from the addresses given at the end of this section. Not all the leaflets are up to date.

IR1	Extra-statutory Concessions
IR4	Income tax and pensioners
IR4A	Income tax – age allowance
IR6	Double taxation relief
IR9	Notes on treatment of livestock kept by farmers and other traders
IR11	Tax treatment of interest paid
IR12	Occupational pension schemes – notes on approval
IR13	Income tax – wife's earnings election
IR14/15	Construction industry tax deduction scheme
IR20	Residents and non-residents – liability to tax in the United Kingdom
IR22	Income tax – personal allowances
IR23	Income tax and widows
IR24	Class 4 National Insurance contributions
IR26	Income tax assessments on business profits – changes of accounting date
IR27	Notes on the taxation of income from real property
IR28	Starting in business
IR29	Income tax and one-parent families
IR30	Income tax – separation and divorce
IR31	Income tax and married couples
IR32	Income tax – separate assessment
IR33	Income tax and school leavers
IR34	Income tax – Pay As You Earn
IR35	Income tax – profit-sharing
IR36	Approved profit-sharing schemes
IR37	Income tax and capital gains tax – appeals
IR38	Income tax – SAYE share options
IR39	Approved savings-related share option schemes
IR40	Income tax – conditions for getting a sub-contractor's tax certificate
IR41	Income tax and the unemployed
IR42	Lay-offs and short-time work
IR43	Income tax and strikes
IR45	What happens when someone dies
IR46	Clubs, societies and associations
IR47	Deed of covenant by parent to adult student
IR51	Business Expansion Scheme

IR52	Your tax office
IR53	Thinking of taking someone on? PAYE for employers
IR55	Bank interest – paying tax
IR56	Employed or self-employed?
IR57	Thinking of working for yourself?
IR59	Students' tax information pack
IR63	Mortgage interest relief at source
IR64	Giving to charity (for businesses)
IR65	Giving to charity (for individuals)
IR66	Stamp duty
IR68	Accrued income scheme – taxing securities on transfer
IR69	Expenses: forms P11D
IR70	Computerised payroll
IR74	Deeds of covenant
480	Income tax – notes on expenses payments and benefits for directors and certain employees
P5	Farmer's guide to PAYE
P7	Employer's guide to PAYE
CA1	Capital allowances on machinery or plant
CA2	Capital allowances on industrial buildings
CA4	Allowances for scientific research
CGT4	Capital gains tax – owner-occupied houses
CGT6	Retirement: disposal of a business
CGT8	Capital gains tax
CGT11	Capital gains tax and the small businessman
CGT13	The indexation allowance for quoted shares
IHT1	Inheritance tax

For **IR12** and **Notes for Guidance on Retirement Annuity Relief**, write to:
　　The Superannuation Funds Office,
　　Lynwood Road,
　　Thames Ditton,
　　Surrey KT7 0DP

For **IHT1**, write to:
　　The Capital Taxes Office,
　　Minford House, Rockley Road,
　　London W14 0DF, *or*
　　16 Picardy Place, Edinburgh,
　　EH1 3NB, *or*
　　Law Courts Buildings,
　　Chichester Street,
　　Belfast BT1 3NU

Inland Revenue concessions

Concessions mean that you are let off paying tax that is technically due. For example, if you are a miner and opt for payment instead of the free coal you are entitled to, you won't have to pay tax on the money you receive instead.

Below we give a brief summary of the income tax concessions in Section A of Inland Revenue leaflet IR1 – this section deals with income tax and individuals. In some cases you'll need to look at the exact wording of the concession. Make sure you also get the supplements to this leaflet: they give details of changes.

A1   **Flat rate allowance for cost of tools and special clothing** – you can claim an allowance if you have to pay for the tools and clothing you need for work. For most kinds of trade, a flat rate is agreed with the relevant trade union(s). If you spend more than the flat rate, you can claim back more

A2   **Meal vouchers** – you won't be taxed on meal vouchers given to you by your employer provided that their value is not more than 15p per working day, the vouchers are non-transferable, and they are used for meals only

A3   **Pensions to disabled employees** – if you retire following an injury at work or because of a work related illness or a war wound, any extra pension paid over and above the amount you would have got if retiring on grounds of ordinary ill health is not taxed. The same applies to a pension awarded solely on one of these grounds. This concession used to be limited to police officers and firemen disabled on duty

A4   **Directors' travelling expenses** – if you're a director of more than one company within the same parent company, you won't be taxed on travelling expenses you receive for business travel from one company to the other(s). This includes hotel expenses, provided they are reasonable and necessary. The same applies if you're an employee of one company and director of another

A5   **Expenses allowances and benefits in kind** – there are three provisions, the most important of which is that you won't be taxed on (reasonable) expenses you receive from your employer when you move house if you are doing so because you take up new employment or you have been transferred within the same organisation. This includes relief for bridging loans provided by your employer. Where the existence of a bridging loan causes tax to be charged on other cheap or interest-free loans that your employer provides you can, from April 1985, claim relief against this extra tax as well

A6   **Miners: free coal and allowances in lieu** – miners do not pay income tax on free coal or on cash they receive in lieu

A7   **Business passing on the death of a trader** – special rules apply if a trader dies and the business passes to the trader's husband or wife who was living with him (or her)

A8   **Loss relief for capital allowances unused on the cessation of a business** – applying normal rules when a business ends could mean that some capital allowances are lost. A special rule allows losses which would otherwise be lost to be set against income in the final year of the business

A9   **Doctors' and dentists' superannuation contributions** – this concession deals with tax relief on personal pension contributions paid by doctors and dentists who also are required to contribute to the NHS superannuation scheme

A10   **Overseas provident fund balances** – no liability to income tax on lump sums received from an overseas provident fund (or something like it) when employment overseas ends

A11   **Residence in the United Kingdom: year of commencement or cessation of residence** – normally, on arrival in the UK in any given tax year, your income for the *whole* of that year (whether or not it was earned in this country) will be subject to UK tax (the same applies if you leave the country). But if you intend to stay for at least 3 years or are coming to work for at least 2 years or if you leave the UK to go and live abroad (intending to live there permanently), you will only be liable for tax for the part of the tax year when you were actually here, provided that you have not been ordinarily resident in the UK prior to or after this stay. There are special rules for Ireland

A12   **Double taxation relief: alimony etc under United Kingdom court order or agreement: payer resident abroad** – if you pay alimony, even if you live abroad, the money you pay counts as income arising in the UK. But relief by way of credit is allowed provided that: you are resident abroad; the money you pay comes out of your income in the country where you are resident and is taxable there; any UK tax you deduct from the payments is accounted for; and the person who receives the money is resident in the UK and effectively bears the overseas tax

A13 **Administration of estates: deficiencies of income allowed against income of another year** – this concession allows relief for higher rate tax to some beneficiaries of an estate if the income of the estate (during the administration period) is a minus figure for tax purposes

A14 **Deceased person's estate: residuary income received during the administration period** – special rules may lower the tax liability of legatees who are not resident or ordinarily resident in the UK

A15 **Dependent relative allowance** – if you contribute less than £75 a year towards the upkeep of a dependent relative, you can claim an allowance for the payment made, even though you don't actually maintain that relative. If two or more contribute, you can each claim part of the allowance in proportion to what you pay

A16 **Annual payments (other than interest) paid out of income not brought into charge to income tax** – if you make covenant payments, maintenance payments or other annual payments from which you deduct tax, you have to account to the Revenue for the tax you've deducted. If your taxable income is lower than the gross amount of the payments, you'll have to hand over extra tax. Concession A16 gives relief against this rule if you make payments late, but – if the payments had been made in the correct tax year – you would have had enough taxable income to cover the payments

A17 **Death of taxpayer before due date for payment of tax** – if this occurs and the executors cannot release the money to pay the tax, interest on the unpaid tax is waived until 30 days from the date on which probate is granted

A18 **Change of accounting basis on the merger of professional firms** – when two or more professional firms merge, top-slicing relief can reduce any extra tax resulting from the merger (ie because one of the firms may have changed its accounting basis)

A19 **Arrears of tax arising through official error** – often partly or completely waived, according to your income, if you haven't been notified by the end of the tax year after the year in which the error occurred. See p454 for further details

A20 **Cessation of trade, profession or vocation** – if you reduce your business or hours of work in order to qualify for a state retirement pension, tax on the business will be assessed as though you had closed down the business and started a new one, if it is to your advantage to do this

A21 **Schedule A: deferred repairs: property passing from husband to wife (or vice versa) on death** – you can set against rents money spent on repairs or maintenance made necessary by dilapidations which occurred while your wife (or husband) was the immediately preceding landlord

A22 **Long service awards** – these are not taxable provided the employee has been working for the employer for at least 20 years and has received no other such award within the previous 10 years and the article doesn't cost the employer more than £20 per year of service. The award must either be a tangible article of reasonable cost or shares in the company you work for (or an affiliated company)

A23 (This concession was superseded by *FA 1986, ss37,38*.)

A24 **Foreign Social Security Benefits** – you don't have to pay tax on these provided they correspond to UK social security benefits which are exempt from tax

A25 **Crown servants engaged overseas** – locally engaged unestablished staff engaged overseas as servants of the Crown won't be liable to UK income tax if they are not resident in the UK for tax purposes and if the maximum rate of pay for their grade is less than the maximum pay of an executive officer working in Inner London

A26 **Sickness benefits** – continuing payment received through an insurance policy because of an accident or sickness is not taxed unless you have been receiving benefit throughout at least one complete tax year. But if you receive such payment from your employer, it does count as taxable income

A27 **Relief for mortgage interest: temporary absences from mortgaged property for up to a year** are ignored when determining if a property is a 'main residence'. This also applies if an employee has to work elsewhere for up to four years, and if a person, working abroad, buys a property in the UK and lives in it for at least three months before returning abroad

A28 **Relief for mortgage interest: residents of the Republic of Ireland** – qualify for UK income tax relief for interest paid on a loan from a lender in the Republic of Ireland, providing certain conditions are met

A29 **Farming and Market Gardening: relief for fluctuating profits** – for the purposes of the averaging provisions in

Section 28 of the Finance Act 1978, 'farming' includes the intensive rearing of livestock or fish on a commercial basis for the production of food for human consumption

A30   **Interest on damages for personal injuries (foreign court awards)** – no liability to UK income tax provided there would have been no liability to income tax on the interest in the country in which the award was made

A31   **Life assurance premium relief by deduction. Pre-marriage policies – premium relief after divorce** – if a husband took out a policy on his wife's life (or vice versa), tax relief on the premiums continues after divorce if they got divorced after 5 April 1979. This rule also applies if the policy was taken out in anticipation of marriage

A32   **Tax relief for life assurance premiums. Position of certain pension schemes which are unapproved after 5 April 1980** – certain non-qualifying policies issued under certain unapproved pension schemes will be treated for tax purposes as though they were qualifying policies

A33   **Lump sum retirement benefits: Standard Capital Superannuation Benefit (SCSB) – Changes after 5 April 1980** – in some circumstances, lump sums from certain 'closed' or 'frozen' pension schemes, which would otherwise be taxable, may have no tax charged on them

A34   **Ulster savings certificates: certificates encashed after death of registered holder** – interest paid after the death of the holder is exempt from income tax if the holder lived in Northern Ireland when the certificates were purchased

A35   **Mortgage interest relief: year of marriage** – if a new home is not bought on marriage but the husband or wife goes to live in the other person's mortgaged home and sells his or her own property, full mortgage relief is still allowable on both homes as long as the second property is sold within 12 months of its being vacated

A36   **Close companies in liquidation: distributions in respect of share capital** – where a close company is in liquidation, and the income is apportioned, liability for higher rate tax is reduced by any capital gains tax paid in respect of the share capital which produced the income

A37   **Tax treatment of directors' fees received by partnerships and other companies** – in certain circumstances, directors' fees will be assessed under Schedule D, rather than Schedule E

A38   **Retirement annuity relief – death and disability benefits**
– if you're employed, and not in an employer's pension
scheme, you could still theoretically lose tax relief on
personal pension payments if you're covered by an
employer's scheme which pays out if you're disabled or
if you die. The concession allows you to get tax relief
on personal pension payments until – if you're disabled
– the tax year in which you receive the disability
pension

A39   **Exemption for Hong Kong officials. Extension of ICTA
1970 s372** – some Hong Kong officials who work in the
UK are not liable to UK income tax

A40   **Adoption allowances payable under Section 32
Children Act 1975** are not liable to income tax.

A41   **Qualifying life assurance policies: statutory conditions**
– the Revenue may count life assurance policies as
qualifying policies even though they have minor
infringements which, technically, mean they aren't
qualifying policies

A42   **Chargeable events: loans to policyholders** – if you take
out a loan on an insurance policy, this can count as a
partial surrender of the policy; it won't do so if the loan
is connected with a retirement annuity contract with the
same insurer

A43   **Interest relief: investment in partnerships and close
companies** – tax relief on loans taken out to invest in
or to lend money to a partnership or close company
won't be withdrawn when the partnership is
incorporated or the company's shares reorganised,
provided that the relief would have been allowed if the
loan had been taken out to invest in the new company

A44   **Education allowances under Overseas Service Aid
Scheme** – there won't be income tax to pay on certain
education allowances payable to public servants from
overseas under the Overseas Aid Scheme

A45   **Life assurance policies: variation of term assured
policies** – a term assurance policy with a term of 10
years or less continues to be a qualifying policy even if
the rate of premium is reduced to less than half,
following a reduction in the sum assured or an
extension of the term (but the total term must still be
less than 10 years)

A46   **Variable purchased life annuities: carry forward of
deficit in capital element** – for annuities where the
amount of any annuity payment doesn't depend on the
length of a person's life. If the tax-free part of the
income – the capital element – comes to more than the

annuity payment, the difference can be carried forward as an allowance in deciding the size of the capital element in the next payment

A47 **House purchase loans made by life offices to staffs of insurance associations** – a loan on a qualifying policy made by a life office to a full-time employee of certain insurance associations won't count as a surrender of rights under the policy

A48 **Transfer of control and management of a partnership outside the United Kingdom** – a partnership trading wholly outside the UK which transfers its control and management overseas won't face a clawback charge for unrecovered stock relief given in the past

A49 **Widow's pension paid to widow of Singapore nationality, resident in the United Kingdom, whose husband was United Kingdom national employed as a Public Officer by the Government of Singapore** – these widows' pensions are exempt from tax

A50 **Job Release Scheme** – payments made under the Job Release Scheme which closed to new applicants on 31 March 1980 are not taxable, even though payments were for a period beginning more than a year before pensionable age

A51 **Repayment supplement: life assurance premium relief** – interest will be paid when clawback of life assurance relief has been too high or where a claim has been made for relief which has not been given through paying lower premiums

A52 **Maintenance payments: concessionary relief** – if you pay maintenance after deducting tax, then, strictly, you should lose the tax relief if you forget to deduct the tax. But the Revenue may allow some relief, limited to the amount the recipient could have claimed if the payments had been properly made

A53 **Stock relief: business passing on the death of a trader** – where concession A7 applies, the surviving spouse can avoid a clawback charge for stock relief

A54 **Members of Parliament: accommodation allowance and expenses** – accommodation allowances paid to MPs for Parliamentary duties from 31 March 1984 are exempt from tax. The exemption may be extended to earlier tax years for which an MP's tax assessment has not been finalised

A55 **Arrears of foreign pensions** – if you receive a foreign pension which is granted or increased retrospectively, tax due on it can be calculated as if the arrears arose in the years to which they relate

New Concessions

The following concessions were included in the latest supplement to IR1, published in June 1987.

Suggestion schemes – certain awards (up to a maximum of £5,000) for ideas put foward through staff suggestion schemes at work will be free of tax

Travelling and subsistence allowance when public transport disrupted – you won't be taxed on (reasonable) extra travel costs of getting to work or the cost of accommodation near work that your employer pays for or reimburses when public transport is disrupted by industrial action

Home to work travel of disabled employees – disabled people who cannot use public transport will not be taxed on the value of special travel facilities or on money provided by local authorities to enable them to get to and from work

Agricultural workers' board and lodging – agricultural employees who receive free board and lodging but are entitled to higher cash wages in lieu may not be taxed on the value of the board and lodging, provided they don't count as higher-paid

Clergyman's heating and lighting etc expenses – clergy who do not count as higher-paid and who perform their duties from accommodation provided by their (mortal) employers, won't be taxed on heating, lighting, cleaning or gardening expenses that their employer meets for them

External training courses – expenses borne by employer – the cost of books and fees your employer pays for you to attend certain external training courses won't be taxed. Provided you are not away for more than twelve months, extra travel expenses and living costs met by your employer while you are on the course may not be taxable either

External training courses – expenses borne by employee – if your employer encourages or requires you to go on a full-time external training course of four weeks or more in the UK and gives you time off work on full pay, you can get tax relief on the cost of books and fees for the course not met by your employer (unless the course is for re-sit examinations). Extra travel expenses or costs of living away from home also qualify for tax relief, unless you're away for more than 12 months.

Workers on offshore oil and gas rigs or platforms – transfers from or to mainland – workers on offshore oil and gas rigs won't be taxed on the value of travel to and from the mainland provided free by their employer, nor on reasonable overnight expenses at the point of departure from the mainland, which their employer pays or reimburses

Employees disabled at work – see concession A3.

INDEX